A History of European Inte
since 1914

A History of European Integration since 1914

PETER M.R. STIRK

PINTER

PINTER
A Cassell imprint
Wellington House, 125 Strand, London WC2R 0BB
127 West 24th Street, New York, NY 10011

First published 1996

British Library Cataloguing-in-Publication Data
A catalogue record for this book is available from the British Library.

Library of Congress Cataloging-in-Publication Data
Stirk, Peter M. R., 1954–
A history of European integration since 1914/Peter M. R. Stirk.
p. cm.
Includes bibliographical references and index.
ISBN 1–85567–411–4. — ISBN 1–85567–412–2 (pbk.)
1. European federation—History. 2. Europe—Economic integration—History. I. Title.
JN15.S776 1996
940.5—dc20 96-13108
CIP

ISBN 1–85567–411–4 (hardback)
1–85567–412–2 (paperback)

Typeset by York House Typographic Ltd, London
Printed and bound in Great Britain by Redwood Books, Trowbridge, Wiltshire

Contents

Preface

Although the Introduction and Conclusion of this history consider the nature of European unity and disunity in the nineteenth century, the focus is on the period 1914 to 1994. The starting-point may seem a little odd. Yet the First World War, like the Second, was to have a profound influence upon European integration, partly because it saw an unsuccessful attempt to unify central Europe under German hegemony and partly because it inaugurated a period of violent instability in Europe. It is a central contention of this book that the forms of integration which we now have in Europe are a product of that instability and can only be understood and assessed in its light. The end of the Cold War division of Europe, with its comparative stability, has created greater room for manoeuvre but also brought back, in thankfully milder form, some of the uncertainties of that earlier period. It is for that reason that as much space is devoted to events after 1989 as to the previous three decades.

The division of Europe was very much the consequence of the failure of Europeans to put their own house in order. It was this that led to the intervention of the two superpowers. Central to Europe's failure was Franco-German enmity and the underlying strength of the German economy. It is for this reason that this book devotes so much attention to the Franco-German relationship. Franco-German antagonism not only hindered integration in the west but also had a decisive impact on eastern Europe. Western disputes blocked any co-ordinated approach to eastern Europe, which then became the victim of a second German bid to reshape Europe. The failure of that venture consigned the two halves of Europe to different courses of integration. Fifty years later, pan-European integration was on the agenda, but still far from being a reality.

The end-point of this book, December 1994, clearly does not have the same significance as 1914. It was chosen in order to bring this account as up to date as possible. Yet it does have a certain convenience. The Essen summit of the European Council was the last attended by Jacques Delors and François Mitterrand, both of whom had great influence on the preceding decade. December 1994 was also the month in which the Conference on Security and Co-operation in Europe became the Organization for Security and Co-operation in Europe.

Convenience of a different kind has also dictated the avoidance of abbreviations where possible. I have also chosen to refer to the 'European Community' where strictly reference should be made to the European Economic Community, European Communities or even European Union. In both cases I have preferred to give precedence to fluidity without, I hope, causing any confusion.

The completion of this book was facilitated by sabbatical leave for which I am grateful to the Department of Politics of the University of Durham. I also owe thanks to Dr Peter Kneen for his helpful response to my frequent queries about eastern Europe.

Peter Stirk
May 1996

In the notes to the chapters the figure in bold refers to the volume number, save in the case of the periodicals listed below where it refers to the part or issue number. *Aus Politik und Zeitgeschichte, Aussenpolitik, Bulletin of the European Communities, Cooperation & Conflict, CSCE Newsletter, Current Digest of the Soviet Press, East European Reporter, Europa-Archiv, Europäische Rundschau, Der Spiegel, Deutschland Archiv, Foreign Affairs, International Security, NATO Review, Paradigms, Problems of Communism, RFE/RL Research Report, The World Today.*

Europe in 1878

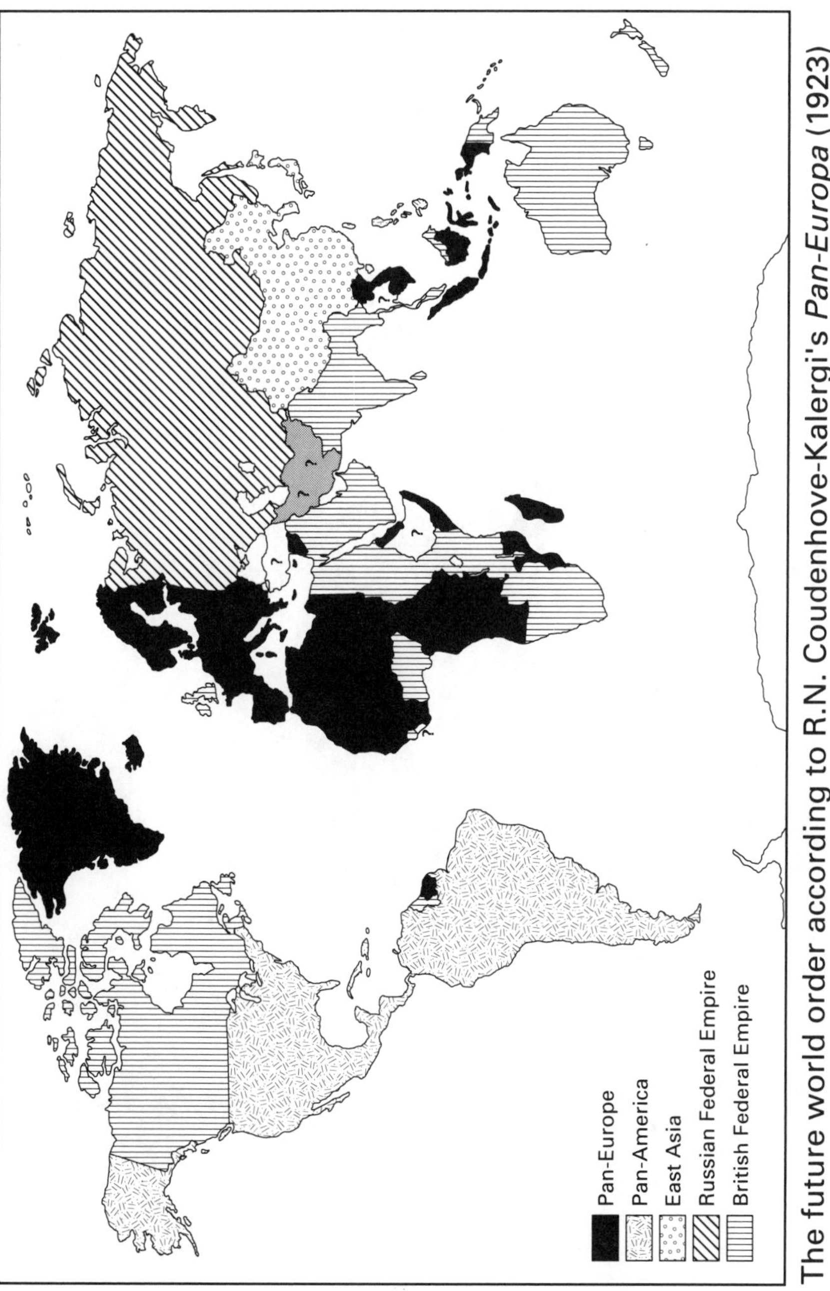

The future world order according to R.N. Coudenhove-Kalergi's *Pan-Europa* (1923)

Eastern Europe according to the Versailles Settlement

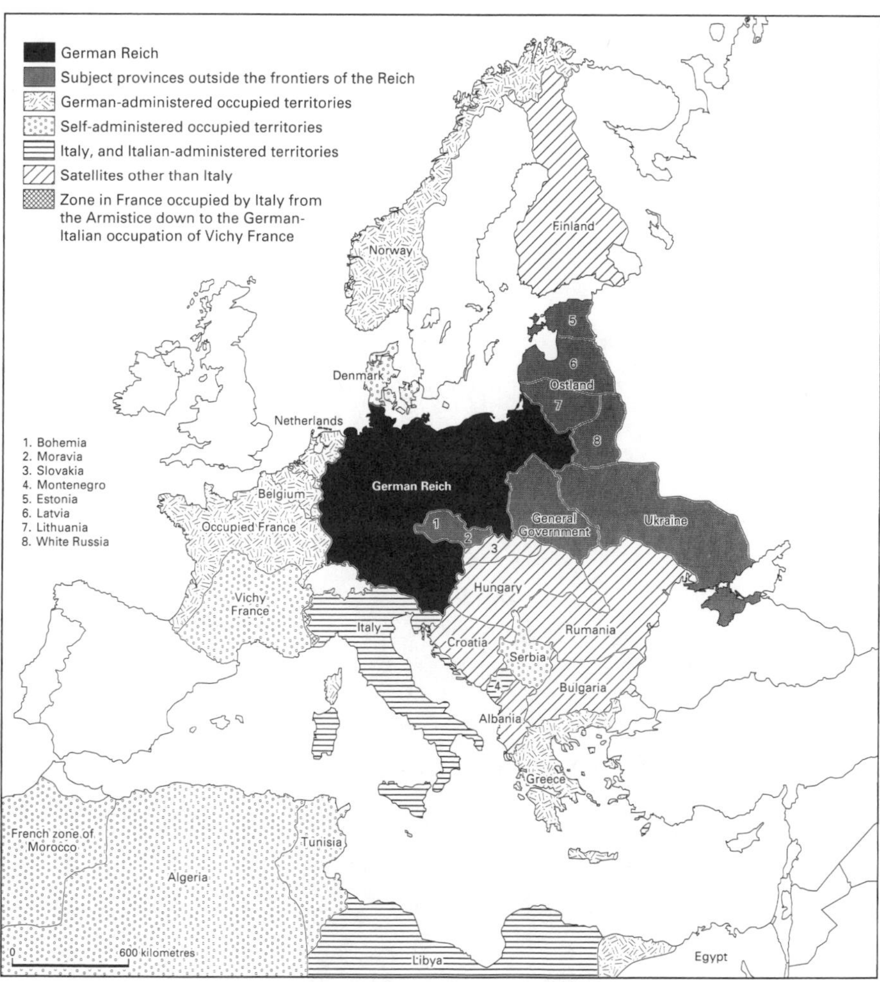

Hitler's Europe before the battles of Stalingrad and Alamein (Autumn 1942)

1

Pre-1914 Origins

In 1914 Europe embarked upon a savage and prolonged conflict which would solve none of its problems and compound most of them. The war itself saw an ambitious attempt by Germany to rip the heart out of Europe and refashion it into a German-dominated Mitteleuropa. The German venture failed because America had entered the lists, becoming in effect the arbiter of Europe's fate. Among the other consequences of the war were the unchaining of several nations and the demise of three empires: one, Russia, succumbing to internal revolution; the second, Germany, suffering military defeat; the third, the Habsburg Empire, disintegrating.

A hundred years earlier the statesmen who gathered in Vienna at the end of the Napoleonic wars drew up a settlement which, though substantially modified in the course of the nineteenth century, would last until 1914. The Vienna settlement was novel in that it not only drew up the terms of the peace but also sought to provide mechanisms to guarantee those terms.[1] The main institutional provision was for periodic conferences of the great powers, the Congress System. The intellectual architect of the Vienna settlement, von Gentz, recognized from the outset that such provisions themselves were of little use. He relied ultimately on the balance of power and the interests of the great powers, the only ones who were capable of disrupting the settlement, in maintaining it.

The territorial distribution reflected this aim and the fear that any threat was most likely to come from France. The Habsburgs acquired more territory in northern Italy, and with it the task of guarding against any French expansion in that direction. Further to the north, Bavaria and, more importantly, Prussia received territories bordering on France in the west of Germany, giving them a direct and immediate interest in resisting French moves there. Equally important was the distribution of power in the centre of Europe. Germany was to be reconstituted as a confederation based on an unequal condominium between the two major central powers, the Habsburg Empire, which had formal precedence in the shape of the Presidency of the Confederation, and Prussia.[2]

The only major loophole was in the south-east of Europe. During the negotiations on the peace settlement Castlereagh had tried to incorporate a guarantee of the integrity of the Ottoman Empire, but the Russian Tsar, Alexander I, refused. His motives were mixed, but Russian ambition to acquire Ottoman territory was certainly among them. The omission was important, for of the empires with European territory it was to be the Ottoman which would suffer the greatest territorial losses before the First World War. Of the others only the Habsburgs would lose any territory, and even then they were compensated by new acquisitions.

It was conflict over the decaying corpse of the Ottoman Empire which provided the spark for the outbreak of hostilities in the twentieth century. More important for the development of Europe, however, was the shift in the balance of power in central Europe. The German Confederation established in 1815 had presented several advantages for its neighbours. First, as a confederation of sovereign princes it was expected to defend the legitimate order against the claims of revolutionary nationalism. Second, with power distributed between two major states and a host of medium and small states, Germany posed less of a threat.[3] The dangers inherent in more unity were evident in the rhetorical question put by the Göttingen historian Alexander von Heeren: 'If this state were a great Monarchy with a strong political unity, armed with all the material forces of state which Germany possesses, what secure peace of mind would there be for them [the other European states]?'[4] Not all of von Heeren's Germany was in fact united in the nineteenth century. The Habsburg lands within the Confederation remained separate from the German Reich. But von Heeren's prediction of the threat to Europe's balance of power was accurate enough.

The threat arose not just from unification but from economic growth in Germany. By the turn of the century the gap was impressive. The German Reich had surpassed even Britain in the production of steel, producing 6.3 million metric tonnes to her 5 million. The Reich dwarfed Austria–Hungary, which had kept pace until the 1850s but could only manage 1.1 million tons in 1900. France too fared little better, producing 1.5 million tons.[5] The foundation of the Reich in 1871 already sounded the alarm bells in London. According to Disraeli, with this 'German Revolution ... [t]he balance of power has been entirely destroyed ... '[6] By 1900 German power was even more impressive, though the conclusion which the British Foreign Secretary drew in 1900 was that Anglo-German friendship should be strengthened.

The rise of a Prussian-dominated Reich has frequently been presented as a virtuous circle in which economic integration, begun by the Zollverein of 1834, promoted economic growth and laid the foundations for unification by Prussian arms and for yet further economic growth.[7] This apparent success story was to exercise a powerful influence in debates on European integration during the twentieth century. Critics and advocates alike of European integration would point to the unification of Germany as a practical example. Economic integration in the form of a customs union would lead, it seemed, inexorably to political unification. Critics added that it was intended to. In fact there was much in the simplistic image of German unification that was misleading. It is true that Prussia soon came to see the Zollverein as a means of gaining influence over fellow German states, though membership of the Zollverein did not prevent several of them fighting on the side of the Habsburgs against Prussia in the war of 1866. Moreover, those states had not joined the Zollverein out of any nationalistic enthusiasm, but primarily for fiscal reasons. They benefited, often disproportionately, from their share of the revenues from the common customs duties. Nor did the customs union itself necessarily bring about any substantial change in the rate of growth, though the low tariff policy associated with it was a significant factor.

At the end of the day it was Prussian arms that ensured unification, in two stages. The first stage, 1866, was the culmination of a long struggle for hegemony between the Hohenzollerns and the Habsburgs and resulted in the exclusion of the Habsburgs from German affairs to the north. The first stage of German unification was therefore also the first division of Germany. The so-called *kleindeutsch* solution unified some Germans, under Prussian leadership, only at the expense of the exclusion of others, albeit the minority. This had not been inevitable. Austria had striven to maintain a looser and broader unity within central Europe. The political framework was provided by the German Confederation. The first real threat to the Confederation came in 1849 with the plan formulated by Baron Joseph von Radowitz. This envisaged a loose union as a substitute for the existing Confederation, and a much stronger Reich which would exclude Austria. As yet, however, Prussia was far too weak to enforce such a solution. Faced with Russia's expression of displeasure the Prussians gave way at Olmütz in November 1849 and agreed to the continuation of the Confederation. The main thrust of Austrian policy continued to be maintaining the Confederation, though they were increasingly willing to co-operate with Prussia in a roughly equal condominium so long as the formal precedence of Austria was maintained. When pushed, however, Austria sought to curb Prussian pretensions.

Amid the manoeuvring for position the Austrians came up with two other solutions which pointed to broader or more intensive integration. One was the brainchild of the Austrian Minister of Commerce Ludwig von Bruck. Bruck's proposal, launched in October 1849, was for a customs union embracing the German states and the Habsburg's non-German lands as well. The proposal was thus a response to the Zollverein as well as a move on the broader stage of central European politics. The implications were quite far-reaching. Bruck was proposing to link the economic fate of Germans and non-Germans. He was also proposing a move towards a more protectionist tariff policy than the one pursued by the existing Zollverein, though he accepted that Austria would also have to meet the Zollverein half-way in this field. On a yet broader canvas Bruck had a vision of a central Europe composed of three federations. In addition to his new Zollverein, the Swiss federation and an Italian federation would form a powerful central European bloc. His political superior the Minister-President Prince Felix zu Schwarzenberg understood little of Bruck's economic reasoning. He did see the possibility of the customs union proposal as a means of weakening Prussian power, of forcing Prussia back within an asymmetric condominium.[8] Prussian officials saw Schwarzenberg's advocacy of the customs union as exactly that, and no more, and successfully fended off the Austrian proposal. The second solution, put forward by Schwarzenberg, was for a reform of the Confederation which would involve the incorporation of all the Habsburg territories into it. Under the existing arrangement only parts of the Habsburgs' lands were included, primarily those inhabited by Germans, though the Czechs too formed part of the 'German' Confederation. Again the Prussians were able to fend off the Austrian move and settled for a restoration of the *status quo ante.*

Both proposals pointed in the same direction: a much broader form of unity than envisaged by Prussia and one which would bind Germans and non-Germans together within a multinational political and economic entity. Both were opposed by Prussia, not out of any great nationalist sentiment – Prussia too was a multinational empire – but out of dynastic interest. Though both proposals were to be revived, their prospects declined with the relative increase in Prussian power. The final conflict came in 1866 when Prussian armies quickly defeated Austria and her allies. The outcome was the dissolution of the Confederation and the confirmation of Prussian hegemony. The Franco-Prussian war of 1870 saw the defeat of the only other power who sought to oppose the consolidation of Prussian-dominated Germany north of Austria.

Even before her military defeat Austria had begun to lose the economic battle, though this was in part because her military commitments imposed a heavy and inhibiting burden upon her economy. The economic victors of the nineteenth century lay to her north and west. It was here that the forces of economic integration operated most fully. When Bruck had pressed for his customs union of an enlarged Mitteleuropa, German industrialists of the Zollverein had shown scant interest. Their markets lay to the north and west, not towards the more slowly developing south. The Zollverein's industrialists were participating in what was a European – or rather a predominantly west European – process of industrialization. The economic historian Sidney Pollard concluded that 'Europe was not a single market merely for commodities: over much of the nineteenth century it also in effect became a single market for capital, skills, enterprise, ideas and technical knowledge.'[9] Until the last quarter of the nineteenth century, governments were promoting this integration to a greater and greater extent. Despite fears of competition from the most advanced industrial nation, Britain, the architects of the Zollverein were, for the most part, persuaded of the benefits of economic competition, and were inclined to pursue a moderate tariff policy. To be sure, their task was made easier by the fact that the politically powerful East Elbian landlords, the Junker, were initially competitive grain exporters. Moreover, as early as 1817 the Prussian King Frederick William III was being told by his advisers that competition, 'far from suppressing home industry, tends to perfect manufacture and induce an extension of activity'.[10] In fact German industry also benefited from the structure of trade with Britain, with some 30 to 50 per cent of British exports to Germany in the period 1815–45 being inputs into the textile industry.[11] Even traditionally protectionist France was drawn towards free trade by the Franco-Prussian Treaty, which Prussia in turn forced upon other members of the Zollverein as a condition of its renewal.

These trends, besides pointing of themselves towards greater European integration, encouraged advocates of unity. In both Britain and continental Europe economic and social trends aroused hope. Belief in the dominant ideology of material progress and the development of societies through more or less fixed stages suggested that societies would become increasingly similar, more inclined towards commerce than warfare, and hence more integrated. The British sociologist Herbert Spencer confidently proclaimed

> that in the tendency to form alliances more or less lasting, in the restraining influences exercised by several governments over one another, in the system, now becoming customary, of settling international disputes by congresses, as well as in the breaking down of commercial barriers and the increasing facilities of communication, we may trace the beginning of a European federation – a still larger integration than any now established.[12]

In Britain sympathy for international co-operation often went hand in hand with suspicion of government, advocacy of free trade and of peace, which it was assumed would be encouraged by free trade. The most direct expression of this came at the end of a brilliant criticism of the European balance of power by Richard Cobden: 'As little intercourse as possible betwixt the *Governments,* as much connection as possible between the *nations,* of the world.'[13] An alternative approach, though sharing the belief that increasing socio-economic homogeneity and integration was the key, was provided by the French technocrat Saint-Simon. In 1814, in a vain attempt to influence the statesmen assembling in Vienna, he published his *De la réorganisation de la société européene,* in which he advocated a federal government independent of the constituent nations and acting in the common interests of the federation.[14] Socio-economic integration might act as a solvent of the existing political institutions but it was no substitute for common institutions. That fact was more widely recognized in continental Europe than in England.

The desire for common institutions did bring some complications with it. If, as was widely assumed, these common institutions would be parliamentary, then a certain political homogeneity of the European states would be required. To the problem of how to unite a series of states of diverging size and power was added the problem of how to unite a series of states of diverging political complexion. One answer, or rather hope, was that the problem would solve itself, the states of Europe would become parliamentary systems which would then unite. In the mean time, however, in response to the Congress of the Friends of Peace held under the presidency of Victor Hugo in 1849, the followers of the Italian republican and nationalist Giuseppe Mazzini denounced any attempt to unite Europe before the triumph of republicanism and nationalism.[15] In some ways even more awkward was the case of countries which had previously been incorporated in the idea of Europe but were seen as irremediably autocratic. In practice this meant above all Russia.

The question of Russia's membership of any European federation or entity was part of a wider complex of issues involving the balance of power, and patterns of political and economic development.[16] What is now recognized as Russia was isolated from European developments for several centuries by the Mongol invasion of the thirteenth century. Only in the sixteenth century was Russia able to shake off the remnants of its subjection and later, in the wake of Peter the Great's reforms, to re-integrate itself into the European society of states.[17] In the nineteenth century, Russia still occupied a dominant place in the calculations of the European balance of power – much to the irritation of Cobden. But a symbolic change had already occurred. At the beginning of the century Russia was regarded as a north European power, along with Prussia and Austria. It was customary to divide Europe in this way: between north and south, not between east and west, save when referring to the eastern (Orthodox) and western (Roman Catholic) churches. Whether condemning Russians as 'northern barbarians' or praising their rulers as the 'star of the north', the geographical designation was the same. Between the end of the Napoleonic wars and the Crimean War Russia was relocated by her neighbours to the east. The change expressed hostility rather than sympathy. It was facilitated by the political connotations of the synonym for 'eastern', 'oriental', where oriental forms of government were assumed to be despotic and alien. By extension so too were 'eastern' forms of government. The changes were accelerated by two events: the failure of the Russian aristocratic rebels, the Decembrists, in 1825 and the suppression of the revolt of the Tsar's Polish subjects in 1830 to 1831. Both, especially as reported by Polish exiles, confirmed the incipient suspicion of Russia as different from western Europe.[18] Russian intervention in the 1848–49 revolutions and then the Crimean War hardened these images. The former made the name of Russia a synonym of autocracy and repression across the political left wing of Europe. The second helped to spread the idea that Europe was threatened by two non-European superpowers: Russia and the United States of America.

Aside from these polemical exchanges there was also a more objective basis for an east–west distinction, though it was not clear cut nor did it necessarily entail any antagonism between the two. Economically, a rough division between western Europe on the one hand and central and eastern Europe on the other can be traced back to the late medieval period. Symbolic of this distinction was the reimposition of serfdom in central and eastern Europe around the turn of the fifteenth to the sixteenth centuries. Though the precise patterns of development varied considerably, the east and to a lesser extent central Europe saw a reassertion of aristocratic power against the incipient freedom of both the peasantry and the towns, with the aristocracy maintaining their economic position by means of corvée labour. The variations were important. The Baltic lands, western Poland, Bohemia and Hungary can be picked out as a middle region distinct from eastern Europe (eastern Poland, south-eastern Europe and Russia). By the first quarter of the nineteenth century in parts of this central European region grain and wool exports were being generated by large farms employing modern techniques – although these were not typical of the agricultural economy as a whole. Bohemia with its comparatively high urban development was economically the most western part of the region.[19]

During the nineteenth century these peoples, whether forming part of the multinational empires or the weak independent states which emerged in the course of the century, sought to catch up with the west. Their motives and methods were not always conducive to sustained economic growth. Landowners, many of whom were hardly competitive in international terms, sought to imitate the fashions and consumption patterns of the advanced west. For many this was economically unsustainable, and the consequences were increasing indebtedness and a search for employment in the state as an escape from their bankrupt estates. This contributed towards a situation where the states of eastern Europe had per capita incomes approximately one-third of that of the most advanced European states, but per capita government expenditures of over three-quarters of those of their richer European neighbours.[20]

One question which arose in this context was whether or not the development of the economically backward was helped or hindered by their relationship with the economically advanced, whether free trade or protection offered the best chance of catching up, whether integration, including perhaps a customs union, or autarky was the best strategy. The debate took place both within independent nations like Romania and within the multinational Habsburg Empire. In the latter the Habsburgs, having temporarily set aside Magyar political autonomy at the end of the 1848–49 revolution, abolished the customs barrier which had divided the Austrian and Hungarian parts of the Empire. Magyar nationalists, following the lead of Louis Kossuth, denounced the union as injurious to Hungarian industrialization. In reality the Hungarian half of the Empire got the better of the deal, marginally. The immediate impact of the customs union was, according to modern commentators, slight, though they make a favourable overall judgement of the arrangement.[21] That Magyar leaders shared this impression is evident from the fact that when they reacquired political leverage, with the 1867 Compromise, they did not seek to revoke the customs union. Their judgement was justified by the subsequent beginning of industrialization in Hungary. Development was led and dominated by food-processing and especially flour-milling, in which Hungary was for a time internationally competitive. Hungary was hurt rather by the general turn towards protection in the last quarter of the nineteenth century. Flour exports from the Empire to Germany, which had amounted to 126,900 tons in 1879, fell dramatically to 22,600 tons in 1880 when confronted with an 8 per cent tariff.[22] Even then the customs union still provided Hungarian flour with a much larger domestic market than it would otherwise have enjoyed. It must be added, though, that the customs union could be exploited to seek profits from protectionism rather than efficiency. Thus the Magyar leader Count Stephen Tisza openly looked forward to a time when the Empire would be a grain importer, for then domestic producers could sell at a price which incorporated the tariff imposed on imports.[23]

The Habsburg customs union, like the Zollverein, produced an environment which was conducive to growth even if neither can be seen as the direct *cause* of growth. The effect of both was also determined by the general development of tariff policy across Europe. Up until the last quarter of the century the trend had been predominantly liberal. Following the British lead in the 1840s, liberalization made substantial strides in the 1860s with the Anglo-French and Franco-Prussian Treaties. But in 1878 Bismarck, as part of a domestic political realignment, moved towards a more protectionist policy. Further increases followed in 1885 and 1887, and, after a brief respite under Chancellor Caprivi, in 1902 (Bülow tariff). In France a succession of increases in the 1880s culminated in the Méline tariff of 1892, imposing an average *ad valorem* rate of 25 per cent on agricultural products and varying rates on industrial goods. Russian policy followed a similar pattern, culminating in the Mendelayev tariff of 1891. By 1894 Italy, which had imposed a moderate tariff in 1878, was one of the most protectionist on the continent. The deteriorating situation was also expressed in a series of tariff wars, including the Franco-Italian of 1887–89, the Austro-Romanian of 1882–98, the Austro-Serb of 1906–14, and even the German–Canadian of 1897–1900.[24]

The pressure for more protectionist policies had grown in the wake of the 1873 depression. This threat induced several schemes for multilateral trade agreements and full-blown customs unions. Even British officials argued for some kind of 'tariff union', and in the mid-1870s first the Chancellor of the Exchequer, Stafford Northcote, and then Lord Derby took up the idea of a tariff congress. A mixture of domestic opposition, especially from the Board of Customs, and the fading of French interest in the scheme sufficed to bury the half-hearted initiative.[25] In fact the German Chancellor Caprivi made more progress in this direction, though he was soon ousted from office.

Outside the corridors of power several advocates of a European customs union were to be found. On the eve of the turn to protectionism the Frenchman Guido de Molinari proposed a central European customs union composed of France, Belgium, Holland, Germany, Denmark, Austria and Switzerland.[26] He drew heavily on the record of the Zollverein for the details of his plan. He sought to reassure prospective members that their customs receipts – still important parts of national budgets – would not suffer greatly. He pointed to the absurdity of improving means of communication and transport only to then cripple the flow of goods by tariff barriers. He claimed that contemporary industry required above all else secure outlets, which the proposed union would provide. Equally significant, he sought to counter the argument that the proposal would meet with immediate opposition from Britain. In the first place, he argued that the union would be open to British membership, holding out the additional prospect that the union might progress to a British approach to tariffs, that is to the use of tariffs for revenue purposes only. In the second place, he claimed that the union would automatically benefit Britain anyway. British goods would have to surmount the common external tariff, but once within the union they could move freely. British membership was, then, optional, but there were distinct advantages to the inclusion of three other major powers. They would balance each other and provide reassurance to smaller powers, whereas a union between say France and Belgium or Germany and Holland would rightly give rise to concern for the long-term independence of the smaller partners.

The Hungarian Guido von Baussern tried to persuade Bismarck of the virtues of an Austro-German customs union in 1880, without success. The idea was, however, taken up, this time from the German side, by Lujo Brentano, a liberal economist in 1884. Brentano's scheme was somewhat broader, incorporating the Balkan states as well. But it fared no better.[27] Yet these ideas were to gain increasing prominence during the next decades. From 1904 the Mitteleuropäische Wirtschaftsverein, founded by the economist Julius Wolff, agitated for a central European customs union. Although the German Foreign Office kept its distance from the Mitteleuropäische Wirtschaftsverein it did in fact have considerable sympathy for the idea.[28] More limited schemes were also floated, including the idea rejected by Molinari of a German-Dutch customs union. Some versions went further than a customs union, envisaging a political alliance as well. A. Sartorius Freiherr von Waltershausen put forward a multi-faceted package which, he claimed, would have brought both sides economic advantages without unduly threatening the independence of the smaller state. This reassurance, even as offered by Waltershausen, was not very persuasive. The small states of Europe, he claimed, need have little fear of conquest: they would be too troublesome to digest. But overseas, things were different. It was there that the boundaries were likely to change. Small powers like Holland lacked the resources to defend their overseas territories. If the Dutch wanted to hold on to their East Indies they needed the protection of a great power, that is, Germany, which would also provide the capital investment which the Dutch could not muster. This would of course entail 'a greater or lesser renunciation of freedom of action in foreign affairs'.[29]

These geo-political strategic considerations were common elements of the Mitteleuropa plans. They were encouraged by German ambitions, especially for the acquisition of overseas colonies; her place in the sun. But they were also part of a much broader consensus that the world was being divided up into potentially hostile trading blocs. Publicists on all sides totted up the surface areas and populations, including colonial subjects, to find some viable size for their preferred option, or to frighten their audiences into accepting the need for action before they were overwhelmed by the colossi of the world. In Germany one of the more raucous prophets of Mitteleuropa, Theodor Schieman, an intimate of the Emperor Wilhelm II, succinctly expressed these attitudes in his suggestions for German policy guidelines: 'central European customs and economic union, a settlement of the colonial question on generous lines, the humiliation of England, the preservation of peace with our allies Austria-Hungary and Italy and the containment of the powerful Russian influence'.[30]

Schieman's list omitted only the American challenge which figured prominently in many other Mitteleuropa projects. Growing American economic competition, the emergence of the United States from its isolation in the war with Spain in 1898, and the formation of the Pan-American League, the significance of which was wildly exaggerated for decades, all seemed to confirm earlier fears that the United States would eventually mobilize its immense resources and challenge Europe.

Yet despite the changes which had taken place over the century Europe still showed signs of continuity. A new German Empire had taken the place of much of the old Confederation, Italy had been united, the Kingdom of the Netherlands had been divided into two, and Sweden and Norway had separated. With the exception of the German Empire, however, none of this really affected the European balance of power. Further east both the Romanov and Habsburg multinational empires had, as yet, withstood the challenge of nationalism. Both remained great powers. Only the Ottoman Empire was visibly crumbling under the pressure of nationalism.

At the beginning of the century nationalism was for most of Europe a weak force, despite fears of France's revolutionary nationalism. As nationalism spread, most liberal nationalists saw it as a force for progress and political and economic integration. As the British historian E. J. Hobsbawm explains, it was assumed that only populations of a certain size could sustain a national identity and a nation-state.[31] Those below the critical threshold, like the Welsh, the Bretons or in some accounts the Czechs, would eventually be subsumed in a larger entity. Their languages would linger on, along with their archaic customs, before finally expiring through lack of interest.

The outcome was, of course, different: nationalism proved to be remarkably virulent and led to disintegration more than integration.[32] The process was slow. As late as 1846 the Habsburgs could stifle a revolt by

Polish nobles, and gain their loyalty thereafter, by the simple expedient of inciting the nobles' fellow nationals, the Polish peasantry, against their masters. Romanian nationalists were later saved from a similar embarrassment only by being promptly evicted by Ottoman troops. Even as nationalism put down deeper roots it could still be contained. The success of the Balkan nations against their Ottoman rulers was in many ways misleading. Only the Serbs gained autonomy, in 1826, by their own efforts. The Greeks required great-power intervention to gain their independence in 1830. Romania was created at the end of the Crimean War to bar the road to Romanov expansion. Bulgaria gained its independence by courtesy of Russian forces in 1878. The Ottomans were still capable of suppressing their subject nations, but they could not withstand any one of the great powers unless aided by some of the others.

The Habsburgs and the Romanovs contained the nationalist pressure, though with significantly different rates of success. Though ruling peoples who were economically and culturally less developed, the Romanovs enjoyed a distinct advantage. The dominant Russian minority accounted for some 44 per cent on its own. Together with other Slavs – Ukrainians and Belorussians – they accounted for three-quarters of the population. By stifling the weak incipient Ukrainian and Belorussian nationalism they were able to give that Slavic bloc some political significance. The Habsburgs were less well placed. Germans accounted for only 24 per cent. Even working on the basis of a condominium with the Magyars (20 per cent) they could not achieve a numerical majority. Slavs constituted a larger group, at 47 per cent, but Slavic identity as opposed to Czech, Polish, Slovene or Croat identity was weak, albeit not insignificant.

The best hope for the Habsburgs was not the equivalent of the Romanovs' Russification of kindred groups and armed suppression of the rest (usually the Poles), but some move to federalism. For over seventy years before the outbreak of war in 1914 federalist projects were formulated to save the Empire. The Empire was not the only source of federal projects in the nineteenth century. German opponents of Bismarck, most notably Konstantin Frantz, upheld a broader federal solution to the German question before and after 1871. In France critics of the centralized French state bequeathed by the Revolution and Napoleon, most notably Proudhon, also appealed to federal solutions. In Britain an Imperial Federation League was formed in 1884. W. T. Stead, an influential journalist, called for a United States of Europe modelled on the United States of America.[33] But it was in the Habsburg lands that the most sustained and intense consideration of federalism took place.

The Empire's ability to implement any of these schemes was severely curtailed after 1866. Fearing a Magyar revolt while Austria faced Prussia,

Emperor Franz Joseph agreed to restore the political power of the Magyars. The outcome, the Compromise of 1867, established a dual Monarchy and made reform much more difficult.[34] The Magyars, who remained a minority in their half of the Habsburg lands, despite years of magyarization, resolutely refused to sacrifice their hegemony. Not that German Austrians were widely committed to federal solutions.

There were two main problems which the federalists faced. One was the current, dualist, structure of the Empire which privileged Germans and Magyars at the expense of Slavs. The second was the ethnic complexity of the region and, it might be added, the small size of some of the would-be nations. The first problem suggested a conceptually simple solution, even if its political realization was bound to be fraught with danger. The solution was for a reform along Trialist lines, giving the Slavs equal weight with the Germans and Magyars. It was a solution which was favoured by the heir to the throne Franz Ferdinand. Even its advocates, however, realized that it would have to be implemented by decree and probably upheld by the sword against a Magyar revolt. The second problem required a more sophisticated approach, which came from the socialist Karl Renner. Renner's proposed solution was a functional differentiation of the state. Economic affairs, for example, would be handled by new territorially defined units. But in cultural affairs people would be represented by their co-nationals wherever they happened to live. In the long run, Renner, like most other socialists and indeed several non-socialists, hoped that common economic interests would cut across and mitigate, if not remove, ethnic tensions. In fact economic grievances were being increasingly viewed from an ethnic stance.

Only in the Habsburg Empire had serious thought been given in the corridors of power to a federal solution, and that was a federal solution for the Empire, not for Europe as a whole. Other, often isolated, figures had argued for a European-wide union either in the form of a full-scale federation or a customs union or some looser confederal form. The predominant trend, as men worried about the increasing tensions of Europe and the exigencies of international trade, was to look beyond the European stage. Schemes for world-wide peace and economic co-operation were increasingly being given prominence. Even advocates of European union would frequently assert that Europe was a first step towards a global solution. Only in central Europe did narrower schemes enjoy great currency. It was these schemes, built around the idea of Mitteleuropa, which would be tested in the First World War.

As Europeans looked back upon the era before the First World War they could, and did, identify contradictory tendencies. Despite the turn to protectionism in the last quarter of the nineteenth century, they could see a pattern of increasing economic integration and impressive, if unevenly distributed and erratic, economic growth. On the other hand, they could see the development of nationalism from a suspect doctrine of limited appeal to the dominant ideology of Europe. Nationalism had, to the agreeable surprise of some governments, exerted a stronger grip on men's loyalties than the international doctrine of socialism. Nationalism had also changed from being a doctrine which promoted integration, that is, larger political units, into one which also threatened to fragment existing states. The severity of the threat varied. For the German Reich it meant the loss of territory. It meant the same thing, though to a greater extent, to Russia. For the Habsburg Empire it potentially meant extinction.

They could also see the great success story of the century: the rise of Germany. For advocates of integration this story offered several lessons. Economic integration, based upon a customs union, appeared to be an attractive strategy. It had produced, it seemed, not only economic integration and growth but had also culminated in political union. Others drew a different lesson: the Zollverein had led to Prussian domination and the creation of a central European state which had undermined the European balance of power. The demise of the Austro-Hungarian Empire naturally attracted attention. To some this only proved the necessity and desirability of the nation-state as the political form for Europe. To others it symbolized a lost opportunity to create a multinational federation which would reconcile the competing claims of the region's diverse ethnic groups. To all its disappearance created a problem simply because it left a power vacuum in its wake.

On the eve of war, the idea of European integration had made little if any progress in the corridors of power. Even among the wider public it was subordinate to schemes of world peace and international arbitration.[35] Yet the nineteenth century did bequeath ideas of federation, of European unity and of a united Mitteleuropa. Equally important, it provided models, albeit only a few, of how these ideas might be implemented. The Zollverein, with its ambiguous message of unity and Prussian hegemony, was the most prominent. The Habsburg Empire provided another model which was similarly ambiguous. On the one hand its simple existence suggested an alternative to the fragmentation which followed its demise. On the other hand it was indicted as the prison house of peoples. In retrospect at least, pre-1914 Europe displayed a level of economic integration which Europe would not regain for decades. Through the gold standard it even provided a model for monetary integration.[36] The world to which Europeans tried to apply these ideas and lessons, fragmentary and ambiguous as they were, was a very different place from the Europe of 1914.

NOTES

1. Wolf Gruner, *Die deutsche Frage* (Munich, 1985), p. 71; F. H. Hinsley, *Power and the Pursuit of Peace* (Cambridge, 1967), p. 196.
2. On the importance of the arrangements in Germany see Gruner, *Die deutsche Frage*, pp. 66–72.
3. See R. Rexheusen and K. -H. Ruffman, 'Russland und die staatliche Einheit Deutschlands im 19. und 20. Jahrhundert', *Aus Politik und Zeitgeschichte*, **9** (1982), p. 13.
4. Cited by H. Gollwitzer, *Europabild und Europagedanke* (Munich, 1964), p. 233.
5. For the production of steel, see Paul Kennedy, *The Rise and Fall of the Great Powers* (London, 1988), p. 257. For the comparison with Austria-Hungary, see Thomas F. Huertas, *Economic Growth and Economic Policy in a Multinational Setting. The Habsburg Monarchy, 1841–1865* (New York, 1977), pp. 10–11.
6. Cited by David Reynolds, *Britannia Overruled* (London, 1991), p. 20.
7. On the Zollverein see the standard work of W. O. Henderson, *The Zollverein* (Cambridge, 1939). For a summary of more recent research, see R. H. Dumke, 'Tariffs and market structure: the German Zollverein as a model for economic integration', in W. R. Lee (ed.), *German Industry and German Industrialization* (London, 1991), pp. 77–115. Among the earlier literature on the viability of the Zollverein as a model of later forms of integration see Wolfram Fischer, 'Der Deutsche Zollverein, die Europäische Wirtschaftsgemeinschaft und die Freihandelzone', *Europa Archiv* (1961), pp. 105–14.
8. On Schwarzenberg see Kenneth W. Rock, 'Felix Schwarzenberg: military diplomat', *Austrian History Yearbook*, **11** (1975), pp. 85–100.
9. Sidney Pollard, 'Industrialization and the European economy', *Economic History Review* (2nd Series), **26** (1973), p. 644.
10. Cited in *ibid.*, p. 642.
11. Richard Hugh Tilly, 'Los von England: Probleme des Nationalismus in der deutschen Wirtschaftsgeschichte', *Zeitschrift für die gesamte Staatswissenschaft*, **124** (1968), p. 187.
12. Quoted in Ludolf Herbst, 'Die zeitgenössische Integrationstheorie und die Anfänge der europäischen Einigung 1947–1950', *Vierteljahreshefte für Zeitgeschichte*, **31** (1983), p. 166.
13. *The Political Writings of Richard Cobden*, Vol. 1 (London, 1867), pp. 282–3.
14. See Derek Heater, *The Idea of European Unity* (Leicester, 1992), pp. 97–108. See also the comments of P. Renouvin, *L'Idéee de fédération europééne dans la pensée politique du XIXe siécle* (Oxford, 1949), pp. 6–7.
15. Renouvin, *L'Idée de fédération europééne*, p. 9.
16. For a survey of these issues as they affected Mitteleuropa, see Peter Stirk, 'The idea of Mitteleuropa', in Peter Stirk (ed.), *Mitteleuropa. History and Prospects* (Edinburgh, 1994), pp. 1–35.
17. See Ekkehard Klug, ' "Europa" und "europäisch" im russischen Denken vom 16. bis zum frühen 19. Jahrhundert', *Saeculum*, **38** (1987), pp. 193–224.
18. Or sometimes as different from Europe at all. According to this version, Russia was not European but Asiatic or half-Asiatic. On this and the above see Hans Lemberg, 'Zur Entstehung des Osteuropabegriffs im 19. Jahrhundert. Vom "Norden" zum "Osten" Europas', *Jahrbücher für die Geschichte Osteuropas*, **33** (1985), pp. 48–91.

19. See the contributions to Daniel Chirot (ed.), *The Origins of Backwardness in Eastern Europe. Economics and Politics from the Middle Ages Until the Early Twentieth Century* (Berkeley, 1989). The division suggested there has similarities to that of Oscar Halecki, *The Limits and Divisions of European History* (London, 1950) and the more recent influential essay by J. Szucs, 'The three historical regions of Europe', *Acta Historica Academiae Scientiarum Hungaricae*, **29** (1983), pp. 741–66.
20. For the general pattern and its impact on incomes and government expenditures, see Andre C. Janos, *Politics and Paradigms* (Stanford, 1986), pp. 87–91 and 166, and for a case study his *The Politics of Backwardness in Hungary 1825–1945* (Princeton, 1982). See also the highly illuminating comments by Z. A. B. Zeman, *The Making and Breaking of Communist Europe* (Oxford, 1991), pp. 42–50.
21. See Huertas, *Economic Growth and Economic Policy in a Multinational Setting*, especially pp. 19–24; John Komlos, *The Habsburg Monarchy as a Customs Union* (Princeton, 1983), *passim*; Derek H. Aldcroft, 'The federal idea in Europe before 1914', in Preston King and Andrea Bosco (eds), *A Constitution for Europe* (London, 1991), pp. 189–92; Péter Hanák, 'Economics, society, and sociopolitical thought in Hungary in the age of capitalism', *Austrian History Yearbook*, **11** (1975), pp. 121–3.
22. Komlos, *The Habsburg Monarchy*, p. 139.
23. Oscar Jaszi, *The Dissolution of the Habsburg Monarchy* (Chicago, 1929), p. 198.
24. Sidney Pollard, *The Integration of the European Economy since 1815* (London, 1981), pp. 56–9.
25. Jack Gaston, 'The free trade diplomacy debate and the Victorian European Common Market initiative', *Canadian Journal of History*, **22** (1987), pp. 59–82. The title of the article is misleading. By Gaston's own account the initiative bears more resemblance to a regional GATT, if that, than to current ideas of a Common Market. It does, however, show that the more imaginative members of the British establishment, sadly few in number, recognized the need for some kind of international co-ordination.
26. G. de Molinari, 'Union douanière de l'Europe centrale', *Journal des Economistes*, **5** (1879), pp. 309–18.
27. On von Baussern see H. C. Meyer, *Mitteleuropa in German Thought and Action* (The Hague, 1955), pp. 59–61. On Brentano see James J. Sheehan, *The Career of Lujo Brentano* (Chicago, 1966), pp. 108–26.
28. R. Fiebig von Hase, 'Die deutsch-amerikanishen Wirtschaftsbeziehungen, 1890–1914, im Zeichen von Protektionismus und internationaler Integration', *Amerikastudien*, **33** (1988), pp. 354–5.
29. A. Sartorius, Freiherr von Waltershausen, 'Ein deutsch-niederländischer Zollverein', *Zeitschrift für Sozialwissenschaft*, **3** (1900), p. 496.
30. Quoted by Fritz Fischer, *War of Illusions. German Policies from 1911 to 1914* (London, 1975), p. 39.
31. E. J. Hobsbawm, *Nations and Nationalism since 1780* (Cambridge, 1990), pp. 30–2. I have relied heavily upon Hobsbawm's book for the assessment of nationalism.
32. For the national problem, see Raymond Pearson, *National Minorities in Eastern Europe 1848–1945* (London, 1983).
33. British political leaders have frequently derided federalism as an 'alien' doctrine. That it is nothing of the sort has been repeatedly demonstrated by M. Burgess. See, for example, his 'Federalism and Empire: Edward Freeman, imperial federation and British federal ideas for the British', in King and Bosco (eds),

A Constitution for Europe, pp. 253–66. See also John Pinder, 'The federal idea and the British liberal tradition', in Andrea Bosco (ed.), *The Federal Idea*, Vol. 1 (London, 1991), pp. 91–118.

34. But not impossible. See Péter Hanák, 'Compromise and disintegration', in Andrea Petö (ed.), *Central European University Yearbook 1993* (Budapest, 1994), pp. 123–34.
35. Hinsley, *Power and the Pursuit of Peace*, emphasizes this. See, for example, p. 116.
36. See Wilhelm Röpke, *International Economic Disintegration* (London, 1942) and M. Panic, *European Monetary Union* (London, 1993).

2

Between Pan-Europa and Mitteleuropa: 1914–39

INTRODUCTION

The First World War marked the end of the nineteenth-century European order and witnessed an attempt to reshape Europe in the form of a German-dominated Mitteleuropa. This was one possible solution of the underlying disequilibrium in Europe created by the growth of economic and military power in central Europe. It was, however, internally flawed. At its heart stood an alliance between two powers with divergent ambitions. The multinational Habsburg Empire sought to use the fruits of victory to resolve the tensions between its constituent nationalities. The German Reich was orientated to Germanic hegemony and increasingly fell under the influence of men more interested in a vast colonial empire stretching deep into Russia. That eastern empire, or Ostraum, had little place for the complex compromises which characterized Habsburg politics. Yet Mitteleuropa failed not because of its internal weaknesses, but because it was overwhelmed by the superior power of its opponents, most notably the United States. From this point on, the United States, whether by its indifference or by its active intervention, became central to the prospects of European integration.

Amidst the chaos and dislocation at the end of the war there were few advocates of full-scale European integration. But there were numerous attempts to halt the fragmentation of Europe, especially among the new states which arose from the ruins of the Habsburg and Tsarist empires. There were even attempts to lay the foundations of Franco-German reconciliation through co-operation in the reconstruction of the exhausted economies of the two countries. None of these succeeded. The new states of eastern Europe were too proud of their independence and too divided by territorial claims. France sought security more through the control of Germany than through reconciliation.

By 1923 the evident failure to establish a stable, let alone a prosperous, order in Europe had prompted some people to turn to the idea of

European union. They did so from across the political spectrum. This fact stands in marked contrast to the late twentieth-century consensus that European union and parliamentary democracy march hand in hand. Early twentieth-century advocates of European integration included authoritarians, nationalists committed to territorial revision of the borders established at Versailles, agrarian radicals and communists.

These men were divided by their vision of European union as well as by their political ideology. Central to their disputes was the membership of any European union, and especially their attitude to Britain. Some pointed to the British Empire and concluded that Britain would have no interest in a European union. Others pointed to the need to include Britain to establish a balance between France and Germany. Most agreed that Franco-German reconciliation was the key. After 1923 improved relations between these two powers seemed to auger well for the prospects of European union. Economic trends were less reassuring. Europe continued to slide towards disintegration. That naturally suggested the need for a customs union, but here the wider context of European integration presented problems. A customs union, by its very definition, would reduce barriers between members, but depending upon its external tariff, it could either promote wider trade liberalization or follow a protectionist course. The latter raised the prospect of antagonizing the United States.

Ever since the success of the Zollverein in the nineteenth century, a customs union had been the most favoured strategy for building a European union. But it was not the only one. In the second half of the 1920s, as politicians hesitated, attention was drawn to the transnational activities of Europe's industrialists. Even politicians upheld businessmen as the trailblazers of integration. Their enthusiasm was misguided. The international cartels which aroused it were fragile. Integration, whether economic or political, depended upon the basic decisions of states.

At the end of the decade choices were being made. Britain preferred a global strategy based on free trade and the League of Nations. But if forced, Britain would retreat into the Empire. Germany was turning back to Mitteleuropa, seeking to build a power base in central and eastern Europe. As these decisions were crystallizing, France officially proposed a European Union. The prospects of such a Union were never good in the 1920s. In 1929 it was definitely too late. The failure of the major western powers to reconcile their differences had profound implications for the rest of Europe, especially for eastern Europe. Eastern Europe had struggled to overcome its economic difficulties in the 1920s. With the onset of the depression the distress in eastern Europe became chronic. But its salvation lay in large part beyond its own control. Integration in the east depended on support from the west, and that, given the divisions between the western powers, was not forthcoming.

In the 1930s economic disintegration was accompanied by political radicalization. Within all camps, even the most unlikely, visions of some form of European union could be found. It was even more apparent now that democrats had no monopoly on European union. But although the idea of European union was espoused in the 1930s, such advocacy was pushed to the margins of political debate. Especially towards the end of the decade, the centre stage was dominated by what seemed the inexorable growth of German power. At the end of the inter-war period Europe was on the eve of a second German bid to reshape Europe.

FORGING MITTELEUROPA

In 1914 the early victories of German forces in the west had induced a wave of speculation and demands for annexation. Publicists and businessmen jostled to outbid each other in the extravagance of their claims on Germany's behalf. Berlin's statesmen were not far behind. Still expecting imminent victory, Chancellor Bethmann-Hollweg formulated his war aims in September 1914. In them he demanded that

> We must create a central European economic association through common customs treaties, to include France, Belgium, Holland, Denmark, Austria-Hungary, Poland, and perhaps Italy, Sweden and Norway. This association will not have any common constitutional supreme authority and all its members will be formally equal, but in practice will be under German leadership and must stabilise Germany's economic dominance over Mitteleuropa.[1]

The devices by which German hegemony would be exercised became clearer later, especially in the plans and treaties formulated towards the end of the war. They included territorial annexation, preferential treatment for German goods, German control of infrastructure, especially ports and railways, and key raw materials, the right to establish military bases and military conventions subordinating the forces of nominally independent states to German control. These devices would have created a zone of German control stretching in the east from Finland, down the Baltic littoral, through the Ukraine to the Crimea and the Balkans and stretching in the west to Belgium and north-western France.

At the heart of the envisaged Mitteleuropa stood the Berlin–Vienna axis. Although Austria-Hungary was included in the September 1914 programme, Bethmann-Hollweg was more specific then about his plans for the west of Europe. Stalemate in the west, military successes in the east and the clamour of the publicists pushed him to focus upon consolidating the Austro-German alliance. The first serious talks on the issue took place in November 1915.[2] From the start an irreconcilable difference of interests was evident. In Berlin a nationalist ethos predominated which was incompatible with the existence of Austria-Hungary as a multinational empire. The Berlin perspective was clear when Bethmann-Hollweg expressed, in August 1915, 'a great concern for the future fate and position of the Germans in Austria'.[3] It became even clearer when State Secretary Jagow recorded his government's position in the November 1915 discussions. According to Jagow's memorandum the Germans had been losing ground within Austria-Hungary to the Slavs. This lamentable development 'would appear to contradict the basis of our alliance and the foreign interests of both signatories'. His conclusion was that Austria should 'return to the Germanic element the leading role which it deserves in the interest of Austria as the German Ostmark'.[4] Vienna protested that it was much more than a German Ostmark and forcefully defended the increasing influence of non-German elements in the empire.

The suspicion that any union of Mitteleuropa would be an instrument of Germanic hegemony pure and simple was widespread and appeared to be confirmed by the more nationalistic of the German publicists. Even those Germans who claimed to desire a more equitable arrangement among the peoples of the region were finding it difficult to convince anyone other than their own nationals. Such was the experience of the most influential of the Mitteleuropa tracts of 1915: Friedrich Naumann's *Mitteleuropa*. Naumann pleaded for greater German appreciation of the diverse identities and customs of Mitteleuropa, but to little avail. His prophecy of a Europe divided by a permanent system of trenches, and of a centrally organized economy in Mitteleuropa, as well as his condescending characterization of other cultures, certainly provided good grounds for suspicion.

Despite his comments on the need for economic union, Naumann gave no detailed consideration to the form and consequences of economic integration in the region. The influential *Verein für Sozialpolitik* did, and concluded in April 1916 that from Berlin's perspective Mitteleuropa made no economic sense save as a wartime emergency measure.[5] Berlin's trade experts and Austria's businessmen were both equally sceptical. The pressure for a customs union was in fact largely political and it came from Berlin. Vienna managed to delay talks on tariff schedules until April 1916. By the middle of the war the speculation and negotiations had achieved little beyond inflaming suspicions of their intentions and provoking the Allies to formulate counter-measures at the Paris Economic Conference. Faced with the prospect of a protectionist Mitteleuropa at the end of the war, Britain and France agreed upon what amounted to the continuation of the wartime blockade after the cessation of hostilities.

As the war progressed and Vienna's financial position became ever more desperate the Austrians began to look with more favour upon the customs union. Agreement was finally reached in October 1918. By then it made no difference. The central powers were facing defeat. The fundamental clash of interest between Berlin and Vienna had, however, persisted until the end, and not only over the economic consequences of unity. A key dispute throughout concerned the fate of Poland. Both agreed that some kind of reconstituted Polish entity was desirable, if only to secure Polish manpower for their cause. But there the agreement ended. Vienna favoured the so-called Austro-Polish solution. Poland would be reconstituted as a part of the Habsburg Empire and, crucially, would provide her Slavic subjects with a status notionally equivalent to her German and Magyar subjects. The Austro-Polish solution would thus be the solution to the long-standing problems of the multinational empire. Although this strategy met with periodic sympathy from Berlin it was rigidly opposed by the increasingly influential Supreme Army Command under Generals Ludendorff and Hindenburg. Both harboured a traditional Prussian suspicion of Vienna. Ludendorff also had an entirely different agenda. The idea of increased unity in Mitteleuropa as a solution to the ethnic entwinement of the region was of no interest to him. He was not even convinced of the economic advantages of the alliance and believed German capital could be more profitably employed in Belgium, Bulgaria and Romania.[6] More importantly, Ludendorff was committed to the creation of a Germanic imperium in the east, including a programme of colonization stretching down to the Crimea. The difference between Vienna's perspective and Ludendorff's has been aptly summarized by the historian of German wartime ambitions Fritz Fischer:

> Germany's great Eastern Idea, which went far beyond Brest-Litovsk, prevented the completion of Mitteleuropa which, in the last phase, was dropped by Germany in favour of absolute domination of the Ostraum – a goal as old as the Mitteleuropa idea itself.[7]

EUROPE AFTER VERSAILLES

With the defeat of the central powers the prospects of a Europe united around Mitteleuropa were shelved. But the image of Mitteleuropa as a thinly veiled scheme for German hegemony would compound the difficulties of finding a solution to the economic problems of the successor states. The outcome of the war, for both western and eastern Europe, was an increased lack of integration. Planning for the post-war world was centred upon the universalist League of Nations. The Charter did include, as Article 21, the provision that 'Nothing in the Covenant shall be deemed to affect the validity of international engagements, such as treaties of arbitration or regional understandings like the Monroe Doctrine.' Despite this concession, inserted by the Covenant's architect Woodrow Wilson, the League was intended to be a global, not a regional, institution.[8] Amidst the popular enthusiasm for Wilson's vision there were few critics who insisted upon the need for European federation as an alternative to the global scheme. The most forthright were Giovanni Agnelli, founder of FIAT, and Attilio Cabiati, an economist, who called in 1918 for a European federation modelled upon the United States of America and insisted that '[a]ny other milder version is but a delusion'.[9]

The United States was no less influential in the economic reconstruction of Europe. At the end of the First World War the United States was hostile to regional schemes and indeed to any official participation in the reconstruction process. A suggestion from Lloyd George in 1919 for an Anglo-American guarantee of a bond issue which would be used to settle reparations payments and war debts was rejected, following Treasury advice to reduce state lending by the United States in favour of private loans. Britain and France also argued for the continuation of wartime agencies for regulating trade, shipping and finance, but these too were blocked. The United States would not even negotiate with her European debtors as a group, preferring bilateral negotiations.[10] Lacking American support for some common reconstruction effort, the Europeans explored the option on their own. The focus of their efforts was the desire to extract reparations from Germany, and the need for German economic recovery at least sufficient to enable her to make these payments.

One approach was tried by the German Minister for Reconstruction, Walther Rathenau, and his French counterpart, Louis Loucheur, at Wiesbaden in June 1921. Together they agreed on a system of payments in kind which eventually led to the signing of an agreement. Behind this agreement lay more ambitious plans for linking western European reconstruction with concerted action in eastern Europe and Russia. This latter idea was taken up by Rathenau and the German industrialist Hugo Stinnes in their approaches to Lloyd George in September and November of 1921.[11] The underlying theme was that the western powers could participate in the development of Russia, expand their industries in the process and generate the wealth to oil the wheels of the network of reparations and debt payments. Lloyd George took up the idea with some enthusiasm and negotiations on an international consortium continued until the Conference of Genoa in 1922. The Soviet authorities regarded the scheme with distrust, seeing it as a device for the capitalist exploitation of Russia. The western powers were divided. German leaders still saw their country as under threat of economic warfare from the Allies, and some advocated a separate deal with the Soviet Union. It is doubtful if the consortium would have had much impact had it come into being. There were disagreements over its organization and control as well as the amount of finance to be at its disposal, with France pushing down the British suggestion of £20 million to a mere £2 million.[12] The scheme was, however, effectively consigned to the graveyard when, during the Genoa Conference, Germany signed the Treaty of Rapallo with Russia, which was subsequently to be invoked as an attempt to secure Russian support for an anti-western strategy.[13]

THE FRAGMENTATION OF EASTERN EUROPE

In eastern Europe too there had been some recognition of the need to halt Europe's fragmentation, not least by the Americans. The dissolution of the Habsburg Empire had not been the original intention of the Allies, and even when political fragmentation became unstoppable there were still hopes that some elements of economic unity could be retained. The successor states, most of whom had mutual territorial grievances, were less accommodating. Alongside their resentment of their former masters, expressed in the obstacles placed upon the supply of coal to Vienna, the successor states were committed to economic independence as well as political independence. One of the few restraints in the initial years was the American Relief Administration, initially a government body but after Congress withdrew authorization in mid-1919 officially private. Its head, Herbert Hoover, also occupied a number of other posts, giving him some leverage over the new states. Consequently, his agents operated the only communications system covering the entire region, which they had inherited from the General Staffs of the central powers. They exercised some control over transport and even arranged barter deals between the states. Some of them were appointed as technical advisers to Austria, Poland, Czechoslovakia and Yugoslavia. In that capacity they helped promote a conference intended to reduce the growing number of import restrictions.[14] The conference was eventually held at Porto Rose in October and November 1921 and a protocol agreeing upon the removal of import restrictions by July 1922 was signed. It was, however, never ratified.

In both west and east there was a recognition that the fragmentation of Europe needed to be resisted. There was, of course, a large gap between the kind of co-operation contemplated in the Wiesbaden agreements or the international consortium and the federalist vision of Agnelli and Cabiati. Positive advocacy of European unity was at best a marginal activity. In the west only the exigencies of reconstruction and the network of reparations and war debts pushed statesmen and their advisers to seek some co-operative solution in reluctant recognition of the fact that unilateral solutions were beyond the power of individual states.

In the east and central European states where borders were less well established, and were patently incongruent with national identities, the reconstruction period still seemed to leave some opening for regional, rather than pan-European, union. Thus the Czech president T. G. Masaryk discussed a federation with Romanian and Yugoslav leaders in 1918, a federation which significantly excluded the enemy states of Austria, Hungary and Bulgaria. A little later the Prime Minister Eduard Beneš did discuss an economic agreement with the Hungarian Prime Minister, Count Paul Teleki, which he suggested could eventually lead to a 'United States of Central Europe'. But nothing came of these schemes save the formation of a set of military alliances, the so-called Little Entente, which linked Czechoslovakia, Romania and Yugoslavia in common opposition to Hungary, who had territorial claims against all three.[15] Further north Estonia had suggested a Baltic federation in 1919 and as late as March 1922 a draft security pact was drawn up, linking Finland, Estonia, Latvia and Poland. Neither made any progress. The omission of Lithuania from the 1922 scheme was significant. The Polish leader Marshall Pilsudski, a man of genuine federalist sentiment, had earlier worked for a Polish-Lithuanian federation, but had misguidedly connived with a coup in Vilnius and then seized the city by force. Territorial ambitions and nationalism easily outstripped both federalist sentiment and pragmatic considerations of the need of small states to co-operate if they were to survive.

A slightly different picture was presented by two groups, especially in the centre and south-east of Europe: the communists and the agrarians. Both favoured federation. The communists, however, were a minority and were on the defensive. In Bulgaria they were crushed in 1919 by Aleksandir Stamboliiski with the aid of Allied troops. Stamboliiski, an agrarian leader, was also an advocate of a union of southern Slavs and the creation of a Green International representing the interest of the peasants who still constituted the majority of east Europe's population. His efforts to begin the process by bringing about a reconciliation with Yugoslavia were cut short when he was assassinated in June 1923. His fellow agrarian and federalist, the Croat Stefan Radich, met the same fate.[16] These faltering efforts at regional unity clearly linked the process of unification with radical reform, with the dictatorship of the proletariat in the case of the communist vision of a Balkan Soviet Socialist Republic and with radical land reform in the case of the agrarians.[17]

COUDENHOVE-KALERGI AND THE IDEA OF PAN-EUROPEAN UNION

The link between social and political form and some kind of union of states was not absent in the west. It was evident in the ideas of an Austrian aristocrat, Richard N. Coudenhove-Kalergi, founder of the Pan-European Union. Coudenhove-Kalergi had been an enthusiastic supporter of Woodrow Wilson and the League of Nations. However, he quickly despaired of the American President's global vision and turned instead to the idea of Europe. As he did so he brought his vision of a new social order for Europe with him. It was not a democratic vision. In a work published in 1923 his sentiment was unambiguous: 'Our democratic era is a miserable interlude between two great aristocratic epochs: the feudal aristocracy of the sword and the social aristocracy of the spirit.'[18] It is not surprising, then, that the first man Coudenhove-Kalergi turned to, in 1922, was Benito Mussolini. Mussolini was not interested. The link between a union of states and the burning issues of Europe's social order were evident to others too. When Coudenhove-Kalergi received funds from the Hamburg banker Max Warburg the latter had been encouraged by one Katherina von Oheimb-Kardorff, who was anxious that the movement for European unity should not fall under the control of proletarians![19]

There were, however, two restraints upon Coudenhove-Kalergi's authoritarian inclinations. He resolutely rejected war as a road to unification and insisted upon the equality of the peoples and states within his proposed union. In his *Pan-Europa*, published in 1923, he set out the stages by which union was to be achieved. Firstly, there would be a Conference of governments; second, a system of arbitration treaties; and third, a customs union. The crowning United States of Europe was to be explicitly modelled upon the American constitution. A House of Peoples would represent the citizens of the union, with each of the three hundred members representing one million peoples. The House of States would consist of one member for each participating state.[20]

The second restraint was Coudenhove-Kalergi's attempt to build his movement on as broad a base as possible. He sought, for example, to win over socialists to his movement and did manage to persuade the SPD President of the Reichstag Paul Löbe to become head of the German section of the movement. He was, in fact, remarkably successful in obtaining the support of people from diverse political camps, from the socialist Löbe to the authoritarian cleric and sometime Chancellor of

Austria Ignaz Seipel. But Löbe was unhappy about the attack on democracy which marked the Pan-European Congress in October 1926, and by the end of the decade the Pan-European Union had acquired the reputation of being anti-socialist.[21]

Coudenhove-Kalergi's main arguments were a blend of the fashionable geo-political calculation and an eclectic cultural anthropology. The former issued in speculation of the division of the world into competing blocs of continental dimensions. Prominent here was the example of the Pan-American league. Coudenhove-Kalergi later recalled that A. H. Fried's *Panamerika* was the first book he read in connection with the Pan-European idea.[22] Like many contemporaries he grossly exaggerated the extent of the integration brought about by the Pan-American League. He could also draw on other examples of this supposed trend, one of which was the British Empire. By pointing to the British Empire as an 'inter-continental' world federation with which Pan-Europe would have to compete, he was excluding Britain from the European union.[23] Russia too was excluded. Indeed, the Russian menace was one of the main motives for Europe's union: 'History gives Europe the following alternatives: either to overcome all national hostilities and consolidate in a federal union, or sooner or later to succumb to a Russian conquest. There is no third possibility.'[24] But the main obstacle to European union was strictly internal. It lay in the relationship between Germany and France.

The year 1923, when *Pan-Europa* was first published, was not a promising one for Franco-German reconciliation. France had not been satisfied by the Treaty of Versailles, which gave her neither the territorial changes nor the Anglo-American commitment which she had sought. She tried to use the periodic crises induced by Germany's difficulty in meeting reparations payments to strengthen her position. This policy culminated in January 1923 when, after Germany's failure to meet scheduled coal deliveries, French and Belgian troops occupied the Ruhr. From her position of occupation France sought to promote separatist tendencies in the Rhineland, ultimately in vain. The occupation itself was also a failure and the French were eventually obliged to withdraw.

The improvement in Franco-German relations from this low point naturally gave encouragement to advocates of European unity. In a Supplement to *Pan-Europa* written in 1926 Coudenhove-Kalergi could look back upon 1924 and claim that '[t]he road was opened to a European understanding'.[25] There was certainly an increase in the activity of the small groups of advocates of European union. April 1924 saw the appearance of an International Committee for a European Customs Union.[26] In Germany a journalist, Dr Alfred Nossig, and the DDP Deputy Wilhelm Heile pursued their own schemes which issued in the creation of competitors for Coudenhove-Kalergi's Pan-European Union.[27] Coudenhove-Kalergi was loosing his brief monopoly of the field. It was not a change he welcomed. Alongside the personal conflicts which marked the relationship between these various groups were disputes which reflected the more substantive problems of inter-war European unity.

One concerned the democratic legitimacy of any move to European union. Coudenhove-Kalergi had set out to recruit a mass organization which would pressure governments into acting. His competitors preferred instead to work through Europe's elites. In practice both followed a similar strategy since Coudenhove-Kalergi never managed to transform his Pan-European Union into a genuine mass organization.[28] So far as any progress was made in the inter-war period it was made at the level of Europe's elites, not the majority of the populations.

Equally important was the issue of membership of any prospective union. Coudenhove-Kalergi excluded Britain and Russia. Heile fiercely advocated the inclusion of both. Heile's argument was that the union would only work if it could not be seen as an arrangement which would lead to German hegemony, and that prospect could only be excluded if Britain were a member. Indicative of the strength with which he held this view was his assertion that Coudenhove-Kalergi's union would be viewed in France as 'German imperialism masked by pacifism'.[29]

Another difference between these two concerned the issue of the revision of the borders drawn at Versailles. Coudenhove-Kalergi insisted that these borders would have to be respected for the foreseeable future if war was to be avoided. He also prophesied that a pan-European conference orientated towards the revision of the Versailles borders would fail.[30] Heile on the other hand was a revisionist. As well as being chairman of the Verband für europäische Verständigung he was Vice-President of the Österreichisch-Deutschen Volksbund whose agenda included the Anschluss of Germany and Austria. He tried to reassure the French that Anschluss would pose no threat. If the German nation were allowed to unite within a single state, Germany would be a satiated power.[31]

TOWARDS FRANCO-GERMAN RECONCILIATION

In the short run international events seemed to confirm the viability of Coudenhove-Kalergi's option. By the Treaty of Locarno of October 1925 the Franco-German and Belgian–German borders were recognized by the signatories, who included Britain and Italy as well, and the parties renounced the use of force. This seemed to justify the growing advocacy of European union evident in the increasing number of journals and other publications devoted to this cause. Equally striking were two speeches by the French Prime Minister Edouard Herriot on 24 October 1924 and 25 January 1925. On the second occasion Herriot spoke of his hope 'one day to see the United States of Europe realized'.[32] On the German side Gustav Stresemann had responded positively to Herriot's first speech, the idea was discussed in the Reichstag in May 1925 and the German SPD included support for a united states of Europe in its September 1925 Heidelberg programme. When the Locarno agreements themselves were reached they were acclaimed by some sections of Europe's press as a step towards the United States of Europe.[33]

The reality of the accords was more prosaic and limited. The German initiative which led to Locarno was motivated by a long-term strategy for removing the limits on German sovereignty imposed by the Versailles Treaty and by the desire to avoid a Franco-British alliance for which the French were pressing. Stresemann himself showed no sign of intending to transform his vague sympathy for Herriot's ideas into concrete action. Stresemann thought in terms of the traditional categories of sovereign states, not of federations or supranational institutions. In the words of Jon Jacobson, the historian of Locarno diplomacy,

> To be a good European during the Locarno era did not mean that one was willing to diminish the sovereignty of one's state; it meant that one did not take unilateral action. One went to Geneva four times a year and there consulted with the other members of the Council of Europe and attempted to act in concert with them.[34]

The detail of the agreements was limited too. For while Germany had recognized her western borders as imposed by Versailles she had resolutely refused to accord the same recognition to her eastern borders. True, Germany had signed arbitration treaties with Poland and Czechoslovakia, the two states against whom Germany had territorial claims. But these treaties did not preclude resort to war if her eastern neighbours refused to comply with an unfavourable arbitration judgement. Nor were the treaties guaranteed by the great powers. The British had explicitly refused any such guarantee for the simple reason that they accepted, in principle, the eventual revision of the eastern borders.[35]

PATTERNS OF TRADE AND THE IDEA OF A CUSTOMS UNION

Nevertheless, the next five years continued to provide encouragement for supporters of European unity. Even before the Locarno agreements the Frenchman Louis Loucheur had called for an economic conference to resolve Europe's problems. Looking back on the inter-war period from the vantage point of 1942 a League of Nations report bemoaned the failure to re-establish 'normal tariffs'. Instead of seeing trade as a 'co-operative activity from the extension of which all stood to benefit', states professed their faith in free trade, but in practice 'trade was consistently regarded as a form of warfare, as a vast game of beggar-my-neighbour'.[36] During the inter-war years two German economists, H. Gaedicke and G. von Eynern, estimated that, adjusting for changes in prices and territorial boundaries, intra-European trade was scarcely higher in the years 1925–30 than in 1909–13. They derived some comfort from the fact that intra-European trade had increased as a percentage of total trade despite the extent of barriers to trade. But they noted that the blanket figures for Europe concealed some important variations.[37] The total trade of the industrial heartland of Europe, which they designated Kerneuropa, had increased but the force of integration was slackening. While this region absorbed some 51 per cent of its exports in the prewar year of 1912 it took only 43 per cent of its own exports in 1929.[38] That the obstacles to trade were mutually damaging was readily conceded by most commentators and ministers. The standard recipe for improvement was a reduction of tariff levels and the maintenance of the Most Favoured Nation (MFN) clause. But other options were being canvassed too, including the idea of a European customs union.

A customs union as a road to integration was, despite competing routes, still the most favoured among advocates of economic integration in the inter-war period. Loucheur's call for an economic conference encouraged speculation on the prospects of a customs union on which the German Foreign Office felt obliged to comment. Initially the suggested response was that Germany was 'not only sympathetic but actively encouraging', though this initial enthusiasm was soon diluted.[39] The eventual circular to German missions still affirmed the goal but listed several problems, among which was the probability that the United States would see the measure as one directed against them. It would also force Britain to choose between Europe and her Empire, a choice Britain would be loathe to take.[40] A prime concern of the German Foreign Office was that the customs union would adopt a protectionist stance against the outside world and especially against the United States. The political economist Wladimir Woytinsky agreed. The success of the slogan of a customs union lay in its ambiguity. A customs union could be concerned primarily with protection against third parties or with liberalizing trade between its members while maintaining a liberal policy towards outsiders. The protectionist course was, he warned, a 'dangerous adventure'. Europe's enemy was not its foreign competitors but its own internal fragmentation.[41]

The conference, when it eventually met in 1927, followed the orthodox path of tariff reduction, which the German Foreign Office had held to be the most promising. Participating states agreed to a convention including the provision that states would adopt free trade policies. The convention was to come into force if eighteen states had ratified it by September 1929. Only seventeen did. By the time the conference met another route to European unity had, it seemed, been opened up.

Throughout the inter-war period, and indeed thereafter, a central issue was the relationship between Europe's heavy industries, and especially the relationship between French and German heavy industry. That relationship had been complicated by the postwar settlement with the iron ore fields of Lorraine returning to France, the customs union between Luxembourg and Germany being dissolved and the Saar being incorporated into a customs union with France, pending the settlement of the fate of the Saar by plebiscite in 1935. For France the aim was to ensure continued access to German Markets after 1925. By the Treaty of Versailles Germany was bound to concede Most Favoured Nation treatment to French products until 1925, and was therefore prohibited from discriminating against French steel. For German heavy industry the prime concern was to ensure market stability amidst the prevailing conditions of an excess of productive capacity. One way of doing this was to regulate the internal market and exclude foreign, especially French, competition.[42] On a broader front the French and German governments were negotiating on a trade treaty to regulate their relationship after Germany regained her tariff sovereignty. The two sets of negotiations, between French and German heavy industry on the one hand and the two governments on the other, were in fact interlinked. Although French and German interests were by far the larger actors, others also played a role, especially the head of the Luxembourg steel firm ARBED, Émile Mayrisch.

INDUSTRIAL CARTELS AND INTEGRATION

Mayrisch was a consistent advocate of industrial co-operation, and in this spirit founded the German-French Study Committee in May 1926. Although officially concerned strictly with Franco-German relations Mayrisch himself had a wider vision of European economic union.[43] It was Mayrisch who revived talks in January 1926 which eventually led to a settlement in the form of the International Steel Cartel.[44] This was a private agreement between industrialists by which they set quotas for steel production and divided up export markets. Thus France was guaranteed 3.75 per cent of the German market and Luxembourg 2.75 per cent. Tariff barriers were circumvented by price-setting agreements, effectively offering rebates for goods having to cross tariff borders. The whole system was regulated through a central treasury into which all members paid. Surcharges were imposed upon producers who exceeded their quota and rebates provided for firms which did not reach their quota.

Once this agreement was in place it proved possible to make progress on the Franco-German trade treaty which was eventually signed in 1927. According to the historian Charles S. Maier, 'both settlements showed that, in the political and economic spheres, nationalist or unilateral solutions had come to appear too costly and even unnecessary'.[45] Many contemporaries of the agreements went further, seeing them as foreshadowing European economic union and even a United States of Europe. The reality of the International Steel Cartel was more problematic than they realized. The Germans soon complained that they had accepted too small a quota and the history of the Cartel was characterized by continual wrangling over shares and the penalty system.[46]

Yet the Steel Cartel did exercise a powerful influence on the minds of advocates of unity. A striking example of its effect was provided by the former French Premier Edouard Herriot in his *The United States of Europe*:

> Whereas attempts at a customs union have failed because they were premature, all the industries are being led by an irresistible movement toward a system of agreements ... It is idle to ask whether Governments can be theoretically disinterested in these agreements. In fact, as the case of the Steel Trust shows, they are constantly concerned with them.
>
> The whole problem to be decided is whether public men will have as much initiative and intelligence as private individuals, or whether in politics, we are going to be content to walk in the old ways, ignoring the great transformation, which is silently creating a new world ... [47]

The case for integrating Europe by means of industrial cartels took diverse forms. One variant, developing a stronger contrast between Herriot's enlightened industrialists and benighted politicians, was that Europe's politicians were beholden to their electorates and could not take the necessary but painful decisions to integrate Europe's economy. Another variant claimed that cartels could help to manage the inevitable rationalization which integration would bring. They would lessen the pain of integration. Yet a third variant started from the observation that tariff reductions were not so much premature as insufficient. In the postwar world, states had learned to use different instruments, especially currency controls, quota systems and health regulations, to regulate trade.

There was some truth in many of these claims. Economic integration required much more than a customs union. Other factors, especially price movements and currency controls, did play a major role in inhibiting the movement of goods. But whether industrialists were more enlightened or more able to mitigate the pain of integration than governments is much more doubtful. The cartels of the inter-war period were animated by a Malthusian economic outlook. The object of the exercise was to lessen competition, to share out what was seen as a stagnant market and to raise domestic prices.

In the second half of the 1920s the prophets of European unity could persuade themselves that events were moving in the desired direction. Their advocacy took place against the background of two complicating factors: fear of the United States of America and, towards the end of the decade, fear of the revival of the idea of Anschluss between Germany and Austria. Throughout the inter-war period, attitudes to the United States were volatile and ambiguous. American efficiency and productive might were admired and feared. The economic competition of the United States seemed so intense that pessimists doubted whether Europe could withstand the challenge. Not only the competition posed by American goods but American investment in Europe seemed to confirm the threat. The United States was also an increasingly protectionist state. The Fordney-McCumber tariff of 1922 had already turned her into the most protectionist of the industrialized states. After the election of Herbert Hoover as President in 1928 speculation on further increases was rife. Tariffs were raised again in 1930 by the Hawley-Smoot tariff. These actions, in connection with increasing economic activity by the United States in Latin America, suggested that the United States was moving to the formation of a continental economic bloc. Europe, it was argued, had to follow suit if she was to survive. This posed particular problems for British businessmen. They were being faced with the uncomfortable choice identified by the German Foreign Office: the choice between Empire and Europe. By the summer of 1930 the consensus among British businessmen was that she should choose the Empire.[48]

BETWEEN PAN-EUROPA AND MITTELEUROPA

The issue of Anschluss posed a different kind of choice: between Pan-Europa and Mitteleuropa. The issues and options emerged in an illuminating meeting between the German State Secretary Schubert and the Czechoslovak Prime Minister Edouard Beneš. In May 1928 Beneš made an unofficial visit to Germany and spoke to the State Secretary while the Foreign Minister Stresemann was ill. On the second day of their discussion they turned to economic matters. Schubert raised the possibility of economic co-operation between Austria, Germany and Czechoslovakia after speaking in more general terms about European economic co-operation. To this Beneš counterposed the possibility of a preference system linking the states of eastern Europe. Schubert objected that 'strictly economically' his scheme was more rational. He had already pointed to the importance of Germany and Austria as export markets for Czech goods. Schubert recorded that Beneš conceded 'to a certain degree' that the German's proposal did indeed make economic sense. But Beneš's prime fear soon became apparent when Schubert suggested a combination of the two schemes. According to Beneš, 'Were a great power included it would immediately mean that this great power would take over the leadership of the association ... '[49] At this point Schubert took up the broader picture again and both men agreed that were there to be an agreement between Germany and France the position would radically change. Then, Schubert's scheme could well be viable.

Although this meeting did not have any impact upon subsequent developments, it clearly exposed the choices and fears in central Europe. Beneš feared a revival of the old Mitteleuropa idea which meant integration under German hegemony. Schubert, who was personally committed to wider economic co-operation rather than to the pursuit of German hegemony, pointed to a way out: central European economic co-operation could be had without raising the prospect of German hegemony if it was part of what amounted to a pan-European economic co-operation.[50]

THE BRIAND PLAN FOR A EUROPEAN UNION

Pan-European union was placed upon the international agenda the next year by the French Prime Minister Aristide Briand. There had been speculation in the press in 1927 – the same year in which Briand agreed to be honorary president of Coudenhove-Kalergi's Pan-European Union – that Briand was thinking of a European federation. But it was more pressing matters that induced him to take the initiative. Briand was still concerned about French security. France's hold over Germany was gradually being weakened, even if French concessions seemed painfully slow and insufficient to Germany. France's efforts to secure allies against any renewal of German aggression had failed again. The attempt to win American backing had issued merely in the Kellog-Briand Pact of 1928 by which the signatories formally renounced war as an instrument of state policy. Against this background Briand began to talk of 'the final liquidation of the war', first using the phrase in September 1928.[51] It was an optimistic term to use given the bitter divisions between Germany and France over the future of the Saar, reparations and the withdrawal of

French troops from the Rhineland. Nevertheless Briand took up the theme in Madrid in June 1929 in a private conversation with Stresemann and referred opaquely to a 'kind of European federation'.[52] It was then debated in the French press – to the surprise and annoyance of the Germans. It was, as yet, far from clear to the German Foreign Office what Briand was aiming at. Schubert was suspicious that Briand was simply trying to direct attention from the problem of the Saar, that any European organization would be used by the French as a protectionist and anti-American tool.[53] He even suggested that Briand envisaged 'a construction in which the predominance in Europe automatically falls to the most powerful', that is, France.[54]

There are indications that Briand himself was not yet sure what he wanted. According to a journalist who accompanied Briand to Geneva for the League of Nations Assembly, he confided:

> We must use the moment when France is giving up military positions to secure ourselves moral positions. Despite everything I will launch the United States of Europe. Now or never is the moment to give the institutions of the League of Nations a new impulse, to awaken a movement of general enthusiasm. Otherwise, everything is finished.[55]

Briand's speech to the League of Nations Assembly did not do much to clarify matters. He spoke of 'une sorte de lien fédéral' but added that he was not suggesting any loss of sovereignty by the participating states. This inconsistency was to recur. He was clear on one issue: 'Evidently the Association will act chiefly in the economic domain: it is the most pressing question.'[56] During an exchange of views between governments on 9 September two questions which were to play a crucial role in responses to Briand's plan were already evident: whether priority was indeed to be given to economic issues and whether or not the proposed arrangement would detract from the institutions of the League.[57] The governments did, however, agree that France should prepare a report which would be discussed at the next meeting of the Assembly of the League of Nations.

Briand's report took some time to prepare, being constantly amended to try to take account of the varied sensitivities of France's neighbours. On the crucial question of the relationship between economic and political matters, Briand and his chef de cabinet, Alexis de Léger, were concerned that the link between the two should be affirmed, and settled on the formulation, 'the necessary subordination of the economic to the political'.[58] The reversal of emphasis, giving priority to political rather than economic problems, was to be important. The final plan was dispatched to the European states on 17 May 1930, the same day on which Coudenhove-Kalergi's Pan-European Union opened its conference in Berlin.

The 'Memorandum on the Organization of a Régime of European Federal Union' asserted the 'necessity of establishing a permanent régime of conventional solidarity for the rational organization of Europe' and promptly turned to reassuring governments that this did not entail any diminution of their sovereignty nor of the authority of the League of Nations.[59] Of the eventual replies to the memorandum only the Netherlands pointed out that it would not be possible to fulfil the memorandum's proposed tasks unless states accepted some limitations upon their sovereignty.[60] With equal alacrity Briand moved to head off the objection that the union would be anti-American in spirit. The substance of the memorandum was divided into three parts. The first was devoted to an 'initial and symbolic pact', though it did not really specify what this would consist of. The second elaborated the institutional machinery of the union. This was clearly influenced by the institutional structure of the League of Nations. There would be a European Conference consisting of government representatives which would be the 'essential directing organ of the European union'.[61] A permanent Political Committee, 'composed of only a certain number of Members', would provide continuity and act as the executive body of the union. Finally, there would be a secretariat.[62] It was thus very much an intergovernmental institution exhibiting none of the federal elements – most crucially the transfer of authority in specified areas to the union – favoured by many of the advocates of European union. Nor did it provide for any means of popular or democratic legitimation, though Briand clearly hoped that the union would inspire popular opinion. The third section was the most problematic, for it contained the formulation agreed by Briand and de Léger: the 'General Subordination of the Economic Problem to the Political'. Reversing the order of priorities set out the previous September, the memorandum insisted that

> The contrary order would not only be useless, it would appear to the weaker nations to be likely to expose them, without guarantees or compensation, to the risks of political domination which might result from an industrial domination of the more strongly organized States.[63]

In the same section the memorandum further muddied the waters by suggesting

> the general development for Europe of a system of arbitration and security, and the progressive extension to the whole European community of the policy of international guarantees inaugurated at Locarno, until such time as special agreements or series of agreements are merged into a more general system.[64]

BRITISH AND GERMAN RESPONSES TO BRIAND

Of the governments to whom Briand presented his memorandum, two were crucial: Germany and Britain. The Germans were suspicious but the response of individuals was varied. Schubert explained to the British Ambassador on 28 May that he saw a 'good core' in the memorandum and laid 'great value' on the economic aims, even if he was unhappy with its political dimension.[65] Other responses were more hostile. Typical was the judgement of the Foreign Minister Curtius on 31 May. Of the political part of the memorandum he wrote, 'There can be no doubt that France is thinking in the first place of perpetuating existing relations to the east and south east of Germany.'[66] The same sentiments dominated a circular to German missions on 10 June 1930.[67] Yet on both the issues which Germany found most worrying, the implications for the borders in the east and the priority of the political dimension, the German Foreign Office was receiving information that Briand was more flexible than they supposed. The most nuanced reports came from the German Ambassador to Paris, Hoesch. On 20 June he distanced himself from the views expressed in the circular of 10 June, arguing that any attempt to read the memorandum as an attempt to assert French hegemony went beyond the available facts. On 26 June he reported that Briand was willing to begin work on the political and economic issues simultaneously, and on 5 July that Briand merely wanted economic issues settled at the highest political level instead of being left to experts, whose record was unimpressive.[68] From both the Belgians and the Austrians the Germans heard that Briand was not committed to the existing eastern borders, but did want to ensure that any adjustments occurred peacefully.[69] But this made little difference. The German cabinet decided to give Briand's memorandum a 'first-class burial'.[70]

The British response was also divided. The Foreign Office considered, but quickly abandoned, the idea that Briand was pursuing an eastern Locarno.[71] While accepting Briand's good intentions, the Foreign Office expressed frequent confusion about what Briand wanted and indulged quite a few prejudices. Despite the fact Briand had disavowed any anti-American motives a document of 30 May declared, 'This is primarily what has always been meant by the "United States of Europe" or "Pan-Europe" and without this it is hard to see that the word "Pan-Europe" can mean anything at all.'[72] Nevertheless the same document advocated 'cordial caution'. There was something worth salvaging from the proposal. As the debate in the British government proceeded, increasing emphasis was placed upon dealing with European issues within the framework of the League of Nations rather than setting up a separate and possibly competing organization.[73] The eventual reply was shorn of some elements of sympathy and understanding by the insistence of the Treasury that 'We ought surely to make it clear that we only accept the introduction of political influences insofar as they help to promote economic union and that we can't encourage any ideas of political union.'[74] The effect of the British reply was at the end similar to that of the German reply. Briand's plan was given a 'first-class burial', that is, it was handed over in September 1930 to a League of Nations committee for further study.

British and German motives had been partly similar. Both were genuinely suspicious that Briand's plan would antagonize the Americans and were concerned to revive a global framework of economic co-operation. Both were genuinely motivated by a concern not to weaken the League of Nations. Britain was also motivated by worries about the impact of such schemes upon its Empire. One of the fears expressed in a Foreign Office memorandum of 3 July was that regional tendencies in general 'might clearly endanger the cohesion of the British Commonwealth of nations'.[75] In Germany there was less readiness to credit Briand with good intentions and an overriding concern with the restoration of Germany's position as a great power. The means to this were spelled out by the Minister Treviranus in June: 'co-operation with the widest possible group of states' and 'the utilization of economic interests for political purposes'.[76]

ANSCHLUSS AND GERMANY'S TURN TO CENTRAL AND EASTERN EUROPE

There was one notable exception to the avoidance of regional strategies: Anschluss. Anschluss had been on the agenda at the end of the First World War and had, for a while, been favoured by the Austrian government. But the way forward was blocked by the Treaty of Saint Germain and by the protocols of 1922 by which Austria's beleaguered finances were restructured. Towards the end of the decade the Anschluss option was being raised again.

The crucial meeting between the German and Austrian Chancellors took place on 22 and 24 February 1930, while the governments of Europe were still waiting for Briand's report. Responding to a comment by the Austrians on Coudenhove-Kalergi's Pan-Europa movement, the German Chancellor Müller expressed his sympathy for the movement but then added, 'Practically, it does not however have the importance which Coudenhove-Kalergi ascribes to it and we hope that Anschluss will come sooner than Pan-Europe.'[77] The idea of Anschluss was not developed further but they did take up the possibility of a customs union. Both governments' experts, Schubert for the Germans and Schüller for the Austrians, argued that it was too early to enter negotiations, that the peace treaties and the 1922 Protocol excluded it, and that there were numerous economic difficulties. But the Austrian Chancellor Schober and the German Foreign Minister Curtius were not deterred. Schober indeed was merely irritated by these objections. Curtius argued that 'there will, undoubtedly, never be a customs union of all Europe' but that neighbouring states could join.[78] Both were agreed the negotiations should begin, in secret.

The negotiations lasted for a year, with the Germans generally being more enthusiastic that the Austrians and Schober being keener than his own officials. The eventual text became public on 19 March 1931. The Protocol affirmed that both countries would retain their independence, that the customs administrations would remain separate, and that the proposed treaty could be denounced at one year's notice. It even stated that 'both parties will in the treaty declare their willingness to enter into negotiations for a similar agreement with any other country expressing such a desire'.[79] The intent was to reassure their neighbours that the treaty would not be a prelude to Anschluss. Neither France nor Czechoslovakia were convinced. Briand saw it as a challenge to his own plan. French suspicions were justified. Elements in the German Foreign Office were not only aiming at Anschluss but also at using the customs union in a broader strategy of revision in eastern Europe. Thus State Secretary Bülow wrote in April 1931:

> Once the German-Austrian customs union has become a reality, I calculate that the pressure of economic necessity will within a few years compel Czechoslovakia to adhere to it ... If we should succeed in incorporating Czechoslovakia in our economic bloc, and if meanwhile we should have established closer economic relations with the Baltic States, then Poland with her unstable economic structure would be surrounded and exposed to all kinds of dangers, we should have her in a vice which could perhaps in the long run make her willing to consider further the idea of exchanging political concessions for tangible economic advantages.[80]

Nor were the assurances about a willingness to enter into similar agreements with other countries entirely sincere. Again in April, Bülow assured President Hindenburg that while, in the light of the Vienna Protocol, Germany could hardly refuse to negotiate with France about a customs union, such an agreement was, at the moment, utopian. Protracted negotiations would be necessary, and if anything did eventually emerge it would be at best a 'partial' customs union.[81]

Bülow's ambitions were, for the time, to be frustrated. Both Germany and Austria were suffering badly from the recession. Austria's finances lay in ruins after the crash of the Credit-Anstalt bank and she was in no position to withstand French financial pressure. Chancellor Brünning and Schober eventually abandoned the project days before the Permanent Court of International Justice declared it was incompatible with Austria's international obligations on 5 September. Its significance lies in the fact that it reflects the growing support in Germany for a central European strategy as an alternative to a policy of co-operation with France, an alternative both to the grandiose visions of Briand and the more limited but still important strategy of behaving as a 'good European' in the sense described by the historian Jacobson.

THE ECONOMIC CRISIS AND EASTERN EUROPE

The economic crisis which formed the backcloth to the proposed Austro-German customs union was tearing apart the interwoven fabric of European trade. Contemporaries were already beginning to write of the 'disintegration' of Europe. Regional solutions were sought most vigorously in an attempt to deal with the impact of the crisis upon Europe's agricultural countries. These were the most dependent upon European trade. They also suffered from the above-average rise of tariffs on foodstuffs. Their exposed position had been the subject of debate throughout the 1920s. Following Alfred Weber it was argued that there were in fact two Europes. The terminology varied as did the precise composition of the two groups, but the basic contrast was between the industrialized countries of western Europe and the agricultural economies of the east.[82] The agricultural economies had embarked upon a haphazard course of industrialization and protection. This was often less a matter of coherent policy than of response to circumstances; for example, the general inflation of tariffs before the World Economic Conference, which they feared would bring pressure to reduce their quota restrictions.[83]

These countries were suffering from a collapse of world food prices led by grain and sugar prices. Dairy produce followed in 1931.[84] At the same time as the world financial markets collapsed they were bereft of the loans upon which they had relied. They now had to export in the face of falling prices and increasing protection, in part simply to service their existing debts. In 1931 debt service as a percentage of exports varied from 16 per cent for Bulgaria to 48 per cent for Hungary.[85] And yet the significance of these countries for the European market was not that great. Before the *annus terribilis* of 1931 they accounted for only 9.5 per cent of Europe's total cereal imports and for derisory shares in total meat and dairy imports.[86]

Under these pressures the agrarian states began to call for some scheme to salvage them. Romanian, Yugoslav and Hungarian representatives met in Bucharest, and agreed to work for preferential treatment of their agricultural exports. In August 1930 the majority of east European states met and renewed the calls for preferential treatment, as well as agreeing to pursue the common organization of their agricultural trade.[87] Yet they could do little without some response from their potential markets in western and central Europe. The response came in 1931 as part of the French reaction to the proposed Austro-German customs union. The French proposal, as communicated to the British government on 4 May 1931, dealt with four issues: the collapse of east and central European cereal markets; the crisis of the industrial countries; the lack of capital and credit in east and central Europe; and Austria's specific problems. In response to the first problem it suggested that preferential treatment be granted to the cereal exporters.[88] The crisis of the industrial countries was to be alleviated by industrial and agricultural ententes accompanied by a lowering of tariffs for fixed contingents of goods regulated by these ententes. Credit would be organized for both the cereal exporters and Austria, while the latter would also benefit from preferential treatment of specified goods by the successor states.

The suggestion of offering preferential treatment was a contentious one, for it ran against the prevailing orthodoxy, that is, the Most Favoured Nation clause. While the French claimed that little opposition would arise to exceptions to the clause, the British disagreed, pointing out that Argentina, Canada and Australia had already declared they would object at the Rome Wheat Conference in March. Britain also reaffirmed its commitment to the 'unimpaired maintenance of the most-favoured-nation treatment'.[89] Nor did Britain favour industrial ententes as envisaged by France. They were said to be limited in effect, difficult to establish and best left to the industrialists themselves. The only part of the proposal to which Britain did not object was the credit proposals. The German response was, not surprisingly, hostile. There was nothing new in the proposals and Germany would not be diverted from the customs union.[90]

The continuing, and indeed worsening, problems of the east European states induced the western powers to make another attempt in the following year. This time the initiative was taken by Britain, who proposed a customs union for some of the successor states.[91] The idea was put to the Germans in January 1932. The response was that the idea was not very promising. This was true, for the British proposal was for a Danubian union, whereas what these states most needed was access to central and west European markets. Germany also stated that she would consider any 'customs union without us as one directed against us'.[92] Nor did the proposal find favour in the Danubian states. Beneš informed the Czech parliament on 22 March that any customs union was out of the question.[93] By the end of February the French had been able to persuade John Simon that a preferential system was after all the only way forward and re-launched their plan of the previous year. The new version, the Tardieu Plan, was put forward in March but was less attractive than the earlier scheme for it was primarily a proposal for a preference system among the Danubian states and left out the crucial concessions by Europe's cereal importers.[94] French and British advocacy of the Tardieu Plan at the Four Power Conference in London in April 1932 did not win over its critics. Nor did a subsequent conference at Stresa in September.

Any co-ordinated attempt to deal with the problem of the two Europes was failing. It was failing because, as Beneš noted, it could only succeed if Europe's great powers acted in concert, and they were far too suspicious of each other to co-operate.[95] Nor was it merely a matter of suspicion. Germany was moving towards the construction of an informal empire in central and eastern Europe. Hence, while she objected to France's multilateral preference system, she was pursuing bilateral preference treaties with east European states. That this was a policy decision is clear from the record of Curtius' statement in the German Cabinet: 'Germany must unconditionally hold fast to the bilateral preference treaties.'[96] In the discussion over the Briand Plan the German Finance Minister was blunter: 'Agrarian co-operation with France should be rejected. Germany would thereby become an importer from the east, by mediation of France, and would thus surrender a trump from its hand ... '[97]

THE RISE OF GERMANY

The political and economic reality of Europe was increasingly shaped in the 1930s by the resurgence of Germany. As yet, few grasped the enormity of Hitler's ambitions, but the increase of German influence and power called forth a succession of largely fruitless attempts to counteract the disruption of the European balance of power. Mussolini had moved to block German expansion, especially in the form of Anschluss, by the Rome Protocols of March 1934 by which Italy, Austria and Hungary agreed upon a programme of political consultation and economic co-operation. Any long-term opposition to German expansion was, however, dependent upon a broader coalition. It was dependent upon co-operation between the two groups which had formed in east central Europe: the Little Entente and the countries of the Rome Protocols. The French did attempt to bring about such an alliance in 1934–35 but their efforts ultimately failed. The proposed Danubian pact would have included mutual recognition of the parties' territorial integrity as well as mechanisms for consultation. Italy, desirous of gaining French acceptance of her ambitions in Africa as well as being fearful of Germany, came close to accepting the pact in January 1935, to the consternation of her

Hungarian ally. Mussolini had in fact indicated that he would make the pact conditional upon settlement of Hungarian grievances, but now seemed less committed. Growing tensions between the Italians and French, especially over the Italian invasion of Abyssinia, abetted by continual Hungarian pressure and signs of an Italian–German reconciliation, eventually undermined the project.[98] The Czech leader Hodza continued to try and reconcile at least the east central European members of the two blocs and made some progress in 1936. But the stumbling-block of the region's ethnic minorities, especially the Hungarian minorities in Czechoslovakia and Romania, remained, and upon this Hodza's efforts foundered in 1937.[99]

Even the attempt to strengthen the Little Entente as a security alliance failed in 1937. Neither Romania nor Yugoslavia would agree to extend the existing provisions by which they agreed to assist each other against Hungarian aggression. The motive, of course, was to avoid being dragged into a war with Germany. Similar problems had arisen earlier with the Balkan Union of 1934. The Union arose from a series of conferences held over the previous three years and was intended to include all the Balkan states, but Bulgaria would not agree to any treaty which sanctioned the existing borders. The other four – Romania, Yugoslavia, Greece and Turkey – proceeded without her, and hence the Union took on an anti-Bulgarian hue. This was not the only limit to the Union. Secret protocols provided for joint action against any Balkan power joining a non-Balkan state in aggression against a member of the Union. But Greece and Turkey, fearful of a war involving a great power, soon entered reservations, effectively nullifying this element of the Union.

PATTERNS OF TRADE IN THE 1930s

The prospects of blocking German expansion were fading both in the economic and political spheres. The German cabinet had agreed in October 1933 to pursue an 'active commercial policy based on reciprocity'.[100] This led to the German–Hungarian treaty of February 1934 by which the two countries established a clearing agreement. A treaty with Yugoslavia followed in May 1934. This was seen by Germany as the first crack in the Little Entente. An agreement with Romania was reached in March 1935. Germany was consciously moving to relocate her trade to the east by means of clearing agreements which minimized the need for payment from her hard-pressed foreign exchange reserves. Trade was being forced into channels dictated by preferential tariffs and the currency controls which the states of central and eastern Europe were adopting. Italy too followed the same path with her Rome Protocol partners, though their co-operation worked only in the exceptional circumstances of the Abyssinian crisis. By the end of 1937 the credits and subsidies granted by the Italians, which had been the linchpin of the system, were ended.[101] The economically much more powerful Germany also experienced problems. Between 1934 and 1936 Germany struggled to raise her exports to her new partners. Her exports were in fact overpriced. Nor did her imports from them reach the projected targets, for the relatively orthodox Schacht worried about the accumulation of large Reichsmark balances in the clearing accounts.

The whole enterprise was based on the assumption that there was a natural complementarity between industrialized Germany and the more agricultural economies of the east. The idea that economic integration should be based upon this kind of relationship was not peculiar to German trading policy. It was also held by many in Britain who envisaged the further development of the Commonwealth and Empire on exactly the same basis. The limits of this strategy were evident in eastern Europe. The eastern states were not content to take German industrial products in return for their raw materials and foodstuffs. They also wanted to dispose of their more profitable exports on the world market in order to obtain the foreign exchange with which they could acquire raw materials for their own industrial development. Hence, in the 1936 clearing agreement with Romania, Germany could secure the desired oil only by paying for 75 per cent of it with long-term investment and arms. As world cereal markets improved in 1936–37, the resort to armaments exports became one of the main means by which the Third Reich maintained the system of exchange.

Towards the end of the decade Germany had succeeded in developing a high profile in the trade of her eastern neighbours, though both Czechoslovakia and Poland held out against the trend. The relationship was, however, highly asymmetrical. For although Germany did manage to relocate some of its trade to the east her major trading partners still lay to the west. The Reichsmark bloc countries with which Germany operated clearing agreements did increase their share of Germany's total imports from 3.9 per cent in the pre-depression year of 1928 to 18.5 per cent in 1939.[102] But this still left Germany heavily dependent upon her traditional markets and suppliers. Germany had succeeded in creating a system of bilateral trading treaties which further weakened the already fragile economic integration between the successor states. It was to be a pattern which would be repeated after the Second World War under the aegis of a different regional hegemon – the Soviet Union. But German hegemony did not solve the problems of the National Socialist planners. They had sought security of raw materials for strategic reasons. On the eve of the

Second World War they were being forced to admit that they had failed.

At the end of the 1930s little progress had been made in halting the slide into protectionism. Europe was less integrated than it had been in the 1920s and even in the years before 1914. Yet the major powers of Europe could not escape from the ties that bound them. Germany's pursuit of autarky within the Reichsmark bloc had failed. Britain's turn to Empire and Commonwealth was more successful, but even here the underlying fragility of the strategy was evident. The share of the Empire in Britain's imports did increase markedly, from 24.5 per cent in 1931 to 37.3 per cent in 1937. But it proved more difficult to expand British exports in that direction. The Empire took 32.6 per cent of British exports in 1931 and 39.7 per cent in 1937.[103]

The division between the two Europes had not been fundamentally altered. It was, moreover, clear that regional integration among the successor states could not transform their economic status. They were dependent upon industrialized Europe, far more so than industrialized Europe was dependent upon them. Regional integration would have been of some help, but it foundered upon the unresolved ethnic complexity and territorial claims of the various states. Versailles had not really created a new set of nation-states. Three of the successor states – Czechoslovakia, Yugoslavia and Poland – were mini-Empires. Bulgaria and Romania still included substantial minorities. The only attempt to deal with this complex reality had been the provision of minority rights guarantees incorporated into the treaties with the successor states, but these had been impossible to enforce.[104]

Germany had begun to rebuild a power base in central Europe, forcing through Anschluss in March 1938 and dismembering Czechoslovakia in 1938 and 1939. Anschluss did awaken fears in Britain about a revival of the Mitteleuropa strategies of the First World War.[105] But these were not sufficient to stop the western great powers consenting to Hitler's acquisition of the Sudetenland. Even when Britain did extend the guarantee to Poland the guarantee demonstrated the limits of Britain's willingness to defend the Versailles order in eastern Europe. For while Britain guaranteed Polish independence she studiously avoided any commitment to Poland's existing territorial boundaries.[106]

The failure of western European states to follow up the first faltering steps towards integration had already had an adverse effect upon central and eastern Europe. It was this part of Europe which would bear the full brunt of Hitler's attempt to recast the European map, in both territorial and ethnic terms. The eastern European states could do little to avert their fate. They were dependent upon the west and the western states were still convinced that they had alternatives to integration. The allure of empires, the misplaced belief that unilateral solutions were still within their grasp, pride in the sovereignty and grandeur of their states, or even the more modest belief that they would be untouched by the coming maelstrom, easily prevailed over the idea of integration.

NOTES

1. Quoted by Fritz Fischer, *Germany's Aims in the First World War* (London, 1967), p. 104.
2. See Richard W. Kapp, 'Bethmann-Hollweg, Austria-Hungary and Mitteleuropa, 1914–1915', *Austrian History Yearbook*, **19–20** (1983–4), especially pp. 229–36.
3. Quoted in *ibid.*, p. 230.
4. Quoted by Stephen Verosta, 'The German concept of *Mitteleuropa*, 1916–1918 and its contemporary critics', in Robert A. Kann *et al.* (eds), *The Habsburg Empire in World War I* (Boulder, 1977), p. 210. On the clash of interest in November 1915 see also Fischer, *Germany's Aims*, pp. 208–12, and Gary W. Shanafelt, *The Secret Enemy: Austria-Hungary and the German Alliance 1914–1918* (Boulder, 1985).
5. Meyer, *Mitteleuropa*, pp. 159–71.
6. Fischer, *Germany's Aims*, p. 435.
7. *Ibid.*, p. 510. See also Meyer, *Mitteleuropa*, p. 290.
8. Ralph White, 'Regionalism vs. universalism in the League of Nations', *Annales d'études internationales* (1970), p. 89.
9. Quoted in D. Weigall and P. Stirk, *The Origins and Development of the European Community* (Leicester, 1992), p. 7.
10. Frank Costigliola, *Awkward Dominion. American Political, Economic, and Cultural Relations with Europe, 1919–1933* (Ithaca, 1984), pp. 34–7.
11. Carole Fink, *The Genoa Conference. European Diplomacy, 1921–1922* (Chapel Hill, 1984), pp. 18–22. See also Peter Krüger, *Die Aussenpolitik der Republik von Weimar* (Darmstadt, 1985), pp. 157–9.
12. Fink, *Genoa Conference*, pp. 102–3. Officially the consortium was to be a private organization.
13. See Hartmut Pogge von Strandmann, 'Rapallo-strategy in preventive diplomacy', in Volker R. Berghahn and Martin Kitchen (eds), *Germany in the Age of Total War* (London, 1981), according to which 'Ever since, Rapallo has been in the eyes of the West the threatening reminder of the possibility of further separate agreements between Germany and Russia', p. 123. See also Robert Himmer, 'Rathenau, Russia, and Rapallo', *Central European History*, **9** (1976), which suggests continuities with the Mitteleuropa idea, p. 158.
14. On the activities of the American Relief Administration see Costigliola, *Awkward Dominion*, pp. 39–49. On the broader problems of economic nationalism in east central Europe see Peter Stirk, 'Ideas of economic integration in interwar Mitteleuropa', in Peter Stirk (ed.), *Mitteleuropa. History and Prospects* (Edinburgh, 1994), pp. 86–111.
15. Borsody, *The Tragedy of Central Europe* (New Haven, 1980), pp. 19 and 34.
16. L. S. Stavrianos, *Balkan Federation* (Hamden, Connecticut, 1964), pp. 202–15.
17. *Ibid.*, p. 224.

18. Quoted by Frommelt, *Paneuropa oder Mitteleuropa* (Stuttgart, 1977), p. 11. On Coudenhove-Kalergi's authoritarianism see also P. M. R. Stirk, 'Authoritarian federalists in Central Europe', in Preston King and Andrea Bosco (eds), *A Constitution for Europe* (London, 1991), pp. 199–212.
19. Frommelt, *Paneuropa oder Mitteleuropa*, p. 15.
20. R. N. Coudenhove-Kalergi, *Pan-Europe* (New York, 1926), pp. 174–6. This is the first English language edition.
21. Frommelt, *Paneuropa oder Mitteleuropa*, pp. 49–50, 62–3.
22. R. N. Coudenhove-Kalergi, *Ein Leben für Europa* (Cologne, 1996), p. 109. In *Pan-Europe* he explained that he was deliberately using the term 'Pan' by analogy with Pan-Americanism and Pan-Hellenism, p. 32.
23. Coudenhove-Kalergi, *Pan-Europe*, p. 4.
24. *Ibid.*, p. 55.
25. *Ibid.*, p. 197.
26. Founded by Charles Gide, E. Stern-Rubarth and Ernö Bleier. See Carl H. Pegg, *Evolution of the European Idea 1914–1932* (Chapel Hill, 1983), p. 33.
27. On these and the developments discussed below see Karl Holl, 'Europapolitik im Vorfeld der deutschen Regierungspolitik', *Historische Zeitschrift*, **219** (1974), pp. 33–94; Jürgen Hess, 'Europagedanke und Nationaler Revisionismus', *Historische Zeitschrift*, **225** (1977), pp. 572–622.
28. Frommelt, *Paneuropa oder Mitteleuropa*, p. 21.
29. Quoted by Holl, 'Europapolitik im Vorfeld der deutschen Regierungspolitik', p. 45. See also Hess, 'Europagedanke und Nationaler Revisionismus', pp. 598–9.
30. Coudenhove-Kalergi, *Pan-Europe*, pp. 125–6. From this perspective Coudenhove-Kalergi was accused of defending French hegemony. He was thus in the unfortunate position of being seen as either an advocate of German imperialism or of French imperialism.
31. Hess, 'Europagedanke und Nationaler Revisionismus', pp. 595–7. Hess points out that this argument was the old one of Rousseau and Herder that peace and self-determination went hand in hand. A more pointed comparison would be with Mazzini.
32. Quoted by C. H. Pegg, 'Die wachsende Bedutung der europäischen Einigungsbewegung in den zwanzigen Jahren', *Europa Archiv*, **24** (1962), p. 866.
33. Walter Lipgens, 'Europäische Einigungsidee 1923–1930 und Briands Europaplan im Urteil der Deutschen Akten', *Historische Zeitschrift*, **203** (1966), p. 65; C. H. Pegg, *Evolution of the European Idea 1914–1932* (Chapel Hill, 1983), pp. 45–7, 51 and 53.
34. Jon Jacobson, *Locarno Diplomacy* (Princeton, 1972), p. 385. See also Lipgens, 'Europäische Einigungsidee 1923–1930', pp. 66–7; Pegg, *Evolution of the European Idea*, p. 55: Werner Weidenfeld, 'Gustav Stresemann-der Mythos vom engagierten Europäer', *Geschichte im Wissenschaft und Unterricht*, **24** (1973), pp. 740–50.
35. Jacobson, *Locarno Diplomacy*, p. 29.
36. League of Nations, *Commercial Policy in the Interwar Period: International Proposals and National Policies* (Geneva, 1941), p. 120.
37. H. Gaedicke and G. von Eynern, *Die produktionswirtschaftliche Integration Europas* (Berlin, 1933), pp. 31–2. This was one of the first books to use the term 'integration'. The authors' use of quotation marks was but one indication of their hesitancy about this terminological novelty.

38. *Ibid.*, pp. 56 and 58.
39. Peter Krüger, 'Die Ansätze zu einer europäischen Wirtschaftsgemeinschaft in Deutschland nach dem ersten Weltkreig' in Helmut Berding (ed.), *Wirtschaftliche und politische Integration in Europa im 19. und 20. Jahrhundert* (Göttingen, 1984), p. 160.
40. 'Runderlass des Reichsministers', 21 January 1926, *Akten zur Deutschen Auswärtigen Politik* (hereafter *ADAP*), Serie B, Vol. 1, doc. 51.
41. Wladimir Woytinsky, *Die Vereinigten Staaten von Europa* (Berlin, 1926), pp. 143–4.
42. French industry also had its protectionists. On the complex pattern of conflicting interests see Charles S. Maier, *Recasting Bourgeois Europe* (Princeton, 1975), pp. 516–45.
43. See Frommelt, *Paneuropa oder Mitteleuropa*, pp. 54–7. Mayrisch also took over the Luxembourg branch of Coudenhove-Kalergi's Pan-Europa Union, though there was little other connection between the two organizations; *ibid.*, p. 63. In 1949, on the eve of the proposals which would lead to the ECSC, Konrad Adenauer would recall discussion in the 1920s with Mayrisch. Hans-Peter Schwarz, *Adenauer. Der Aufstieg: 1876–1952* (Stuttgart, 1986), p. 684.
44. On Mayrisch's role see Jacques Bariety, 'Le rôle d' Émile Mayrisch entre les sidérurgies allemande et français aprés la première guerre mondiale', *Relationes Internationales*, **1** (1975), pp. 123–34.
45. Maier, *Recasting Bourgeois Europe*, pp. 542– 3.
46. For an example of the disputes from the German side see *ADAP*, Serie B, Vol. 9, doc. 147. For a sceptical account of the whole agreement see Daniel Barbezat, 'Cooperation and rivalry in the International Steel Cartel, 1926–1933', *Journal of Economic History*, **49**(1989), pp. 435–47, which argues that rivalry was the predominant theme.
47. Edouard Herriot, *The United States of Europe* (London, 1930), pp. 152.
48. Robert Boyce, 'British capitalism and European unity between the wars', in Stirk (ed.), *European Unity in Context*, p. 80.
49. *ADAP*, Serie B, Vol. 9, doc. 30. For a detailed account of the discussions and the context, see Peter Krüger, 'Benes und die europäische Wirtschaftskonzeption des deutschen Staatssekretärs Carl von Schubert', *Bohemia*, **14** (1973), pp. 320–39.
50. On Schubert's views see Krüger, 'Beneš und die europäische Wirtschaftskonzeption des deutschen Staatssekretärs', especially pp. 333, 338.
51. Jacobson, *Locarno Diplomacy*, p. 287.
52. *ADAP*, Serie B, Vol. 12, doc. 19.
53. *ADAP*, Serie B, Vol. 12, docs 138 and 139.
54. Quoted by Lipgens, 'Europäische Einigungsidee 1923–1930', p. 76.
55. Quoted by Ferdinand Siebert, *Aristide Briand 1862–1932. Ein Staatsman zwischen Frankreich und Europa* (Zürich, 1973), p. 498.
56. Speech to the Assembly, 5 September 1929, in Odile Keller and Lubor Jilek (eds), *Le Plan Briand d'union fédérale européene* (Geneva, 1991), p. 2.
57. Most agreed that the emphasis should be placed upon economic co-operation. But see the Yugoslav delegate's response: 'C'est le sentiment d'insécurité politique qui fait obstacle au libéralisme économique . . . ', *ibid.*, p. 9.
58. Cornelia Navari, 'The Origins of the Briand Plan', in Andrea Bosco (ed.), *The Federal Idea*, Vol. 1 (London, 1991), p. 226. This is the best account of the development of the plan.

59. 'Memorandum on the organization of a Régime of European Federal Union', *International Conciliation*, Special Bulletin (June 1930), pp. 327–35.
60. Keller and Jilek (eds), *Le Plan Briand*, pp. 54–5.
61. 'Memorandum on the organization of a Régime of European Federal Union', p. 339.
62. *Ibid.*, pp. 341 and 343.
63. *Ibid.*, p. 343. This fear was evident in the Yugoslav response to Briand in September and in Beneš' discussions with Schubert in 1928.
64. *Ibid.*, p. 345.
65. *ADAP*, Serie B, Vol. 15, doc. 53.
66. *Ibid.*, doc. 56.
67. *Ibid.*, doc. 70.
68. *Ibid.*, docs, 90, 100, 121.
69. *Ibid.*, doc. 64. See Lipgens, 'Europäische Einigungsidee 1923–1930', pp. 328–41, for an account of these and other sources.
70. Quoted in Lipgens, 'Europäische Einigungsidee 1923–1930', p. 346.
71. *Documents on British Foreign Policy* (hereafter *DBFP*), Series 2, Vol. 1, doc. 189.
72. *DBFP*, Series 2, Vol. 1, doc. 189. On Britain's response see Karl-Dietrich Erdmann, 'Der Europaplan Briands im Licht der englischen Akten', *Geschichte im Wissenschaft und Unterricht*, **1** (1950), pp. 16–32; Robert Boyce, 'Britain's first "no" to Europe', *European Studies Review*, **10** (1980), pp. 17–45; Ralph White, 'Cordial caution: the British response to the French proposal for European Federal Union of 1930', in Bosco (ed.), *The Federal Idea*, Vol. 1, pp. 236–62.
73. For the details of this, see White, 'Cordial caution', pp. 244–6.
74. Quoted in *ibid.*, p. 251.
75. *DBFP*, Series 2, Vol. 1, doc. 193.
76. *Akten der Reichskanzlei. Kabinette Brünning I und II*, Vol. 1, doc. 55.
77. *Akten der Reichskanzlei. Das Kabinett Müller II*, Vol. 2, doc. 453. On the customs union see the contrasting interpretations of O. Hauser, 'Der Plan einer Deutsch-österreichischen Zollunion von 1931 und die europäische Föderation', *Historische Zeitschrift*, **179** (1955), pp. 45–92; F. G. Stambrook, 'The German–Austrian Customs Union Project of 1931', *Journal of Central European Affairs*, **21** (1961), pp. 15–44. Stambrook has the better of the argument.
78. *Akten der Reichskanzlei. Das Kabinett Müller II*, Vol. 2, doc. 453.
79. Art. 1, 'Protocol of Vienna', in *Documents on International Affairs 1931* (Oxford, 1932).
80. Translated as an Appendix to Stambrook, 'The German–Austrian Customs Union Project', p. 43. Bülow was not interested in 'palliative remedies', to Germany's disagreements with Poland. See his response to Coudenhove-Kalergi's suggestions in April 1931, *ADAP*, Serie B, Vol. 17, doc. 72.
81. *ADAP*, Serie B, Vol. 17, doc. 89.
82. On this see *ibid.*, pp. 46–8. The most widely cited was F. Delaisi, *Les Deux Europes* (Paris, 1929). The best categorization is probably provided by Hilde Monte, *The Unity of Europe* (London, 1943). For recent attempts to use this framework, see David Arter, *The Politics of European Integration in the Twentieth Century* (Aldershot, 1993).
83. A. Basch, *The Danube Basin and the German Economic Sphere* (New York, 1943), p. 26.
84. H. Liepmann, *Tariff Levels and the Economic Unity of Europe* (London, 1938), pp. 108–9.

85. A. Teichova, 'East-central Europe and south-east Europe, 1919–1939', in Peter Mathias and Sidney Pollard (eds), *The Cambridge Economic History of Europe*, Vol. 8 (Cambridge, 1989), p. 948.
86. Basch, *The Danube Basin*, p. 40.
87. Liepmann, *Tariff Levels*, p. 350; Jacques Bariety, 'Der Tardieu-Plan zur Sanierung des Donauraums', in Josef Becker and Klaus Hildebrand (eds), *Internationale Beziehungen in der Weltwirtschaftskrise 1929–1933* (Munich, 1980), pp. 366–7.
88. The memorandum to the British government was prefaced with the comment that the Austro-German customs union was 'politically a prelude to Anschluss'; *DBFP*, Series 2, Vol. 2, doc. 31. This comment was absent from the shorter memorandum to the German government, delivered on 11 May; *ADAP*, Serie B, Vol. 17, doc. 126. The concession extended by preferential treatment was niggardly, for the French suggested there be assurances that the cereal exporters would not take advantage of the situation to increase their production.
89. *DBFP*, Series 2, Vol. 2, doc. 37.
90. *ADAP*, Serie B, Vol. 17, doc. 132.
91. On this see F. G. Stambrook, 'A British proposal for the Danubian States: the Customs Union Project of 1932', *Slavonic and East European Review*, **42** (1963–4), pp. 64–88.
92. *Ibid.*, p. 87.
93. Edvard Beneš, *Die Probleme Mitteleuropas* (Prague, 1932), p. 38. So too was any 'international organization', 'confederation' or similar proposal.
94. According to Stambrook, 'A British proposal for the Danubian States', p. 80, the French did later include the concession of preferences by the great powers. This does not, however, seem to have been widely understood at the time.
95. On this see Stirk, 'Ideas of economic integration in interwar Mitteleuropa', pp. 86–111.
96. *Akten der Reichskanzlei. Kabinette Brünning I und II*, Vol. 2, doc. 296.
97. *Ibid.*, Vol. 2, doc. 68.
98. See Jens Petersen, *Hitler–Mussolini. Die Entstehung der Achse Berlin–Rom 1933–6.* (Tübingen, 1973); M. Sz. Ormos, 'Sur les causes de l échec du pacte danubien (1934–35)', *Acta Historica Academiae Scientarum Hungericae*, **14** (1968), pp. 21–81.
99. Royal Institute of International Affairs, *South-Eastern Europe. A Political and Economic Survey* (London, 1939), pp. 43–4.
100. David E. Kaiser, *Economic Diplomacy and the Origins of the Second World War* (Princeton, 1980), pp. 73–4.
101. Basch, *The Danube Basin*, pp. 161–4.
102. A. S. Milward, 'The Reichsmark bloc and the international economy', in H. W. Koch (ed.), *Aspects of the Third Reich* (Basingstoke, 1985), p. 358.
103. Jürgen Wendt, *Appeasement 1938. Wirtschaftliche Rezession in Mitteleuropa* (Frankfurt am Main, 1966), p. 52.
104. See Pearson, *National Minorities in Eastern Europe 1848–1945*, pp. 141–6.
105. For details, see Wendt, *Appeasement 1938*, pp. 39–68.
106. See Alan J. Foster, 'Britain and east central Europe 1918–48', in Stirk (ed.), *Mitteleuropa*, pp. 112–28.

3

Making the New Europe in the Second World War: 1940–45

INTRODUCTION

The Second World War presented an even greater challenge than the First. The greater success of German forces gave the victorious National Socialists the opportunity to set about building a New Order in Europe. The political structure which emerged was a complex mosaic, formed by a mixture of military exigencies and National Socialist doctrine. In the west at least, during the first year of occupation, National Socialist intentions were unclear. Indigenous fascists, and not only they, faced with the prospect of indefinite German hegemony, sought to find a place for themselves and their nations in the New Order. But hopes that Hitler would concede to the defeated nations some measure of independence, in return for collaboration, were frustrated. Despite the rhetoric of the New Order, the political structure of occupied Europe was chaotic.

It was less easy for the National Socialists to tolerate chaos in the economic field. Initially, a policy of simple plunder ran alongside grandiose plans, including customs unions and currency unions. Both met obstacles. A more rational economic policy was adopted, if only in the interests of exploiting Europe's resources for the prosecution of the war. At the same time, plans for long-term economic integration ran up against the National Socialist desire to reduce many of the defeated nations, especially in the east, to a colonial status. Yet the rhetoric of the New Order created uncertainty among Germany's opponents about the economic reality and prospects of Europe under German hegemony.

The resistance was also divided. On the one hand, the experience of defeat induced many to turn to the idea of European unity as the only way to put an end to the continent's recurrent civil wars. On the other hand, the slogan of European unity had been appropriated by the occupier and the collaborationists, and seemed tainted. Radical reconsideration of the political order of Europe was not restricted to the resistance. Especially in the dark months of 1940 British ministers and officials contemplated a sacrifice of sovereignty which had previously been advocated only by politically marginal groups. Yet Britain too, like her opponent, failed to clarify her policy, albeit for different reasons. Britain's hands were tied by the fear that any explicit and detailed vision of Europe's future would antagonize the United States. Exiled governments were less constrained, or so it seemed at first, and eastern European exiles drew up ambitious plans for future federations.

For all the parties concerned, the German invasion of the Soviet Union in the summer of 1941 marked a turning-point. For the collaborationists, the anti-Bolshevik crusade was welcomed as the common cause which would unite Germany and the defeated nations of the west. Again this met with Hitler's opposition. The reality of German policy after the summer of 1941 was marked by two trends. First, the National Socialists radically increased their efforts to create a racial hierarchy in Europe, a hierarchy in which Jews would not even be allowed to exist. Second, National Socialist technocrats were pushed to seek yet more rigorous economic integration.

For the resistance the second half of the war saw a growth in advocacy of a post-war European federation, though this view was neither universal among the resistance, nor was it shared by the majority of the occupied peoples. For most, liberation would signify national liberation, not the dawn of a united Europe. What liberation would really mean depended less on the wishes of the inhabitants of occupied countries and more on the intentions of the Allied powers.

On some issues policy became brutally clear. Stalin would not tolerate federations in eastern Europe, at least not ones formulated by exiled governments. The Soviet Union played an important, if unknowing, role in the dismissal of another option: an Atlantic security system. The idea of an Atlantic security system, which took the form of the North Atlantic Treaty four years after the war had ended, ran up against the need to keep the wartime allies together. For the implicit threat, which the Atlantic security system would guard against, came from none other than the wartime ally, the Soviet Union. The United States also excluded options of European unity, seeing these as a threat to ideas of a new international organization as well as a threat to global free trade.

On two crucial issues Allied policy was either inadequate or unsettled. Despite repeated debates, policy towards Germany after the war remained uncertain. The possibilities ranged from dismemberment and deindustrialization to decentralization and rapid rehabilitation. Unable to agree upon either, the Allies approached the end of the war on the basis of an amalgam of both. On the issue of post-war reconstruction the fault was one of omission. There were plans for immediate relief and visions of a stable long-term order, but no mechanism for getting from one to another. Neither for the first nor for the last time, the crucial phase of reconstruction failed to receive the attention it needed.

The war years witnessed a remarkably rich debate upon the idea of European union and of regional federations within Europe. That debate took place in isolated resistance groups as well as the corridors of power. But the option of European union had been squeezed from the agenda. Over five years after Germany embarked upon its bid to reshape Europe, the Allied governments were no nearer to agreement on a viable future for Europe than they were at the beginning of the war.

THE POLITICAL STRUCTURE OF THE NAZI NEW ORDER

The Third Reich had embarked upon its bid to fashion a new Europe without any coherent plan for what it would do in the wake of the anticipated victory. It was not that the Nazis were devoid of images of Europe and of a European order. They had, however, never really tried to reconcile the conflicting alternatives espoused by the various ideologues and paladins of the Third Reich. There was one pre-eminent goal, pre-eminent in that it lay at the heart of Adolf Hitler's ideology, and that was the pursuit of *Lebensraum* in the east. The pursuit of *Lebensraum* had begun in 1939 with the attack upon Poland, but it was not until the victories in the west in 1940 that the Nazis were forced to give serious consideration to Europe's future.

By then Hitler's contempt for many of Europe's states had already been made clear. Czechoslovakia had been divided in March 1939 into a satellite Slovak state and a Protectorate of Bohemia and Moravia. Typically, the form of the latter was not decided until the evening of Hitler's entry into Prague. According to the Decree of 16 March, the occupied territories were 'incorporated into the territory of the Greater German Reich' though the Protectorate was to be 'autonomous and shall govern itself'.[1] That this autonomy was to be limited was clear from the subordination of the Czech authorities to the Reich Protector. Poland was divided between Germany and the Soviet Union. Within the German-occupied areas, approximately half of the former Polish territory was incorporated directly into Germany, with the fate of the remainder being uncertain. Hitler considered allowing a Polish 'statelet', primarily as a bargaining counter for peace negotiations with the west. But as the possibility of peace in the west faded even this shadow of independence disappeared from the Nazi agenda.[2] The General Government, as the Nazis designated the remainder of Poland, was from the outset destined to be the starting-point of Nazi racial engineering in the east. As Hitler had explained to his military leaders in 1939, his war aims did not consist of 'the attainment of specific boundaries, but in the physical destruction of the opponent'.[3] In the east Hitler gave free rein to his belief that Slavs were incapable of forming and maintaining a state, by dismembering Poland and inaugurating a policy of eliminating any potential political leadership.

In the west the constraints, both practical and ideological, were more substantial. Although Hitler was contemptuous of western Europe's smaller states, and determined that France should never again enjoy the status of a great power, western Europe did not form part of the main *Lebensraum* for German colonists. To the contrary, the Danes, Norwegians and Dutch were regarded as 'Germanic' peoples who would, at some point, be incorporated into the Greater German Reich. On the day on which German troops crossed the Danish border Hitler declared 'Just as Bismarck's Reich arose from the year 1866, so will the Great Germanic Reich arise from this day.'[4] The Reichskommisar for the Netherlands, Seyss-Inquart, was more guarded in addressing the Dutch population in May 1940 but was quite explicit about the presumed kinship of Germans and Dutchmen. He reassured the Dutch that

> It will, however, be my concern that the Netherlands nation, akin in blood to the German nation, shall not be subject to living conditions less favourable than those necessitated by the community of fate and the destructive tendencies of our enemies at this time.
>
> As Reich Commissioner I have to safeguard the interests of the Reich in the Netherlands territories placed under the protection of German troops and I shall safeguard them. The Netherlands nation, in fulfilling the duties resulting from the common task, will be able to secure its country and its liberty for the future.[5]

Four days later he was speaking of the role of the Netherlands in the 'new Europe'. On 26 July he was even more fulsome, and spoke of a 'new Europe of solidarity and cooperation' in which the 'special talents of every nation will enjoy a greatly enlarged field of action'.[6] Both Seyss-Inquart and the Reichskommisar for Norway, Terboven, were sincere in their desire to win over their new subjects to a policy of collaboration, even if they were less than honest in implying this would bring with it long-term independence. Both hoped that the kindred nations could be guided along a path of self-Nazification, but were intelligent enough to realize that the self-proclaimed indigenous Nazi leaders, Vidkun Quisling and Anton Mussert, were neither popular enough nor skilful enough to be of much use.[7]

For the first few months at least of the Nazi occupation the future of Europe under Nazi hegemony was not clear to the conquered peoples. Nor indeed was it clear in the minds of the Nazi leadership. The ambiguity left scope for those who wished to adapt to the New Order, or at least who hoped that they might be able to pursue an independent path within it. Among the most vigorous supplicants were Mussert, Quisling and the Belgian fascist Leon Degrelle. Mussert was calling for a League of Germanic peoples as early as 27 August 1940.[8] In October Quisling suggested a Pan-Nordic Federation in which Norway would be a 'free, indivisible, and independent state'.[9] Degrelle's position was less favourable since, as a Walloon, his credentials as a member of the Germanic community were dubious. Nevertheless, he called for an enlarged Belgium, incorporating parts of both the Netherlands and France, which would be a *Germania inferior* and would mediate between 'German and Latin civilizations'.[10] The fate of these schemes revealed the futility of the collaborationists' pleading for a place in the New Order which would concede to their countries some measure of independence. Quisling continued to seek a peace treaty with Germany linked with a scheme of federation well into 1943, despite the fact that Hitler had made the German position clear in the summer of 1942. Quisling had sent yet another memorandum on the New Order in February 1942, accompanied by a draft peace treaty. In this memorandum, he laid great stress on Norway regaining the right to dispatch ambassadors abroad, and sought to persuade Hitler this was of advantage to Germany.[11] Hitler responded some months later, in August. There was to be no peace treaty for the duration of the war, and when Norway did find out what its future would be this would be by means of a 'one-sided declaration by the Reich government'. On the question of ambassadors Hitler was unequivocal: 'Norwegian representation abroad is out of the question, not even mere trade representation.'[12] Degrelle's experience was even more bitter. By the beginning of 1943 there was little left of his earlier hopes for Belgium. He now accepted the division of Belgium into two Reichsgaue, the northern Flemish part possibly being incorporated into a Gau with the Netherlands. As the Foreign Office observed, Degrelle's motive was quite simple. He was loathed by his fellow Belgians and was desperately seeking a position for himself as head of the prospective Wallonian Gau.[13]

The response to Quisling's plea of February 1942 is of broader significance. It reflected Hitler's typical aversion to making decisions and his fear of entering negotiations at a time when Germany needed at least the passivity of the subject populations in western Europe. But it also embodied the general principles of the New Order. These were set out quite clearly by Werner Best, one of the most vocal architects of the New Order.

According to Best the creation of a Grossraum 'assumes that the Grossraum is consciously shaped as a unit by a single political will, which, in the völkisch-organic world-view is only conceivable as that of a particular people or its leadership'.[14] In other words the New Order would be shaped by Germany. The 'leading nation' would not send ambassadors to even the most favoured of the other nations of the Grossraum. Its representatives would, rather, be 'administrative authorities'. It would only send ambassadors to the 'leading nations' of other Grossräume.[15] By implication the other nations would not be able to dispatch ambassadors.

Best's outline was somewhat ahead of the reality of the New Order for, in the west, Germany did maintain ambassadors in two occupied countries, Denmark and France. The comparatively lenient treatment of Denmark owed less to the supposed Germanic character of the Danes than to the Danish government's decision not to resist the German invasion. In France an armistice brought about a division of the country, into an occupied zone in the north and west and an unoccupied zone controlled by the Vichy government of Marshall Pétain. There were divisions among both the Germans and the members of the Vichy regime about France's place in the New Order. On the German side ambassador Abetz was the most energetic advocate of a Franco-German reconciliation. A meeting between Pétain and Hitler at Montoire in November 1940 was meant to symbolize a step in this direction, but in fact issued in nothing more than a declaration of Vichy's willingness to collaborate. Pétain's regime did not, however, take the step of entering the war against England, and the Germans later complained that the promise of Montoire had not been fulfilled.[16] Part of the problem was that the Vichy regime did not know exactly what Hitler's intentions were. Thus in May 1941 Admiral Darlan 'pointed out [to Hitler] that at the moment France was unfortunately marching "in the dark" '. Typically, his plea for enlightenment was ignored.[17]

Politically, Europe under Nazi hegemony remained a complex mosaic of occupation regimes and satellites which even the Nazis found difficult to deal with. Yet, as late as March 1944, Rosenberg's plea for a more unified approach met with the reply 'that the Führer does not place the slightest weight on the uniform construction of the authorities and administrative organs of the various areas under German control'.[18] Direct incorporation into the Reich, *de facto* incorporation, the extension of German administrative control under civil administrations and control by the military authorities jostled side by side. Usually the pattern of occupation chosen in the wake of invasion would remain in place until the Germans were driven from the area concerned, though there were some exceptions. Hitler retreated behind the assertion that the final shape of the New Order would not be determined until complete victory had been achieved.

THE ECONOMICS OF THE NAZI NEW ORDER

It was not so easy to tolerate chaos in the economic field. Germany had entered the war without an adequate economic base and became increasingly dependent upon the utilization of economic resources upon a European scale for the prosecution of the war. The initial policy was as simple as it was crude: plunder. In the General Government, plunder was associated with a deliberate policy of deindustrialization. Production was to be reduced to the minimum required to keep the Polish population alive. But even here the absurdity of this policy eventually made itself felt as, in January 1940, the General Governor, Frank, was able to persuade Hitler and Göring to set the remaining factories to work in the interests of the German war effort.[19] The Protectorate of Bohemia and Moravia, despite its Slavic population, had been spared this fate. Its economy was evidently too important.

In the west too the initial policy was one of plunder. German agencies seized raw material stocks, financial assets and rolling stock and transported them to the Reich. Yet at the same time officials in the Foreign Office had begun the process of planning for the post-war world. In a memorandum of 30 May Carl Clodius of the Foreign Office advised against a policy of plunder, and argued for the integration of the Netherlands, Belgium, Luxembourg and Norway into the Greater German economy by means of a customs union and a currency union. His colleague, Karl Ritter, offered a more expansive vision on 1 June and by the middle of June Gustav Schlotterer had entered the lists on behalf of the Ministry of Economics. Schlotterer saw no need for a currency union – the predominance of the Reichsmark would suffice – but he did see a role for industrial agreements, under the control of the Reichsgruppe Industrie, which would create a 'rational division of labour between the European countries'.[20] Some clarification of policy was achieved in a meeting of 22 June 1940 chaired by Funk. The Minister expressed considerable reservation about the idea of customs unions. 'It was', he said,

> fantasy to talk at this stage of a unified economy on a European scale, and in the same way it was harmful to use slogans like 'currency and customs union' and expect them to solve all our difficulties. A currency or customs union could only be envisaged with a country having a similar standard of life to our own. This was not the case in south-eastern Europe, for instance,

> and it was not at all in our interest to confer on that area a similar standard of life to ours.[21]

Countries which fell into the more privileged category were to 'be organized similarly to ourselves and treated more generously in the matter of payments'.[22] By 'organized similarly to ourselves' he meant that they were to adopt organizations for the regulation of production modelled on those in the Third Reich. The issue of customs unions, even in countries judged to have analogous standards to Germany, proved more difficult. Customs unions were created with Luxembourg, the Netherlands and the Protectorate of Bohemia and Moravia. Yet in the case of Denmark the negotiations petered out in 1940 despite initial interest from both sides. In the case of Slovakia it was the Germans who broke off the discussion. Although the German official Wiehl reported the agreement of both sides that a union was desirable on 27 July, he was obliged to report to the German Commercial Policy Committee, on 9 August, 'the Führer's decision that treatment of the question of economic federation with Slovakia be postponed until later'.[23] The underlying difficulties are easy to discern. On the Slovak side there was a desire to avoid being classified along with the agrarian states of the east and to find a way of utilizing its trading credit, currently locked in non-transferable Reichsmarks in Germany.[24] On the German side Slovakia simply did not figure among the privileged states of the New Order. Among the latter there were fears of long-term subordination to Germany, a concern that domestic price levels would be disrupted, or that a customs union might have little effect in the light of government control of trade.[25]

Considerations of the long-term character of the economic New Order proved to be something of an irritation to the Reich. As early as 9 August 1940 the Commercial Policy Committee was warning that public discussion of such issues was undesirable, and even agreed to restrict the more voluble German speculators.[26] Internal discussions did continue through 1940 and, with less intensity, 1941, until, at the instigation of military and economic leaders, Hitler agreed in February 1942 to ban all further planning for the postwar order.[27]

THE BRITISH RESPONSE TO THE CHALLENGE OF THE NEW ORDER

Although public discussion eventually proved to be an embarrassment, the initial speculation had caused some alarm among the Nazi's opponents. This was especially true of Funk's speech of 25 July 1940. Funk held out the prospect for a post-war order of guaranteed markets, stable prices and exchange rates, 'a rational economic division of labour', and a united

Europe able to negotiate from a position of strength with third parties.[28] In Britain this speech and others were seen as a dangerous challenge to the will of the occupied peoples to resist Germany, and was judged sufficiently serious for the Cabinet to commission the economist John Maynard Keynes to draft a counter-proposal.[29] Similarly, in a leading British economic journal, G. W. Guillebaud argued that Germany would not seek to impoverish the conquered states: it was not in her economic interest to do so. The New Order, with stable prices and exchange rates, was, he claimed, quite viable economically. The only reason for rejecting it was that it was designed to support a 'one-sided German hegemony'.[30] Such views were in fact widespread and were to outlive the end of the Second World War.[31] They were not, of course, undisputed. Paul Einzig replied at length to Guillebaud's article. Showing a greater awareness of Hitler's priorities, he referred to Nazi plans for the settlement of Germans in occupied countries and a preference for relying upon force rather than conciliation. On the economic front he argued that there would be no stability of prices or exchange rates and that the much-vaunted clearing system would merely serve to exact tribute. Furthermore, any international division of labour would be manipulated to Germany's advantage.[32] Einzig had the better of the argument, though the picture was not as straightforward as either of them imagined. German economic policy was being forged largely on an *ad hoc* basis between competing agencies within the occupation regime. While some quickly saw the need for a rational utilization of the productive capacities of the occupied territories, Göring continued to insist upon a right of plunder and repeatedly complained that the peoples of occupied Europe were too well fed.

The reality of the economic New Order was in place by the summer of 1941. Europe's trade had been relocated and was held in place by a system of clearing agreements, some inherited from the pre-war period, relating to east European states, others more or less imposed upon the occupied countries of the west. The pattern of trade was heavily focused on Germany to the detriment of traditional partners, even where they too formed part of the New Order. Whereas Norway had exported some 90 million kroner of goods to Belgium, Holland and France in 1938, she exported a mere 8.4 million in 1944.[33] Germany's eastern allies were not immune to this trend: Bulgarian, Hungarian and Romanian dependency upon trade with Germany increased above the already high pre-war levels.[34] The promise which Funk had made was that there would be a transition from an essentially bilateral trading pattern with Germany at the centre to a genuinely multilateral system. But as the more honest German commentators acknowledged this remained an unfulfilled promise. As one noted in 1942, the main difficulty was the debts accumulated by Germany through the clearing system.[35] In Belgium the debts accumulated by Germany by the end of the first quarter of 1944 were estimated to be RM 4,288, which equalled three-quarters of the amount paid by Belgium in occupation costs.[36] As Einzig had claimed, the clearing agreements became mechanisms for the exaction of tribute for the prosecution of the war.

EARLY RESPONSES FROM THE RESISTANCE

The challenge which all this posed to the occupied peoples of Europe was an enormous one. It was not only that they had suffered military defeat, though this was a severe shock, especially in the case of Poland and France. They were also exposed to economic exploitation and worse still to the increasingly apparent racist policies of the Nazi regime. As if this were not enough, some societies were internally divided by the existence of collaborationist regimes, again most strongly in the case of France. One response to this by the incipient resistance movements was to turn to the idea of European integration, though this was by no means an automatic step. One obstacle to advocacy of European integration was the fact that the idea of Europe was one which the Nazis and their collaborators had appropriated. As late as April 1943 one of the leading members of the French resistance, Paul Bastid, warned:

> Without realizing it, false ideas have taken root among us. In this article I would like to slay one of these monsters.
>
> It is an idea that presents itself in a seductive form, with what appear to be highly respectable guarantees. I refer to the idea of 'Europe'.[37]

But many more drew a clear distinction between the Nazi New Order and the idea of Europe. This presented particular difficulties for Germans who opposed Hitler. One who took an unequivocal stance quite early was Helmuth von Moltke. In April 1941, under the heading 'Expected political and military situation at the end of the war', he wrote:

> Germany has been defeated, i.e. she is no longer in a position to continue the war ... For our purposes, the possibility of a German victory is of little interest since it would defer the conditions on which the fulfilment of our objectives depends to a much later period.[38]

The Europe which Moltke envisaged was to be radically different from the prewar order. There would be an 'inter-European economic bureaucracy' and a five-member European cabinet and a legislative body which would be 'responsible to the individual citizen' rather than to the member states of the European union.[39] But these institutional arrangements would not suffice. For Moltke, isolated with a small number of friends in a hostile society, nothing less than some kind of moral renewal was required to break the hold of the nation-state. The hold of the nation-state was also of concern to two Italian opponents of the New Order, Altiero Spinelli and Ernesto Rossi. For them, however, it was less a question of moral renewal than of interests and political leverage. According to their Ventotene Manifesto of August 1941,

> In the brief, intense period of general crisis [at the end of the war] (when the States will lie broken, when the masses will be anxiously waiting for a new message, like molten matter, burning and easily shaped into new moulds capable of accommodating the guidance of serious internationalist-minded men), the most privileged classes in the old nationalist systems will attempt, by underhand or violent methods, to dampen the wave of internationalist feelings and passions and will ostentatiously begin to reconstruct the old State institutions.[40]

What distinguishes both Moltke's speculations and the Ventotene Manifesto, albeit in quite different ways, is their awareness of the enormity of the changes they were demanding, and of the resistance which they would face. What both wanted was a thoroughgoing federation which would displace both the institutions and the political loyalties of the old Europe. Others showed less insight, though they were not thereby less sincere or clear cut in their advocacy of federation. As yet, however, in western Europe at least, these views were very much those of a minority. More widespread advocacy of European federation would not really begin until the second half of 1941.[41]

THE DEVELOPMENT OF THE DEBATE IN BRITAIN

It was not only in occupied Europe that the Nazi challenge forced a reconsideration of Europe's political order. In Britain even government ministers advocated the option. On 8 September 1939, only days after the outbreak of the war, Lord Davies invoked everything from the foundation of the United States of America to the views of the German philosopher Kant in an unrestrained plea for British commitment to a United States of Europe. More briefly Anthony Eden, then Minister of Dominions, wrote that 'the only possible solution is some kind of federation' and went on to refer to a 'defence scheme, a European customs union and common currency'.[42] Their comments were made against the background of increasing public debate about the possibility of federation, much of it driven forward by the activities of Federal Union, an organization formed by a clique of British federalists which soon had a membership in excess of ten thousand.[43]

While somewhat ambivalent about the public clamour, the British political establishment did pay serious attention to the idea of a federation, largely in order to cement the Anglo-French alliance and to provide the French with an alternative to a postwar policy of occupying parts of Germany. With these aims in mind Sir Orme Sargent, on 28 February 1940, advocated an Anglo-French union which would entail a substantial sacrifice of sovereignty on Britain's part. More significantly, he won the approval of Prime Minister Chamberlain. The internal debate continued over the following four months with advocates of full-scale federation arguing with those who favoured a temporary arrangement for the duration of the war and others who preferred something closer to the British Commonwealth, which was, they claimed, 'based primarily on a common outlook and common interests, rather than on an elaborate constitutional organization'.[44] Although the debate was to continue after the capitulation of France, it was the imminence of French surrender that induced the British government to offer an 'indissoluble union' to France. The offer was rejected.[45]

Despite Churchill's resolve to fight on alone, the desperate plight of Britain continued to induce radical speculation upon the future. From Stafford Cripps, then Ambassador to Moscow, came the suggestion of an Anglo-American union modelled on the offer to France. Cripps was in no doubt that Britain would play the junior role: 'Britain would become merely the European outpost of an Anglo-Saxon group concentrated in the west.'[46] Although it was quickly pointed out that the United States itself would have little interest in this, the idea formed part of a broader stream of opinion which looked to Anglo-American or Atlantic co-operation as an alternative to a continental commitment.

Within beleaguered Britain the debate on the postwar order continued with Churchill consenting to the establishment of a cabinet committee on war aims. Churchill himself, however, was reluctant to tie his hands by any explicit statement, for a variety of reasons. One was that a statement would probably divide the cabinet, a fear shared by the Labour leader Clement Atlee. He also pointed to uncertainty about the situation at the end of the war. Equally important was the desire to avoid any explicit commitments which might antagonize the United States, upon whom Britain depended for the resources to continue the war. Churchill's view prevailed and there was to be no statement of war aims until the Atlantic Charter was published in 1941. That document, agreed between Roosevelt and Churchill, was studiously vague and served primarily as a substitute for any more precise definition on both sides of the Atlantic.[47]

By then a rough consensus had emerged on two important issues in Britain. The first concerned Germany. Spurred by the rhetoric of the New

Order, and especially Funk's speech, the cabinet had commissioned Keynes to draft a reply. In his draft, which was ready in December 1940, Keynes, who had been a severe critic of the reparations burden imposed on Germany at the end of the First World War, proposed to assure the Germans that they too would share in the postwar prosperity. 'It would', he argued, 'be senseless to suppose that her neighbours can develop an ordered, or a prosperous, or a secure life with a crushed and ruined Germany in their midst.'[48] He even conceded that 'Germany must be expected and allowed to assume the measure of economic leadership which flows naturally from her own qualifications and her geographical position.'[49] That proved too much and was subsequently edited out. But it did point to a genuine dilemma: there could be no European reconstruction without German reconstruction, but the latter was bound to conjure up fears of German hegemony.

The second concerned the fate of eastern Europe. From the outset there was interest from the British foreign policy establishment, and from the east Europeans, in the idea of an east-central European federation. The idea, of course, long pre-dated the outbreak of war. But this time the drive for a federation was led by the Polish exile leader General Sikorski and was to be built around a Polish–Czech federation. By March 1940 the Czech leader Beneš had given his blessing to the scheme in principle.[50] As yet, however, Beneš was more interested in securing Allied recognition, which he duly gained in the wake of France's defeat. Towards the end of the year Polish-Czech discussions accelerated, but Beneš had reservations. In the first place Poland was simply much larger than Czechoslovakia and Beneš was highly suspicious of Poland's authoritarian past and the dominance, as he saw it, of the Polish aristocracy in Polish politics. Alongside these internal considerations, and a minor territorial dispute between the two parties,[51] lay the question of the Soviet attitude to the plan. Beneš, mindful of western betrayal at Munich, was concerned that the plan must be acceptable to the Russians. Despite these reservations, and no doubt encouraged by the lack of opposition from Soviet officials whom he sounded out, Beneš agreed to go ahead with a joint communiqué on 11 November 1940. Formal negotiations began in the following year.

The British response to this was largely positive. According to F. K. Roberts of the Foreign Office,

> We have already welcomed the Polish-Czech federation, which is clearly necessary to balance German strength and we should, I think, share the Polish hope that it will expand to cover other nations. Such a federation is unlikely to become a dangerous expansionist Power as, for example, a nationalist Poland might.[52]

Roberts also wrote, in words that were to be taken up by Foreign Minister Eden, 'It is to be hoped that the Poles are right in assuming that Russia will be content to think of herself mainly as an Asiatic Power and will not consider herself threatened by the Polish–Czech Federation.'[53] It was a rash hope. The Soviet Union had, it must be remembered, joined the Third Reich in invading Poland in 1939. But the picture seemed to change when, in the summer of 1941, Hitler launched operation Barbarossa: the invasion of the Soviet Union.

THE NAZI NEW ORDER AFTER THE INVASION OF THE SOVIET UNION

The invasion of the Soviet Union changed the strategic balance of the war and also refocused the ideological dimension. Anti-Bolshevism now came to the fore and was consciously used by the Nazis with headlines like 'Europe Rises up Against Bolshevism'.[54] The collaborators needed no encouragement in order to take up the theme. Pétain openly welcomed the development and saw it as the opportunity for Franco-German co-operation against a common enemy. Indeed the enthusiasm of the French collaborationist press went too far for Hitler's taste. According to Martin Borman's record of a meeting on 16 July,

> By way of introduction the Führer emphasised that he wished first of all to make same basic statements. Various measures were now necessary; this was confirmed, among other events, by the assertion in an impudent Vichy newspaper that the war against the Soviet Union was Europe's war and that, therefore, it had to be conducted for Europe as a whole.[55]

Although Hitler typically vacillated or issued ambiguous instructions, he remained firm in his opposition to any precise or specific outline of Europe's future. As the German offensive on the eastern front slowed in the autumn of 1942 functionaries of the propaganda apparatus drew up schemes for a revival of plans for the New Order and sought to maximize the linkage between anti-Bolshevism and European unity, but the old difficulties recurred. At each military setback advocates of a more positive use of the European theme would revive the idea, only to meet with Hitler's hesitation and then resistance. Thus as the summer offensive of 1942 ground to a halt at Stalingrad, Goebbels, and even Ribbentrop, sought to win over Hitler. The response was a Hitler decree according to which, 'The planning, preparation and execution of demonstrations of a European or international kind . . . must cease.'[56] The defeat at Stalingrad at the beginning of 1943 induced another surge of enthusiasm for the European theme. Ribbentrop even established a European Committee to draft a charter of a European confederation, but again nothing came of this.[57]

German propaganda did however try to exploit the idea of Europe in different ways. The Third Reich was presented as a guardian of European independence and culture against American imperialism and Russian Bolshevism, both of which were described as tools of the Jews. Britain was relegated to the sidelines; she would merely lose her Empire to the Americans. The main theme, however, was an attempt to invoke fear of the Soviet Union. In occupied Europe German newspapers printed articles with headlines like 'Roosevelt's World Order. The Sacrifice of Europe to the Soviets Confirmed.'[58] There was an attempt to appeal to old European prejudices, to a fear of American domination and a hostility to American culture, to a fear of Bolshevism and an Asiatic Russia, supplemented by the venom of Nazi racial theories. The more intelligent Nazis had indeed correctly identified the main elements of European prejudices about the looming superpowers but, aside from an increasingly beleaguered collaborationist minority, Nazi propaganda was too readily compared with the reality of occupation and the increasing probability of German defeat.

The reality of occupation had become harsher and more brutal in the wake of the invasion of the Soviet Union. Denmark increasingly lost its relative autonomy after the appointment of Werner Best as Reichsbevollmächtiger in November 1942 and Vichy France was occupied in the wake of Allied victories in North Africa, again in November. The occupation regime in western Europe was, despite its brutality, still far removed from events taking place in the east. There the Final Solution was in full swing. At some point early in 1941 Hitler had taken the decision to murder Europe's Jewish population.[59] From then on resources needed by the German military would be diverted to a genocidal campaign. Not even the crude consideration of the utility of exploiting Jewish labour could long delay transportation to the camps and death. The extermination of the Jews was intended to be followed by an even more wide-ranging programme of racial engineering in eastern Europe. It had in fact already begun, with German minorities being relocated and indigenous peoples being expelled or designated as fit for Germanization. Not long after the invasion of Poland the Germanization of the territories incorporated into the Reich had begun and in the spring of 1940 the same fate was decreed for the General Government. Associated with this process was a systematic attempt to eliminate the elite of Polish society.[60] Of the remainder only some 3 per cent of the population was judged to be fit for Germanization, in contrast to the Protectorate, where Hitler had agreed that the majority of the Czechs could be assimilated.[61]

The fate of those not considered fit for Germanization was part of the subject matter of the General Plan East, the blueprint for the future of eastern Europe. According to one version of this plan between 16 and 20.4 million Poles were to be transported from the General Government and dumped in Siberia. Warming to his theme the author of the document, Erhard Wetzel, speculated that Walloons, Czechs and Hungarians could also be dispatched to Siberia and perversely added,

> here the European idea in all its aspects would have meaning, while it would be dangerous for us in the settlement area of the German Volk, since it would mean ... the acceptance of the idea of racial mixture even for us ... The greatest misfortune which could threaten the German Volk would be the triumph of the pan-European racial idea, which could only have as a consequence a great European racial swamp.[62]

While Nazi ideologues gave vent to their hatred of the pan-European idea the Third Reich's economic directors were being forced into an attempt to integrate the European economy.[63] Although the foundations were laid by others the new policy came to fruition under Albert Speer. Speer sought to maximize use of the industry of occupied Europe to remedy the deficiencies in the Reich's output. Orders were increasingly allocated to occupied Europe. Speer followed a conscious policy of using French industry to produce consumer goods, thereby releasing capacity in Germany for war *matériel*. He established an increasingly uniform planning apparatus in western Europe integrating German officials and those of occupied Europe. His efforts have led the British historian A. S. Milward to conclude that 'Speer's views on the industrial organization of Europe, although primarily inspired by the immediate need to increase war production, fitted ... quite comfortably into the line of German liberal capitalist thought stretching from the work of Rudolf Delbrück to the Common Market.'[64] Although this assessment glosses over the distinctive characteristics of the European Economic Community, it is a clear testament to the scale of integration Speer was obliged to pursue.

But alongside Speer's policy lay another strategy embodied in Gauleiter Sauckel. Sauckel had been appointed Plenipotentiary for Labour Mobilisation with the brief to recruit foreign labour for German factories. Sauckel, a radical Nazi of the old school, distrustful of Speer and his connections with big business, set about his task with vigour. Although Speer had originally supported this policy it soon came into conflict with his own. Western industry could not work on German orders if its labour force was being rounded up by Sauckel's agents. Speer responded by bringing in a system of 'protected' factories, protected that is from Sauckel. The high-point of Speer's strategy came in September 1943 when he met the French Minister Bichelonne. The two technocrats agreed upon a programme of collaboration, including a committee for

European armaments production and protection for designated factories.[65] Yet Speer could never win a clear-cut victory over Sauckel. Hitler, equivocal as ever, advised trying to combine both approaches. Nor could German industry, even with the improved exploitation of the resources of occupied Europe, keep pace with Allied output. The sheer weight of Allied resources gradually ground down the Third Reich.

RESISTANCE PLANS FOR A UNITED EUROPE

The combination of the increased brutality of the occupation regimes and the prospect of liberation induced more of the resistance groups to give consideration to the post-war order, and many turned to the idea of a European federation when they did so. Those who did were often vague about the constitutional details, and those who were precise often differed. There was a general, if unsurprising, consensus that the federation or confederation should guarantee peace within the union and have responsibility for external affairs. In some accounts the member states would be deprived of national armies entirely.[66] Typical too was a strong emphasis upon human rights, upon the idea that federal guarantees of human rights should prevail over national law which failed to guarantee them.[67] The influence of the United States was evident in a proposal for a legislature composed of a House of Federal Representatives and a Federal European Senate, though the same proposal opted for a three-man Directorate instead of a President.[68]

It was not so much the constitutional details which concerned them as the general motives for having a federation and the crucial question of membership. A particular problem here, of course, was the fate of Germany. French and Dutch socialists agreed that a democratized Germany should be included, though their warnings against a 'vengeful peace' suggest that they knew they were out of step with popular opinion.[69] That most people who withstood the allure of collaboration thought mainly in terms of national liberation is confirmed by an early report of Visser t'Hooft, a Dutch cleric, who reported in November 1941 that 96 per cent of the population were 'ardently nationalistic'.[70]

The problem was not only that the peoples of occupied Europe would have to be won over to federalism. As the Italian federalists argued in November 1943, 'a European federation will not come about unless the peoples compel their diplomats to establish it'.[71] For Spinelli, as indeed for several others, what was at stake was both the future international order in Europe and its socio-economic order. The defeat of the nation-state was bound up with the overthrow of the old economic order and the installation of a broadly socialist Europe.

That combination, though fairly widespread among the resistance was not undisputed. For example, *Trouw,* the journal of the right wing of the Dutch resistance, asked rhetorically, 'How can a country like ours, with territory extending over four continents, be confined to the straitjacket of a European federation, when the war has only just demonstrated how closely the different territories are bound together?'[72] Yet the author of this question did not opt for a simple reassertion of the national autonomy and Empire. He recognized the need for an international organization, but it had to be, he claimed, world-wide. In this he was probably influenced by growing awareness of Allied planning, but the choice between a European or world-wide organization had been one which had divided the resistance from the outset.

The main trends of Allied planning for the post-war world were becoming more and more apparent from the winter of 1943–44 onwards. At the same time Allied armies were beginning to make substantial inroads into Nazi-held Europe. Their presence and intentions were regarded with ambivalence by some. The most directly threatened were the Polish federalists. According to one source, 'The present war had revealed the true aims of Soviet policy for the first time ... Russia had decided to move westward. Russian imperialism is like a nightmare of destruction overshadowing the whole of European civilization.'[73] Nor was fear of Soviet hegemony limited to Poles. Alfred Delp, a German Jesuit and member of von Moltke's Kreisau group, speculated upon Russian intentions a mere month before his execution in 1945. His description of 'Slavs' as a destructive and alien force differed little from Nazi propaganda. For Delp Europe was in fact threatened by two alien cultures: the Russians and the Americans, who, he wrote, 'are thrusting irresponsible hands into our lives from all directions'.[74] It was not necessary to view the Allied powers as culturally alien in order to be concerned. With considerable prescience the Dutchman Hans-Dieter Salinger cast doubt upon the Allied plans for a new League of Nations. Predicting the collapse of Allied unity in a postwar world, he anticipated a divided Europe which would 'become a deployment zone in peacetime and a battlefield in war'.[75]

There was, of course, little these men could do to influence events. They were far from the corridors of power, still hunted by the police of the occupier, isolated from each other and often unrepresentative of prevailing sentiment in their own societies. Yet they did reflect a willingness to develop prewar ideas of European unity in a more radical direction, and a few of them, including Altiero Spinelli, would survive to argue for federation from positions of some influence. Spinelli had seen the difficulties more clearly than most, even if he overestimated the plasticity of loyalties and political cultures in the wake of the war. He also sought to establish links between the resistance groups and to promote a political movement committed to federalism. In both he achieved a limited success, but it was a decidedly limited success. Europe's fate would not be determined by those who had resisted the New Order from within.

SOVIET POLICY AND IDEAS OF FEDERATION IN EASTERN EUROPE

In the summer of 1941 British policy on the post-war order was still undecided. The only official commitment was the Atlantic Charter. Its vague promises were, however, of little reassurance to the new participant in the war, the Soviet Union. Britain and the Soviet Union had agreed, on 12 July, to aid each other and not to sign a separate peace with Germany, but there the matter remained until November. Then, on 8 November, Stalin wrote complaining about the lack of any agreement on war aims. The note presented the British with a considerable dilemma. As one Foreign Office official commented some days later, 'The difficulty here arises that we have not made up our own minds on the questions of the economic and political postwar settlement and that we are committed to the Americans not to undertake during the war commitments which would bind us at the peace and after.'[76] Pressured by Stalin, Britain sent to Moscow Anthony Eden, who was quite aware that Stalin would press for acquiescence in the Soviet Union's territorial expansion. During their conversations Stalin did duly ask for British recognition of the Soviet frontiers of 1941. He also suggested the division of Germany into three, the assignment of East Prussia to Poland, and he indicated that he would not oppose 'federal relationships' in Europe.[77]

Despite the commitment to the Americans, Eden was inclined to make concessions to the Soviets. His position sprang from a recognition of Soviet power and a desire to try to win Stalin over to a policy of joint decision-making and co-operation. The problem was that Churchill was opposed to concessions, as indeed was Roosevelt, who objected to any Anglo-Soviet treaty at all. In May Roosevelt agreed to avoid at least public criticism of the treaty and Stalin had dropped his insistence upon explicit territorial concessions, probably in response to the deteriorating military situation on the eastern front.[78]

By then doubts had arisen about Stalin's apparent willingness to sanction federations in eastern Europe. The Soviets had been prodded into a response by the progress made by the east Europeans. In January 1942 agreement was reached on both a Polish–Czech union and a Yugoslav–Greek union. In both cases the proposed union was of a rather limited, intergovernmental, nature since one party to each union was considerably less enthusiastic than the other. While Sikorski had proposed a Supreme Council, including representatives from the legislatures of the two states, with the ability to take binding decisions, Beneš preferred a more confederal structure. In the case of the Balkan states it was the Yugoslavs who pressed for the more far-reaching union and the Greeks who wanted a more circumspect document.[79]

At first the Soviet Ambassador adopted a favourable attitude, but in February the Czech envoy in Moscow, Fierlinger, reported Soviet hostility. Critical comments also came from Soviet officials and the Soviet radio. As yet Beneš was still not sure of how firm Stalin's opposition was, though Soviet resistance to the inclusion of a clause expressing support for federations in the Anglo-Soviet treaty reveals his underlying hostility. The true Soviet position was eventually made clear to the Czechs on 16 July by Ambassador Bogomolov. By the end of the year Beneš told his cabinet he had decided to drop the idea. Sikorski, for the Poles, had clung to the idea more vigorously. He made two journeys to the United States, where he sought to enlist the Americans and gained the impression that they would be more supportive than they actually intended. He even suggested to Beneš that they sign an act of confederation and present the Russians with a *fait accompli*, but Beneš would not agree. The proposed Greek–Yugoslav union fared no better, and for similar reasons.[80] Although hopes were to remain in British and American minds that the Russians would permit some kind of federation in east-central Europe, there was, as one British official noted, never much evidence that they would, although there was to be one exception to their generally hostile attitude.

WESTERN EUROPEAN EXILES AND THE DEBATE ON AN ATLANTIC SECURITY SYSTEM

Exiles from western Europe had also been forced to undertake a fundamental reappraisal of their long-term position. The most vigorous initiative here came from the Norwegian Foreign Minister Trygve Lie. As early as December 1940 he had proclaimed the need to renounce Norway's traditional policy of non-alignment and in the following year he made a series of increasingly precise comments on a regional security system. Lie was thinking in terms of an Atlantic security system, involving both the British and the Americans, within which 'the smaller countries would perform definite tasks of a regional character'.[81] The Dutch joined the Norwegians in this campaign and, in 1942, offered Britain bases on Dutch territory as part of an Atlantic security system.[82] There was considerable interest in these ideas among Britain's foreign policy establishment. The Foreign Research and Press service prepared a highly positive confidential report in October. Eden even tried to persuade the war cabinet to raise the issue with the Americans, but in the same month the cabinet decided to give priority to the Four Power Plan.

One interesting casualty of Norwegian enthusiasm for an Atlantic system was the alternative of a Scandinavian defence system. In numerous schemes for a postwar Europe it was suggested that Europe should be reconstituted as a series of confederations, and one of these was usually a Scandinavian bloc. There was, moreover, considerable popular support for Nordic co-operation. Scandinavian critics of an Atlantic security system quickly pointed to its incompatibility with Nordic union. British advisers were aware of the divergent interests and fears of the Scandinavians and estimated, correctly, that Sweden and Finland would probably not opt to join an Atlantic system.[83]

THE UNITED STATES AND PLANNING FOR A POSTWAR WORLD

The Four Power Plan, to which the British cabinet gave precedence over these ideas of an Atlantic system, was not to receive its final shape until July 1943, and even then it retained an ambiguity which bedevilled Anglo-American planning. The ambiguity arose because of American preference for a global approach and American suspicion that Britain preferred a regionalist approach. In reality both camps were internally divided and sought to fuse elements of global and regionalist approaches. The waters were muddied, again in both Britain and America, by the peculiarities of foreign policy-making in the two wartime states, and more precisely by the character of the two leaders. Both had a tendency to ignore their foreign policy specialists, though Roosevelt was more guilty of this than Churchill. Both were prone to making *ad hoc* comments whose import was as expansive as they were vague.

In America the State Department had been working on schemes for the postwar order even before the United States entered the war. Much of this speculation strongly endorsed some kind of European integration. Almost none of it seems to have reached President Roosevelt. Worse still for the advocates of European integration, Secretary of State Cordell Hull was highly suspicious of regionalism, that is regionalism outside the American hemisphere. Hull was committed to the principles of free trade and critical of anything which suggested a protectionist bloc: hence his constant pressure upon Britain to renounce the protectionist economic policies surrounding the Empire and Commonwealth. It was a vision to which Roosevelt subscribed.[84]

While Hull supplied an economic vision the political vision of the postwar world was more Roosevelt's own. The first clear, if brief, statement of it came in response to the Soviet Foreign Minister, Molotov, in

May 1942. Roosevelt stated that 'the United States, England and Russia and perhaps China should police the world and enforce disarmament by inspection'.[85] It was this idea of the Four Policemen which the British took up in drafting their own Four Power Plan and sought to reconcile with the idea of some kind of regional arrangement. In the Foreign Office care was taken to ensure that the regional arrangement would not offend the Americans. According to one draft, ' "Regionalism" should be held to mean not the establishment of the power of any one great power in any particular region, but rather should connote districts in which one of the great Powers should have primary responsibility for defence against Germany or Japan.'[86]

Churchill was less cautious. He wrote to Roosevelt in February 1943 suggesting 'an instrument of European government' along with a similar arrangement for the Far East.[87] He repeated the idea, with variations, in a speech in March and at an Embassy lunch in Washington in May. It was the suggestion of some institutional regional arrangement which caused the problem. According to Harry L. Hopkins, at a meeting with Eden shortly after Churchill's March speech,

> The President and Welles were very emphatic that the United States could not be a member of any independent regional body such as a European Council; they felt that all the United Nations should be members of one body for the purposes of recommending policy ... That there would be under this body regional councils with similar advisory powers ... but, finally, that the real decisions should be made by the United States, Great Britain, Russia and China ... [88]

Roosevelt's position was hardly consistent – he even referred to regional 'security commissions' – but Churchill's comments had conjured up the idea of 'independent' bodies, and hence of spheres of influence, while Roosevelt was committed to the idea of his Four Policemen co-operating to govern an otherwise disarmed world.[89] With Cordell Hull there to pounce upon anything which strayed from a global approach, European integration was increasingly excluded from the decision-making agenda.

Eden continued to press for some kind of European agency and won over a reluctant cabinet to approval of a United Nations Commission for Europe in June 1943. In the *aide-mémoire* which Eden sent to Washington on 16 July 1943 he referred to the Commission for Europe and suggested that various other authorities, covering shipping, inland transport, telecommunications, propaganda, reparations and 'other economic problems', should all be subordinated to the Commission.[90] The initial response was that any such commission should confine itself to matters relating to the Axis states lest it 'impede the later establishment of a general international organization'.[91] A few days later a memorandum for the President was more pointed: the whole thing smacked of Churchill's regionalism. With some exaggeration the memorandum declared that the commission, as proposed by Eden, 'would be essentially a kind of super-government for Europe'.[92] Although Roosevelt had previously been ambiguous about regional bodies he had now been convinced that they posed a threat to his global international organization.[93] It was too late for Eden to influence the Americans. In August at the Quebec Conference Eden and Churchill accepted Hull's proposal to proceed with the planning of a world-wide international body.

The issue was raised again, from an unexpected quarter, at the Teheran Conference, the first meeting of the three Allied leaders. As Roosevelt pressed his global organization Stalin countered with the suggestion of separate councils for Europe and the Far East. Roosevelt immediately noted that this was Churchill's proposal again and said that public opinion in the United States would not support it. Quite why Stalin raised this option is unclear, but it is doubtful that he was seriously interested. As other comments he made at Teheran reveal, the overriding fear of the Soviets was a postwar revival of Germany, and Stalin assumed that any European federation would be dominated, sooner or later, by Germany. The Soviet position on east European federations was made crystal clear. The Soviet Union was opposed, seeing them as an anti-Soviet cordon sanitaire.[94]

In the preparations for the Teheran Conference Eden had managed to salvage something from his proposals for a Commission for Europe, in the form of a European Advisory Commission. This commission was given a highly restricted brief, though Eden was able to win some expansion of its role at the Teheran Conference itself. This turned out to be a very partial victory, for Cordell Hull kept a careful watch to ensure that the European Advisory Commission did not exceed its brief. Again the fear was that it might impede the formation of the global organization. Quite how suspicious Hull was is evident from the fact that he felt it necessary to warn the European Advisory Commission's American representative, Ambassador Winant, that the Commission must not do anything which 'might be construed or interpreted as paving the way for a European control body'.[95]

The British were not, of course, proposing a European federation, though they did see the need for federations in eastern Europe, and advisers in the foreign policy establishment had drawn a more general conclusion, namely that

> The exaggerated encouragement given in the last peace settlement to the claims of small nations to independent sovereignty has now given way to a

> natural reaction in favour of regional groupings, by means of which it is hoped that the necessary protection may be afforded to States which experience has shown to be too weak to stand alone.[96]

On the broader canvas of Europe as a whole Eden argued for a kind of intergovernmental, and in fact Allied, control of European-wide functional bodies. He argued for a co-ordination of Allied occupation policies, immediate relief aid and an Allied policy towards longer-term problems of reconstruction. The Americans, especially Roosevelt and Hull, confounded Eden's argument with Churchill's vaguer speculations, and saw Eden's plan as a threat to their world-wide organization, in much the same was as Briand's critics saw his European union as a threat to the League of Nations. The outcome was not only a defeat for the idea of a European Commission with some authority, but also an artificial divide between the problems of occupation policy, the problems of immediate relief in liberated Europe and the problems of longer-term reconstruction.

THE GERMAN PROBLEM

These problems applied particularly to Germany, where the picture was clouded by differences between Allied leaders and their advisers, a failure to define policy clearly and uncertainty between the Allies about each other's true intentions. Uncertainty about Germany brought with it uncertainty about the fate of Europe as a whole. This at least was clear to the advisers in both Britain and the United States. In 1943 British Foreign Office officials were coming to agree that the only long-term solution was the integration of a unified Germany into Europe, especially west Europe. They did see a dismembered Germany as the best political solution, but only if this came about as a result of spontaneous separatism, and that they dismissed as implausible. Moreover, economic unity, essential to the integration of Germany into the European economy, would lead to political unity much as it had done in the nineteenth century. The solution, they decided, lay not in dismemberment but in decentralization. American officials came to broadly similar conclusions.[97]

But Churchill and Eden on the one hand and Roosevelt on the other were not necessarily in step with their officials. In March 1943, during talks in Washington, Roosevelt and Eden 'agreed that, under any circumstances, Germany must be divided into several states, one of which must, over all circumstances, be Prussia'.[98] Roosevelt was even firmer in this conviction than Eden. On the eve of the Moscow and Teheran Conferences the President 'stated categorically that he favours partition of Germany into three or more states'.[99] Churchill was not far behind, frequently speculating on the division of Germany and hiving off part of southern Germany into a Danubian federation. Yet despite this enthusiasm for division the Allied leaders failed to come to any clear decision at Teheran and referred the matter to the European Advisory Commission.

The following year the British representative on the European Advisory Commission, Sir William Strang, raised the issue of dismemberment, but neither of his partners was in a position to make any concrete suggestions and the issue then effectively disappeared from the agenda.[100] The idea did reappear, in bizarre form, in September 1944 at a meeting between Churchill and Roosevelt in Quebec. Here they agreed to a modified version of a document put forward by the American Secretary of the Treasury, Henry Morgenthau. Morgenthau's plan associated dismemberment with the drastic deindustrialization of the Ruhr and Saar. In the final document signed by the two leaders this was described as part of a programme 'looking forward to converting Germany into a country primarily agricultural and pastoral in its character'.[101] In both America and Britain ministers and officials were quick to point out the absurdity of this idea and both men effectively backed away from the agreement. Germany was too important to Europe as a whole to be consigned to such a fate. The result was that the issue was still undecided when the Allied leaders met at Yalta in January 1945. There they did agree to assert their right to 'take such steps, including the complete disarmament, demilitarisation and the dismemberment as they deem requisite for future peace and security'.[102] But they were still clearly divided and uncertain about how far to exercise this right.[103]

During the previous year Germany had figured in a broader debate upon the security of western Europe in the postwar world. The initiative for the debate came from several sources including Dutch and Belgian exiles who took up their earlier schemes for an Atlantic defence system. This time it was Spaak, the Belgian Foreign Minister, who took the initiative, suggesting a western bloc reaching from Norway to the Iberian peninsula.[104] Significantly, Spaak noted that this might promote the division of Europe into two blocs. The same supposition was made, and accepted, by Britain's Chiefs of Staff. According to a Foreign Office report of their views,

> The military say, quite rightly, that the only power in Europe which can, in the foreseeable future, be a danger to us is the Union of Soviet Socialist Republics. They go on to argue that the only way to meet that potential danger is to organise against it now, and in pursuance of that policy they have recently advanced as an argument in favour of the dismemberment of Germany the theory that we might then be able to use the man-power and resources of north-west Germany in an eventual war against the Russians.[105]

Although the debate continued for some time, there was considerable alarm in the Foreign Office lest the Soviets hear of these comments. At a time when there was suspicion on both sides that one half of the Allied effort might still consider a separate peace with Germany, the concern is understandable. Furthermore, Churchill was not convinced, in part because of his reluctance to contemplate the kind of commitment to the continent that the western bloc would entail.[106]

TOWARDS THE END OF THE WAR

Yet Churchill too was increasingly concerned by the sheer military weight of the Soviet Union in a post-war world. The fact had made some impression on American minds too. One of the documents they took to the Quebec conference was a military estimate that Russia would dominate post-war Europe. Britain, unaided, might at best retain some influence in the Mediterranean.[107] Roosevelt, though occasionally making similar geo-political calculations, placed his hopes on the strategy of post-war co-operation with Stalin while Churchill became more and more concerned about Soviet intentions as well as power. There was persistent wrangling over the fate of Poland, both its territorial location and the political complexion of its postwar government, with Stalin breaking off relations with the exiled Polish government when the Poles (rightly) charged the Soviets with responsibility for the murder of Polish officers at Katyn. It was, however, disagreements over the Balkans which led to the famous percentages deal. The deal was reached during Churchill's October 1944 visit to Moscow and consisted of a division of responsibility, with Britain being assigned 90 per cent influence in Greece, Russia 75 per cent in Bulgaria and the two having an equal share in Yugoslavia. These three countries are of particular interest since two of them, Bulgaria and Yugoslavia, provide the only case in which Stalin favoured a federation. The idea of a south-Slav federation had a long history but the immediate initiative had been taken by the communist leaders Tito and Dimitrov early in 1944, with Stalin's approval. In January 1945, however, they were told any idea of federation would have to be postponed on account of British opposition to the idea.[108]

As the war drew to a close there were signs that Allied co-operation was giving way to Allied dissension. Neither was favourable to European unity. Allied co-operation entailed the exclusion of European unity as a potential threat to four-power condominium veiled by an all-embracing United Nations. Allied dissension meant each saw federations proposed or supported by the other as hostile. While the war continued neither side could persist in supporting partial integration, lest that rupture the alliance and threaten the all-important unconditional victory over Germany.

For the French exile, Jean Monnet, the issue was more urgent. He argued that,

> To enjoy the prosperity and social progress that are essential, the states of Europe must form a federation or 'European entity' which will make them a single economic unit. The British, the Americans and the Russians have worlds of their own into which they can temporarily withdraw. France is bound up in Europe. She cannot escape. Her life depends on solving the European problem.[109]

His conviction was not shared by the French leader, de Gaulle, who still thought in traditional terms of the restoration of the grandeur of France and of obtaining security against a postwar Germany by territorial acquisitions in the Rhineland.[110] There would, as Spinelli had predicted, be a battle between advocates of federation and advocates of restoration, and the latter would use the symbols of statehood and nationality to bolster their claim to postwar loyalties. Spinelli erred only in grossly overestimating the immediate prospects of the federalists.

These arguments would be fought out amidst a Europe whose economy and trade had been dislocated by war. It was also a Europe in which the initiator of this catastrophe, Germany, still invoked fear and hatred of the kind which led the American Morgenthau to respond to suggestions that the Ruhr should be kept working with these words:

> Just strip it. I don't care what happens to the population ... I would take every mine, every mill and factory, and wreck it ... Steel, coal, everything. Just close it down. I am for destroying it first and we will worry about the population second.[111]

The Second World War had witnessed the most brutal attempt to shape Europe during this century and its consequences would mark the character of Europe for over forty years after its end. Although most accounts treat the Nazi bid to construct a New Order as a manifestation of a superheated nationalism, in the eyes of many contemporaries the conduct of the war raised the prospect of a Europe integrated under German hegemony. The experience of the Nazi challenge forced many more to doubt the viability of the pre-war system of nation-states, and to turn to ideas of federation and union which still go beyond anything achieved today. Some of these ideas were discussed by governments and their advisers, though they were gradually eliminated from the agenda, largely at the instigation of the superpowers.

Nor was this the limit of the impact of the New Order. The mass murder of European Jews and the immense population movements, both during and after the war, transformed the ethnic structure of Europe, especially in the east. In this sense, a return to pre-war Europe after 1945 was an impossibility. Europe had been irrevocably changed. In 1945 Europe had also been weakened. American and Soviet armies stood in the centre of the continent. This time there would be no rapid withdrawal to feed the delusion that Europeans were the masters of their own fate.

NOTES

1. R. Lemkin, *Axis Rule in Occupied Europe* (Washington, 1944), p. 343. On the background to the Decree see V. Mastny, *The Czechs under Nazi Rule* (New York, 1971), pp. 47–50.
2. J. Noakes and G. Pridham (eds), *Nazism 1919–1945*, Vol. 3 (Exeter, 1988), doc. 645. For evidence of the confusion over the remainder of Poland, see also docs 646–8 and Arnold Toynbee and Veronica Toynbee (eds), *Hitler's Europe* (London, 1954), pp. 553–5.
3. Hans Umbreit, 'Auf dem Weg zur Kontinentalherrshaft', in B. R. Kroener *et al.*, *Das Deutsche Reich und der Zweite Weltkrieg*, 5/1 (Stuttgart, 1988), p. 29.
4. Hans-Dietrich Loock, 'Zur "Grossgermanischen Politik" des Dritten Reiches', *Vierteljahreshefte für Zeitgeschichte*, **8** (1960), p. 39.
5. Proclamation of 15 May 1940, in Lemkin, *Axis Rule in Occupied Europe*, p. 448.
6. W. Lipgens (ed.), *Documents on the History of European Integration* (hereafter *DHEI*), Vol. 1 (Berlin, 1984), pp. 72–3.
7. On this see Loock, 'Zur "Grossgermanischen Politik" des Dritten Reiches', pp. 41–2, 46.
8. *Ibid.*, p. 53.
9. Lipgens (ed.), *DHEI*, Vol. 1, doc. 10, p. 79.
10. *Ibid.*, doc. 9, p. 78.
11. *ADAP*, Serie E, Vol. 1, doc. 248. On Quisling's efforts in general see Paul M. Hayes, *Quisling* (Newton Abbot, 1971), pp. 278–96.
12. *ADAP*, Serie E, Vol. 3, doc. 182. The marginally milder version of the decision as communicated to Quisling is in doc. 293.
13. *ADAP*, Serie E, Vol. 5, doc. 51. For the further development of this idea, see *ibid.*, Vol. 6, doc. 139.
14. Werner Best, 'Grundfragen einer deutschen Grossraum-Verwaltung', in *Festschrift für Heinrich Himmler* (Darmstadt, 1941), p. 34.
15. *Ibid.*, pp. 54–5.
16. An early offer by Laval to enter the war, in the wake of the sinking of the French fleet at Mers el Kebir, met with the brusque reply: 'We do not need your help, which would not amount to much anyway.' Quoted in Paul Kluke, 'Nationalsozialistische Europaideologie', *Vierteljahreshefte für Zeitgeschichte*, **3** (1955), p. 253.
17. *Documents on German Foreign Policy* (hereafter *DGFP*), Series D, Vol. 12, doc. 491.
18. Quoted in C. Madajczyk, 'Die Besatzungssyteme der Achsenmächte', *Studia Historicae oeconomicae*, **14** (1980), p. 117.
19. Umbreit, 'Auf dem Weg zur Kontinentalherrschaft', p. 218.
20. Annexe II, J. Freymond, *Le IIIe Reich et la réorganisation économique de l'Europe 1940–1942* (Leiden, 1974).
21. Lipgens (ed.), *DHEI*, Vol. 1, p. 63.
22. *Ibid.*, p. 64.
23. *DGFP*, Series D, Vol. 10, docs 246 and 320.
24. *Ibid.*, doc. 246.

25. On Czech fears about price levels see Mastny, *The Czechs under Nazi Rule*, p. 71. For Danish comments that a customs union was pointless under wartime conditions, see *DGFP*, Series D, Vol. 10, doc. 382.
26. *Ibid.*, 320.
27. Freymond, *Le IIIe Reich et la réorganisation économique*, p. 142.
28. Lipgens (ed.), *DHEI*, Vol. 1, pp. 65–71.
29. See the Introduction to R. A. Blasius (ed.), *Dokumente zur Deutschlandpolitik*, I Reihe, Vol. 1, pp. xxvi–xxvii; Albrecht Tyrrell, *Grossbritanien und die Deutschlandplanung der Allierten 1941–1945* (Frankfurt am Main, 1987), pp. 34–5.
30. G. W. Guillebaud, 'Hitler's new economic order for Europe', *Economic Journal*, **50** (1940), p. 458.
31. See the references in Anthony McElligott, 'Reforging Mitteleuropa. The economic impact of integration under German hegemony', in Stirk (ed.), *Mitteleuropa*, p. 130.
32. Paul Einzig, 'Hitler's "New Order" in theory and practice', *Economic Journal*, **51** (April 1941), pp. 1–18.
33. Milward, *The Fascist Economy in Norway*, p. 146.
34. McElligott, 'Reforging Mitteleuropa', p. 141.
35. B. Benning, 'Europäische Wähungsfragen', *Die Deutsche Volkswirtschaft*, **9** (1942), p. 304.
36. C. Buchheim, 'Die besetzten Länder im Dienste der Deutschen Kriegswirtschaft während des Zweiten Weltkrieges', *Vierteljahreshefte für Zeitgeschichte*, **34** (1986), p. 133.
37. Lipgens (ed.), *DHEI*, Vol. 1, p. 301.
38. *Ibid.*, p. 385. Others speculated upon a united Europe under German leadership, albeit a Germany that had dispensed with Hitler; *ibid.*, pp. 398–9.
39. *Ibid.*, pp. 385–6.
40. In Weigall and Stirk (eds), *Origins and Development of the European Community*, p. 31. On the background to Spinelli's federalism see Pinder, 'Federalism in Britain and Italy', in Stirk (ed.), *European Unity in Context*, pp. 201–23.
41. This is the impression created by the selection of documents in Lipgens (ed.), *DHEI*, Vol. 1. See also the editorial comment on pp. 210–11, 223, 248, 559. See also J. C. H. Blom and W. ten Have, 'Making the New Netherlands: ideas about renewal in Dutch politics and society during the Second World War', in Smith and Stirk (eds), *Making the New Europe*, pp. 106–7.
42. *Dokumente zur Deutschlandpolitik*, I Reihe, Vol. 1, pp. 5–9 and 11.
43. On Federal Union see R. Mayne *et al.*, *Federal Union: The Pioneers* (London, 1990); R. A. Wilford, 'The Federal Union campaign', *European Studies Quarterly*, **10** (1980), pp. 101–14.
44. The latter view was that of the Post-War Reconstruction Group on 12 July 1940. See *Dokumente zur Deutshclandpolitik*, I Reihe, Vol. 1, pp. 171–2. It was, in its vagueness, a typically British response.
45. For two contrasting views of the debate and the offer, see A. Bosco, 'Federal Union, Chatham House, the Foreign Office and Anglo-French Union in spring 1940', in A. Bosco (ed.), *The Federal Idea*, Vol. 1 (London, 1991), pp. 291–325; A. Schlaim, 'Prelude to downfall: the British offer of union to France, June 1940', *Journal of Contemporary History*, **9** (1974), pp. 27–63.
46. Henry Butterfield Ryan, *The Vision of Anglo-America* (Cambridge, 1987), p. 18.

47. See the Introduction to *Dokumente zur Deutschlandpolitik,* I Reihe, Vol. 1, by R. Blasius, pp. xxvii–xxxi.
48. *Dokumente zur Deutschlandpolitik,* I Reihe, Vol. 1, p. 246.
49. *Ibid.*
50. For British interest, see Detlef Brandes, 'Konföderationspläne im 2. Weltkreig', *Sudosteuropa Mitteilungen,* **23/4** (1983), p. 3. For Sikorski's initiative, see Piotr S. Wandycz, 'Recent traditions of the quest for unity', in J. Lukaszewski (ed.), *The Peoples' Democracies after Prague* (Bruges, 1970), pp. 42–3; and S. M. Terry, *Poland's Place in Europe* (Princeton, 1983). The following survey is based on these works.
51. Wandycz, 'Recent traditions of the quest for unity', pp. 43–4, 47.
52. *Dokumente zur Deutschlandpolitik,* I Reihe, Vol. 1, p. 229.
53. *Ibid.*
54. R. E. Herzstein, *The War That Hitler Won* (London, 1980), p. 370.
55. In Weigall and Stirk (eds), *Origins and Development of the European Community,* p. 27. On Pétain's reaction see R. O. Paxton, *Vichy France* (New York, 1972), pp. 127–8. For an assessment of the theme, see M. L. Smith, 'The anti-Bolshevik crusade and Europe', in Smith and Stirk (eds), *Making the New Europe,* pp. 46–65.
56. With typical equivocation, the decree went on to specify who was authorized to sanction such events if they did prove to be necessary. Lipgens (ed.), *DHEI,* Vol. 1, pp. 108–9. See also Longerich, *Propagandisten im Krieg,* pp. 97–100.
57. For the documents, see Lipgens (ed.), *DHEI,* Vol. 1, pp. 122–62. See also Robert Edwin Herzstein, *When Nazi Dreams Come True* (London, 1982), pp. 232–47.
58. *Brüsseler Zeitung* (21 April 1943). On these themes see Herzstein, *The War That Hitler Won*; Peter Stirk, 'Anti-Americanism in National Socialist propaganda during the Second World War', in Smith and Stirk (eds), *Making the New Europe,* pp. 66–86.
59. Richard Breitman, *The Architect of Genocide* (London, 1991), p. 153.
60. See the documents in Noakes and Pridham (eds), *Nazism,* Vol. 3, especially nos 681 and 683.
61. See J. T. Gross, *Polish Society under German Occupation* (Princeton, 1979), p. 49; Mastny, *The Czechs under Nazi Rule,* p. 128.
62. In Weigall and Stirk (eds), *Origins and Development of the European Community,* p. 29. On the General Plan East see Ralph Giordano, *Wenn Hitler den Kreig gewonnen hätte* (Hamburg, 1989), pp. 153–200; Götz Aly and Susanne Heim, *Vordenker der Vernichtung* (Frankfurt am Main, 1993), pp. 394–440.
63. The following relies primarily upon the works of A. S. Milward, *The French Economy*; *War, Economy and Society 1939–1945* (London, 1977); 'French labour and the German economy, 1942–1945', *Economic History Review,* **23** (1970), pp. 326–31; 'German economic policy towards France, 1942–1944', in K. Bourne and D. C. Watt (eds), *Studies in International History* (London, 1967), pp. 423–443.
64. Milward, *The French Economy,* p. 148.
65. *ADAP,* Serie E, Vol. 6, doc. 338. See also the works of Milward listed in note 63 above.
66. Thus the Italians T. Galimberti and A. Repaci in April 1943, Lipgens (ed.), *DHEI,* Vol. 1, p. 498. See also the Frenchman F. Gerard in November 1943, *ibid.,* pp. 323–4.
67. For example, H.-D. Salinger of the Netherlands in 1944, *ibid.,* p. 599.

68. Thus M. A. Rollier, January 1944, *ibid.*, p. 530.
69. *Ibid.*, pp. 305, 573–4, 577.
70. *Ibid.*, p. 563.
71. *Ibid.*, p. 667.
72. *Ibid.*, p. 586.
73. *Ibid.*, p. 647.
74. *Ibid.*, p. 448.
75. *Ibid.*, pp. 594–5.
76. G. Ross (ed.), *The Foreign Office and the Kremlin. British Documents on Anglo-Soviet Relations 1941–45* (Cambridge, 1984), p. 81. On the effect of the note see also Tyrrell, *Grossbritanien und die Deutschlandplanung der Allierten*, pp. 58–9 and 67.
77. *Ibid.*, p. 82. There is some disagreement about Stalin's attitude on the latter point. See Wandycz, 'Recent traditions of the quest for unity', p. 55.
78. Ross (ed.), *The Foreign Office and the Kremlin*, pp. 17–24 and 82–105; Tyrrell, *Grossbritanien und die Deutschlandplanung der Allierten*, pp. 68–73.
79. The Greeks actually agreed to something more substantial than they wanted as a result of Foreign Office pressure; Brandes, 'Konföderationspläne im 2. Weltkreig', pp. 6–7. On the differences between Poland and the Czechs see Wandycz, 'Recent traditions of the quest for unity', p. 54.
80. *Ibid.*, pp. 54–8; Brandes, 'Konföderationspläne im 2. Weltkrieg', pp. 5–9.
81. Quoted by J. Eisen, *Anglo-Dutch Relations and European Unity 1940–1948* (Hull, 1980), p. 9. See also O. Riste, 'Norway's "Atlantic Policy" ', in A. de Staerke (ed.), *NATO's Anxious Birth* (London, 1985), pp. 19–29.
82. Eisen, *Anglo-Dutch Relations*, pp. 9–10. It is interesting to note that the Dutch insisted on keeping these efforts separate from the schemes of the east Europeans; *ibid.*
83. *Dokumente zur Deutschlandpolitik*, I Reihe, Vol. 3, pp. 561–6 and 883–90. On the failure of an earlier scheme for Nordic defence co-operation see A. Upton, 'The crisis of Scandinavia and the collapse of interwar ideals, 1938–1940', in Stirk (ed.), *European Unity in Context*, pp. 170–87.
84. Warren S. Kimball, *The Juggler. Franklin Roosevelt as Wartime Statesman* (Princeton, 1991), pp. 43– 61 and 187–9.
85. *Ibid.*, p. 85.
86. *Dokumente zur Deutschlandpolitik*, I Reihe, Vol. 3, p. 669.
87. In Weigall and Stirk (eds), *Origins and Development of the European Community*, p. 33.
88. Robert E. Sherwood, *The White House Papers of Harry L. Hopkins* (London, 1949), p. 715.
89. For the reference to 'security commissions', see Kimball, *The Juggler*, p. 96.
90. *Dokumente zur Deutschlandpolitik*, I Reihe, Vol. 4, p. 446. For the background, see Tyrrell, *Grossbritanien und die Deutschlandplanung der Allierten*, pp. 109–20.
91. *Dokumente zur Deutschlandpolitik*, I Reihe, Vol. 4, p. 450.
92. *Ibid.*, p. 464.
93. Cordell Hull claimed the credit for this. See his *Memoirs*, Vol. 2 (London, 1948), p. 1646.
94. William H. McNeill, *America, Britain and Russia. Their Cooperation and Conflict 1941–1946* (London, 1953), pp. 356–7; Ross (ed.), *The Foreign Office and the Kremlin*, p. 140.
95. *Dokumente zur Deutschlandpolitik*, I Reihe, Vol. 4, p. 740 (23 December 1943).

96. Memorandum of G. M. Gathorne-Hardy, 6 July 1942, *ibid.*, Vol. 3, pp. 561–2.
97. For the British view, see Tyrrell, *Grossbritanien und die Deutschlandplanung der Allierten*, pp. 140–53; for examples of the American view, see *Dokumente zur Deutschlandpolitik*, I Reihe, Vol. 4, pp. 38–43 (12 January 1943) and 140–5 (29 January 1943).
98. *Ibid.*, p. 223. The antipathy towards Prussia was shared by the British in general.
99. On 5 October 1943; *Dokumente zur Deutschlandpolitik*, I Reihe, Vol. 4, p. 584.
100. See F. King, 'Allied negotiations and the dismemberment of Germany', *Journal of Contemporary History*, **16** (1981), pp. 586–7.
101. Quoted by Herbert Feiss, *Churchill Roosevelt Stalin* (Princeton, 1967), p. 370.
102. *Foreign Relations of the United States* (hereafter *FRUS*), *The Conferences at Malta and Yalta*, p. 978.
103. See *ibid.*, pp. 624–8.
104. John Baylis, 'British wartime thinking about a post-war European security group', *Review of International Studies*, **9** (1983), p. 269. For this whole debate, see *ibid.*, pp. 265–81; Tyrrell, *Grossbritanien und die Deutschlandplanung der Allierten*, pp. 445–58; documents 27–8 in Ross (ed.), *The Foreign Office and the Kremlin.*
105. *Ibid.*, p. 161.
106. Baylis, 'British wartime thinking about a post-war European security group', p. 278.
107. *The White House Papers*, p. 744.
108. Wandycz, 'Recent traditions of the quest for unity', pp. 75–6. For the official reasons given by Britain, see *FRUS, The Conferences at Malta and Yalta*, pp. 876–7, 881–2, 890–1, 939, 981.
109. Lipgens (ed.), *DHEI*, Vol. 2, p. 304.
110. W. Lipgens, 'Bedingungen und Etappen der Aussenpolitik de Gaulles 1944–1946', *Vierteljahreshefte für Zeitgeschichte*, **21** (1973), pp. 65–6, 68–9.
111. Quoted in Gregory A. Fossedal, *Our Finest Hour. Will Clayton, the Marshall Plan and the Triumph of Democracy* (Stanford, 1993), p. 164.

4

The Reconstruction of Europe under Superpower Hegemony: 1945–49

INTRODUCTION

In the immediate post-war world the fragile superpower co-operation, not European union, dominated the agenda. The few statesmen and officials who showed any interest in European union were usually unable to gain even the consent of their own governments, let alone other states. In the west the only two powers who could have taken a lead, Britain and France, were weakened by the war and divided over policy towards occupied Germany. It was the stagnation of economic reconstruction which began to change this picture, and to change the policy of the United States in 1947. Fearful that economic hardship would lead to the spread of communism in western Europe, the United States offered aid, soon known as the Marshall Plan, on condition that the Europeans co-operated for their own salvation. Co-operation soon came to mean economic, and political, integration, by means of which Europe, or at least western Europe, would come to resemble the United States rather than the old Europe of pre-1939. The change of policy was decisive. From being an indifferent or hostile observer of plans for European integration, the United States became a vigorous advocate. Ironically, the Europeans proved reluctant, especially Britain.

Some of the eastern European states, notably Poland and Czechoslovakia, had wanted to participate in the Marshall Plan but were blocked by Stalin. East European co-operation, in the shape of a Bulgarian–Yugoslav federation, was vetoed in 1948, but after considerable equivocation from Moscow. This coincided with the consolidation of the eastern bloc, and revealed the underlying difference between the attitude of the two superpowers to their respective spheres of influence in Europe. The United States could contemplate, with relative equanimity, a united western Europe strong enough to say no to both the Soviet Union and the United States. True, American ministers and officials were tempted to force the pace when the Europeans seemed to retreat into their nationalist shells, and sometimes succumbed to the temptation. But western Europe as a Third Force was, in principle, seen as desirable. Stalin did not envisage a similar status for eastern Europe. For many Europeans the idea of a Third Force meant something different. It meant a united Europe which could stave off the incipient division into east and west. That vision faded in 1948. The consequences were most dramatic of all for occupied Germany. Here, the division of Europe meant the division of Germany as well.

The Marshall Plan had played an important role in the division of Europe, but had proven unable to bring about integration in the west. The Soviet response to the Marshall Plan, the Council for Mutual Economic Assistance, Comecon, fared even worse. It too symbolized the division of Europe, but made no contribution at all to integration, at least in its early years. In the east, fundamental disagreements about the desirability and course of integration were decisive. In the west, Germany remained a key problem.

Initially, the Federal Republic of Germany was a member of neither the Council of Europe nor the North Atlantic Treaty. Both of these had been created with some reluctance, and for quite different purposes. Yet they symbolized the tension between strictly European integration and Atlantic integration which was to dog the progress of western integration over the next two decades. At the end of the 1940s European integration was fragmentary and sometimes antagonistic. Equally important, the German problem was unresolved.

IMMEDIATE PROSPECTS

Presiding over the fate of Europe at the end of the war were the Allied powers. Of the big three, Britain was in the weakest position. As a British official put it in a memorandum headed 'Stocktaking After V.E. Day',

> Our own position . . . is very different from what it was at the end of the last war, when we and France shared and disputed, and eventually lost, control of Europe. This time the control is to a large degree in the hands of the Soviet Union and the United States, and neither of them is likely to consider British interests overmuch if they interfere with their own and unless we assert ourselves.[1]

The two overarching powers were committed, uneasily and with considerable mutual suspicion, to a policy of continuing the wartime collaboration through the newly established United Nations and four-power control of Germany. Despite the agreements reached at Yalta for the dismemberment of Germany, enthusiasm for that option was waning. On 8 May 1945, the day before the Soviet Union accepted the capitulation of the German armies, Stalin had declared that the Soviet Union 'does not intend either to dismember or to destroy Germany'.[2] For different reasons Stalin's allies had no interest in the division of Germany either. At the first postwar conference at Potsdam the Allies agreed only upon measures for the control of Germany during the occupation. According to these 'for the time being, no central German Government shall be established', though centralized administrative departments were to be permitted in order to facilitate their commitment to treat Germany as a 'single economic unit'.[3] In brief there was no consensus on Germany's long-term future and hence no consensus on Europe's future.

It was clear, however, that European union was not on the agenda. Of the postwar governments only those of the Netherlands and Italy made tentative proposals for some kind of European union in 1945. Both met with indifference.[4] Contrary to the expectations of the more radical federalists there was to be no popular revolt against the old world of nation-states. There would be no congress of European peoples to impose a federation. The reality was grasped quite early by Spinelli. Others clung to the idea of a mass movement with as much obduracy as futility. As late as October 1946 Umberto Campagnola was able to persuade the majority of the Italian Mouvemente Federaliste Europeo to support the idea of a popular movement to force governments to federate.[5] The first year of peace was one of immense disappointment for Europe's federalists. For all the horrors of the war the basic loyalties of Europe's peoples remained tied to the nation-state.

Only among the smaller states was there any sign of interest in federation. The Netherlands and Belgium managed to agree, in April 1946, to reaffirm their commitment to establish a customs union, though it would take them until 1948 to bring this into being and their union was, as they knew, no substitute for broader arrangements involving the larger states which constituted their vital markets. In the east there were occasional signs that the Yugoslavs and Bulgarians were still interested in the idea of union, when Dimitrov welcomed the abolition of monarchy in September 1946 as 'a step toward Slavic federation'.[6] A Yugoslav–Albanian agreement of December 1946 also referred to 'a wide co-ordination of economic plans, unions of customs' areas, and standardization of currency'.[7] Both of these initiatives were, however, dependent upon the toleration of the Soviet Union and neither was being pushed very hard, in the interests of avoiding any aggravation of the precarious co-operation between the superpowers.

THE FIRST STEPS TOWARDS A WESTERN BLOC

By the end of 1946 that co-operation was extremely fragile. A change in the general climate in Washington was heralded by George Kennan's famous 'Long Telegram' of 22 February 1946 which attacked the underlying assumptions of Roosevelt's policy of co-operation with the Soviet Union. It would take some time before Kennan's strictures became the prevailing orthodoxy in Washington. Such sentiments were more welcome to the British Foreign Secretary Ernest Bevin. Bevin had been attracted from the start by the idea of a western bloc incorporating a revived western Germany, but was hindered both by the reluctance of the United States and opposition from his colleagues. His task was complicated by the conflict of interest between France, which would form the starting-point of any prospective western bloc, and Britain, over the fate of Germany. France's favoured policy remained the separation of the Ruhr and the Rhineland.[8] Bevin himself had some sympathy for the separation of the Ruhr, which, he claimed, might constitute the 'first foundation ... of something like the Economic United States of Europe'.[9] Faced with the same arguments against separation which had been used during the wartime planning, Bevin backed down but won Cabinet approval for international control of a socialized Ruhr on 17 April 1946. The implications were quite clear. According to the Cabinet the scheme

> faced the fact that Europe was now being divided into two spheres of influence, and it would give us an opportunity to prove that we could build up in Western Germany, under a democratic system, an efficient industrial organization which challenged comparison with that which was being created under a different system in Eastern Germany.[10]

The rejection of the separation of the Ruhr as an option inevitably made co-operation with France more difficult. An Anglo-French treaty, however, seemed more urgent than ever to Britain, albeit for somewhat different reasons than in 1945. It was no longer just a first step towards a western bloc but also a case of strengthening pro-western elements in France herself. Ironically it was the resignation of General de Gaulle on 20 January 1946 which was the cause of the alarm. Seeing de Gaulle as the only force holding together the coalition which governed France, a near hysterical Foreign Office joined Bevin in speculating upon the probability of civil war and a communist take-over in France.[11] Such motives were still at work a year later when the long-awaited Anglo-French Treaty was eventually signed at Dunkirk on 4 March 1947. The Dunkirk Treaty was a straightforward alliance, by which the two states promised to support each other in the event of any renewal of German aggression. According to Article 2, if either party was attacked the other would 'at once give the High Contracting Party so involved in hostilities all the military and other support and assistance in his power'.[12] But the Dunkirk Treaty solved none of the underlying problems. It had proved possible to sign it only because the French had dropped their insistence upon tying the treaty to agreement on policy towards Germany. French policy towards Germany remained unchanged. Nor was the treaty seen in France as a step towards a western bloc.[13] Nor did it include anything of Bevin's grander vision of a western European economic bloc and customs union. The latter was buried by opposition from Bevin's own colleagues.

By the time the Dunkirk treaty was signed the failure to reach agreement on Germany was increasingly apparent. So too were the probable consequences. Within the American State Department some officials sought to escape from the drift to division. One of these, Charles P. Kindelberger, wrote with considerable prescience on 5 April 1946, 'It seems clear to us . . . that we must either re-assert our faith in a European solution, other than relatively exclusive blocs; or we must, increasingly, find ourselves, *de facto*, in support of the British bloc conception'.[14] By a 'European solution' Kindelberger and his colleagues meant a European organization, within the framework of the United Nations, which would include a set of committees or commissions co-ordinating European policy in specific sectors like fuel and power, trade, transport, finance and planning.[15]Despite some interest shown by the Secretary of State, Byrnes, he did not refer to this option in the Council of Foreign Ministers meeting which began in April 1946. Indeed, when the Conference resumed in July after a break he took a step which would later facilitate the division of Germany. He offered to join the United States' zone with any other zone or zones in the interests of moving towards treating Germany as a single economic unit.[16] By the end of the year Britain and the United States had agreed to merge their zones. They had taken the first step towards the formation of a western German state.

TOWARDS THE MARSHALL PLAN

At the end of 1946 European industrial production had managed to crawl back to 83 per cent of its 1938 level, but fell back to 78 per cent in the first quarter of 1947. Food production had still not recovered its prewar level. The crucial commodity of coal also lagged behind prewar figures with the shortfalls arising largely from Britain and even more so from Germany, which produced only 66 million tons in 1946 compared with a prewar output of 159 million tons. European trade was failing to keep pace with this level of recovery, with exports reaching 59 per cent of their 1938 level in the third quarter of 1946.[17] The significance of these and similar figures is disputed, but what is clear is that a faltering economic recovery was combined with a chronic dollar gap. Europe's balance of trade with the

United States was bad enough in 1946, with a deficit of $2356 million, but in 1947 this rocketed to $4742 million.[18]

In the wake of the severe winter at the beginning of 1947, which served to dramatize Europe's plight, American officials became alarmed, both by the economic difficulties and their perceived political consequences. The answer, which was becoming common currency, was some form of European integration backed by American aid. That same answer doubled as a solution to the German problem. It was a solution which was developed most vigorously by junior officials like Paul Porter of the American Economic Mission in London, who, in a memorandum of 14 January, argued for the internationalization of the Ruhr as one of the first steps to economic unification, free trade and greater prosperity. The alternative, he warned, was a relapse into autarchy, political instability and the spread of communism. Outside the administration the Republican John Foster Dulles pointed to America as a model for Europe. Economic unity, he said, would provide a market 'big enough to justify the modern methods of cheap production for mass consumption'.[19] What changed these ideas from being the subject matter of public commentary into the subject matter of policy deliberation was the instruction, on 4 March 1947, from Acting Secretary of State Dean Acheson, for a study of global requirements for aid. Later, in April, the newly formed Policy Planning Staff was instructed to devote its attention to the same issue. Its memorandum of 23 May formed the basis of discussion with Secretary of State George C. Marshall on 28 May. Just before that, Under-Secretary of State for Economic Affairs Will Clayton added to the general sense of foreboding by writing, 'Europe is steadily deteriorating. The political position reflects the economic. One political crisis after another merely denotes the existence of grave economic distress. Millions of people in the cities are slowly starving.'[20] A week later, on 5 June, Marshall made a speech at Harvard which was later seen as the launch of the Marshall Plan. In fact the speech was far less precise than the various reports and memoranda which preceded it. The speech itself was notable only for three things. There was a clear expression of American willingness to provide further aid. There was an insistence that such aid would be 'directed not against any country or doctrine but against hunger, poverty, desperation and chaos'. Finally, there was an insistence that the Europeans take the initiative in drawing up a 'joint' programme.[21]

Even American officials were to complain that there was no plan as such on 5 June, or indeed till much later. That was true, and reflected in part continuing debate about the 'plan' within the American administration. It also reflected the decision that any plan would have to be devised by the Europeans and not just imposed by the United States. That decision was one of several key choices which the United States had to make. Two other vital choices concerned whether or not to include the Soviet Union and eastern Europe, and Germany's role in the plan.

THE MARSHALL PLAN AND EASTERN EUROPE

Despite the openness of Marshall's offer the clear expectation was that the Soviet Union would not participate. Nor was such participation desired. Eastern European participation was more welcome, but only at the price of drawing closer to the western world and away from the Soviet Union. The participation of eastern European states had advantages but it was not essential. The point was put clearly by Will Clayton on 29 May:

> Mr Clayton expressed the strong view that, while Western Europe is essential to Eastern Europe, the reverse is not true. Coal and grains from Eastern Europe are important to Western Europe, but these products will be exported westward in any event because the necessity of obtaining vital foreign exchange for necessary products from the west creates a suction which the U.S.S.R. is incapable of counteracting ... It was concluded, therefore, that a European economic federation is feasible even without the participation of Eastern European countries. There was general agreement, however, that the plan should be drawn with such conditions that Eastern Europe could participate, provided that the countries would abandon near-exclusive Soviet orientation of their economies.[22]

Clayton was substantially right on all counts.

For Ernest Bevin, the prospect of Soviet participation was even more unwelcome than for the Americans. Bevin manoeuvred from the outset to secure the exclusion of Russia. Bidault also favoured the exclusion of the Soviet Union but was anxious to avoid being seen to divide Europe over Marshall's offer, for fear of the domestic criticism this would arouse.[23] After preliminary consultations between themselves, the two western Foreign Ministers met with Molotov in Paris on 27 June. Though showing concern about the threat to national sovereignty, Molotov appeared to be negotiating in good faith. But on 2 July, after receiving instructions from Moscow, Molotov declared that the Soviet Union would not participate.

By then both the Poles and Czechoslovaks had expressed their keen interest in the plan.[24] The Polish Ambassador to Washington even cited the 'fact that Poland had decreased the proportion of her exports going to the Soviet Union as evidence of Poland's desire to integrate her economy with that of Western Europe'.[25] The Soviet decision, though it evidently caused concern to the Poles, did not lead to an automatic rejection of participation in the conference, set for 12 July, which was to discuss the European response to Marshall's offer. The Czech government in particular was keen to proceed, and at first there did not seem to be a Soviet veto. On 8 July, however, Moscow opposed any participation. The Czechoslovak government, which had already announced its involvement, argued for participation at a meeting with Stalin on 9 July, pointing to Czechoslovak dependence on trade with the west. Stalin was unmovable. With a mixture of crude threats and offers to take Czechoslovak goods he bullied the Czechoslovak representatives into submission.[26] Neither Poland nor Czechoslovakia participated in the conference. That did not mean that further co-operation was excluded. Poland continued to export large quantities of coal to western Europe, supplying 25 per cent of western coal consumption in 1949, and lobbied hard for loans from the World Bank. The Poles even conceded that the bank should have a 'certain voice' in allocating coal exports as a condition of the loan, which rather contradicted the official objection to participation in the Marshall Plan, namely that it would infringe national sovereignty. Polish efforts to limit the impact of the Cold War were ultimately fruitless.[27]

GERMANY AND THE MARSHALL PLAN

The other key decision concerned Germany's role. Here the Americans were divided among themselves. General Clay and the War Department gave priority to German recovery, arguing that Germany would drag the rest of Europe behind it on the road to recovery. They were encouraged in this by the Hoover Report of March 1947 which was forthright enough to elicit this response from one White House official: 'there must be other approaches to these problems than the revival of a German colossus along the lines suggested by Mr. Hoover'.[28] The State Department fought back, arguing for a balanced approach to European recovery. Both wanted the same thing in the end: European recovery. But the difference of emphasis was significant. The army wanted to give priority to 'making the German economy self-sustaining and thus reduce or eliminate the present costs of occupation'.[29] The State Department, more sensitive to French fears of a revived Germany, wanted to tie German recovery in with European integration.[30] The problem became acute amidst the negotiations with the Europeans on the Marshall Plan. The occasion for the dispute was not the Plan itself but an Anglo-American decision to raise the level of German steel capacity and hence, so the French feared, divert German coal from French steel furnaces to German furnaces. Bidault claimed that lifting restrictions on Germany would undermine his government, and stall the whole programme of European recovery. But all that Bidault could achieve was a face-saving formula, whereby the French were officially consulted before the decision was made public. On 28 August

German steel capacity was raised to 11 million tons.[31] France had accepted the Anglo-American *fait accompli*, but only because she was unable to block it.

THE DEBATE OVER A CUSTOMS UNION

The dispute over Germany took place amidst the negotiations in Paris, which began on 12 July, to formulate the European response to Marshall. As the negotiations progressed the Americans became increasingly frustrated with the hesitancy and caution of the Europeans, and were increasingly inclined to revise their commitment to let the Europeans take the initiative. The Americans were, at this point, committed to a much more ambitious form of integration than the Europeans. They were also divided among themselves about which form of integration to press. They were divided roughly into what the American historian Michael Hogan has described as free traders and planners.[32] Will Clayton was an unequivocal free trader, as became clear even before the Paris Conference opened, when Clayton held talks with the British in June. Clayton stated that the 'United States would like some proposals regarding a closer integration of the European economy'.[33] Bevin countered that obligations under the International Trade Organisation, meaning the commitment not to discriminate against certain trading partners, were incompatible with European integration. Clayton referred to the Benelux customs union and 'said this certainly did not violate ITO rules'.[34] But another of Bevin's examples, a bilateral deal with France including a planned specialization of labour between the two, did. In other words a customs union was acceptable, preferential agreements were not. To be more precise, Britain's system of imperial preferences was also unacceptable.[35] Clayton wanted more than just a customs union, though. He also wanted rapid progress on currency convertibility and a currency union. This, in the long term, was what the planners wanted too. But their priorities were different and their willingness to rely on government intervention, rather than the working of the free market, was greater. For the planners the priority was increased production and supranational planning. The planners gained the upper hand when Under-Secretary of State Lovett wrote to Clayton on 26 August:

> While in many respects the long-run gains of European economic integration in terms of specialization of production and economic location – achieved ideally through both a customs and a currency union – would be the most beneficial consequences of a recovery program, these goals must be in perspective in relation to more urgent short-term needs.[36]

Lovett even stated that schemes reducing trade barriers might be acceptable even if they were preference systems.

The European response to the customs union issue was a mixed one. Although Bevin continued to harbour some sympathy for the idea, the economic ministries in Britain remained opposed. So far as it conceded the advantages of a customs union at all, the Board of Trade saw them arising from a customs union between Britain and 'primary producing countries' or 'countries whose industries were primitive compared with those of the United Kingdom'.[37] There was a complete failure to grasp the fact, long since evident, that economic growth would take place disproportionately between advanced industrial economies.[38] The most that Britain would agree to in the General Report of the Committee of European Economic Co-operation was a Study Group to examine the issue of a customs union. The French and the Italian governments went further, declaring their readiness to enter into negotiations on a customs union.[39] France, however, was, at the end of the day, only interested in a customs union which included Germany, a union which would enable the French to whittle down German tariffs while retaining their own quantitative controls on France's imports. The traditionally low tariff countries of the Netherlands and Belgium were equally desirous of incorporating Germany, a rapidly revived Germany, and also of dismantling the system of quantitative restrictions which the French wanted to keep.[40]

In the short run the Europeans were agreed on one thing: extracting as much aid as possible and minimizing the extent of co-ordination demanded by the United States. It was this which led to American insistence upon a revision of the draft report, scaling down the total figure from $29 billion over four years to a little over $19 billion. The United States was far from happy with even the modified report, but decided that it might suffice to persuade Congress and accepted that this was as far as the Europeans could be pushed, for the moment. The United States would, in fact, continue to push for the duration of the Marshall Plan.

The Report did suffice, and the Economic Co-operation Act was enacted on 3 April 1948. The Act did not include everything the Europeans wanted. It approved aid, of $5.3 billion, only for the first year. The Act was also the product of intense in-fighting within Washington and was very much a compromise measure designed to secure bipartisan support. Among the compromises were the creation of a separate agency, the European Co-operation Administration, to administer the aid programme and the appointment of a Special Representative to handle relations with the Europeans.[41] Both measures were intended to prevent State Department control of the programme and to emphasize the non-political nature of the aid. In the same spirit, Senator Vandenberg, who played a key role in securing bipartisan support, vetoed the appointment of the Under-Secretary of State as head of the Economic Co-operation Administration and secured the position for Paul G. Hoffman. Hoffman in turn insisted upon Averell Harriman, then Secretary of Commerce, as the first Special Representative. The character and background of both men were significant. Hoffman was president of the Studebaker Corporation and Harriman had a Wall Street background. Both had been prominent members of the Committee for Economic Development which advocated government intervention to secure high employment and economic growth. It also rejected the antipathy to labour and trade unions found in more traditional American business circles. The future, according to the Committee, lay in economic growth and prosperity which in turn would bring with it social harmony. Hoffman, Harriman and many of the men from the business and trade union worlds whom they brought with them, were to proffer this same vision to Europe.[42] European co-operation, which meant for these men European unification, preferably following the American model, also entailed a refashioning of Europe's socio-economic structure.

PROSPECTS OF INTEGRATION IN EASTERN EUROPE

By the time the European Co-operation Act was signed by President Truman the options for European unity were being narrowed in both the east and the west, though this by no means meant that the road forward was either clear cut or agreed. In the east there were signs of co-operation. An agreement between Czechoslovakia and Poland of 4 July 1947 provided for co-operation in a series of fields, which was intended to 'promote industrial development and progress in both countries and to avoid unnecessary investment'.[43] Hungary and Yugoslavia had also agreed to a joint investment and commodity exchange programme. On the other hand, the Soviet Union was imposing joint companies with east European partners. The companies enjoyed substantial privileges and were effectively under Soviet control.[44] The two trends pointed to a choice between integration under Soviet hegemony and a more autonomous east European integration which would haunt the region over the following decades. Neither had, as yet, progressed very far.

The most ambitious project was undoubtedly the continuation of Yugoslav and Bulgarian plans first elaborated towards the end of the Second World War. After lying dormant since the end of the war, the plan was revived when Tito and Dimitrov met at Bled in Yugoslavia in July 1947. Among the forms of co-operation they agreed to was preparation for a customs union.[45] The Bled agreement was followed by no less than seven bilateral regional treaties, including a Bulgarian–Romanian treaty of 16

January 1948 which again referred to a customs union.[46] Stalin was furious about the Bled agreement. His main complaint was that they had not consulted Moscow, but he also warned the two parties that they were giving the west an excuse to expand its activities in Greece and Turkey, and he instructed them to do nothing more until the peace treaty with Bulgaria came into effect in September. Both obeyed and duly consulted Moscow before signing a formal treaty in November. By then a second issue was coming to a head. Yugoslavia had been exerting increasing influence over Albania, with Soviet approval, but in December Stalin announced that there were 'new issues' and called the Yugoslavs to Moscow. On 17 January 1948 he warned them against undue haste and against appearing to impose unification on Albania.[47] Around the same time three other developments heightened the tension. The Romanian-Bulgarian Treaty was signed on 18 January. On 19 January Tito tried to push the Albanian leader into accepting the deployment of Yugoslav troops to ward off the threat from Greek royalists – a threat the Soviets did not believe existed. Furthermore, Dimitrov held a press conference in which he referred to a possible federation between not only the socialist Balkan countries but also Hungary, Czechoslovakia, Poland 'and perhaps Greece'.[48] After some hesitation Dimitrov's comments were roundly condemned by *Pravda*, on 28 January. Tito backed down over the deployment of Yugoslav troops, but Stalin was not placated so easily this time. Both the Yugoslavs and the Romanians were summoned to Moscow. At the key meeting on 10 February Stalin ruled out any participation of Romania as nonsense. He also reaffirmed his warnings of 17 January about the treatment of Albania. He did sanction Albanian membership of a prior federation of Bulgaria and Yugoslavia. The latter, moreover, was to be a federation of equals. This touched on a sore point in Yugoslav–Bulgarian relations, for the Yugoslav preference was for the incorporation of Bulgaria as one element on a par with the other members of the Yugoslav federal state.[49]

Stalin's motives are not easy to pin down. Dimitrov's more ambitious speculations must have induced a comparison with wartime plans for confederation which Stalin had vetoed. It is also clear that the Yugoslavs had acted on several occasions without consulting Moscow and thereby violated the underlying hierarchy of the new eastern Europe.[50] They were probably tainted by association with the Soviet leader A. Zhdanov, of whom Stalin was increasingly suspicious.[51] It is equally clear that regional conflicts of interest between the Bulgarians, Yugoslavs and Albanians had not been overcome, and would have intensified as progress was made towards any actual federation. Both borders and national identities were still far from secure and agreed.[52] The mutually suspicious parties failed to reconcile their differences. The Yugoslavs denounced Bulgaria as a 'Trojan horse' on 1 March. The following month Yugoslavia was condemned by Cominform (Communist Information Bureau) and excluded from the socialist camp. A little over one year later, in July 1949, Dimitrov was dead, probably at Stalin's instructions. An Eastern European federation led by communists disappeared from the agenda.

A THIRD WAY?

The consolidation of the eastern bloc under Soviet hegemony had an important influence in narrowing options in the west. Throughout 1947 there had been widespread, if uneven, interest in western Europe in the idea that Europe might pursue a 'third way' or become a 'third force'. The term was, like the very idea of European integration, elastic and varied in its meaning, if not downright opaque. It was used by a senior official of the State Department, Hickerson, in January 1948, in the context of discussions about a prospective European defence system. Hickerson 'had envisaged the creation of a third force which was not merely the extension of US influence but a real European organization strong enough to say "no" both to the Soviet Union and to the United States, if our actions should seem so to require'.[53] This idea remained an important strand in American thinking for some time. It also provides a useful comparative perspective on the problem faced by Dimitrov and Tito: Stalin did not want them to gain sufficient independence to be able to say no.

Hickerson emphasized one common theme in advocacy of Europe as a third force, but he was talking about a western defence organization and it was precisely a division into east and west which most European advocates of the third force idea wanted to avoid. They wanted, of course, to avoid the division of Europe into two opposed political camps, but they also wanted to avoid the division of Europe into two opposing social and economic systems. Once again the debate about the unity, or disunity, of Europe was a debate about its internal socio-economic structure. The point was made as late as 6 January 1948 by the French socialist Léon Blum:

> Between the United States, 'champions of individual liberty and the rights of man' but where the capitalist economy is fully maintained ... in all its inhumane severity, and the Soviet Union, which has destroyed capitalist private property but has also eliminated all individual, civic and social liberties, there is a place for nations which want both personal liberty and a collective economy, democracy and social justice ... It is neither an exaggeration nor a presumption to affirm that democratic socialism represents at present the predominant aspiration of old Europe, especially of

> Western Europe ... The international third force is therefore really a force. And in order to act as a force it must become conscious of itself, of its nature and of its immediate mission.[54]

Blum's hopes for the realization of this force were based, as were those of his British counterparts, upon the prospects of an Anglo-French axis. Encouraged by the electoral victory of the British Labour Party in July 1945, Blum had argued in August for the formation of a 'western family' of nations, built around an Anglo-French alliance, which would act as a bridge between the two superpowers.[55] In Britain left-wing members of the Labour Party, convinced that socialism would sweep the continent, drew similar conclusions; the alternative, they feared, was war.[56] In Britain the progress of the third force idea was bound up with criticism of Ernest Bevin's foreign policy. His slavish obedience to American policy was, his critics claimed, needlessly antagonizing the Soviet Union. Criticism of Bevin became almost a ritual at Labour Party conferences. Eventually the critics grouped together under the slogan 'Keep Left'. Their high-point came with the Dunkirk Treaty, which they saw as the basis of a European security pact 'strong enough to hold the balance of world power'.[57] The accumulating pressure of Soviet distrust of European union made their position an increasingly difficult one, as did Marshall's offer of 5 June. The latter, or rather Molotov's withdrawal from the Paris negotiations, imposed a strain upon the French socialists too, though Blum clung to the idea with increasing desperation. The greater strength of the idea in France arose from its greater domestic significance. In Britain the left-wing critics of Bevin were ill-organized and increasingly marginal. In France one element of the idea of a third force acquired added significance in the autumn of 1947. As the French communists adopted a harder line in the wake of the formation of Cominform in September, and with the Gaullist municipal electoral successes in October, the third force became identified with the defence of the Fourth Republic against communists and Gaullists.

The autumn of 1947 also saw a brief diplomatic initiative for a third force. Ironically the initiative came from Ernest Bevin, who periodically sought to increase his freedom of manoeuvre *vis-à-vis* the United States, while keeping in sight the need for American backing against the Soviet Union.[58] During 1947, with this goal in mind, Bevin suggested using Africa as the basis for the development of Anglo-French co-operation as a prelude to broader western European co-operation in the development of Africa.[59] The latter would provide raw materials and markets for Europe and would constitute an alternative to multilateral global trade. This option seemed more attractive as Britain, which had introduced limited convertibility of sterling in July as part of its obligations under the

Loan Agreement with the United States, faced a massive drain of gold and dollars. Convertibility was suspended on 20 August.[60] The following month Bevin discussed the option of a third force with the French Premier, Ramadier. But nothing came of Bevin's initiative. Bevin had not prepared the French for his initiative and, more importantly, was faced with opposition to his idea of 'Euro-Africa' from his own colleagues.[61] In reality Africa simply could not play the economic role envisaged for it.

Towards the end of 1947 the prospects of a third force were fading. Among the federalists the idea of a third force had proved even more attractive. But, as early as the August 1947 Montreux conference of the Union Européene Fédéralistes, H. Brugmans argued that a start had to be made in the west. The earlier hope that the third force would be a way of keeping all of Europe together was being reluctantly abandoned.[62] In Britain, the idea of a third force, already seriously weakened by the debate over the Marshall Plan, was effectively undermined by the Prague coup at the beginning of 1948.[63] It would survive longer in France and in the western zones of Germany.

The consequences of a failure of the third force idea were much greater in Germany than elsewhere. For Germans it was a question not just of the unity or independence of Europe, but the unity of Germany herself. In 1947 and the first half of 1948 unity still seemed to be an option. The Marshall Plan, though later seen as a decisive step in the division of Europe, was not widely perceived at the time as entailing the division of Germany.[64] Quite how the third force idea might help Germany recover, without being divided, was however rarely clarified. The most imaginative solution came from the socialist Carlo Schmid. At the end of 1947 Schmid pleaded for a Scandinavian union and a Franco-Benelux union, both of which would subsequently merge. As for Germany, he stated,

> It seems to me preferable for Germany to remain in its present interim state ... until some progress has been made towards creating the unions described above. The latter will then have provided Europe, apart from Germany, with a secure economic and political superiority such as to dispel much of the fear that at present acts as a bad counsellor ... It will then be easy for the rulers of European states to convince their peoples that a Germany enjoying equal rights need not necessarily be presumed to be an aggressor.[65]

Within months Schmid's strategy was buried by the first steps towards the creation of a purely west German state and towards a western military alliance. Of federations in western Europe there was still no sign. There was however still considerable fear of Germany. There was also considerable doubt about western Europe's economic recovery. At the end of 1947 the Marshall Plan was still in the process of being formulated and Europe's future as a whole remained uncertain.

THE LIMITS OF INTEGRATION THROUGH THE MARSHALL PLAN

The United States continued to hope that the successor to the Committee for European Economic Co-operation would provide the basis for strong European co-operation. The negotiations leading up to the Convention for European Economic Co-operation of 16 April 1948 proved, however, to be disappointing for those genuinely committed to integration. The problem was that the European governments were not committed.[66] From the beginning the United States Ambassador to France, Caffery, was suspicious of the British approach. He reported that the British

> argue that their proposal for placing [the] principal emphasis on [the] role of national representatives [will] insure governmental support. British also argue that given uncertainties as to form of act and wishes of administrator, there must be great flexibility, and that consequently statement of functions of organization should be limited to broad generalities.[67]

Caffery suspected, rightly, that the British aim was to ensure that a weak organization emerged. The British government was successful in its aim and was, ironically, aided by American miscalculation. Lovett assumed that the organization would develop in the desired direction if it had 'important functions to perform', an 'effective organizational structure' and the appropriate personnel.[68] In fact the United States relied upon the first and third of these conditions. Lovett considered the structure of the Organization for European Economic Co-operation (OEEC), which was established by the April Convention, adequate. Yet this merely provided that 'decisions shall be taken by mutual agreement of all the Members'. The only qualification was that 'The abstention of any Members declaring themselves not to be interested in the subject under discussion shall not invalidate decisions, which shall be binding for the other Members.'[69] There were also real problems with the functions ascribed to the OEEC given that the Administrator of the Economic Co-operation Administration (ECA) and its country missions were to play the major role in ascertaining the aid requirements of countries, with the OEEC playing a co-ordinating role.[70] As the limitations became increasingly apparent, Hoffman and Harriman embarked upon an ill-fated attempt to remedy the situation by persuading the Europeans to appoint 'a man of international political position as a type of director general'.[71] The man they had in mind was Spaak, but he was unacceptable to Britain, as indeed was the whole conception. Eventually, in January 1950, Dirk Stikker, more acceptable to Britain than the federalist Spaak, was appointed 'Political Conciliator', a post with no authority.[72]

The United States did exercise more leverage through the ECA itself, though again there were limitations. The ECA seemed to be in a strong position by virtue of its control of the counterpart funds which accrued from the sale of United States' aid within the various European countries. These sums, in local currencies, were intended to fund investment which would fuel recovery. In fact they were used for diverse purposes and a running battle developed between the ECA and the European governments over the use of counterpart funds. The counterpart funds became entangled in a broader conflict between the American vision of Europe's socio-economic order and the policies of the European governments. Concerned about living conditions in France, the ECA sought to force France into a much-needed programme of housing construction. Successive French governments evaded the pressure, citing impending governmental crises in order to wring the funds from the ECA. At the end of the day only 3 per cent of counterpart funds in France were spent on housing.[73] In Italy the government stubbornly refused to use counterpart funds to combat recession, and the ECA eventually gave way. Similarly, in Germany, Ludwig Erhard refused to raise taxes, despite the fact that the ECA withheld counterpart funds to try to force his hand, and resisted ECA demands for increased expenditure on housing.[74] In other words, the European states clung to their domestic programmes and priorities despite ECA pressure.

That did not mean that the ECA and the European governments were continually opposed. They often found that the ECA could be an ally in disputes with other United States' agencies or provide a useful scapegoat for unpopular policies at home.[75] So too could the very image of America herself. This became the focus of the Technical Assistance Programme whose origins lay in a meeting between Stafford Cripps and Hoffman in July 1947 when the two men agreed to establish an Anglo-American Council on Productivity. Although it was officially to promote exchanges and mutual learning by both parties, it was really a mechanism for disseminating American industrial practices in Britain. The Council funded exchange visits by groups of industrialists and trade unionists who subsequently prepared a whole series of reports upon selected industries. Later, similar organizations were established in other Marshall Plan countries. The reports set out from the assumption that American productivity was much higher than European levels and sought to disentangle the factors unique to the United States and those which could be transferred to Europe. Much was made of the supposed harmony of management-labour relations, of the American work ethic, but also of levels of investment, the amount of electrical power at the disposal of American workers, and the standardization of products intended for a high-wage, mass-consumption market. The praise of American practices naturally aroused criticism. In a booklet intended for American students the ECA warned, 'The argument you may most frequently hear is that the Marshall Plan is a means of imposing the American economic system on Europe.'[76] Communists denounced the entire programme in lurid tones and even the president of the British TUC Congress of 1948 lamented that

> If American practice is held up to us as a pattern to follow, and when the mechanical equipment of our factories is contrasted with those of America, we are not being conservative or obstructive in saying that the productive techniques which have been carried further in other countries, we invented.[77]

Behind the self-defence of the Americans and the offended pride of the British lay a significant dispute, but not only between Europeans on the one hand and Americans on the other. True, the ECA did uphold America as a model, not only in terms of 'know-how' and management–labour relations, but as an integrated economy with standardized products and mass consumption, all of which was supposedly conducive to social and political stability. For some Americans this was the essence of Americanism. As the trade union leader James Carey put it, 'The idea of the simultaneous increase of production and mass consumption is the most typical American product that we can export.'[78] This image was often attractive to European socialists, who invoked it in their conflicts with employers even when they knew that it was being presented through rose-tinted spectacles. America, the image as much as the reality, was being used as a tool in domestic conflicts about modernization versus protectionism, investment levels, the role of labour and trade unions as well as the distribution of national income across social classes.[79] The impact of these efforts has proved impossible to assess with any precision. The Europeans did increasingly accept the central message that growth was the solution and also that productivity and mass consumption were the road to growth, though that idea was not as distinctly American as Carey implied. So, too, European socialist parties increasingly de-emphasized the traditional rhetoric of class conflict in favour of strategies of corporatism and prosperity. But these were long-term trends with indigenous European roots. During the Marshall Plan years European socialists, and for that matter European businessmen, maintained their own agenda, prominent among which were nationalization in Britain and the extension of workers' rights through co-determination in Germany. Where they failed to implement traditional strategies, as the German socialists failed to implement widespread nationalization, this was less because of American pressure than because of a failure of commitment or because they could not surmount domestic opposition.[80] Where European elites found that the American model was simply inappropriate, they ignored it. Thus, for the Italian business community the way forward lay in the utilization of cheap labour to increase exports, not capital investment to raise productivity and sales to the undeveloped domestic market.[81]

In the summer of 1948, when the productivity drive was being discussed by Cripps and Hoffman, the Americans were struggling to make progress on the revival of intra-European trade. A major obstacle, which threatened to choke the recovery, was the payments crises which arose from the imbalances in intra-European trade. An early and partial payments agreement signed in November 1947 managed to cope with a mere 2 per cent of payments debts.[82] A little more success was achieved when the United States agreed to back a revived scheme in October 1948. This time intra-European trade debts would, in effect, be financed by transfers of Marshall Plan aid. Although the programme was extended in 1949, it was a cumbersome system which failed to cope with the unanticipated shifts in European trade in 1949.[83]

ECONOMIC INTEGRATION IN THE EAST AND THE FOUNDATION OF COMECON

Economic integration in eastern Europe was not making much more progress. A Soviet press communiqué of January 1949 did announce the creation of the Council for Mutual Economic Assistance (Comecon). It referred to western boycotts of trade with the east and the refusal of eastern Europe to submit to the 'dictatorship of the Marshall Plan, which would have violated the sovereignty and the interests of their national economies'.[84] It said little about the purposes of Comecon and even less about its structure, specifying that it would take decisions only 'with the agreement of the interested countries' and that there would be a rotating chairmanship.[85] The paucity of this document and the fact that Comecon did not even publish a Charter until 1960 have naturally aroused some doubt as to the purpose of the launch of the organization. It seems probable, however, that the announcement embodied the remnants of a much more substantial plan aimed at genuine regional integration. According to one document, the members of the eastern bloc had intended to establish a Secretariat General with control of funds of 100 million roubles. Furthermore, the document stated that 'Beginning with this year the economic plans of all member countries will be drawn up in conformity with the advice of the Council.'[86] To facilitate this the Council was given extensive rights to obtain information on economic performance. Quite why this more ambitious agenda was abandoned is unclear. Stalin's suspicion of multilateral organizations and preference for bilateral, *ad hoc* and party-controlled agreements, along with the economic nationalism, of which there was to be evidence later, may well have played a part.

THE GERMAN PROBLEM

As European trade and production slowly revived, the pressure to resolve the German problem grew. The decisive steps were taken in the spring and summer of 1948 as the western powers moved towards fusion of the three western zones and then the creation of a west German government. This still caused alarm in France, but there was little the French could do to stop the process. Even the threat of restricting Marshall Plan aid, upon which the French zone was dependent, was mobilized to bring France into line. The result of the London Conference which met between February and June was the Six Power Agreement of 1 June 1948.

This Agreement placed the west Germans in a considerable dilemma. They were anxious to gain as much control over their destiny as possible, but reluctant to go ahead with the formal constitution of a state which would be but part of Germany. At a meeting in Koblenz on 8–10 July Carlo Schmid was able to hold his colleagues to the idea of a provisional arrangement. As Clay later recalled, this amounted to refusing to accept responsibility for a separate government. Later in the month, however, under pressure from Clay and the British Military Governor Robertson, as well as from Ernst Reuter, Mayor of Berlin, the Germans gave way, with some formal reservations.[87] Schmid's scenario whereby European unification should precede the establishment of a German state was being reversed.

It was typical of the uncertainties of these years that shortly after the Germans were pushed into agreeing to a western state the option of German unity was revived in the State Department by George Kennan as an explicit alternative to the 'London Programme'. Kennan argued that current policies would cement the division of Europe. He even claimed, mistakenly, that the economic viability of the western zones was dependent upon a revival of east–west trade.[88] Even while the German Parliamentary Council was drafting the new constitution Kennan's Policy Planning Staff produced 'Program A', fleshing out his alternative which involved withdrawal of both western and Soviet forces from Germany. Although these ideas met with interest, as well as some immediate hostility, they, like the earlier proposals of 1946, were not submitted to the Council of Foreign Ministers for which they were intended.[89]

As part of the price for securing French assent to the Six Power Agreement the United States and Britain had agreed to the creation of an International Authority for the Ruhr. The London Conference's paper on the Ruhr failed, however, to include the provision for ownership and control of Ruhr coal and steel which had been the French government's ambition. Spurred on by the French National Assembly, the government returned to the theme of ownership later in 1948; to no avail. By the time the Authority came into existence in the following year the French had already lost the battle.[90]

THE COUNCIL OF EUROPE

More progress was made in two directions in 1948, culminating, in April and May 1949 respectively, in the signing of the North Atlantic Treaty and the Statute of the Council of Europe. Although both were significant milestones in the development of European integration, neither included Germany. Both were the product of divergent aims and left everyone partially satisfied at best. The first governmental initiative which eventually led to the Council of Europe was taken by Bidault in July 1948, when he proposed the creation of a European Assembly and also issued a dramatic plea for European economic union. The idea of a European Assembly was, of course, a constant theme among the federalist pressure groups and federalist elements of Europe's political parties. These had managed to raise the profile of the idea of a European Assembly at the Hague Congress of May 1948. There the delegates called for the 'convening, as a matter of real urgency, of a European Assembly chosen by the Parliaments of the participating nations'.[91]

The Hague Congress was presided over by Winston Churchill, who had enjoyed an undeserved reputation as a supporter of European integration since a speech in Zurich in September 1946. More acute observers noticed that the Zurich speech did not envisage British membership of the proposed union.[92] Churchill's prominence at the Hague was one of the reasons which explain the antipathy of the British Labour Party to the Congress. The party had been pressured to support the Congress by its own, if few, federalist members and, more importantly, by the French Section Française de l'Internationale Ouvrière (SFIO), which saw the Congress as an opportunity to cement Anglo-French co-operation on the basis of a socialist-led Europe, that is on the basis of Europe as a third force. At a conference at Selsdon Park the French party was able to persuade the Labour delegates to agree to a resolution supporting the idea of a United States of Europe, but was less successful in overcoming Labour hostility to the forthcoming Congress. At a further conference in Paris on 24–25 April 1948 the Labour Party refused to back the Congress and forbade party members to attend. In the interests of socialist unity the SFIO reluctantly adopted the British line.[93]

Despite their surrender to the dictates of socialist unity in April, the SFIO pressed the French government to take steps towards a European Assembly. When Bidault was forced from office his successor Robert Schuman took up the theme, though on a less ambitious scale, in August. Bevin and the British government were suspicious of French motives and hostile to the whole idea. They were also under pressure from the Americans not to reject the idea outright. The British response to this dilemma was a counter-proposal for a Council of Ministers. When Britain reluctantly conceded that there should also be an Assembly, Bevin sought to constrain the Assembly as tightly as possible, wanting the delegates to be appointed by the governments and to vote *en bloc*. Again a compromise was reached, with delegates being allowed to vote freely and the manner of their selection being left to each member state. On this basis the Statute of the Council of Europe was signed on 5 May 1949.[94] Britain had managed to cripple the Council but not to strangle it. It had no substantial powers and the Assembly was purely advisory, but it did provide a platform for advocates of political integration, much to Bevin's irritation. As he lamented in October 1950,

> To the majority of governments which set it up the Council of Europe was not an instrument for the immediate political unification of Europe, but part of the general material and moral build up of which other parts are represented by the OEEC, the Brussels Treaty and the North Atlantic Pact.
>
> From the outset this conception has broken down ... the Consultative Assembly has tended naturally to consist largely of enthusiasts for European federation. It is therefore biased in favour of federal solutions to an extent which wholly invalidates its claim to represent European opinion as a whole.[95]

THE NORTH ATLANTIC TREATY

Bevin had less reason to complain of those other elements of the 'material and moral build up'. At the end of 1947, he raised the idea of a 'sort of spiritual federation of the west' with Marshall and later, on 22 January 1948, devoted a speech to the theme of western union.[96] On both occasions rhetorical flourishes were given precedence over clarity. Western union, he proclaimed, 'is more a brotherhood and less of a rigid programme'.[97] He was not even sure whether western union required further treaties, 'understandings' might suffice. There were of course more precise considerations in the background, such as the view of the British Chiefs of Staff that any defence of western Europe required

American involvement or the French pressure for an alliance with the United States.[98] Bevin too referred to one clear option, namely the conclusion of treaties similar to the Dunkirk Treaty with other western states, though this was no more than a possibility.[99] As so often, Bevin, convinced that something needed to be done but unsure as to what, had grasped an existing model and speculated upon its extension. The State Department was not convinced of the virtue of the Dunkirk Treaty as a model for future development. It was, after all, specifically directed against Germany and could hardly serve as the basis of a wider western union of which Germany would eventually be a part. But the United States also had a recent model at hand, the Rio Treaty.[100] The Rio Treaty was an intra-American regional security pact rather than a traditional military alliance directed against specific enemies.

Bevin had also indicated, in a memorandum sent to the United States on 13 January, the importance of the 'backing of the Americans and the Dominions'.[101] Two weeks later the British Ambassador, Lord Inverchapel, conveyed Bevin's view that the treaties would be ineffective unless there was an assurance of American support, and proposed Anglo-American talks on western security. The United States was sympathetic but raised two obstacles. Firstly, Congress was still considering the Marshall Plan legislation and it would be unwise to complicate this by introducing a new set of proposals. Secondly, Marshall wanted the Europeans to display their unity and resolve first, before any negotiations on a commitment by the United States. The same formula was being deployed as with economic recovery, the initiative had to come from the Europeans, though this time without even a general American promise equivalent to Marshall's speech.[102]

The Europeans, that is the British, French and Benelux states, proceeded to negotiate, disagreeing over whether or not to include provisions against Germany similar to those in the Dunkirk Treaty. The Benelux states were opposed, France was insistent, but eventually a compromise was reached and the threat of German aggression was relegated to the preface of the treaty. The core provisions conformed to the type of regional security pact favoured by the United States and Benelux.[103] The Treaty creating the Brussels Pact was signed on 17 March 1948.

By then Bevin had further clarified his ideas and increased the pressure on the United States. Opportunity was provided by speculation about Soviet approaches to Norway concerning a possible Soviet–Norwegian pact similar to one negotiated with Finland. Bevin exploited these hints to the hilt. On 11 March he urged 'very early steps, before Norway goes under, to conclude ... a regional Atlantic Approaches Pact of Mutual

Assistance'.[104] Bidault had also sent alarmist messages to Washington and, equally important, the Americans were moving towards accepting the idea of talks. The Europeans were duly informed on 12 March that the United States was ready to discuss the issue.[105]

That still left a great deal to determine, including whether or not a pact or treaty was necessary at all, who should be included in any defence arrangement and, assuming a treaty was desirable, precisely what provisions it should include. All points were contentious. George Kennan was doubtful about the need for new military alliances and insisted that the main issue was European economic recovery. This was an important point since Secretary of Defense Forrestal had justified the Marshall Plan to Congress on the grounds that it was an alternative to greater American military commitments. The whole point was to help the Europeans to stand on their own feet. Kennan also argued that the Europeans already had sufficient guarantee of support from the United States by virtue of the presence of American troops in Europe. Marshall agreed.[106]

Despite these reservations the United States was moving towards the conclusion of a treaty. Tripartite, and secret, negotiations between the United States, Britain and Canada had begun on 22 March 1948. By 1 April the negotiators had agreed upon the need for an Atlantic Treaty, discarding the alternative of a presidential declaration reassuring the Europeans of American support. This was facilitated by the fact that the American negotiating team was dominated by advocates of an alliance, including Hickerson, but they were far from having overcome all domestic opposition to the idea of a treaty.[107]

One major obstacle was Congress. Hickerson and the other advocates of the treaty were in effect asking Congress to abandon the basic principles which had governed United States' foreign policy since its inception. The proposed treaty would tie the United States, during peacetime, to Europe, violating George Washington's advice against 'entangling alliances'. A decisive step forward was taken when the Senate sanctioned the Vandenberg Resolution on 11 June, according to which the Senate approved 'Association of the United States, by constitutional process, with such regional and other collective arrangements as are based on continuous and effective self-help and mutual aid, and as affects its national security.'[108]

Backed by this resolution, talks, this time including France and the Benelux states, began in July. Two major points of dispute were the nature of the guarantees and the territorial extent of the alliance. The Europeans, especially the French, wanted stricter guarantees than the Americans. In fact the French wanted an automatic commitment to go to war in the event of a member of the alliance being attacked. The Americans argued for a looser commitment, citing constitutional obstacles to any automatic commitment.[109] The draft treaty, produced at the end of December, came quite close to French wishes.[110] The French also eventually won the inclusion of Italy in the alliance, against the wishes of most of the others. This southward extension of the Atlantic alliance had not been part of Bevin's original conception, and Britain headed the opposition to Italy's inclusion. The Italians themselves were undecided about membership and eventually opted for inclusion on political grounds. Even then, Truman was only persuaded to accept Italy on 2 March 1949 in the context of France's threat not to ratify the treaty without Italy.[111] In the north there was a similar uncertainty about the geographical extent of the alliance. Norway was considered essential for strategic reasons, as in Bevin's proposal of 11 March. But until quite late the inclusion of other Scandinavian states, or the alternative possibility of a Scandinavian defence union loosely linked to the alliance, was undecided.[112]

When the treaty was signed on 5 April 1949, the article covering the defence guarantees had been modified in the light of Senatorial opposition. France now had to be satisfied with article 5, by which, in the event of an attack, each promised to 'assist the Party or Parties so attacked by taking forthwith, individually and in concert with other Parties, *such action as it deems necessary*, including the use of armed force, to restore and maintain the security of the North Atlantic area'.[113] The change was significant in limiting the commitment of the United States. Vandenberg's reasons for insisting on this were linked to the fact that the idea of an Atlantic treaty had itself become entangled in another issue, namely military aid for Europe. France, again, was the most insistent upon this, to the frequent irritation of the Americans.[114] Senator Taft, an opponent of the treaty, pointed to article 3. According to this the parties, 'by means of continuous and effective self-help and mutual aid, will maintain and develop their individual and collective capacity to resist armed attack'.[115] Taft warned that this could be construed as an open-ended commitment of military aid, but Vandenberg and the new Secretary of State, Acheson, denied that it would.[116] Taft's fears were to prove closer to the truth than the reassurances of Vandenberg and Acheson. Yet that was not clear to Congress. The North Atlantic Treaty was approved in large part because of its apparent limitations. There was as yet no North Atlantic Treaty Organisation, no vast military apparatus.

When the treaty was signed there was no agreement on American military aid and no agreement on Germany. Both issues were raised while the European ministers were in Washington to sign the treaty. The ink was scarcely dry on the treaty when the members of the Brussels Pact lodged a formal request for American military assistance, citing article 3 of the North Atlantic Treaty. This brought into focus an underlying problem of postwar reconstruction and integration. The problem was spelled out the following day, 6 April, by the Italian Ambassador, who had been instructed to state that,

> since Italy is engaged in the effort of achieving economic recovery through the assistance generously granted by the American Government in the framework of the European Recovery Program, it would be harmful to increase military production to such an extent as to endanger the successful pursuance of economic recovery.[117]

Many within the State Department agreed with him. The policy of the United States had been based upon the assumption that the communist threat to Europe was not military, but political. The solution, as Kennan continued to argue, was economic recovery and political stability, both of which would be promoted by European integration. To the extent that a military threat gained predominance, a shift towards an Atlantic dimension and Atlantic integration rather than strictly European integration became much more likely.[118]

THE LIMITS OF INTEGRATION IN THE WEST

Wherever the emphasis was put, on Atlantic or European integration, the greatest unresolved problem was Germany. The day before the signing of the treaty, President Truman called the European ministers to a private meeting during which he and Acheson bluntly set out the position of the United States. When Schuman suggested that the ideal solution for Germany was 'perpetual neutralization', Acheson promptly quashed the idea. The way forward, he said, was to integrate Germany into western Europe by tying Germany into the OEEC and a 'Council and parliament of Europe', and 'by combining any future German armed forces into a unified Western defense'.[119]

Progress was made in integrating Germany into the European economy when the Federal Republic joined the OEEC in October 1949. German entry into the organization was a highly significant political step, since this was the first international organization of which the newly established Federal Republic became a member. German economic policy was also changing as the Economics Minister, Ludwig Erhard, embarked upon a policy of trade liberalization which was soon to transform his country into the second most liberal European trading nation.[120]

Despite this there was substantial frustration throughout 1949 in the United States about the lack of progress towards economic integration in Europe. Within the ECA a group around Assistant Deputy Administrator Richard Bissel placed renewed emphasis upon trade liberalization as part of a grander scheme to force the pace of economic and political integration. Bissel and his colleagues drew directly from the experience of the United States in formulating their prescription for Europe. They took the Interstate Commerce Commission and the Federal Reserve Bank as models and argued for the establishment of analogous European bodies. The hope was that such institutions would educate Europeans in the art of co-operation and would lead, as the advocates of functionalism would later put it, to the 'spill over' of co-operation into new institutional forms.[121]

Progress was in reality slower as the Europeans put forward divergent schemes for the removal of quotas and argued over the extent and mechanism of a prospective payments union. Inspired by the ideas of Bissel's group and irritated by the lack of real progress, Hoffman decided to increase the pressure in a speech to the OEEC in October 1949. Hoffman's speech was less ambitious than he had originally intended. The State Department was able to dissuade him from effectively making further aid conditional upon the establishment of a central bank. Nevertheless, Hoffman's speech was a forthright statement of the United States' expectations. European integration, he insisted 'is not just an ideal, it is a practical necessity'.[122] United States pressure for trade liberalization and a payments union did eventually bear fruit, though not until the following year and not with the supranational institutional apparatus which had been desired.

ATLANTIC VERSUS EUROPEAN INTEGRATION

Institutional innovation did take place within the framework of the Atlantic Treaty, largely as a precondition of the military aid for which the Europeans were clamouring. Congress insisted that the aid would be forthcoming only if article 9 of the treaty, providing for the creation of an Atlantic Council and subordinate bodies, was implemented. The underlying principle was the same one enshrined in the Marshall Plan: aid went hand in hand with institutionalized co-operation and mutual help. Accordingly, on 17 September 1949, the North Atlantic Council met for the first time and laid out the institutional structure of the alliance, including a Standing Group restricted to the United States, Britain and France, and five Regional Planning Groups, of which the United States was a member of only two. With these measures agreed, the Mutual Defense Assistance Act was passed on 6 October. The basis for the militarization of American aid to Europe had been laid.[123]

The Atlantic Alliance's institutional structure already indicated two outstanding problems. The Standing Group picked out the three largest members of the Alliance, causing some concern to the smaller members.

But those three were of a clearly different status. The main problem was not the unavoidable superiority of the United States. It was rather the relationship of France to the other two. For France the fear was that an Anglo-Saxon special relationship would relegate her to second-class status. Her ambition, which would complicate relationships within the Alliance for the next decade and a half, was a genuine triumvirate, or, at least, equality with Britain. The second problem was evident from United States membership of only two of the Planning Groups, those responsible for the defence of Canada and the United States and the North Atlantic. The absence of United States participation in the strictly European Planning Groups reflected the American desire to limit its commitment.

In the second half of 1949 these issues, concerning strategies of European integration, the tension between Atlantic and European integration, the extent of the military commitment of the United States to Europe, and military versus economic aid, were becoming increasingly entangled. They were all complicated by a reassessment of the roles which the United States expected various European countries to play. The key change in emphasis concerned Britain. The most clear-cut assertion of the new policy came from Kennan. Kennan argued that Britain should develop closer economic ties with the United States and Canada, leaving continental Europe to progress towards integration on its own. The suggestion was not supported by the majority of the State Department, who continued to feel that Britain was necessary as a counterweight to Germany in any European union. It did, however, find favour with Secretary of State Acheson.[124] In October, shortly before his speech to the OEEC, Hoffman reassured the British that the United States understood that Britain could not be integrated in Europe to the extent that questioned its wider commitments.[125]

The corollary of this new understanding for the British position was a call for France to take the lead in integrating the continent, including Germany. The combination of these two strategies, closer co-operation between Britain and the United States and French leadership of continental European integration, worried Paris, and the Americans had to reassure the French that the United States did not intend to 'abandon' France. They also pointed out that the expectations of some commentators about an American–Commonwealth union were hardly practicable.[126] There was, however, no modification of the call for a French initiative. The United States was less forthcoming about what that initiative should be.

The only alternative to this unspecified French initiative was to use existing machinery, that is the Atlantic Alliance. From October 1949

American officials gave serious consideration to the possibility of developing the North Atlantic Treaty Organisation as a framework for economic as well as military co-operation. The objective was twofold: to drive forward the process of integration and to incorporate the Federal Republic into the integration process.[127] In retrospect it is easy to see the enormous obstacles to this strategy. It raised the question of the relationship between NATO and the OEEC, it would place the issue of German rearmament on the immediate agenda, above all else it would raise the issue of how far the United States would submit to the authority of a North Atlantic organization with an expanded remit. The policy of the United States had been to stand as an external sponsor, insisting upon steps towards integration by the Europeans but regulating its relationship to the European states by bilateral agreements. In the field of defence the United States had to go further and participate in the common organization, but it is notable that in this case the extent of integration was far weaker than that which the Americans held up as the goal for European economic and political union.

At the end of 1949 the outlook was not so different from December 1948 when the State Department had summarized the outlook for the immediate future. The prospects were for broad economic co-operation through the OEEC, broad political co-operation through a 'Council of Europe', narrower security co-operation through an Atlantic Pact, and the development of 'more limited sub-regional groups such as the Benelux union'.[128] Furthermore, the Americans predicted that 'Integration will thus proceed at a different pace in the various fields of interest and with somewhat different participants in each case. This is desirable if the pace is not to be set by the slowest.'[129] It was a good prediction of the evolution of Europe's post-war architecture.

At the end of 1949 the most pressing problem was Germany. Thus far, the halting steps towards European, and Atlantic, integration had taken place largely without Germany. The Federal Republic had been accepted into the OEEC, but the Federal Republic still operated under a regime of 'dual power'. The Occupation Statute of May 1949 not only reserved a whole series of powers, including foreign affairs, but also specified that the 'Occupation authorities ... reserve the right ... to resume, in whole or in part, the exercise of full authority'.[130] German industry was still faced with a programme of dismantling which stood in stark contrast to the calls for integration, though the Allied Powers did concede some exemptions in the Petersberg Agreements of November 1949. The extent to which the relics of an earlier policy towards Germany poisoned the atmosphere is evident from the fact that when Adenauer presented the Petersberg Agreement to the Bundestag, he was denounced by Schumacher as the

'Federal Chancellor of the Allies'.[131] Such rhetoric fed fears in the west that the west Germans might be tempted to align themselves with the Soviet Union for the sake of the reunification of Germany. The risk had been raised by General Clay on the occasion of his departure from Germany. As Oberdirektor Pünder recalled, Clay invoked the temptation of Christ, and warned the Germans against succumbing. According to Pünder, 'Much depends upon a clear and clever attitude from the Germans. The western allies demanded, above all, a clear confession to *their* ideology, as embodied in the ideas of the Marshall Plan.'[132]

The western allies had less reason to fear than they supposed. The west Germans had largely accepted the idea of the Marshall Plan. That also meant, in practice, the division of Germany and Europe. Integration would proceed along different paths in east and west, to the long-term detriment of the eastern part of Europe. The simple fact was that the west did not really need the east for its economic recovery and prosperity. In eastern Europe, integration was cut short by both the vagaries of power politics within the Soviet bloc and the lingering suspicions associated with economic nationalism, as well as the more justified fears of subordination to hegemonic powers, which long pre-dated the Soviet hold over the region. In the west, the American forecast of December 1948 would hold good. Integration would proceed at different paces and with diverging membership according to the particular field.

NOTES

1. Ross (ed.), *The Foreign Office and the Kremlin*, p. 211.
2. Quoted in King, 'Allied negotiations and the dismemberment of Germany', p. 591.
3. *Documents on British Policy Overseas (hereafter DBPO)*, Series 1, Vol. 1, doc. 603.
4. The initiatives were made by de Gasperi and Spaak. W. Lipgens, *A History of European Integration*, Vol. 1: 1945–1947 (Oxford, 1982), pp. 256 and 260.
5. *Ibid.*, p. 277.
6. Quoted in Wandycz, 'Recent traditions of the quest for unity', p. 79.
7. Quoted in I. T. Berend, 'The problem of eastern European economic integration in a historical perspective', in I. Vajda and M. Simai (eds), *Foreign Trade in a Planned Economy* (Cambridge, 1971), p. 12. These phrases were backed up by a series of Yugoslav–Albanian mixed companies. See W. Hildebrandt, 'Die Aussenpolitischen Beziehungen der FVRJ', in W. Markert (ed.), *Osteuropa Handbuch. Jugoslawien* (Köln, 1954), p. 163.
8. S. Greenwood, 'Ernest Bevin, France and "Western Union": August 1945–February 1946', *European History Quarterly*, **14** (1984), p. 321.
9. Memorandum of 16 December 1945 quoted by Anne Deighton, *The Impossible Peace* (Oxford, 1993), pp. 63–4.
10. *Ibid.*, p. 66.

11. Greenwood, 'Ernest Bevin, France and "Western Union" ', pp. 330–5. See also J. Charmley, 'Duff Cooper and Western Union', *Review of International Studies*, **11** (1985), pp. 53–64.
12. Andrew and Frances Boyd, *Western Union* (London, 1948), p. 234.
13. See John W. Young, *France, the Cold War and the Western Alliance* (Leicester, 1990), pp. 138–9; G. H. Soutou, 'George Bidault et la construction europĕene 1944–1954', *Revue d'histoire diplomatique*, **105** (1991), pp. 269–72. According to the latter, Bidualt's policy had nothing to do with European unification but was aimed at creating a network of bilateral alliance along classical lines.
14. W. W. Rostow, *The Division of Europe after World War II: 1946* (Aldershot, 1982), p. 61.
15. *Ibid.*, pp. 94–101. Other versions of the proposal are also included.
16. Deighton, *The Impossible Peace*, pp. 96–101; John Gimbel, *The Origins of the Marshall Plan* (Stanford, 1976), pp. 104–11. Both agree that Byrnes had no intention of laying the basis for the division of Germany.
17. A. S. Milward, *The Reconstruction of Western Europe 1945–51* (London, 1984), pp. 8 and 35; Michael Hogan, *The Marshall Plan* (Cambridge, 1987), p. 30.
18. Milward, *The Reconstruction of Western Europe*, p. 27. Whereas early commentators emphasized the severity of the crisis, Milward and others have questioned this. See for example Milward's statement that 'All that was immediately at stake was a malfunction of international trade and payments, itself partly due to the very success of economic recovery'; *ibid.*, p. 55. On the same page, however, he writes that '1947 did constitute a crisis with the most profound implications'. For helpful assessments of the debate, see W. Diebold, 'The Marshall Plan in retrospect', *Journal of International Affairs*, **41** (1988), pp. 421–35 and the introduction to C. S. Maier (ed.), *The Marshall Plan in Germany* (Oxford, 1991).
19. M. J. Hogan, 'The search for a "creative peace": the United States, European unity, and the origins of the Marshall Plan', *Diplomatic History*, **6** (1982), p. 275. There are now numerous accounts of the origins of the Marshall Plan.
20. *FRUS*, 1947, Vol. 3, p. 230.
21. *Ibid.*, pp. 237–9.
22. *Ibid.*, p. 235.
23. *Ibid.*, pp. 258–60; William C. Cromwell, 'The Marshall Plan, Britain and the Cold War', *Review of International Studies*, **8** (1982), pp. 238–42. Cromwell emphasizes the 'crucial British role' in the exclusion of the Soviet Union.
24. For this point and the following, see Sheldon Anderson, 'Poland and the Marshall Plan, 1947–1949', *Diplomatic History*, **15** (1991), pp. 473–94; Karel Kratky, 'Czechoslovakia, the Soviet Union and the Marshall Plan', in O. A. Wested *et al.* (eds), *The Soviet Union in Eastern Europe, 1945–89* (Houndmills, 1994), pp. 9–25; Karel Kaplan, 'Stalin, Czechoslovakia, and the Marshall Plan', *Bohemia*, **32** (1991), pp. 133–44.
25. *FRUS*, 1947, Vol. 3, p. 261.
26. There is a record of the meeting in Kaplan, 'Stalin, Czechoslovakia, and the Marshall Plan'.
27. Anderson, 'Poland and the Marshall Plan, 1947–1949', pp. 477–94.
28. Quoted in Gimbel, *The Origins of the Marshall Plan*, p. 184.
29. Quoted in Scott Jackson, 'Prologue to the Marshall Plan', *Journal of American History*, **65** (1979), p. 1062.

30. *Ibid.*, pp. 1063–4; M. Hogan, *The Marshall Plan* (Cambridge, 1987), pp. 58–9. See also W. D. Miscamble, *George F. Kennan and the Making of American Foreign Policy, 1947–1950* (Princeton, 1992), pp. 58–9.
31. I.M. Wall, *The United States and the Making of Postwar France* (Cambridge, 1991), pp. 74–89; Gimbel, *The Origins of the Marshall Plan*, pp. 225–35, 252–3.
32. Hogan, *The Marshall Plan, passim.*
33. *FRUS*, 1947, Vol. 3, p. 281.
34. *Ibid.*, p. 282.
35. Clayton's linkage of European integration and a reduction of imperial preferences is emphasized by Fossedal, *Our Finest Hour*, pp. 246–53.
36. *FRUS*, 1947, Vol. 3, p. 386.
37. Memorandum of 10 October 1947 quoted in Milward, *The Reconstruction of Western Europe*, p. 241.
38. *Ibid.*, pp. 241–3. Milward is scathing in his criticism of the British failure of vision.
39. Committee of European Economic Co-operation, *General Report* (London, 1947), p. 20.
40. Hogan, *The Marshall Plan*, pp. 63–6.
41. There is a succinct summary of these developments in Henry Pelling, *Britain and the Marshall Plan* (Houndmills, 1988).
42. On this see Charles S. Maier, 'The politics of productivity', *International Organization*, **31** (1977), pp. 607–33. Maier summarizes their position well: 'The true dialectic was not one of class against class, but waste versus abundance'; *ibid.*, p. 615. See also M. Hogan, 'American Marshall Planners and the search for a European neocapitalism', *American Historical Review*, **90** (1985), pp. 44–72 and *The Marshall Plan*. On the broader theme of growth see D. Ellwood, 'The Marshall Plan and the politics of growth', in P. Stirk and D. Willis (eds), *Shaping Postwar Europe* (London, 1991), pp. 15–26.
43. Berend, 'The problem of eastern European economic integration in a historical perspective', p. 11. It is far from clear that this and other examples substantiate Berend's claims that 'most of the European socialist countries considered economic integration as inevitable'; *ibid.*
44. See Nicolas Spulbar, *The Economics of Communist Europe* (London, 1957), pp. 198–201. T.G. Patterson emphasizes that these did not account for substantial parts of the east European economies, *Soviet–American Confrontation* (Baltimore, 1973), p. 104.
45. *Documents on International Affairs 1947–8*, p. 94.
46. Wandycz, 'Recent traditions of the quest for unity', pp. 80–1.
47. Leonid Gibianski, 'The 1948 Soviet–Yugoslav conflict and the formation of the "socialist camp" model', in Wested *et al.* (eds), *The Soviet Union in Eastern Europe*, p. 35. According to V. Dedijer, *Tito Speaks* (London, 1953), p. 320, Stalin said, 'Yugoslavia is free to swallow Albania.' Others repeat this statement, but Gibianski says there is no archival evidence to support it. The precise motives and even statements in this whole affair are still unclear, though the fog is beginning to lift.
48. *Documents on International Affairs 1947–8*, p. 98.
49. See G. Ra'anan, *International Policy Formation in the USSR* (Hamden, Conn., 1983), pp. 139–40 and 147–8.

50. This is emphasized by Gibianski, 'The 1948 Soviet–Yugoslav conflict and the formation of the "socialist camp" Model'.
51. This is emphasized by Ra'anan, *International Policy Formation in the USSR*.
52. See any of the above accounts for details. There is an important general comment in R. N. Berki, 'Postwar misery in eastern Europe: glosses on an Hungarian perspective', in Stirk and Willis (eds), *Shaping Postwar Europe*, pp. 53–67.
53. *FRUS*, 1948, Vol. 3, p. 11. The discussion took place on 21 January.
54. Quoted in Michael Newman, 'Léon Blum, French socialism and European unity, 1940–50', *Historical Journal*, **24** (1981), pp. 196–7.
55. W. Loth, *Sozialismus und Internationalismus* (Stuttgart, 1977), 78–82.
56. Jonathon Schneer, 'Hopes deferred or shattered: the British Labour left and the Third Force movement, 1945–49', *Journal of Modern History*, **56** (1984), p. 202.
57. W. Lipgens and W. Loth (eds), *DHEI*, Vol. 3, doc. 673. See also M. Newman, *Socialism and European Unity* (London, 1983), pp. 138–40.
58. The difficulty in defining the balance between the two underlies much of the disagreement about Bevin's policy. For a very helpful guide to the state of the debate, see John W. Young, *Britain and European Unity, 1945–1992* (Houndmills, 1993), pp. 14–18.
59. On this see John Kent, 'Bevin's imperialism and the idea of Euro-Africa 1945–49', in M. Dockrill and J. W. Young (eds), *British Foreign Policy 1945–56* (Houndmills, 1989), pp. 47–76.
60. It was not convertibility itself that was the main cause of the drain. See Alec Cairncross, *Years of Recovery* (London, 1985), pp. 121–64.
61. I have taken the term from Kent, 'Bevin's imperialism and the idea of Euro-Africa 1945–49'. On the Bevin–Ramadier talks see Young, *France, the Cold War and the Western Alliance*, pp. 168–9.
62. W. Loth (ed.), *DHEI*, Vol. 4, doc. 10. See also Lipgens, *A History of European Integration*, pp. 579–85.
63. Schneer, 'Hopes deferred or shattered', pp. 212–13.
64. Klaus Schwabe, 'German policy responses to the Marshall Plan', in Maier (ed.), *The Marshall Plan and Germany*, p. 234. But see W. Loth, 'Deutsche Europa-Konzeptionen in der Eskalation des Ost-West-Konflikts 1945–1949', *Geschichte in Wissenschaft und Unterricht*, **35** (1984), pp. 457–9.
65. Lipgens and Loth (eds), *DHEI*, Vol. 3, doc. 152. On these ideas see Hans-Peter Schwarz, *Vom Reich zur Bundesrepublik* (Stuttgart, 1980), pp. 568–88. Something like Schmid's scenario eventually took place almost fifty years later. It is important to recall that although the idea of a third force appealed to many European socialists it did not appeal to all. Indeed the association of the third force idea with European union did much to discredit the idea in the eyes of the Dutch Labour Party. See W. Asbeek Brusse, *The Dutch Social Democrats and Europe*, EUI Colloquium Papers, 306/88, p. 5.
66. On the negotiations see Milward, *The Reconstruction of Western Europe*, pp. 168–79.
67. *FRUS*, 1948, Vol. 33, p. 402.
68. 8 April 1948, *ibid.*, p. 414.
69. Article 14 of the Convention, Boyd and Boyd, *Western Union*, p. 153. This amounted to what would now be called a right to opt out. It is undoubtedly an improvement upon the *liberum veto*, but that is all.

70. For examples of the difficulties, see the reports of Harriman, 4 July, and Hoffman, 13 July, *FRUS*, 1948, Vol. 3, pp. 464–5, 467–9.
71. Harriman, 31 July 1948, *ibid.*, p. 473. On the whole episode see Milward, *The Reconstruction of Western Europe*, pp. 183–95; Hogan, *The Marshall Plan*, pp. 156–61.
72. Hogan, *The Marshall Plan*, pp. 330–1; Milward, *The Reconstruction of Western Europe*, pp. 190–5.
73. Wall, *The United States and the Making of Postwar France*, p. 183.
74. James Edward Miller, *The United States and Italy, 1940–1950* (Chapel Hill, 1986), p. 255; *Akten der Vorgeschichte der Bundesrepublik Deutschland 1945–1949*, Vol. 5, pp. 355–60; Werner Abelshauser, 'American aid and West German recovery', in Maier (ed.), *The Marshall Plan and Germany*, p. 400.
75. See, for example, Pelling, *Britain and the Marshall Plan*, pp. 59–61, 73–4, 97.
76. *The Marshall Plan. A Program of International Cooperation* (Washington, DC, n.d.), p. 34.
77. Quoted in Stirk, 'Americanism and anti-Americanism in British and German responses to the Marshall Plan', in Stirk and Willis (eds), *Shaping Postwar Europe*, p. 30.
78. In a memorandum of 22 January 1952, quoted in Werner Link, *Deutsche und amerikanische Gewerkschaften und Geschäftsleute 1945–1975* (Düsseldorf, 1978), p. 131.
79. *Ibid., passim*; Volker Berghahn, *The Americanization of West German Industry, 1945–1973* (Leamington Spa, 1986); Peter Stirk, 'Americanism and anti-Americanism in British and German responses to the Marshall Plan'; P. P. D'Attore, 'Americanism and anti-Americanism in Italy', in Stirk and Willis (eds), *Shaping Postwar Europe*, pp. 27–42 and 43–52. For a more critical approach, see A. Carew, *Labour under the Marshall Plan* (Manchester, 1987).
80. On the much-discussed German case see Werner Link, 'Der Marshall-Plan und Deutschland', *Aus Politik und Zeitgeschichte*, **50** (1980), pp. 11–14.
81. This was despite the fact that this aspect of the Marshall Plan was pursued with greater vigour in Italy than any other country. See P. P. D'Attore, 'Americanism and anti-Americanism in Italy', and *ERP Aid and the Politics of Productivity in Italy during the 1950s*, EUI Working Paper no. 85/159.
82. Hogan, *The Marshall Plan*, pp. 119–21.
83. *Ibid.*, pp. 165–75; Milward, *The Reconstruction of Western Europe*, pp. 258–81; Barry Eichengreen, *Reconstructing Europe's Trade and Payments* (Manchester, 1993), pp. 18–22.
84. Quoted in G. Schiavone, *The Institutions of Comecon* (London, 1981), p. 14.
85. *Ibid.*, p. 15.
86. J. M. Brabant, 'Another look at the origins of east European economic cooperation', *Osteuropa Wirtschaft*, **24** (1979), p. 264. My account follows Brabant. A. Korbonski, 'CMEA, economic integration, and Perestroika, 1949–1989', *Studies in Comparative Communism*, **23** (1990), p. 50, sees the creation of the CMEA as part of the consolidation of Soviet hegemony following the expulsion of Yugoslavia from Cominform. P. J. D. Wiles, *Communist International Economics* (Oxford, 1968), p. 313, sees it as the 'last fling' of the Zhdanov–Voznesenski policy, but does not elaborate.

87. On this see Schwarz, *Vom Reich zur Bundesrepublik*, pp. 574–88; Lucius D. Clay, *Decision in Germany* (London, 1950), pp. 409–10; Wilfried Loth, *The Division of the World 1941–1955* (London, 1988), pp. 206–7.
88. *FRUS*, 1948, Vol. 2, pp. 1287–97.
89. *Ibid.*, pp. 1325–40. On the whole issue see Miscamble, *George F. Kennan and the Making of American Foreign Policy*, pp. 145–74.
90. See R. Poidevin, 'Frankreich und die Rurhfrage (1945–51)', *Historische Zeitschrift*, **228** (1979), pp. 324–8; J. Gillingham, *Coal, Steel and the Rebirth of Europe 1945–1955* (Cambridge, 1991), pp. 157–62.
91. *DHEI*, Vol. 4, doc. 76. On the Hague Congress see also docs 69–79.
92. *DHEI*, Vol. 3, doc. 193.
93. On these developments see *DHEI*, Vol. 4, docs 106 and 107; John T. Grantham, 'British labour and the Hague "Congress of Europe": national sovereignty defended', *Historical Journal*, **24** (1981), pp. 443–52; W. Loth, *The SFIO and the Beginnings of European Integration, 1947–54*, EUI Colloquium Papers 301/88.
94. See A. H. Robertson, *The Council of Europe* (London, 1956); G. Warner, 'Die Britische Labour-Regierung und die Einheit Westeuropas', *Vierteljahreshefte für Zeitgeschichte*, **28** (1980), pp. 316–20.
95. *DBPO*, Series 2, Vol. 1, doc. 172.
96. Quoted in N. Petersen, 'Who pulled whom how much? Britain, the United States and the making of the North Atlantic Treaty', *Millennium*, **11** (1982), p. 94.
97. Quoted in Weigall and Stirk (eds), *The Origins and Development of the European Community*, doc. 3.7.
98. Petersen, 'Who pulled whom how much?', pp. 95–6; I. M. Wall, 'France and the North Atlantic Alliance', in F. H. Heller and J. R. Gillingham (eds), *NATO: The Founding of the Atlantic Alliance and the Integration of Europe* (New York, 1992), p. 47.
99. See the memorandum outlining his forthcoming speech to the United States, *FRUS*, 1948, Vol. 3, pp. 3–6.
100. See the views of John Hickerson on 19 January and 21 January, *ibid.*, pp. 6–7 and 9–12. Hickerson even raised the issue of participation by the United States.
101. *Ibid.*, p. 5.
102. *Ibid.*, 13 January 1948, pp. 3–6; 27 January 1948, pp. 12–16; 2 February 1948, pp. 17–18.
103. For details of the negotiations, see John Baylis, 'Britain, the Brussels pact and the continental commitment', *International Affairs*, **60** (1984), pp. 623–9.
104. *FRUS*, 1948, Vol. 3, p. 47.
105. *Ibid.*, pp. 49–50. On these events see Petersen, 'Who pulled whom how much?', pp. 97–100.
106. *FRUS*, 1948, Vol. 3, 20 January 1948, pp. 8–9 and 29 April 1948, pp. 108–9; Timothy P. Ireland, *Creating the Entangling Alliance* (Westport, Conn., 1981), pp. 59–60, 69.
107. On these negotiations see Cees Wiebes and Bert Zeeman, 'The Pentagon negotiations March 1948: the launching of the North Atlantic Treaty', *International Affairs*, **59** (1983), pp. 351–63. On the strength of reservations on the American side see pp. 361–3.
108. *FRUS*, 1948, Vol. 3, p. 136.
109. For the difference, see the preliminary report of 9 September 1948, *ibid.*, p. 247.

110. *Ibid.*, 24 December 1948, p. 335.
111. E. Timothy Smith, 'The fear of subversion: the United States and the inclusion of Italy in the North Atlantic Treaty', *Review of International Studies*, **8** (1987), pp. 139–55; 'United States security and the integration of Italy into the western bloc, 1947–1949', in Heller and Gillingham (eds), *NATO*, pp. 73–97; Wall, 'France and the North Atlantic Alliance', pp. 45–56.
112. N. Petersen, 'Britain, Scandinavia and the North Atlantic Treaty 1948–49', *Review of International Studies*, **8** (1982), pp. 251–68.
113. Article 5, North Atlantic Treaty. For French dissatisfaction with this, see Vincent Auriol, *Journal du Septennat 1947–1954*, Vol. 3 (Paris, 1977), pp. 127, 151, 159–60.
114. See, for example, *FRUS*, 1948, Vol. 3, 20 August 1948, pp. 218–20.
115. Article 3, North Atlantic Treaty.
116. Alan K. Henrikson, 'The creation of the North Atlantic Alliance 1948–1952', *Naval College War Review*, **32** (1980), pp. 22–3; Ireland, *Creating the Entangling Alliance*, pp. 131–46. See also Vandenberg's concern about the effective linkage between the pact and aid in Arthur H. Vandenberg, Jr (ed.), *The Private Papers of Senator Vandenberg* (London, 1953), p. 479.
117. *Documents on International Affairs 1949*, p. 264.
118. For French attempts to blur the tension, see P. Guillen, 'La France et la question de la défense de l'Europe Occidentale', *Revue d'histoire*, **144** (1986), pp. 83–4.
119. Cees Wiebes and Bert Zeeman, 'Eine Lehrstünde in Machtpolitik', *Vierteljahreshefte für Zeitgeschichte*, **40** (1992), pp. 417–18. This rather undermines Miscamble's argument that Acheson was still considering Kennan's Program A. *George F. Kennan and the Making of American Foreign Policy*, pp. 166–74.
120. Schwartz, 'European integration and the "special relationship" ', in Maier (ed.), *The Marshall Plan in Germany*, pp. 184–5.
121. Milward, *The Reconstruction of Western Europe*, pp. 285–6.
122. Quoted in E. van der Beugel, *From Marshall Aid to Atlantic Partnership* (Amsterdam, 1966), p. 182. See also Milward, *The Reconstruction of Western Europe*, pp. 297–8.
123. Ireland, *Creating the Entangling Alliance*, pp. 155–62; Lawrence S. Kaplan, *A Community of Interests: NATO and the Military Assistance Programme, 1948–1951* (Washington, 1980), pp. 23–47; Henrikson, 'The creation of the North Atlantic Alliance, 1948–1952', p. 26.
124. Schwartz, 'European integration and the "special relationship" ', pp. 177–9. Kennan had suggested something similar, if not as clear cut, in a memorandum of 4 September 1947, *FRUS*, 1947, Vol. 3, pp. 397–405.
125. Hogan, *The Marshall Plan*, pp. 275–6.
126. Auriol, *Journal du Septennat*, Vol. 3, 1949, entries for 22 and 28 September, pp. 330–2 and 336–7.
127. Ireland, *Creating the Entangling Alliance*, pp. 166–7.
128. *FRUS*, 1948, Vol. 3, 3 December 1948, p. 302.
129. *Ibid.*, p. 303.
130. W. Benz (ed.), *Deutschland seit 1945* (Munich, 1990), p. 201. The characterization of the regime as one of 'dual power' is taken from Ludolf Herbst, *Option für den Westen* (Munich, 1989), pp. 59–60.
131. *Ibid.*, p. 68.
132. *Akten der Vorgeschichte der Bundesrepublik Deutschland 1945–1949*, Vol. 5, 10 May 1949, pp. 414–15.

5

The Years of Growth and the Foundation of the Communities: 1950–60

INTRODUCTION

The great unresolved problem in 1950 was Germany. It had been clear even during the Second World War that western Europe could not prosper without the German economy, and could not be secure without the integration of German military potential. France reluctantly accepted this logic in two initiatives. The first, the Schuman Plan, led to the European Coal and Steel Community. By the time the treaty was signed, in April 1951, France had taken the second, more ambitious, initiative. This was for the creation of a European army under the control of a European Defence Community. German rearmament could be tolerated, so the argument ran, if German forces were integrated into a supranational structure. Although France initiated this idea it was France which, in 1954, effectively rejected the Defence Community. Yet France could not hold out against American pressure for German rearmament. The solution was found in allowing the Federal Republic to rearm under the nominal supervision of a Western European Union. In reality, Germany rearmed within the framework of the Atlantic Alliance.

The Soviet response was to establish the Warsaw Pact in 1955. This was very much a response to German rearmament, not to the Atlantic Alliance itself. The Soviet Union had lived with the latter since 1949, without moving to establish a counterweight. The Warsaw Pact was neither a response to, nor a replica of, the Atlantic Alliance. The Atlantic Alliance was far from being a supranational body, the Warsaw Pact even less so. If the east lagged behind the west in terms of military integration, it lagged even further behind with respect to economic integration. Here, the problems arose both from the inherent problems of integrating planned economies, and from the historical legacy of the region.

In the west, market economies provided a more fertile ground for integration. A customs union, long considered as the royal road to integration formed the core of the European Economic Community. Yet the latter would not have come into being without a less well-known body: Euratom. It was Euratom which initially attracted France. The customs union, which had been placed on the agenda by the Netherlands, posed a threat to traditional French protectionism. Yet the one was not to be had without the other. The linkage between the two ensured that the Treaties of Rome were signed in 1957.

A customs union also posed a threat to Britain. The fear was that British goods would be locked out if the Economic Community took a protectionist turn. The British alternative was a European free trade area embracing all of western Europe. But this was vehemently opposed by France, both on economic and political grounds It was France that killed off the negotiations on the British proposal. That left Britain, and others who baulked at the commitments of the European Economic Community, to form the European Free Trade Association at the end of the decade. Economically western Europe was now divided into the six of the Community and the seven of the Free Trade Area.

Western divisions were greeted in the east as proof of capitalist antagonism. Yet conflicts of interest, in both the military and the economic fields, were also evident in the east. So too was the assertion of the sovereignty of states. At the end of the day, all of the fora of integration which included either of the superpowers had failed to develop the supranational traits of the European Communities. This was true of the Atlantic Alliance, of Comecon and the Warsaw Pact.

ECONOMIC INTEGRATION OF THE FEDERAL REPUBLIC AND THE SCHUMAN PLAN

The prospects of the integration of the Federal Republic at the beginning of 1950 were not good. France was still fearful and suspicious of the German state and relations between them were soured by the question of the future of the Saar. The Saarland, a small part of the former Germany but rich in coal, had not been included in the Federal Republic in 1949. France had established a customs barrier between the Saar and other German territories and, more importantly, intended to prevent any reunification of the Saar with the Federal Republic. For the Germans, the fate of the Saar was important in two ways. They claimed it as German territory in its own right. They also argued that to renounce the claim to the Saar would undermine their refusal to accept the Oder-Neisse as the eastern limit of Germany.[1]

It is hardly surprising that the dispute over the Saar marred the first French state visit, by Foreign Minster Robert Schuman, to the Federal Republic in January 1950. Less than a week before his visit the French government had announced that it was entering into negotiations with the Saar government about the economic and political status of the territory. Worse was to come. On 2 March the French High Commissioner announced to Adenauer that the conventions with the Saar would be signed the next day. Adenauer immediately responded that it was 'highly improbable' that the Bundestag would accept membership of the Council of Europe in those circumstances.[2]

Yet two months later, on 9 May 1950, Robert Schuman issued a declaration which led to the signature of a treaty creating the European Coal and Steel Community less than a year later. According to the declaration,

> the French Government proposes that Franco-German production of coal and steel as a whole be placed under a common High Authority, within the framework of an organisation open to the participation of other countries of Europe.
>
> The pooling of coal and steel production should immediately provide for the setting up of common foundations for economic development as a first step in the federation of Europe ... [3]

There was nothing startling in Schuman's choice of coal and steel. There had been several suggestions that Franco-German reconciliation should be built around co-operation in this sector. Adenauer, who had been consulted about the declaration on 8 May, recalled on several occasions that he had been in favour of such a strategy in the 1920s.[4]

It was the fact that Schuman made the offer at all that was surprising. France was under pressure from the United States to take some kind of initiative. More importantly, France was being pressed by the Americans and British to raise the German steel quota at the London Foreign Ministers Conference, which was due to open on 10 May. In broader terms, France was faced with the prospect that controls on German industry would be abandoned whether France approved or not. This was clear to Jean Monnet, France's Planning Commissioner, who formulated the proposals which led to Schuman's declaration. Monnet was concerned to secure the future of the French modernization plan, which he felt was threatened by German revival. The picture he painted for Schuman on 4 May was indeed bleak: 'Germany expanding, German dumping on export markets, a call for the protection of French industries; the halting or camouflage of trade liberalization; the reestablishment of pre-war cartels ... France fallen back into the rut of limited, protected production.'[5] The only alternative was the creation of a system which would permit 'joint expansion, in competition but without domination'.[6]

The responses to Schuman's declaration were varied. Adenauer had strong political reasons for welcoming the move, especially since it was made clear that Germany would be treated as an equal partner in the negotiations. Political leaders in Italy and the Benelux states largely welcomed the plan, though there were some suspicions about French intentions, especially in the Netherlands. Britain was even more suspicious.

Britain's initial response was one of irritation that the French had acted without giving Britain prior warning. Until the matter was studied further, British ministers decided 'to adopt a very cautious and non-committal attitude'.[7] In the following weeks British ministers and officials tried to learn more about the French plan, with limited success. It was clear that the implications of the plan were potentially serious. According to an early assessment the economic impact on the United Kingdom would be slight in the short run, but disadvantageous in the long run.[8] The outcome was that Britain was willing to enter into negotiations, but not on the terms desired by the French. France wanted a prior commitment to the principle of a treaty establishing a High Authority. This was unacceptable to Britain. After being pressed by France on 25 May, and again on 30 May, Britain declined to participate. Given French insistence upon prior commitment this was a predictable outcome. As a Foreign Office official summarized,

> It has been . . . accepted by Ministers as a basis for policy, that we should not become involved in Europe in the economic sphere, beyond the point of no return. To contemplate, even in principle, on agreement to pool the British coal and steel industries with those of other Western European countries, and make their operations subject to the decisions of an independent European authority which are binding on H.M.G., would imply a readiness to accept a surrender of sovereignty in a matter of vital national interest which would carry us well beyond that point.[9]

The underlying suspicions of western Europe held by the Labour Party were almost brutally set out in a statement by the Party's National Executive Committee. This included the famous assertion that 'we in Britain are closer to our kinsmen in Australia and New Zealand on the far side of the world, than we are to Europe'.[10] The document went further, asserting that, apart from Britain and Scandinavia, western Europe lacked the 'civic and administrative traditions' essential to democratic socialism. Even the United States was judged to be 'more progressive' than most of Britain's western European neighbours.[11]

It was less predictable that the French would insist upon the commitment. Indeed the French government raised no objection to the Dutch position, which consisted of accepting the French memorandum, and then issuing a unilateral declaration stating that the Netherlands would not sign the treaty if they found it objectionable. But Britain insisted that her reservations be entered in her formal response, and France insisted that the British response include accepting the French memorandum with its statement of a commitment to sign a treaty. This has led to suggestions that France deliberately sought to exclude Britain and that Monnet was the main force behind this decision. Monnet did, in fact, on this occasion and subsequent ones, show great concern about the principle and symbols of the supranational bodies he espoused. The reason why Monnet and Schuman placed so much importance on British statements of intent was probably accurately summarized by the British Ambassador to Paris. The fear, he said, was that an uncommitted Britain would seek to undermine the supranational elements of the plan and this 'would free the Germans from the commitment to these ideas'.[12]

One of the numerous reservations which were raised in the British discussions was the impact of the proposed community upon other institutions. Stafford Cripps worried that it might signal a move away from an Atlantic Community. The Chiefs of Staff had more specific concerns. The policy of the proposed community would have to be compatible with the Atlantic Alliance's requirements, lest rearmament were threatened. Spierenburg, head of the Dutch delegation to the negotiations, related the concerns of his government about the possible impact on the OEEC.[13] Dutch concern about the OEEC, which was shared by the British, was understandable, for Stikker was about to submit his own plan for trade liberalization on a sectoral basis to it. Within the French government Bidault, though he supported the Schuman plan, also had other irons in the fire. He had put forward, on 16 April, a proposal for an Atlantic High Council to co-ordinate defence and economic policy. According to this scheme the Council, on which France, Britain and the United States would have permanent seats, would act as the Atlantic Alliance's executive arm.[14] Although the architecture of the European house was still fragmentary it was already proving difficult to add a new element without calling into question the status of the rest.

NEGOTIATING THE EUROPEAN COAL AND STEEL COMMUNITY

Much, of course, depended upon the eventual shape and policies of the Coal and Steel Community, and they had still to be determined. The only thing which was clear at the beginning was that there was supposed to be a High Authority. Quite what that meant was not clear. The term had been suggested to Monnet by Paul Reuter, who explicitly drew on American models like the Tennessee Valley Authority.[15] Monnet explained to British officials in May that the members of the Authority would be independent. They would be neither representatives of the industries nor of the governments. This was essential, he explained, if a genuine community view was to prevail. Moreover, the High Authority's writ was to be directly binding upon member states. He did concede that there would have to be some mechanism of appeal against the decisions of the High Authority.[16] Beyond this there was little to constrain the Authority.

It was this lack of restraint which worried some of the parties to the negotiations, which opened on 20 June. The main disputes concerning institutional matters were conducted between the French, usually supported by the Germans and Italians, and the Benelux states, with the Dutch being the most vocal in their opposition.[17] The Belgians were concerned to secure a permanent court of arbitration and Monnet had already made some concession to Belgian concerns when he distributed a working document on 24 June. This envisaged both a court and a parliamentary assembly. There was, however, no council of ministers, and it was this that the Dutch were most insistent upon.[18]

For Monnet it was a battle between his own conception of a genuinely supranational body, which he interpreted as one free from interference by governments, and the Dutch attempt to install an intergovernmental watch-dog over the High Authority. The clash between the two became evident when they dealt with the source of the High Authority's power. For Monnet, the Authority would receive its power from a treaty ratified by national parliaments. According to the Dutch, it would receive its power from a treaty concluded by the governments. This dispute became bound up with the allocation of powers between the High Authority, the Council of Ministers, which Monnet reluctantly accepted as part of the institutional structure, and the parliamentary assembly. The German delegates, Walther Hallstein and Carl Friedrich Ophüls, sought to utilize the disputes to introduce a strong federal element. They suggested that the Council of Ministers and the Assembly should constitute a Congress following the American model. This, however, found no favour with the French, who persisted in trying to defend the status of the High Authority.[19]

By 9 November 1950, when the first draft of the treaty was ready, these disputes had been settled by a series of compromises which produced a complex network of decision-making powers, rights of consultation and co-determination. The Assembly emerged as much the weaker of the Community's institutions, with nothing more than the power to pass a motion of censure in the entire High Authority. It was a power it never used. The High Authority retained the decision-making initiative but was dependent upon the authorization of the Council of Ministers in specific cases. Given the apparent weakness of the small powers, they had been remarkably successful in curtailing the High Authority.

There had also been disputes over the economic aims of the Community. The general principle of a common market free from customs barriers and quotas still left a whole series of issues, including the extent of the Community's authority over wages, investment and prices, the level of the Community's external tariff, as well as the problem of the transitional period, during which weaker producers would enjoy some protection while they modernized their facilities in preparation for the rigours of the market. This was especially important for Belgium, with its relatively high level of wages and large number of inefficient coal producers. Belgian efforts to secure a harmonization of wages, around the higher Belgian level, failed, despite some sympathy in the French camp. But Belgium did secure generous treatment for the transitional period through a system which effectively provided for German subsidy of Belgian coal production. At the end of the day, acrimonious though the disputes were, a compromise could be found to satisfy the smaller producers like Belgium and Italy without asking other members to pay too high a price.

A much bigger problem was presented by Monnet's proposal to commit the Community to the principles of competition. Historically, co-operation in the coal and steel sectors had taken the form of cartels intended to bolster prices and stability by market-sharing and price-fixing measures. Yet in Monnet's eyes these traditional practices were incompatible with the modernization programme to which he was committed. Any revival of cartels also threatened to undermine American support. Despite initial hesitations the American foreign policy establishment was reassured that 'Monnet is [the] leading advocate [of] real anti-cartel legislation and [a] policy of expansion in production.'[20] The Americans were aware that there was a risk that the plan could 'degenerate into a super-cartel', and that some protection of European industries was inevitable. But the risk was judged to be worth taking because of the potential economic and political advantages.[21]

The American prescription of competition challenged both French industry's protectionist heritage and the German tradition of sanctioning cartels. There was, here, a fundamental divergence of outlook. German courts had long accepted that cartels could in principle be in the public interest. The American tradition, though often neglected in practice, tended to assume that cartels were against the public interest. The potential clash was all the greater since coal and steel were among the most highly organized sectors of German industry. This conflict, aligning Monnet and the Americans against the German tradition, reached its crisis-point at the beginning of 1951. By then the negotiations on the Schuman Plan had been complicated by the emergence of another problem: the prospect of German rearmament.

GERMAN REARMAMENT AND THE EUROPEAN DEFENCE COMMUNITY

The British chiefs of staff had speculated upon this option even before the end of the war. From 1947 even leading French generals accepted the necessity of a German contribution to western defence. But the need for German rearmament was resolutely rejected by the majority of the French officer corps and by France's political leaders.[22] The atmosphere in which these differences were expressed was transformed by the North Korean invasion of South Korea on 25 June 1950. Analogies were quickly drawn. In the far east, in a divided country, a Soviet proxy, the North Koreans, sought to reunify the country under communist hegemony. Pessimists found a similar scenario in the heart of Europe. Konrad Adenauer took up the analogy in one of his meetings with the Allied High Commissioners on 17 August. He claimed to have no doubt that Stalin intended exactly the same fate for Germany as was unfolding in Korea. His fears seemed confirmed by the formation of a large, armed Volkspolizei in east Germany. In response he asked for a Federal German police force of 150,000 men.[23]

There was an increasingly strong consensus, at least among the Anglo-Saxons, that German rearmament was necessary. In Britain the favoured strategy was to consent to Adenauer's request for a large police force and, in the long run, to integrate Germany into the Atlantic Alliance. The American High Commissioner, John McCloy, argued for a European army, and a sympathizer in the State Department suggested that the Schuman Plan might serve as a model for this European defence force. The Defense Department was not impressed by this option, not least because it saw nationalism as an essential motive for the willingness to fight. In other words, Germans would fight in defence of their homeland, but not for Europe.[24]

The United States seemed to be in a strong position to press its case. Western Europe was dependent upon American aid for the restoration of its defence capacity. Yet even with the Mutual Defense Assistance Programme and increased European defence budgets, the Europeans wanted something more. They wanted greater American commitment, in the form of more American troops in Europe and an American commander of NATO forces in Europe. At the insistence of the Defense Department, Secretary of State Dean Acheson attempted to exploit European dependence at the New York Foreign Ministers conference in September 1950. In the so-called 'one-package' proposal he offered increased American troop commitments in return for immediate German rearmament. The French Foreign Minister, Schuman, though he had been forewarned of the American proposal, would not even agree at first to accept the principle of German rearmament. Even under American pressure, he conceded, at the end of September, no more than that Germany 'should be enabled to contribute to the build-up of the defence of Western Europe'.[25]

Under persistent American pressure, the French desperately sought an alternative which would keep Germany out of the Atlantic Alliance, and place the maximum number of constraints upon German rearmament. Their solution was announced to the French National Assembly on 24 October 1950 by Prime Minister Pleven. The Pleven Plan proposed the creation of a European army under a European Minister of Defence. Pleven specified that the 'contingents furnished by the participating States would be incorporated in the European Army at the level of the smallest possible unit'.[26] He added that 'participating states which currently have national forces at their disposal would retain their own authority so far as concerned that part of their existing forces which was not integrated by them into the European army'. There was, of course, only one state which did not currently have national forces: Germany. The implication was that all future German troops should be part of the European Army, but that France and the others should contribute to the European Army while retaining their own national forces. German freedom of manoeuvre was also to be constrained by restricting the size of national units in the European Army. There would be no German divisions. It was also part of the French agenda that there would be no German Ministry of Defence.

The Pleven Plan was clearly discriminatory. It was seen by the United States and Britain as little more than a means of delaying German rearmament. In Britain it also aroused the suspicion that further European integration would weaken Atlantic unity. Bevin even declared himself to be in favour of an Atlantic Army which 'eliminates the European federal concept from N.A.T.O. defence and replaces it by an Atlantic federal concept, which is in line with our own general political thinking'.[27] The suggestion that any kind of federal concept formed part of British policy was an exaggeration, but the emphasis upon Atlantic cooperation was not.

The outcome of these differences was a dual set of negotiations. In the Petersberg Hotel in Bonn the Allied High Commissioners discussed rearmament with the Germans, while in Paris the French called a conference, to which the Germans were invited, to discuss a European Army. None of the major parties was in a hurry. In his 24 October 1950 announcement Pleven had suggested that discussions about a European Army should begin only after the treaty on the Coal and Steel Community was signed. The French were determined to secure the Schuman Plan first. The point, of course, was to establish institutionalized control of the economic basis of any future German war machine, before permitting the re-emergence of German soldiers.[28] The Germans were more interested in the Petersberg negotiations, in which they aimed at German rearmament on the basis of equality and within the framework of the Atlantic Alliance.

FINALIZING THE EUROPEAN COAL AND STEEL COMMUNITY

France was successful in her insistence upon the prior signature of the Schuman Plan treaty before any significant progress was made on German rearmament, though success was neither guaranteed nor easy. The main difficulty concerned the structure of the German economy. For Monnet and his American allies there were three problems: the extent of concentration of German industry, especially the steel industry; the extent to which steel concerns owned coal mines (*Verbundwirtschaft*); and the existence of a coal sales agency, that is a coal cartel. These issues were linked to the coal and steel treaty in so far as Monnet insisted upon articles prohibiting cartels and other restrictive practices. The dispute with the Germans had become particularly intense from September 1950 onwards. On 12 October Adenauer complained that experts on deconcentration, who had failed to have any influence in their own country, were now seeking to implement their ideas in other states. He meant the American Robert Bowie, Monnet's friend and collaborator. On 12 December he told the High Commissioners that German industrialists saw the *Verbundwirtschaft* as vital, and that if it was undermined there would be no majority in the Bundestag for the treaty.[29] Such brinkmanship was not confined to the Germans. In December Monnet threatened to break off the negotiations entirely if there was no genuine decartelization. Again, when Hallstein proposed to drop the offending articles of the treaty Monnet threatened to pull out.

The impasse was finally broken by the Americans. On 4 March the American High Commissioner, McCloy, dictated the terms of an agreement to Adenauer. Twenty-four separate steel companies were to be formed, there would be limits on the ownership of coal producers by steel concerns, the coal sales agency was to be replaced by 1952, and the Germans would have to bring in anti-cartel legislation. Under American pressure Adenauer consented. With these problems apparently resolved, the way to signing the treaty was open. The treaty establishing the European Coal and Steel Community (ECSC) was duly signed on 18 April 1951.[30]

THE REJECTION OF THE EUROPEAN DEFENCE COMMUNITY

The summer of 1951 witnessed another French success. In June, Monnet was able to persuade Eisenhower of the virtues of the Pleven Plan. With this conversion of the Americans the situation changed drastically. It became clear to the Germans that the Americans were 'resolved to exert massive pressure on anyone who now wanted to break out of the defence community'.[31] This was a major disappointment for the Germans, who had sought to push through their preference for rearmament within a NATO framework at the Petersberg negotiations. Nevertheless there were compensations. There was genuine and widespread concern within Germany itself about rearmament. The SPD was opposed and there was a substantial protest movement which also appealed to young Catholics, who otherwise formed part of Adenauer's electoral support. By linking rearmament with a European goal Adenauer could hope to pull back some of these waverers.[32] Even more important was that Adenauer was engaged in negotiations for an end to the occupation statute and the restoration of German sovereignty. The two sets of negotiations were closely tied together. Indeed according to article 11 of the eventual General Treaty ending the occupation, the General Treaty would come into force only after the treaty establishing the Defence Community.[33] The connection between the two treaties was symbolized by the signature of the General Treaty on 26 May and the Defence Community Treaty on 27 May 1952.

The treaty which France signed on 27 May was no longer the treaty embodied in the Pleven Plan. The same fate had in many ways befallen the Schuman Plan, but this time the discrepancies between the plan and the treaty were more serious. The Pleven Plan had prescribed discrimination against Germany. It was precisely this discrimination which enabled the French government to win support from the National Assembly on 26 October 1950. The Germans, however, had stubbornly and skillfully whittled away the discriminatory character of the treaty. Towards the end of 1951 the French conceded the face-saving idea that national contributions to the army should take the form of the *groupement* of 12,000 to 15,000 men. In reality this amounted to accepting German divisions. The French had already conceded that Germany would have its own defence ministry. France even lost the battle over the shape of the Defence Community's executive. France had wanted a single Commissar, whom they intended should be French, assisted by deputies. The Germans and Italians pushed through their preference for a collegial body.[34]

Other states had also managed to change the shape of the treaty, most notably Italy. The Italians had been unenthusiastic about the Pleven Plan from the outset. They feared that the Defence Community would weaken NATO or refocus its attention on central Europe, to the neglect of the Mediterranean theatre. Just as they had worried that the 1949 debate on rearmament would lead to economic burdens which would damage economic recovery, so too they worried about the economic impact of this new organization. Under attack from domestic critics for subservience to the Americans, de Gasperi sought a way out by transforming the Defence Community into a full-blown European Political Community.[35] The stimulus for the Italian initiative came from Altiero Spinelli.

Spinelli, in classic federalist tradition, wanted the parties to create a constituent assembly which would draft a treaty establishing a political community. While Spinelli sought to commit the government in advance to the political community, the Italian government's position was somewhat weaker. Yet de Gasperi was able to persuade the other states in December 1951, despite strenuous objection from the Netherlands, to incorporate an article according to which the Assembly of the Defence Community was to draft a constitution, which might later be submitted to member governments.[36] This task was later entrusted to an *ad hoc* assembly which reported in March 1953. Not only did this Statute of the European Community prescribe a federal constitution, it also, at the insistence of the Dutch Foreign Minister Johan Beyen, dealt with economic integration. According to article 82, the Community 'shall establish progressively a common market among the Member States'.[37]

The Defence Community had turned into an extensive edifice which extended into the political and economic relations of member states and affected the commitments of non-member states. Both Britain and the United States offered new guarantees, and Britain signed a treaty with the Defence Community states on 27 May 1852. There had never been any real prospect of British membership of the Defence Community, but given this basic fact Britain did undertake quite extensive commitments, in the hope of ensuring the success of the Community and hence German rearmament.

Despite the advent of a new Conservative government in October 1951, there was little change in the basic British attitude to European integration. Britain would not commit herself to supranational integration but did not want to be wholly excluded either. In 1952 British ministers sought to resolve this dilemma by proposing that the Council of Europe be used as an overarching framework within which the Coal and Steel Community and the Defence Community could be grouped. For Foreign Minister Eden this had several advantages, including that of avoiding the 'reduplication of European bodies'.[38] A more radical strategy was suggested by Harold Macmillan. If the Defence Community did succeed, the aim should be '*to subordinate the Continental Federation to the Council of Europe rather than to subordinate the Council to the Continental Federation*'.[39] In the event that it did not, he proposed British membership of a 'European Union or Confederation organised along Commonwealth lines'.[40] The foreign Office was sympathetic to Macmillan's first point but argued that the second was implausible; the whole purpose of the six was 'to achieve European unity on federal lines'.[41] When the British proposal was put forward in the Council of Europe, on 20 March, it met with considerable sympathy. Yet others, above all Monnet, saw it as a direct challenge to the process of supranational integration. This was indeed the clear implication of Macmillan's stance, but not so much of Eden's. The Eden plan was less an insidious attempt to undermine Monnet's supranationalism than a confused attempt to reconcile the irreconcilable. As a British official put it to Monnet in August 1952, by way of recommendation of the Eden plan, 'some method must ... be found of linking together all the activities of Western European countries – whether supra-national or intergovernmental'.[42] The difficulty was in finding a way of doing this without undermining either.[43] By the end of the year it was clear that Eden's plan would not be implemented. Britain's position remained an uncomfortable one, recognizing the virtues of greater continental co-operation but worried about being wholly excluded. Within these self-imposed constraints, however, Britain had done all it could to ensure the progress of the Defence Community.

Yet all this was not enough to secure the future of the Community. The underlying problem was that France feared being locked into an arrangement with a Germany which was not only economically stronger, but which would also be militarily stronger. French military resources were being drained by her attempt to retain control of Indo-China, and the pressure worsened as more troops were withdrawn from Europe to deal with unrest in Tunisia and Morocco. France, like Britain, was being torn between empire and Europe. One solution was to ensure that French and German forces would remain balanced by restricting the number of German troops. But, as the French generals pointed out in February 1953, this would undermine western defence efforts. For France's generals the Defence Community would only 'crystalize' the discrepancy between France and Germany. They much preferred to 'dissolve' it within a NATO framework where they expected to be supported by the United States and Britain.[44]

Faced with increasing domestic opposition to a treaty which no longer seemed to serve its original purpose, French Prime Ministers sought to revise the treaty as a condition of its ratification. Their efforts were directed at two goals. First, they sought to weaken the supranational control over French forces and to extract part at least of the symbol of French statehood, its army, from the Community. The second goal was to reintroduce elements of discrimination against Germany. The first attempt, of February 1953, was largely successful. But the second, more drastic and discriminatory set of protocols, which they proposed at the August 1954 Brussels conference, met with opposition from the other states. Unable to secure his goal, the French Prime Minister submitted the treaty to the French National Assembly, which rejected it on 30 August.[45]

Alternatives had been under active consideration for some time. Adenauer speculated upon the possibility of a German–American alliance as early as October 1953 and had to be warned by General Grünther, NATO's Supreme Allied Commander in Europe (SACEUR), and Foreign Minister Dulles, that there was no alternative to the Defence Community.[46] Dulles also threatened an 'agonizing reappraisal' of American policy towards Europe if the treaty was not ratified, though the French, who were the target of this threat, were not convinced. The French General Staff, anticipating the failure of the Defence Community, favoured an enlargement of the Brussels Treaty Organization to provide a framework for German rearmament. It was indeed this option which Eden took up and campaigned for during the autumn of 1954.

Compared with the protracted deliberations over the Defence Community, Eden rapidly won support for his proposal. There was, as he warned the French, no longer an alternative to German rearmament.[47] The Paris Agreements provided for German membership of NATO and, along with Italy, of the Brussels Pact. The enlarged Brussels Pact or Western European Union was to act as a mechanism for monitoring German rearmament. Britain, as part of the price for winning agreement to Eden's alternative, had to guarantee that it would not withdraw its current forces committed to NATO command in Europe against the wishes of its Brussels Pact partners. This was a substantive commitment, though it was a commitment to the kind of intergovernmental organization which Britain favoured.

As with the Defence Community, German rearmament was tied to a restoration of German sovereignty. Ironically the Federal Republic gained more from the General Treaty of the Paris Agreements than it would have done from its 1952 predecessor. Whereas the 1952 treaty still provided for Allied rights to declare a state of emergency in Germany, this provision disappeared from the 1954 treaty. There were other improvements. The 1952 text carefully avoided the word sovereignty, conceding only that the 'Federal Republic should have full authority over its internal and external affairs'.[48] The 1954 text conceded 'the full authority of a sovereign state', though like its predecessor it specified that the Allies retained their rights 'relating to Berlin and to Germany as a whole, including the reunification of Germany and a peace settlement'.[49] This did not suffice to gain the Paris Treaties universal assent in Germany. The SPD condemned them for consolidating the division of Germany. The SPD favoured economic integration with the west but claimed that military integration was, at best, premature. The dissent was not confined to the SPD, but Adenauer prevailed and the Treaties were ratified.[50]

THE SOVIET RESPONSE TO GERMAN REARMAMENT

France was not the only country to have reservations about German rearmament. The Soviet Union had warned that the eastern bloc would have to take steps to co-ordinate its defence if German rearmament went ahead. It is notable that the Soviet Union had lived with the existence of NATO since 1949 without taking such steps. German rearmament was a different matter. Even so, there were differences of emphasis among the Soviet leadership. Molotov spoke in February 1955 about the need to 'defend socialist achievements' against 'militarism' and 'German revanchists'.[51] However, Premier Bulganin took a more moderate line. Though hostile to the Paris Agreements, he did affirm the possibility of the 'co-existence of different social systems' at the founding conference of the Warsaw Treaty Organization.[52] The treaty itself showed strong similarities to the North Atlantic Treaty, including the provision that in the event of an attack upon a member state the others would assist it with 'all the means it considers necessary'.[53] There were also notable differences. The preamble explicitly mentioned the Paris Agreements and article 11 specified that the treaty would cease in the event of the establishment of a general European security system.

There were also signs of some reluctance to fully integrate the German Democratic Republic within the system. The Democratic Republic was a signatory to the treaty, which included provision for a Joint Command in article 5. But in a communiqué issued on 14 May, the same day as the signature of the treaty, it was stated that 'The question of the participation of the German Democratic Republic in measures concerning the armed forces of the Joint Command will be examined at a later date.'[54] This led the French Foreign Office to speculate that eastern European states, namely Poland and Czechoslovakia, might have expressed strong objections to the full integration of the eastern bloc's Germans.[55] The Democratic Republic did not have to wait long, however, before it was accorded equal status. Its forces were duly integrated into the Joint Command by a decision of the Warsaw Pact in January 1956.[56]

Despite the establishment of the Warsaw Pact there was little sign that it was used to promote integration to the same extent as NATO. The Soviet Union relied instead predominantly upon bilateral treaties, signed in 1956 and 1957, which regulated the presence of Soviet forces on the territories of the eastern bloc states. In comparison the Atlantic Alliance had embarked upon a programme of integration, backed by American military aid, in the early 1950s. The Temporary Council Committee established in September 1951 carried out a review of defence requirements and assessed defence efforts in terms of percentages of GNP. Its report was accepted at the Lisbon Council meeting the following February and its practices were carried forward in a process of annual reviews.[57] Yet there were clear limits to how far this integration might go. The United States exempted itself from close examination of its defence efforts on the grounds that it already contributed 14 per cent of its GDP to defence.[58] The real obstacle, however, was that the United States would not accept the restriction of its own freedom of manoeuvre.

HISTORICAL AND STRUCTURAL OBSTACLES TO INTEGRATION IN THE EAST

The Soviet bloc also lagged behind the west in terms of economic integration. Comecon was largely dormant in the first half of the 1950s and its central organ, the Assembly, did not even meet between November 1950 and March 1954.[59] During these years the eastern European states had embarked upon a programme of forced industrialization in imitation of the Soviet model. Investment was concentrated upon the capital goods sector to such an extent that by 1953 the inadequate provision of consumer goods threatened to induce political instability. The response, facilitated by the death of Stalin in the same year, was the 'new course' which redirected production to the consumer goods sector.

This sudden switch brought with it tensions between the eastern European states with their heavily skewed patterns of trade. The problems emerged most clearly in the relation between Romania and Czechoslovakia. As the Romanians redirected some of their agricultural production to domestic consumption, Czechoslovak machinery exports were reduced. The Romanians added to the problem by trying to tie their agricultural and raw material exports to exports of their generally poor industrial goods. When the Czechoslovaks refused to accept this linkage Czechoslovak–Romanian trade deteriorated further.[60]

The Romanian attempt to artificially boost machinery exports formed part of their drive for industrialization, as did a strategy of import substitution. This drew implicit criticism from Czechoslovak commentators and the Party called, in 1956, for a study of the 'political economy of the division of labour among the countries of the socialist camp'.[61] The Romanian reply was evident in the following year. It was argued that if profitability alone guided choices about what to produce, 'a country with a weakly developed industry would find that the importation of finished products was more advantageous than their production. Such a conclusion would be tantamount to forsaking industrialization.'[62] This is the classic argument for the protection of underdeveloped economies against superior competitors. It was, of course, not new in Romania, but harked back to the use of the same arguments before the Second World War.[63] While these arguments were voiced most often and more publicly by the Romanians, they were found elsewhere. According to a Polish communist,

> Given the present structure of world prices and domestic costs, our comparative advantage lies – generally speaking – in raw materials rather than in fabricated products ... If we were guided strictly by profitability considerations ... we should increase the share of raw materials in our exports at the expense of finished products ... [but] ... This would be contrary to the long-run interests of our economic development.[64]

The pattern of economic integration in eastern Europe was further influenced by the predominance of the Soviet Union and by the problems of trading between planned economies. Soviet dominance did have some advantages, in so far as trade with the Soviet Union acted as a buffer mitigating the effect of declines in intra-east European trade. The ideological hegemony of the communist parties also inhibited the more blatant and petty forms of discrimination which had been evident in the inter-war period. But Soviet predominance also reinforced the tendency to bilateralism, which was inherent in trade between planned economies lacking convertible currencies. Concentration of trade on the Soviet Union itself in 1952 varied from 32 per cent for Poland to 58 per cent for both Romania and Bulgaria.[65]

In the years after Stalin's death some of the cruder forms of economic hegemony were dismantled. The privileged joint Soviet–east European companies established in the wake of the war were largely dissolved in 1954. The Soviet Union relaxed its control over and monopolization of Danubian transport. At the same time Soviet commentators began to emphasize the need for multilateral co-operation, at first in technical and cultural fields.[66] This new concern with integration fed through into an attempt to breathe life into Comecon. Beginning with the fourth session of the Assembly in 1954, the groundwork was laid for an attempt to co-ordinate the national plans of member states. It is unlikely that this would have succeeded, but the disruption caused by unrest in Poland and the Soviet-led invasion of Hungary in 1956 certainly helped to bury the more grandiose versions of plan co-ordination.[67] There was, however, one lasting achievement from this period. At the Seventh Assembly meeting in May 1956, Comecon transformed its temporary working groups into Standing Commissions.[68] Comecon was beginning to develop an institutional framework within which further attempts at integration could be made.

Despite the difficulties faced by the Soviet bloc, its record of economic growth, and especially its extremely high level of capital investment, looked impressive in the mid-1950s. That record worried American officials. According to one memorandum, 'the USSR will, by 1975, have overtaken Western Europe's aggregate GNP, unless political and economic decisions are made to increase its power and accelerate its growth'.[69] They added that without this growth the western world would be unable to assist the underdeveloped countries who would consequently look to the Soviet Union as a model. The conclusion was clear: 'It is in the context of these potentialities and these dangers that the form and purpose of European integration should be considered.'[70] The United States would continue to back efforts towards European integration, though, in the light of the failure of the Defence Community, it would adopt a lower profile in the future.

THE FIRST STEPS TOWARDS A CUSTOMS UNION AND AN ATOMIC ENERGY COMMUNITY

There had been little break in speculation upon further integration in western Europe. France still looked for some progress in military co-operation and suggested an armaments pool, but this met with little enthusiasm from her prospective partners.[71] One of the opponents of the armaments pool was the Netherlands' Foreign Minister Beyen, who returned to his earlier ideas of a customs union. Beyen had not acted immediately after the failure of the Defence Community, in part because he saw little point while Mendès-France remained French Prime Minister. But in February 1955 Mendès-France was replaced and the way was clear for a revival of the customs union project.

Beyen's support for a customs union reflected the dependence of the Netherlands upon foreign trade and her dissatisfaction with existing trade liberalization measures within the OEEC. The latter, confined to the removal of quantitative barriers, did not concern tariffs and excluded governments purchases.[72] The Netherlands was also concerned by Franco-German negotiations, in the autumn of 1954, about a trade and investment agreement which seemed to threaten a return to a policy of bilateralism.[73] Beyen's solution was a detailed treaty specifying an automatic progression to a customs union and a low external tariff. For Beyen this would preclude a return to the inter-war situation where economic recovery was wrecked by a retreat into protectionism. It also offered a guarantee against what he saw as the vices of sectoral integration. As he made clear in a memorandum of 4 April 1955, he believed that sectoral integration, following the model of the Coal and Steel Community, favoured the development of cartels and was inimical to the interests of consumers.[74]

Beyen's memorandum was a response to another proposal for European integration, along sectoral lines. The sectoral or functionalist approach was still very much in favour. It enjoyed the support of Monnet and the Americans, as well as the Assembly of the Coal and Steel Community, which had called for an extension of the High Authority's competence to cover gas, electricity, transport and atomic energy. Atomic energy seemed particularly promising to Monnet. In April 1955 his colleague on the High Authority, Albert Coppe, assured the Americans that it 'would identify the community with the power of the future and capture the public imagination'.[75] By July the Americans were sufficiently persuaded to discourage alternative plans to use the OEEC as a framework for co-operation in atomic energy. They also saw an opportunity for the United States to act as an 'outside catalyst' by supporting integration in this field. After all, an external stimulus had worked in the past with the creation of the OEEC, NATO and the WEU. Moreover, there were 'few vested interests' in the new field of atomic energy and hence, it seemed, fewer obstacles to overcome.[76]

Monnet had been able to persuade Spaak to take up the idea of sectoral integration with the result that Spaak and Beyen emerged as the leading advocates of divergent approaches to European integration. When the Benelux states were presented with these proposals they avoided the difficulty of choosing between them by the simple expedient of forwarding both to the Council of Ministers of the Coal and Steel Community on 18 May 1955. When the Ministers met, at Messina, at the beginning of June, they were no more able to resolve the problem than the Benelux states. They did manage to agree to create a study group which would produce a report on everything from the 'better co-ordination of air transport', to 'a common organization which would have the responsibility and the facilities for ensuring the peaceful development of nuclear energy', and 'a common European market, free from all customs duties and all quantitative restrictions'.[77] It was subsequently agreed that the study group should be chaired by Spaak.

The Messina resolution had been drafted in haste and, as the French Foreign Office recalled, did not commit the governments to anything.[78] French reservations, though stronger than those of the others, were understandable. The disparities between the partners were substantial and the precise shape of any further integration was still undecided. Differences existed not only between states but, with equal if not greater vehemence, within the foreign policy establishments of the various countries. The two central questions were whether or not to continue along the functional road to integration and whether or not to enter into a customs union.

In Germany Ludwig Erhard answered no to both questions. He had spoken against any extension of the type of integration embodied in the Coal and Steel Community, with the backing of German industry. Erhard, as an economic liberal, was suspicious of the *dirigiste* tendencies of the High Authority. His antipathy to sectoral integration with strong supranational authorities was shared by Italian industry. According to the French Ambassador, a paper which voiced the concerns of Confindustria opposed 'sectoral integration and the multiplication of specialised supranational authorities . . . In the place of a Europe of nation states . . . [such integration] . . . would substitute, not a united Europe, but a series of fiefdoms dominated by technocrats and planners.'[79] Erhard's economic liberalism also led him to prefer global liberalization, by means of intergovernmental co-operation, with an emphasis upon the convertibility of currencies.

Somewhat confusingly, Erhard and his allies were labelled 'functionalists', on account of this emphasis upon global intergovernmental co-operation, while his opponents were designated 'institutionalists', on account of their preference for sectoral integration under the aegis of supranational authorities.[80] While the terminology, rooted in the ambiguity of the idea of functionalist integration, was confusing, the conflict of policy preferences was clear enough.[81] It was only with considerable difficulty that German ministers and officials were able to agree upon a joint approach. At a meeting of 22 May they agreed upon support for a customs union, largely because customs unions were compatible with the global trading regime as defined by GATT. The resulting German memorandum also supported the Benelux proposals for further sectoral integration. Erhard's consent to a customs union had been hesitant. His underlying antipathy would later break through.[82]

The French establishment was no less divided, even if the tone of their disputes lacked the doctrinal flavour evident in Germany. The Foreign Ministry tended to favour increasing European trade while at the same time continuing France's preferential trading regime with her overseas territories. The economic argument, that France would profit from trade with complementary economies, was bolstered by a grander vision of Eurafrican co-operation. Here the key role would be played by an international bank which would finance the development of Africa.[83] The initial reaction of the Foreign Ministry was consequently hostile. After listing a series of specific obstacles, a memorandum of 18 May 1955 concluded that it would be better to warn France's neighbours that she was not ready to enter a common market.[84] There were, however, countervailing opinions which were gaining strength in 1955 as France continued to enjoy a balance of payments surplus.[85]

LINKAGE BETWEEN THE EUROPEAN ECONOMIC COMMUNITY AND EURATOM

More important at the beginning, however, was the link which was established between the common market and co-operation in the field of atomic energy. Atomic energy was seen as the fuel of the future. There was no doubt that France had to develop an atomic industry; any country which did not would soon become 'underdeveloped', since it would be deprived both of a vital energy source and the associated technical and scientific developments.[86] Equally important was France's relationship to Germany in this field. It was true, the French argued, that Germany lagged far behind France in atomic energy. But Germany possessed a reservoir of scientists and a 'remarkable chemical industry' which would facilitate rapid development. Faced with this prospect, France's officials invoked the arguments which they said lay at the beginning of European political integration: the need to control Germany without discriminating against her, the economic and technical advantages of co-operation and the grand gesture furthering the unification of Europe.[87]Against this background, the Committee of National Defence authorized the Minister of Foreign Affairs, on 30 March 1955, to enter into negotiations for a European atomic energy organization.

Out of the package of proposals embodied in the Messina resolution, covering several areas of sectoral integration and the idea of a common market, only atomic energy and the common market emerged as viable steps forward. The nature of each, and the link between them, remained disputed. France made some concessions in a memorandum to the other government on 14 October 1955, but added a substantial list of qualifications. Among the most important of the latter was the suggestion that there should be an initial stage during which customs duties would be reduced in steps by a total of 30 per cent. At the end of this the governments would consider how to proceed further in the light of a report to be prepared by a 'common magistracy' of independent personalities. During this first stage they would begin to implement measures to bring about equal pay between men and women, to harmonize the length of the working week and the number of paid holidays. The memorandum also called for a substantial investment and readaptation fund and the right to reintroduce duties if faced with a balance of payments crisis.

The reference to a harmonization of the costs of labour became a favourite theme of French negotiation and was not resolved for another year. French concerns centred around their supposed lack of competitiveness because France had adopted more generous social provisions than her neighbours. It was, however, far from clear that France was disadvantaged in this way. The government authorized or received several studies on the competitiveness of the French economy during this period, though it is doubtful if they were of much help. The conclusions and methods were too diverse to indicate a clear judgement.[88] Nevertheless, France sought to make progress towards a customs union dependent upon harmonization of these social charges, and upon a subsequent intergovernmental agreement at the end of the first stage.

These reservations struck at the heart of Beyen's plan for a customs union. For Beyen the vital point was that there should be an automatic progression from one stage to another, culminating in a full customs union. Automatic progression was important, because without it there was a risk that the reduction of tariffs would be stalled. The member states would then be left with lower tariffs between themselves, but far short of free trade, and no common tariff. In fact they would be operating a simple preferential system. As a French memorandum recognized, that would be unacceptable to other European countries, to the United States and to Canada.[89]

Not long after the French memorandum, one clear decision was reached: Britain would not join. Britain had participated in the Spaak committee, but in the internal debate the same arguments used at the time of the Schuman Plan were rehearsed. Entry into the common market would weaken ties with the Commonwealth and the wider world, might lead to politically unacceptable federalism and would expose British industry to competition.[90] The Permanent Secretary to the Treasury regretted that Britain had ever been involved in the negotiations and warned that 'we must not let ourselves be misled by the kind of mysticism which appeals to European catholic federalists and occasionally – I fear – to our Foreign Secretary'.[91] He had no cause for concern. Foreign Secretary Macmillan was occupied with other matters and his fellow ministers were disinterested or opposed. On 7 November, Spaak forced the issue by asking for a declaration of commitment. The British representative was unable to give one.

There was one substantial difference between the Schuman Plan negotiations and the common market negotiations. This time the British government sought to push through an alternative. It was agreed in November that Britain should suggest the creation of a free trade area embracing the OEEC countries. Speculation on this culminated in a sharp response from Beyen and Spaak at a meeting of the Western European Union Council on 14 December 1955. Macmillan had only succeeded in antagonizing his colleagues. Britain did not give up the idea, partly because of a persistent belief that the free trade area had a strong appeal to elements of the German cabinet, especially Erhard. Erhard was indeed interested. Erhard's sniping at the idea of a customs union among the six had induced Ophüls of the Foreign Ministry to ask for a clear ruling on policy as early as July 1955. It was not, however, until January of the following year that Adenauer finally moved. On 19 January he formally wrote to his ministers invoking his constitutional authority to set the guidelines of government policy. In fact Erhard continued to snipe, but he could do little more so long as Adenauer remained committed to integration among the six.[92]

Despite reservations on all sides, the Spaak report was finally completed and officially released on 21 April 1956. The French Foreign Ministry complained that on almost every point the Spaak report's recommendations diverged from French demands, as set out in their memorandum of October 1955. The report clearly defined not just the first stage of tariff reduction but the entire process, it did not make social harmonization obligatory, it went beyond the OEEC programme for the abolition of quantitative restrictions, it did not allow for the unilateral implementation of safeguard clauses, and it had produced recommendations for an institutional framework that were modelled on the Coal and Steel Community.[93] The Spaak report was animated by a vision of growth and integration through competition which was explicitly justified by reference to the virtues of the United States. It was a vision with which Robert Marjolin, an adviser to the new Foreign Minister, Christian Pineau, agreed. But when he spoke in favour of the report at an interdepartmental meeting he met, as he recalled, with an 'icy reception'.[94] The French foreign policy establishment was far from convinced and promptly set about reasserting its original position.

France was much happier with the report's recommendations for atomic energy, especially its silence on the use of atomic energy for military purposes.[95] This had been a prime aim for France all along. For France, atomic weapons were 'the right of entry into the club of the great [powers]'.[96] Pressure for a commitment to purely peaceful uses had come from Monnet and the public statements of his Action Committee. The United States, which was in a position to supply the Europeans with vital raw materials and technical knowledge, was sympathetic to Monnet's goals but was also wary of exerting public pressure, lest this induce a wave of anti-American sentiment.[97]

The advantages of Euratom and the risks entailed in the common market induced Pineau to suggest that the six proceed to sign the Euratom treaty before the common market treaty. The Germans, however, feared that if France succeeded in obtaining integration of atomic energy first, it would allow the negotiations on the common market to stagnate. In order to exclude this possibility, the cabinet agreed, on 9 May 1956, that the two treaties were tied together.[98] The linkage was reaffirmed when the ministers met in Venice at the end of May to consider the Spaak report. Hallstein, Beyen, Gaetano Martino and Joseph Bech all insisted that the two treaties were bound together. France would return to the idea of giving priority to Euratom, but the resolve of the others was clear enough at Venice. France was still seeking satisfaction on the harmonization of social costs, on the inclusion of overseas territories and weakening the automatic progression towards a customs union. The others were opposed in varying degrees, the Netherlands being the most resolute. Despite these strong differences, the parties agreed to enter into formal negotiations which began on the 26 June.

They were soon complicated by developments beyond the territories of the six. In July, in response to British initiatives, the Secretary General of the OEEC formally put forward the idea of a free trade area which would encompass the customs union of the six within a wider framework. Britain still doubted that the common market negotiations would succeed and did not feel herself to be under great pressure. Erhard, of course, was pleased by the initiative and hoped to bring the six back from what he described as an 'exaggerated conception' to a more pragmatic course.[99] While the mood in Britain was still calm, Adenauer was alarmed, but not by the free trade area proposals. In June *The New York Times* reported that Admiral Radford had suggested substantial withdrawal of American troops from Europe. Even when Secretary of State Dulles offered assurances of American commitment, Adenauer remained suspicious. Fearful that he might be abandoned by the United States, Adenauer was receptive to French suggestions of the need for closer European defence cooperation. It was against this background that Adenauer was tempted by Monnet's suggestions, on 12 September, that they should go ahead with the Euratom treaty. It was only with difficulty that von der Groeben,

Hallstein and Etzel were able to hold Adenauer to the line agreed on 9 May.[100]

FROM A NEGOTIATING CRISIS TO THE ROME TREATIES

The following month the negotiations among the six were in crisis. The negotiations on Euratom were making progress, though even here there were outstanding problems. The French wanted the community to be the owner of all fissile material and to exclude private ownership. Minister Franz-Joseph Strauss and German industry saw this as a device to control German industry. Strauss declared that for Germany it was 'radically unacceptable'. The French pointed to the American and British practice of excluding private ownership, but Strauss replied that the analogy was irrelevant. Their insistence upon public ownership reflected the priority they gave to military uses of atomic energy, whereas Germany had renounced atomic weapons.[101]

The crisis, however, concerned the common market. The main stumbling-block was the old French demand for the harmonization of social costs. Marjolin was not convinced of its importance and described this 'sacred cow' of the French negotiating position as 'nonsense'.[102] Nevertheless, it had become a point of principle for the French. But both sides were looking for a way of breaking the impasse. The inevitable compromise took place amidst the tensions caused by the Anglo-French landings in Egypt, as part of the response to the Egyptian nationalization of the Suez canal. At a meeting between Mollet and Adenauer the French were relieved to find that Adenauer was prepared to satisfy their demands for harmonization 'in principle'.[103] The outcome of their agreement, as refined in subsequent negotiations, was that by article 119 of the treaty establishing the European Economic Community the states committed themselves to ensuring 'that men and women would receive equal pay for equal work'.[104] On another demand, concerning the length of paid holidays, the experts had decided that the difference between the states was less than previously thought, so the treaty could merely confirm 'the existing equivalence between paid holiday schemes'.[105] That left French concern about the length of the working week and the associated extent of overtime pay. This issue was resolved by a protocol, which allowed France to invoke safeguards if overtime hours and pay did not approximate French standards by the end of the first stage. Although Erhard protested that this was economic nonsense, in retrospect the issues hardly look substantive with the exception of the idea of equal pay, which was the least contentious. However, as the economic historian A. S. Milward has emphasized, the underlying concern, that the treaty should not endanger the postwar consensus on the welfare state, was important.[106] Yet, at the end of the day, the social provisions of the treaty were minimal. The French had accepted the idea, as Foreign Minister Pineau recorded on 8 November, that '[t]he equalization of living standards and condition of work will be assured in time by the operation of the common market itself . . .'[107]

With the breakthrough on harmonization, work could resume. The Euratom treaty was nearing completion, but was losing some of its attraction for France. The French had begun the process of weakening the treaty themselves, by insisting upon their right to utilize atomic material for military purposes.[108] The controversial issue of ownership was settled late in the day, at the Brussels conference in February 1957. The community would own special fissile material but 'member states, persons or undertakings shall have unlimited right of use and consumption' subject only to safety considerations.[109] By then it was clear to the French that there was little prospect that the community would support an isotope separator, which had been one of the 'principal attractions of Euratom' for France.[110] Equally significant was the admission that Euratom would not be a major instrument of European integration. The reason 'is not to be found in the inadequacies of the treaty but in the fact that nuclear energy does not play an economic role which allows it to bear forth a major political idea'.[111] The idea of Europeans united around a vision of the brave new world of atomic energy had evaporated even before the treaty was signed.

About the same time as the French Foreign Ministry drew these disappointing conclusions about Euratom, it also took stock of the common market treaty. The treaty, it noted, had been conceived along a 'strictly liberal perspective'.[112] It noted that this was not the only conceivable road to integration. Integration could have been pursued along the lines of an 'essentially organic plan'. By this was meant a co-ordination of economic and financial policy as well as commercial policy, state intervention and planning.[113] It was this alternative vision of European integration that was held up by the critics of the treaties like Mendès-France. In the preliminary National Assembly debates on the common market treaty in January 1957 he put forward a vision of integration built around the activities of a European Investment Bank, which would, he claimed, avoid the damaging growth of regional disparities that would be the outcome of the treaty. The problem of regional disparities had been raised from the outset by the Italians. Pointing to Italy's own experience in the 1860s and to the experience of the United States after their civil war, they argued for extensive public investment to offset the trend towards divergence.[114] The treaty which emerged, however, trusted in the market and economic growth, which, it was assumed, would percolate through the regions.[115] There was to be a European Investment Bank, but not of the kind desired by Mendès-France. At German insistence, its financial resources and scope of action had been carefully defined and limited.

An essentially liberal conception of the rules of economic competition was also forced through by the combined efforts of the German and Dutch negotiators against French resistance. There was, however, an interesting difference between the competition rules enshrined in the Treaty of Paris of 1951 and the common market treaty. Whereas the former, according to article 66, required the 'prior authorization' of any 'concentration between undertakings', the latter, in article 86, merely forbade the 'abuse ... of a dominant position within the common market'.[116]

Before the treaty could be signed there were two more major disputes which had to be resolved: the issue of overseas territories and the decision-making mechanisms of the community. Neither was settled until 1957. Agreement on the overseas territories was finally reached in February. The key lay in agreement to a programme of investment in the overseas territories of member states. This meant primarily Belgian and especially French territories. Of the total of 581 million units of account, of which France and Germany were to supply 200 million each, French territories alone were to receive 511 million. France had attained a major goal. Unable to finance modernization programmes in her overseas territories, France was desperate to obtain European, and especially German, support. It was a price Adenauer was willing to pay.[117]

Agreement on the decision-making mechanisms was also reached in February. There was considerable difficulty in reconciling the French preference for intergovernmental mechanisms and the Dutch insistence upon more federalist procedures. Clarity was not aided by the fact that the German negotiators were divided. The outcome was a complex variety of decision-making procedures which varied according to the particular task at issue. The general principle was that the Council of Ministers could decide by majority only where the treaty specified that the Council could act only on a proposal from the Commission. Where the Council did not require a Commission proposal, either unanimity or a special qualified majority was required.[118] As the French Foreign Ministry had observed on an earlier set of compromises concerning the relative powers of the community's institutions and member states, the compromise greatly improved the prospects of the ratification of the treaty. At the same time, it was quite possible that those same compromises would prejudice the successful application of the treaty in the future.[119]

With the remaining compromises in place the treaties were signed at Rome on 25 March 1957. Quite what the implication of these treaties would be was far from certain. The public impact of what was to be seen as a momentous step forward was hardly reassuring. Even among the most enthusiastic nation, Germany, only 64 per cent of respondents to a questionnaire had heard of the common market and only 52 per cent were certain that the Federal Republic was a member.[120] It was now clear, at least to the initiated, that it was the European Economic Community rather than Euratom that was the decisive forum of integration. That the customs union, which formed the core of the Economic Community, would bring great benefits was something its advocates assumed without any detailed quantitative study. When such studies were conducted in the early 1960s the consensus among economists was that the direct benefits brought by the customs union were rather minimal.[121] Much depended upon the rate of the external tariff which the Economic Community was to establish. In principle the norm was to be the mean of existing tariffs in force on 1 January 1957. American businessmen, who had looked on inter-war proposals with great suspicion, were sanguine. They did expect their exports to be disadvantaged, but there were compensations. According to a report drafted for the Secretary of State for Economic Affairs, 'The prospect of a high income market of over 250 million people unimpeded by internal trade barriers and surrounded by barriers against outsiders is apparently looked upon as a juicy opportunity for direct investment abroad by U.S. manufacturers.'[122]

The United States was also concerned by the continued complexity of Europe's institutional architecture, and especially by repeated British initiatives. The latest of these was the Grand Design of Foreign Minister Selwyn Lloyd for a common parliamentary body for Europe's various institutions. The initiative succeeded in irritating Spaak, while the Americans response was more nuanced, but clearly concerned by the British 'tendency [to] blur [the] vital distinction between merely cooperative arrangements (OEEC) and genuine integration'.[123] Selwyn Lloyd's Grand Design made little progress, but British pressure through the OEEC for a European free trade area was more difficult to resist.

THE FREE TRADE AREA DEBATE

The British case was aided by the fact that the OEEC working party on a free trade area reported, in January 1957, that it was 'technically possible' to establish a free trade area which would also embrace the customs union of the six.[124] Although the moment was not opportune, in the light of the irritation already caused by Selwyn Lloyd's Grand Design, the British government took the initiative in a memorandum of February 1957. The memorandum explained that Britain could not contemplate entering a customs union, since this would have adverse effect upon imports from the Commonwealth. Instead, she proposed a free trade area which would reduce and eventually eliminate tariffs on industrial goods. Foodstuffs were not to be included, in part because of British desire to maintain preferential arrangements with the Commonwealth.[125]

Despite considerable criticism of Britain's desire to keep the benefits of Commonwealth preferences, while enjoying the advantages of European free trade, the OEEC Council agreed to further studies. With the success of the Rome treaties as a spur, the British governments began to push harder, and to make some concessions. Prime Minister Macmillan was ready to consider a Council of Ministers with majority voting, at least in some areas. In October, Maudling, who had been appointed Special Minister for the free trade zone, even conceded that there would have to be some special arrangement including agriculture. With these concessions, the others agreed, in October 1957, to set up an Intergovernmental Committee which elected Maudling as chairman.[126]

The French response came in February 1958, in a memorandum putting forward a host of conditions which were unacceptable to Britain, and to many members of the six. France insisted that tariff reduction be preceded by social harmonization, that there should be different timetables for different industrial sectors, that Commonwealth preferences were to be excluded, and that unanimity would be required during the transitional phase. On many of these issues France was refusing to make the kind of concessions it had already made in the common market. A compromise proposal was made by the Italian Minister Carli which involved a certain harmonization of external tariffs along with compensatory taxes when tariffs diverged by a given percentage. For the British, however, this looked too much like a customs union for comfort.

The underlying divergence of conception emerged in the protracted dispute over rules of origin. The French argued that third parties could gain an unfair advantage by exporting to member states with a low external tariff, and then transhipping the goods to member states with higher external tariffs. The British countered that this could be avoided by rules of origin which would exclude such goods from the free trade regime. Differences arose over the operation of such rules. For France, they were acceptable only if they acted as a temporary substitute for a common external tariff which substantially discriminated in favour of trade among member states. For the German liberals around Erhard, however, loose rules of origin were quite acceptable, since high tariff countries would be under pressure to lower their tariffs. In a sense both the French and the German liberals wanted the same thing, tariff harmonization, but the crucial difference was that while the liberals wanted harmonization around a low, non-discriminatory tariff, the French wanted to discriminate.[127]

In the end France was able to push other members of the six into adopting a hard line, as the price for agreeing upon a common position at all. But there was no genuine consensus among the six, let alone among the OEEC states as a whole. Desperate to save the negotiations, Erhard proposed to go to Paris himself and asked Adenauer to put pressure on the French. In a strongly worded letter the Chancellor declared Erhard's visit was 'absolutely impossible'.[128] The following day, on 14 November 1958, the French Information Minister Jacques Soustelle declared that the British idea of a free trade zone was unacceptable. The British took this as the occasion to suspend the negotiations, though Soustelle, strictly speaking, had not said anything new. In reality France was opposed to any kind of free trade zone, not because of concern about competition from third parties, but for fear of competition within the free trade area.[129]

One of the casualties of the collapse of the free trade area negotiations was the idea of a Nordic customs union. The Scandinavian states hoped to boost their still underdeveloped manufacturing industries by means of a customs union while continuing their traditional exports, especially to the United Kingdom, under the aegis of the free trade area.[130] They had appointed a committee to study a customs union in 1954 whose final report appeared in October 1957. A year later, with the collapse of the free trade area negotiations, the Nordic customs union was shelved as Sweden and Norway, followed by a more ambivalent Denmark, sought to salvage something from the wreckage. The Swedish Minister Gunnar Lange was one of the first to suggest a free trade area among the seven as an alternative. Swedish and British industrial associations added their voices in support of the idea. The ensuing negotiations began in earnest in March 1959, and by July Ministers were able to agree the basic text of a treaty. In accordance with the original British idea, it was to be a free trade area for industrial goods, though concessions had to be made to Portuguese and Norwegian fishing interests and to Danish bacon exporters.[131] It was far from being the first choice of any of the members, and its precarious nature was evident in article 42, which permitted member states to withdraw from the Association on twelve months' notice. The European Free Trade Association was essentially an intergovernmental organization dominated by a Council of Ministers which operated mainly by unanimity. Whereas the Economic Community was a juridical body whose law could be enforced by a Court of Justice, the Free Trade

Association could only resort to retaliation in the event that member states failed to abide by their obligations.[132]

OBSTACLES TO INTEGRATION IN THE EAST

The Soviet Union promptly proclaimed that the formation of the Free Trade Association was proof of their argument that western European integration was impossible.[133] Yet efforts to cement integration in the eastern bloc, though seen as increasingly urgent, were proving equally difficult. After the disruption of 1956, Moscow was reasserting its hegemony. In November of 1957 a conference of communist parties proclaimed the leading role of the Soviet Union, and in the following year there was a renewed burst of forced industrialization and collectivization of land.[134] But there was no intention of returning to the autarkic policies of the first phase of industrialization. As Khrushchev explained,

> Capitalist experts have found out that it is mass production which renders production cheap and economic. We Marxists, too, have to see the importance of this problem. The sooner and the better we develop the division of labour between our countries, the greater our economies will be.[135]

In the preceding month, June 1957, the Eighth Comecon session had increased the number of Standing Commissions and called for the adoption of ten- to fifteen-year plans for some industrial sectors. The Eighth session also agreed to introduce a multilateral clearing system, which was to be operated by the Soviet State Bank in Moscow, in an attempt to overcome the obstacles to trade posed by the lack of convertible currencies. Later in the same year the Standing Commission on Foreign Trade drew up a set of conditions governing the sale and delivery of goods. These efforts were, however, only partially successful. The clearing system was a failure, with, for example, only 1.5 per cent of Bulgaria's trade being cleared multilaterally over the next four years.[136]

Part of the problem lay in the diversity of prices within the bloc. It was this problem which the Comecon sought to resolve in June 1958 with the Bucharest Price Principle. This principle was really a set of guidelines for deriving the foreign trade prices for intra-Comecon trade from prevailing world market prices. The latter were judged to be distorted by the inequities of capitalism, including the existence of monopolies and imperialistic practices. The reality was that the guidelines still left substantial scope for bilateral haggling, which continued to prevail. Despite this freedom of manoeuvre some members of the Comecon were far from happy with the arrangement. Echoing the arguments of the inter-war economist M. Manoilescu, a Romanian communist claimed that

> Countries that have a centuries-old lead in developing skills and in raising their labour productivity are in a favourable position because they do not have to sell at prices below world market values and are able therefore to export goods whose international value exceeds their national value. In underdeveloped countries, on the other hand, national value is in excess of international value.[137]

The conclusion was clear. Romania was being systematically disadvantaged.

After this outburst the Romanians were relatively quiet. According to the economist Montias, the reason was probably that they were seeking to extract credits from the Soviet Union to help with their ambitious plans for the development of the chemical and steel industries. In both cases they were to be bitterly disappointed.[138] Romania did, however, have an alternative. Ironically, because of her raw-material resources she was able to obtain some of the materials from the west, in return for directing her valuable raw materials away from the Soviet Union. The consequence was that the Soviet share of Romanian trade dropped from 51.5 per cent in 1958 to 41 per cent in 1961.[139]

Romania was more successful in extracting concessions in another field. Just over a year after signing an agreement on the stationing of Soviet troops in Romania, the Romanians managed to persuade the Soviet Union, in May 1958, to withdraw. This may well have been in exchange for Romanian agreement to further integration in Comecon. There were three sessions of the Comecon Council in 1958, the last of which saw agreement on the construction of the 'friendship' pipeline to supply the eastern bloc with Soviet oil. In 1959 the pace continued with a further two sessions, including the Twelfth, in December 1959, which agreed upon, and published, the Council's Charter. The Polish representative, Jaroszewicz, proclaimed that 'The publication of the Council's Charter ... puts an end once and for all to the speculations of certain foreign economic circles about the alleged supranational character of the Council.'[140]

Jaroszewicz's denial did not put an end to such speculation, but his claim about the principles of the Charter was accurate. Article 1 bluntly affirmed that 'The Council is based on the principle of the sovereign equality of all member-countries.'[141] The Charter provided for making 'decisions on procedural matters, which were binding on member states, and 'recommendations' on economic co-operation which had to be ratified by members 'in conformity with their respective national legislatures'.[142] But in both cases members could declare their disinterest and were in no way bound by any subsequent decision or recommendation. The Charter was no more supranational than the Convention establishing the Organization for European Economic Co-operation, and less so than the Council of Europe.[143]

Integration in the east could not, of course, be implemented by the same methods as in the west. Tariff barriers did not have the same significance, given the absence of convertible currencies and the existence of planned economies. Integration in the east could be advanced only by either the co-ordination of economic plans or agreements on product specialization. In some ways this made integration in the east more difficult in principle. Governments could not divest themselves of responsibility for economic outcomes by leaving decisions to a hopefully benign common market. The political origin and significance of economic outcomes was blatant.

OBSTACLES TO ATLANTIC INTEGRATION

Both east and west, despite – or rather precisely because of – the division of Europe, were bound together, especially in their common concern about the fate of Germany. Proposed solutions came from each side. All of them foundered upon the entwinement of the German question with broader considerations of security. The British Prime Minister, Eden, initiated a round of proposals with his suggestion for the unification of Germany and a security pact at the Geneva summit of July 1955.[144] George Kennan added fuel to the fire with his call for military disengagement and the neutralization of Germany in 1957, the same year in which the Polish Foreign Minister, Adam Rapacki, put forward the first version of his proposal for starting with a nuclear-free zone embracing both German states, Poland and Czechoslovakia.[145] The complications and risks entailed by these ideas were spelled out forcefully by the Secretary General of NATO, Spaak, in the following year. Disengagement, he said, was out of the question because it would lead to an American withdrawal from Europe.[146] The neutralization of Germany appealed to neither Spaak nor the United States. According to Secretary of State Dulles, neutralization 'would leave Germany free to blackmail both sides'.[147] The only acceptable solution was to continue to tie Germany into the west. The full ramifications of the German question had, surprisingly, been underestimated by Kennan in 1957. He later recalled that

> I quite failed to realize ... the intensity of the fear that the spectre of a reunited Germany aroused in Western countries, the depth of the attachment there to the programs already evolved for uniting Western Germany economically with the rest of Western Europe and militarily with the

> Atlantic Community . . . This was a project that assumed the continuation of a divided continent . . . [148]

The Atlantic Community to which Kennan referred was the defence alliance, cemented by an integrated command structure, into which the North Atlantic Treaty had grown. For some it ought to have been much more, for others it was already too much. Among the former the publicist George Catlin called unequivocally for an Atlantic union bolstered by the 'Atlantic Economic Area' and a level of integration equal to that achieved in Europe.[149] In 1959, the year in which Catlin renewed his call for Atlantic union, there was indeed growing advocacy of transatlantic economic co-operation, often in the form of a remodelled OEEC.[150]

Pressure had come earlier for strengthened political consultation within the Atlantic Alliance. The dilemmas this involved emerged clearly in meetings between Dulles and the Federal Republic's Foreign Secretary, von Brentano, in 1957. Von Brentano was worried by a growing sentiment that the alliance was actually 'disintegrating', and wanted more rigorous political consultation, but at the same time he conceded that he did not want to inhibit the United States' freedom of action. For the United States, Dulles expressed similar sentiments. The problem, he noted, was that 'We cannot pool all of our sovereignties and work as a single unit but must find a way to concert our efforts within the limits inherent in the situation.'[151] The North Atlantic Council had already commissioned a report by Three Wise Men on precisely this issue, which had been approved in December 1956 but signally failed to solve the problem.[152] The problem was indeed insoluble, both because of the character of the organization and the unequal distribution of forces within it. The United States, as the guarantor of western security and pre-eminent nuclear power, claimed a right to act as it saw fit. But that claim raised doubts in the minds of her allies, both about American willingness to stand firmly by the Europeans, and about the consequences of American initiatives of which they might have little forewarning. The problem, grounded in the realities of military power, was also enshrined in the North Atlantic Treaty. As the Americans noted in July 1959, the treaty 'creates a framework within which sovereign nations unite for the common defense. NATO is thus an alliance of sovereign nations, and is not a supranational organization.'[153]

While the lack of integration worried many members of the alliance, General de Gaulle was concerned that NATO was in fact already a supranational organization. He was even more concerned by what he saw as France's inferior status *vis-à-vis* the Anglo-Saxons. It was this that led to his memorandum of September 1958, in which he called for a triumvirate of the United States, Britain and France which would deal not just with the North Atlantic area but global security issues as well.[154] As a French diplomat later conceded, de Gaulle was looking for something similar to the relationship between the wartime big three. For de Gaulle it was a matter of the status of France. Existing arrangements did not take into account the 'rebirth of France, her ability now to play a greater role in the world'.[155]

Although anxious not to offend de Gaulle's sensitivities, the United States had no intention of acceding to his suggestions. Nor, of course, were the other members of the alliance especially pleased by the idea. But as de Gaulle's vision of a triumvirate ran into opposition, so his suspicions of the alliance grew stronger. After a dispute over the technicalities of NATO's command structure, France withdrew her naval forces in the Mediterranean from NATO. In the note confirming the French decision, priority was given to France's 'own national tasks', which were said to be also 'of prime importance for the Alliance as a whole'.[156] De Gaulle drew a similar distinction at the beginning of the following year. In a conversation with General Norstad about a co-ordinated air defence system de Gaulle explained that

> The French were willing to give all the means and forces in this forward area for the battle in Germany, but if this battle were lost, the countries of Europe, France and Great Britain would still have to defend themselves. The first battle in Germany would be integrated and the second would not ... They must preserve the national entity; and that was all.[157]

De Gaulle's position in 1960 was rather similar to the conditions which France had sought to impose on the eve of the rejection of the European Defence Community: only those forces in the forward area, that is Germany, would form part of an integrated defence. De Gaulle was expressing a traditional French position, but from a more consistent standpoint and with much greater sensitivity to the symbolic status of his country.

At the same time as de Gaulle set limits to the alliance, others were pressing for even greater Atlantic integration. One dimension under consideration was economic co-operation. There was interest on both sides of the Atlantic in reshaping the OEEC, in order to try to bridge the gap between the six of the European Community and the seven of the imminent Free Trade Area. Britain was especially enthusiastic about this possibility, but the gap between the six and seven was too large. There were also limits to the commitment of the United States. She would act as a sponsor to talks between the Europeans, but an Atlantic free trade area, as favoured by some in Britain, was out of the question.[158] In the end the OEEC was remodelled, becoming the Organisation for Economic Co-operation and Development in 1960. The new body included the United

States and Canada but was not a forum for Atlantic integration. Instead, the OEEC's successor was orientated in large part to the underdeveloped world.

By the beginning of the 1960s the institutional unity of Europe had made remarkable progress, but so too had its fragmentation. Europe had developed a complex set of institutional arrangements which brought together parts of Europe at the expense of excluding others and tied European states to extra-European powers. As early as May 1951 this had led Dirk Stikker to hope that he might see some simplification of the 'architectural style of the House of Europe'.[159] His hope was disappointed. Although the rhetoric of Europe's architecture did not become widespread until much later, the problems posed by it were already evident in the 1950s.

NOTES

1. Hence Kurt Schumacher's claim that 'If we silently tolerate that [the separation of the Saar] in the west then we lose the juridical, moral, and in part also the political ground in our struggle to win back the territories east of the Oder–Neisse line'; quoted in Rudolf Hrbek, *Die SPD–Deutschland und Europa* (Bonn, 1972), p. 108.
2. *Akten zur Auswärtigen Politik der Bundesrepublik Deutschland. Adenauer und die Hohen Kommissare 1949–1951*, Vol. 1, doc. 9. The tension surrounding these events is admirably conveyed by Herbst, *Option für den Westen*, pp. 11–34.
3. Quoted in Pascal Fontaine, *Europe – A Fresh Start. The Schuman Declaration 1950–1990* (Luxembourg, 1990), p. 44.
4. *Akten zur Auswärtigen Politik der Bundesrepublik Deutschland. Adenauer und die Hohen Kommissare 1949–1951*, Vol. 1, doc. 13; 'Konrad Adenauer und der Schuman-Plan. Ein Quellenzeugnis', in K. Schwabe (ed.), *Die Anfänge des Schuman-Plans 1950/51* (Baden-Baden, 1988), p. 137.
5. R. Vaughan (ed.), *Postwar Integration in Europe* (London, 1976), p. 53.
6. *Ibid.*, p. 53. The role of Jean Monnet has proved contentious. While some accounts do border on hagiography, critics have argued that the national interests of France played a greater role than considerations of European unity. According to Milward, *The Reconstruction of Western Europe*, p. 340, 'The Schuman Plan was invented to safeguard the Monnet Plan.' F. M. B. Lynch, 'Resolving the paradox of the Monnet plan', *Economic History Review*, **37** (1984), p. 242, writes of 'couching the plan in the rhetoric of European integration, so dear to the Americans'. Such assessments are, however, exaggerated and difficult to reconcile with Monnet's persistent enthusiasm for European integration.
7. *Documents on British Policy Overseas* (hereafter *DBPO*), Series 2, Vol. 1, doc. 3 (10 May 1950). For the development of British attitudes, see Roger Bullen, 'The British government and the Schuman Plan May 1950–March 1951', in Schwabe (ed.), *Die Anfänge des Schuman-Plans*, pp. 199–210.
8. *DBPO*, Series 2, Vol. 1, doc. 18 (11 May 1950).
9. *Ibid.*, doc. 75 (2 June 1950).
10. Labour Party, *European Union* (London, 1950), p. 4.

11. *Ibid.*, pp. 7 and 9. For reactions to this document, see Warner, 'Die Britische Labour-Regierung und die Einheit Westeuropas 1949–1951', pp. 324–5. For a spirited refutation of the British assertions, see André Philip, *Die Sozialismus und die europäische Einheit* (Gelsenkirchen, 1950).
12. *DBPO*, Series 2, Vol. 1, doc. 103 (16 June 1950). See also Young, *Britain and European Unity, 1945–1992*, p. 31.
13. *DBPO*, Series 2, Vol. 1, docs 3 (10 May 1950), 16 (11 May 1950), 106 (17 June 1950).
14. On the Stikker plan see W. Asbeek Brusse, 'The Stikker Plan', in R. T. Griffiths (ed.), *The Netherlands and the Integration of Europe 1945–1957* (Amsterdam, 1990), pp. 69–92. On Bidault's plan and his attitude to the Schuman Plan see Soutou, 'George Bidault et la construction européene', pp. 293–5. See also Wall, *The United States and the Making of Postwar France*, p. 193.
15. P. Gerbet, 'La Haute Autorité de la CECA', in E. V. Heyen (ed.), *Die Anfänge der Verwaltung der Europäischen Gemeinschaft* (Baden-Baden, 1992), p. 13.
16. *DBPO*, Series 2, Vol. 1, docs 25 (16 May 1950) and 45 (25 May 1950).
17. For the following, see in addition to J. Monnet, *Memoirs* (London, 1976): Hanns-Jürgen Küsters, 'Die Verhandlungen über die institutionelle System zur Gründung der Europäischen Gemeinschaft für Kohle und Stahl', in Schwabe (ed.), *Die Anfänge des Schuman-Plans*, pp. 73–102; Ulrich Lappenküper, 'Der Schuman Plan', *Vierteljahreshefte für Zeitgeschichte*, **42** (1994), pp. 418–24; R. T. Griffiths, 'The Schuman Plan', in R. T. Griffiths (ed.), *The Netherlands and the Integration of Europe* (Amsterdam, 1990), pp. 118–21.
18. For Monnet's draft, see *FRUS*, 1950, Vol. 3, pp. 727–38.
19. Kevin Featherstone sees the technocratic emphasis of Monnet as the source of the democratic deficit which aroused much attention during the problematic ratification of the Maastrict Treaty; 'Jean Monnet and the "democratic deficit" in the European Union', *Journal of Common Market Studies*, **32** (1994), pp. 149–70. While his criticisms of Monnet are well argued, he does neglect the significance of Benelux insistence upon increasing governmental influence rather than democratic legitimacy.
20. *FRUS*, 1950, Vol. 3, p. 699 (12 May 1950).
21. *Ibid.*, pp. 720–4 (6 June 1950).
22. Pierre Guillen, 'Die französische Generalität, die Aufrüstung der Bundesrepublik und die EVG (1950–1954)', in H-E Volkmann and W. Schwengler (eds), *Die Europäische Verteidigungsgemeinschaft* (Boppard, 1985), pp. 125–8.
23. *Akten zur Auswärtigen Politik der Bundesrepublik Deutschland. Adenauer und die Hohen Kommissare 1949–1951*, Vol. 1, doc. 15. Adenauer had asked for 25,000 men already in April.
24. *Ibid.*, pp. 24–5; T. A. Schwartz, *America's Germany. John J. McCloy and the Federal Republic of Germany* (Cambridge, Mass., 1991), pp. 129–33.
25. Edward Fursdon, *The European Defence Community* (London, 1980), p. 85. For these developments, see also Ireland, *Creating the Entangling Alliance*, pp. 199–207; Kaplan, *A Community of Interest*, p. 115.
26. Weigall and Stirk (eds), *The Origins and Development of the European Community*, p. 76.
27. *DBPO*, Series 2, Vol. 2, doc. 115 (24 November 1950). On this see also Dockrill, *Britain's Policy for West German Rearmament*, pp. 49–50.
28. On the linkage see Herbst, *Option für den Westen*, pp. 94 and 97.

29. *Akten zur Auswärtigen Politik der Bundesrepublik Deutschland. Adenauer und die Hohen Kommissare 1949–1951,* Vol. 1, docs 18 and 21.
30. On these developments see Lappenküper, 'Der Schuman Plan', pp. 429–33; J. Gillingham, 'Solving the Ruhr problem: German heavy industry and the Schuman Plan', in Schwabe (ed.), *Die Anfänge des Schuman-Plans,* pp. 422–32; *Coal, Steel and the Rebirth of Europe,* pp. 268–80.
31. Note of the German military expert Ulrich de Maiziére (13 August 1951), quoted in Paul Noack, 'EVG und Bonner Europapolitik', in Volkmann and Schwengler (eds), *Die Europäische Verteidigungsgemeinschaft,* p. 250.
32. *Ibid.*, p. 244; D. C. Large, 'Grand illusions: the United States, the Federal Republic of Germany and the European Defence Community, 1950–1954', in J. M. Diefendorf *et al.* (eds), *American Policy and the Reconstruction of West Germany* (Cambridge, 1993), p. 386.
33. The text of the treaties can be found in *Documents on International Affairs 1952.*
34. For early differences, see the interim report of the Paris negotiations of 24 July 1950 in *Akten zur Auswärtigen Politik der Bundesrepublik Deutschland. Adenauer und die Hohen Kommissare 1949–1951,* Vol. 1, Appendix 15. For French concessions, see Fursdon, *The European Defence Community,* pp. 123–4; Dockrill, *Britain's Policy for West German Rearmament,* pp. 90–4; Wilfried Loth, *Der Weg nach Europa* (Göttingen, 1990), p. 96.
35. On Italian motives see Antonio Varsori, 'Italy and the European Defence Community: 1950–54', in Stirk and Willis (eds), *Shaping Postwar Europe,* pp. 100–11 and, more generally, 'Italy between Atlantic Alliance and EDC, 1948–1955', in E. de Nolfo (ed.), *Power in Europe II* (Berlin, 1992), pp. 260–99.
36. For the details and an assessment, see W. Lipgens, 'EVG und politische Föderation', *Vierteljahreshefte für Zeitgeschichte,* **32** (1984), pp. 637–88.
37. Draft Treaty embodying the Statute of the European Community, in European Parliament, *Selection of Texts Concerning Institutional Matters of the Community from 1950–1982* (Luxembourg, n.d.). The importance of Beyen in the history of European integration is emphasized by A. S. Milward; see *The European Rescue of the Nation-State* (London, 1992), pp. 185–90.
38. *DBPO,* Series 2, Vol. 1, doc. 435 (17 March 1952).
39. *Ibid.*, doc. 429 (29 February 1952). There has been considerable dispute over the attitudes of British ministers. For an assessment, see John W. Young, 'Churchill's "no" to Europe', *Historical Journal,* **28** (1985), pp. 923–37.
40. *DBPO,* Series 2, Vol. 1, doc. 429 (29 February 1952).
41. *Ibid.*, doc. 430 (8 March 1952). This was somewhat of an exaggeration.
42. *Ibid.*, doc. 484 (29 August 1952).
43. British officials privately conceded that Monnet had a point. See *ibid.*, doc. 496 (8 September 1952).
44. Guillen, 'Die französische Generalität, die Aufrüstung der Bundesrepublik und die EVG', p. 146.
45. For these developments, see Fursdon, *The European Defence Community;* K. Weidenfeld, 'Konrad Adenauer und die EVG', in Volkmann and Schwengler (eds), *Die Europäische Verteidigungsgemeinschaft,* pp. 265–6.
46. Hans-Peter Schwarz, *Adenauer. Derr Staatsman 1952–1967* (Stuttgart, 1991), p. 123.
47. Anthony Eden, *Memoirs. Full Circle* (London, 1960), p. 171.

48. *Documents on International Affairs 1952*, p. 106. See also Ludolf Herbst, *Option für den Westen* (Munich, 1989), pp. 103–4.
49. Wolfgang Benz (ed.), *Deutschland seit 1945* (Munich, 1990), pp. 203–4.
50. On the attitude of the SPD see Hrbek, *Die SPD–Deutschland und Europa*, pp. 197–218.
51. R. A. Remington, *The Warsaw Pact. Case Studies in Communist Conflict Resolution* (Cambridge, Mass., 1971), p. 12.
52. *Ibid.*, p. 13.
53. Article 4, in H. F. van Panhuys, L. J. Brinkhorst and H. H. Maas (eds), *International Organisation and Integration* (Leyden, 1968), p. 1026.
54. Curt Gasteyger (ed.), *Europa zwischen Spaltung und Einigung 1945–1990* (Bonn, 1991), doc. D:34.
55. *Documents diplomatique française* (hereafter *DDF*), 1955, Vol. 1, doc. 287 (17 May 1955). The memorandum also considered several alternative explanations.
56. This occurred at the first meeting of the Political Consultative Committee. Gasteyger (ed.), *Europa zwischen Spaltung und Einigung 1945–1990*, doc. D:35.
57. Kaplan, *A Community of Interest*, pp. 163–4. C. S. Maier, 'Finance and defense: implications of military integration 1950–1952', in Heller and Gillingham (eds), *NATO*, pp. 213–40, emphasizes the importance of the achievement, especially of the principle of 'collective scrutiny of budgetary data related to defence', p. 345.
58. Kaplan, *A Community of Interest*, p. 163.
59. The Assembly was in fact a council of ministers.
60. J. Montias, 'Background and origins of the Romanian dispute with Comecon', *Soviet Studies*, **16** (1964), pp. 127–8; *Economic Development in Communist Rumania* (Cambridge, Mass., 1967), pp. 46–7.
61. Quoted in *ibid.*, p. 190.
62. *Ibid.*, p. 194.
63. On the continuities and differences see J. Montias, 'Economic nationalism in eastern Europe: forty years of continuity and change', *Journal of International Affairs*, **20** (1966), pp. 45–71.
64. Quoted in J. Montias, *Central Planning in Poland* (Westport, Conn., 1962), p. 281.
65. D. T. Cattell, 'Multilateral co-operation and integration in eastern Europe', *Western Political Quarterly*, **13** (1960), p. 64. L. Pryor, 'Forms of economic co-operation in the European communist bloc: a survey', *Soviet Studies*, **11** (1959–60), p. 193, argues that the extent of bilateralism has been exaggerated. It is, however, not the simple distribution of trade alone which matters, but also the convertibility of the resulting balances. This is brought out in a comparison of prewar Hungarian and postwar Dutch reliance upon German markets by Milward, *The European Rescue*, p. 139.
66. Spulbar, *The Economics of Communist Europe*, pp. 201–6; Cattell, 'Multilateral co-operation and integration in eastern Europe', pp. 66-7.
67. *Ibid.*, p. 67.
68. Schiavone, *The Institutions of Comecon*, pp. 20–1.
69. *FRUS*, 1955–57, Vol. 4, doc. 133 (6 December 1955).
70. *Ibid.* Similar comments on comparative growth were voiced in a report on 'The future of NATO' in March 1956. Anticipating continued rapid growth in the Soviet bloc, its authors suggested that the United States and Canada should join

a reformed OEEC in order to meet the Soviet challenge in the battle for growth. See Pascaline Winand, *Eisenhower, Kennedy and the United States of Europe* (New York, 1993), pp. 128–9.

71. See Hanns-Jürgen Küsters, *Fondements de la communauté économique européene* (Luxembourg, 1990), pp. 38–40; *DDF*, 1955, Vol. 1, doc. 62.
72. See Milward, *The European Rescue*, pp. 175–6.
73. *Ibid.*, p. 192.
74. Loth, *Der Weg nach Europa*, p. 115.
75. *FRUS*, 1955–57, Vol. 4, doc. 89 (20 April 1955).
76. *Ibid.*, doc. 109 (5 July 1955). Self-avowed functionalists tended to favour integration in areas where vested interests were presumed not to exist or where issues of 'high politics' were presumed to be absent. Such instances proved more difficult to find than the functionalists supposed.
77. Messina Resolution, *Selections*, pp. 96–7. They also agreed upon a successor to Jean Monnet as head of the High Authority.
78. See the useful summary of the French negotiating position in a memorandum of 7 May 1956, *DDF*, 1956, Vol. 1, doc. 302. Messina implied 'an intention to agree and not a decision, an engagement, to agree'. The reservation is an interesting one in the light of disputes over British unwillingness to enter into open-ended commitments.
79. In a report of 4 February 1956, *ibid.*, doc. 75.
80. For these distinctions, see Küsters, *Fondements de la communauté économique européene*, pp. 58–64; 'Adenauers Europapolitik in der Gründungsphase der Europäischen Witrschaftsgemeinschaft', *Vierteljahreshefte für Zeitgeschichte*, **31** (1983), pp. 652–3. For French awareness of the disputes among the Germans, see *DDF*, 1955, Vol. 1, doc. 297 (25 May 1955).
81. For the ambiguity of the concept of functionalism as espoused by Mitrany, see *A Working Peace System* (London, 1943).
82. Küsters, *Fondements de la communauté économique européeene*, pp. 62–3.
83. Frances M. B. Lynch, 'Restoring France: the road to integration', in A. S. Milward *et al.*, *The Frontier of National Sovereignty. History and Theory 1945–1992* (London, 1993), pp. 62–3; R. Girault, 'La France entre l'Europe et l'Afrique', in E. Serra (ed.), *The Relaunching of Europe and the Treaties of Rome* (Baden-Baden, 1989), pp. 351–78 – see especially p. 356, where Girault describes Robert Schuman's enthusiasm for this idea.
84. *DDF*, 1955, Vol. 1, doc. 288. See also a memorandum of 26 May 1955, doc. 301.
85. Milward, *The European Rescue*, pp. 202–3.
86. Memorandum of end April/beginning of May, *DDF*, 1955, Vol. 1, doc. 239.
87. *Ibid.*
88. For an assessment, see Lynch, 'Restoring France: the road to integration', pp. 78–84.
89. *DDF*, 1956, Vol. 1, doc. 67 (2 February 1956). For American insistence upon the importance of automatic progression, see *FRUS*, 1955–57, Vol. 4, doc. 180 (13 July 1956). For Dutch reaction to the French proposals, see R. T. Griffith and W. Asbeek Brusse, 'The Dutch cabinet and the Rome treaties', in Serra (ed.), *The Relaunching of Europe*, pp. 469–72.
90. Simon Burgess and Geoffrey Edwards, 'The six plus one: British policy-making and the question of European economic integration, 1955', *International Affairs*, **64** (1988), p. 407.

91. *Ibid.*, p. 404.
92. Küsters, *Fondements de la communauté économique européene*, pp. 93, 119–20.
93. *DDF*, 1956, doc. 302 (7 May 1956).
94. Robert Marjolin, *Memoirs 1911–1986* (London, 1989), p. 285.
95. *DDF*, 1956, Vol. 1, doc. 227 (8 April 1956). It was agreed that Spaak could personally write to the governments with his recommendation of a moratorium.
96. *DDF*, 1955, Vol. 1, doc. 239 (30 April 1955).
97. American policy is surveyed in J. E. Helmreich, 'The United States and the formation of Euratom', *Diplomatic History*, **15** (1991), pp. 387–410.
98. Küsters, 'Adenauers Europapolitik in der Gründungsphase der Europäischen Witrschaftsgemeinschaft', p. 660. According to the Italian Minister Martino, Adenauer had even suggested that the five, excluding France, should proceed with the common market on their own if France could not be won over; *FRUS*, 1955–57, doc. 162 (1 March 1956).
99. G. Brenke, 'Europakonzeptionenen im Widerstreit. Die Freihandelszonen-Verhandlungen 1956–1958', *Vierteljahreshefte für Zeitgeschichte*, **42** (1994), p. 598. On the free trade area see also Küsters, *Fondements de la communauté économique européene*, pp. 171–82; Miriam Camps, *Britain and the European Community* (London, 1964).
100. Alfred Grosser, *The Western Alliance* (London, 1980), pp. 167–8; Küsters, *Fondements de la communauté économique européene*, p. 196; 'Adenauers Europapolitik in der Gründungsphase der Europäischen Witrschaftsgemeinschaft', pp. 661–4.
101. *DDF*, 1956, Vol. 2, doc. 192 (18 September 1956).
102. Quoted by Milward, *The European Rescue*, p. 212.
103. *DDF*, 1956, Vol. 3, doc. 146 (8 November 1956).
104. Article 119, Treaty establishing the European Economic Community.
105. Article 121. See also Milward, *The European Rescue*, p. 214.
106. Milward, *The European Rescue*, p. 216.
107. *DDF*, 1956, Vol. 3, doc. 146 (8 November 1956).
108. As Spaak mentioned to the Americans, *FRUS*, 1955–57, Vol. 4, doc. 220 (8 February 1957).
109. Article 87 of the Treaty establishing the European Atomic Energy Community. On the compromise see P. Weilemann, 'Die Deutsche Haltung während der Euatom-Verhandlungen', in Serra (ed.), *The Relaunching of Europe*, p. 542.
110. *DDF*, 1956, Vol. 3, doc. 316 (21 December 1956).
111. *Ibid.*
112. *DDF*, 1956, Vol. 3, doc. 262 (5 December 1956).
113. *Ibid.*
114. On Mendès-France see F. O'Neil, *The French Radical Party and European Integration* (Farnborough, 1981), pp. 92–3. On the Italian viewpoint, see F. Roy Willis, *Italy Chooses Europe* (New York, 1971), pp. 54–7.
115. For a critical assessment of this assumption see T. Cutler *et al.*, *1992 and the Struggle for Europe* (Oxford, 1989).
116. Küsters, *Fondements de la communauté économique européene*, p. 247.
117. *Ibid.*, pp. 257–68. For the broader picture, see Lynch, 'Restoring France: the road to integration'; R. Girault, 'La France entre l'Europe at l'Afrique'.
118. Küsters, *Fondements de la communauté économique européene*, p. 274.
119. *DDF*, 1956, Vol. 3, doc. 262 (5 December 1956).

120. W. Loth, 'Deutsche Europa-Konzeptionen in der Gründungsphase der EWG', in Serra (ed.), *The Relaunching of Europe*, p. 601.
121. Milward, *The European Rescue*, pp. 121–3.
122. *FRUS*, 1955–57, Vol. 4, doc. 236 (24 May 1957).
123. *Ibid.*, doc. 227 (6 March 1957).
124. OEEC, *Report on the Possibility of Creating a Free Trade Area in Europe* (Paris, 1957), p. 27.
125. United Kingdom Memorandum to the Organisation for European Economic Co-operation, *A European Free Trade Area* (London, 1957). According to Miriam Camps, Britain was unwise to confound an outline of the free trade area and her own negotiating position, *Britain and the European Community*, p. 111.
126. Brenke, 'Europakonzeptionenen im Widerstreit', p. 600.
127. *Ibid.*, pp. 610–11.
128. Quoted by S. Huth, *British and German Relations between 1955 and 1961*, Ph.D., Cambridge University, 1992, p. 116. See also Brenke, 'Europakonzeptionenen im Widerstreit', p. 622.
129. *Ibid.*, pp. 612, 623–4.
130. The British proposal, excluding agricultural products, created a problem for Denmark. On this and Scandinavian strategies in general see V. Sorensen, 'Between interdependence and integration: Denmark's shifting strategies', in Milward *et al.*, *The Frontier of National Sovereignty*, pp. 88–116. See also H. Pharo, 'The Norwegian Labour Party'; U. Olssen, 'The Swedish Social Democrats', in Richard T. Griffiths (ed.), *Socialist Parties and the Question of Europe in the 1950s* (Leiden, 1993), pp. 201–20 and 221–38. Pharo is sceptical about the Nordic union.
131. Danish interests were satisfied by means of bilateral agreements. See Camps, *Britain and Europe.*
132. For a useful comparison, see Fischer, 'Der Deutsche Zollverein, die Europäische Wirtschaftsgemeinschaft und die Freihandelzone', pp. 105–14.
133. P. Luif, 'Die Entstehung der EFTA', in P. du Bois and B. Hurni (eds), *EFTA from Yesterday to Tomorrow* (Geneva, 1988), p. 70.
134. F. Fetjö, *A History of the People's Democracies* (Harmondsworth, 1974), pp. 138–9, 144–5.
135. Quoted in D. D. Finley, 'A political perspective of economic relations in the communist camp', *Western Political Quarterly*, **17** (1964), p. 305.
136. E. E. Hewett, *Foreign Trade Prices in the Council of Mutual Economic Assistance* (Cambridge, 1974), p. 14.
137. Quoted in Montias, *Economic Development in Communist Rumania*, p. 195. The Bulgarians claimed that even using world market prices as a base meant reflecting the imperialist exploitation of less developed economies by imperialist ones; Hewett, *Foreign Trade Prices*, p. 164.
138. Montias, *Economic Development in Communist Rumania*, pp. 199–200, 203–5. According to P. J. D. Wiles, the Soviet Union had threatened to cut off steel supplies to Romania in 1957 since the latter persisted in producing a type of truck not allocated to her by the CMEA; *Communist International Economics*, p. 324.
139. J. Montias, 'Background and origins of the Rumanian dispute with Comecon', p. 136.
140. Quoted in Schiavone, *The Institutions of Comecon*, p. 25.
141. Quoted in *ibid.*, p. 175.

142. Article 4, *ibid.*, p. 177. For an assessment, see W. E. Butler, 'Legal configurations of integration in eastern Europe', *International Affairs*, **51** (1975), pp. 525–6.
143. Compare article 20 of the Statute and article 4 of the Charter for similarities. The Statute did provide for a Consultative Assembly which could at least embarrass the Committee of Ministers.
144. A. Eden, *Memoirs. Full Circle* (London, 1960), pp. 295–311; see especially p. 305 for the linkage between the two.
145. Rapacki continued to push the plan in subsequent years. See Adam Rapacki, 'The Polish plan for a nuclear-free zone today', *International Affairs*, **39** (1963), pp. 1–12.
146. *FRUS*, 1958–1960, Vol. 7, Part 1, doc. 143 (7 May 1958).
147. *Ibid.*, doc. 152 (5 July 1958). For a fuller specification, see the National Security Council report of 7 February 1958, *FRUS*, 1958–1960, Vol. 9, doc. 243.
148. Quoted in W. F. Hanrieder, *Germany, America, Europe* (New Haven, 1989), p. 88.
149. George Catlin, *The Atlantic Community* (London, 1959). Catlin had published much of this work during the war years.
150. Camps, *Britain and Europe*, p. 239.
151. *FRUS*, 1955–1957, Vol. 4, doc. 63 (23 November 1957). See also doc. 64.
152. The Report is printed as Appendix 2 in NATO, *Facts about the North Atlantic Treaty Organization* (Paris, 1962).
153. *FRUS*, 1958–1960, Vol. 7, Part 1, doc. 218 (20 July 1959).
154. *FRUS*, 1958–1960, Vol. 7, Part 2, doc. 45 (17 September 1958). The memorandum even considered revising the North Atlantic Treaty as part of this process.
155. *Ibid.*, doc. 81 (15 December 1958). For the views of the French diplomat Alphand, see doc. 77 (4 December 1958).
156. *FRUS*, 1958–1960, Vol. 7, Part 1, doc. 196 (6 March 1959).
157. *Ibid.*, doc. 249 (21 January 1960).
158. On this see Camps, *Britain and Europe*, pp. 272–3. For American rejection of the Atlantic free trade area, see *FRUS*, 1958–1960, Vol. 7, Part 1, doc. 85 (11 December 1959). A later report by Bowie considered an 'Atlantic Confederation' as 'premature'; *ibid.*, doc. 266 (August 1960).
159. *FRUS*, 1951, Vol. 4, doc. 1.

6

The Development and Limits of Integration in the 1960s and 1970s

INTRODUCTION

The 1950s had seen the completion of the long process of postwar reconstruction. In the next decade the pursuit of growth continued to bear fruit, albeit with markedly less success in the eastern half of Europe. Even in the west new strains appeared. In the United States an adverse balance of payments had already inaugurated great debate on the role of the United States in the world economy at the end of the 1950s. In 1960 the western world began to implement *ad hoc* measures to support the dollar which served as the basis for international trade. The rate of growth of the Federal Republic of Germany no longer outstripped that of its European neighbours, but the strength of her economy, and increasingly of the Deutschmark, once again pressured France into seeking to contain her neighbour by further integration at the end of the 1960s.[1] Yet France's turn to integration was preceded by an obstinate defence of sovereignty under President de Gaulle. De Gaulle's vision of 'a Europe of states' brought him into conflict with advocates of supranationalism. His vision of 'Europe from the Atlantic to the Urals' brought him into conflict with President Kennedy's grand design. This clash reflected the persistent tension between Atlantic and European integration. The outcome was that both the Economic Community and the Atlantic Alliance reached the point of crisis in the middle of the decade.

Resistance to the pressures of integration and the asymmetries of the balance of power and level of economic development was also pronounced in the east. Here eastern Europe's 'Gaullists', the Romanians, held out against Soviet pressure for integration. Despite the rhetoric of socialist internationalism and the even more important reality of Soviet power, Romania stubbornly defended the symbols of sovereignty and the perceived dictates of the national interest. Neither Romania nor France, neither Nicolae Ceauşescu nor Charles de Gaulle, sought a retreat into splendid isolation. Nor were the concerns they expressed the sole property of these nations or these men. But both did exercise an influence which seemed disproportionate to the underlying strengths of their economies and military establishments. Both did unequivocally demonstrate that faith in the European nation-state was far from dead.

The 1970s saw the enlargement of the European Communities. With British entry the question which had agitated the inter-war advocates of European unity was resolved, in principle at least. In the details of the Community's development British reservations persisted. Enlargement was linked with an expansion of the Community's agenda into sensitive areas like monetary union. Fearful of an even greater loss of sovereignty, the member states responded by strengthening the intergovernmental elements of the Community. Despite these limitations, the Community exercised considerable influence upon the members of Comecon. Capitalist integration was forging ahead of socialist integration. Reforms at the beginning of the 1970s failed to bring about any substantial improvement. Indeed, it seemed to some that eastern Europe had become an economic liability for the Soviet Union.

Relations between the two halves of Europe had shown some signs of improvement in the early and mid-1970s. The high-point was the 1975 Helsinki Act of the Conference on Security and Co-operation in Europe. Here, it seemed, was a bridge between east and west. But at the end of the decade the rhetoric of the Cold War was revived. That in turn aggravated tensions between the United States and the Europeans, for the latter had more to lose from the reversal of *détente* than the former. European integration was still stamped by the division of Europe whose roots lay in the failure of Europe's states to resolve their own problems decades earlier.

DE GAULLE'S VISION OF EUROPE

De Gaulle was motivated by both considerations of French interests and a vision of Europe, a Europe of states stretching from the 'Atlantic to the Urals'. Quite what de Gaulle had in mind by this phrase still puzzles historians.[2] It is clear that it was an alternative vision to the dominance of an ideologically defined Cold War division of Europe. It was, hence, a Europe which would enjoy greater independence from both superpowers. It was a conception which rested upon confidence in a national identity conferred by the one and indivisible republic that was France. That confidence in national identity was not necessarily shared by de Gaulle's German neighbours, for whom the relationship between state and nation was a more complicated matter.[3]

Yet de Gaulle needed the co-operation of the Federal Republic if his vision was to have any hope of becoming a reality. He had made a good start with his first meeting with Adenauer, in September 1958, a few days before his memorandum to Eisenhower and Macmillan calling for a reform of the Atlantic Alliance. He strengthened his hand in November 1959, when the Soviet Union called into question the status of Berlin. In November, and again in the following year, de Gaulle emphatically supported Adenauer's insistence that no concessions be made, against Anglo-American equivocation. Adenauer was grateful.

Later, in July 1960, at a meeting in Rambouillet, de Gaulle put before Adenauer his ideas for European intergovernmental co-operation, as well as expounding his criticisms of the Commission and the current state of the Atlantic Alliance. He had raised these issues, in more moderate form, the previous year, but his partners would only agree to regular consultation on political co-operation.[4] De Gaulle was slowly revealing proposals for what amounted to a revision of the entire process of integration. In a press conference on 5 September 1960, he gave vent to his suspicion of the Commission, that is of 'certain, more or less extra-national, organisms' which were of some technical use but lacked the authority to deal with political issues.[5] The way forward, he said, lay in improved intergovernmental co-operation in the fields of politics, economics, culture and defence. To this he added a European assembly and a referendum to legitimate the entire procedure.

When the members of the Community met to discuss de Gaulle's proposals in February 1961 most were prepared to establish a committee to prepare for regular meetings of heads of state or governments. Foreign Minister Josef Luns of the Netherlands, however, firmly resisted, arguing that the proposal was a threat to the Community's method of supranational integration and to co-operation within the Atlantic Alliance, that it ignored British interests, and that they were being presented as a Franco-German *fait accompli*.[6] The Netherlands only consented to consider proposals on further co-operation, although it did agree later, after considerable pressure had been exerted, to hold regular meetings. With the reluctant assent of the Netherlands the six enshrined their consensus in the Bonn Declaration. The Bonn Declaration of 18 July 1961 also committed the six to establish a committee, which was 'to submit proposals on the means which will as soon as possible enable a statutory character to be given to the union of their peoples'.[7]

Luns' concern about British interests reflected traditional Dutch sympathy for Britain and the rapidly changing British position. During the second half of 1960 there were a series of signs that Britain was reconsidering her decision not to join the Communities. The potential obstacle was quite evident: de Gaulle. Conscious of this, Macmillan prepared a memorandum at the end of 1960 in which he suggested that 'We could woo the French more easily by backing their great power ambitions – that is, by putting real life into tripartism . . . We might even be able to persuade the Americans to give the French some help in their nuclear plans.'[8] There was in fact little prospect of the Americans being persuaded. In the late 1950s consideration had been given to helping the French, but, by October 1957, Eisenhower had opted for a policy of opposing France's nuclear weapons programme.[9] Moreover, at the same time as Macmillan was formulating his 'Grand Design', including the idea of trilateralism, Eisenhower, in the last month of his office as President, agreed that the United States should propose a multilateral nuclear force within the framework of NATO. The nuclear warheads would, however, remain firmly under American control.[10]

As the British government groped its way towards a formal application it had to take account of both old (the Commonwealth) and recent (EFTA) commitments.[11] Neither process was easy. Britain promised to protect the interests of its existing partners in order to win their acquiescence, a promise which complicated negotiations with the six. That there had been a fundamental change in Britain's evaluation of its position was clearest in its relationship with the Commonwealth. At the end of the September 1962 conference of Commonwealth Prime Ministers, the British made clear that

> The broad concept that raw materials were to be exchanged for processed goods had become outdated, and that all the Commonwealth countries were increasingly making their own goods and trying to export them. He [Macmillan] could not see how Britain could maintain alone her free-entry system when a tariff structure was being built up against it in many parts of the Commonwealth, with protection for home industries.[12]

Britain had finally, if belatedly, accepted the logic of post-war economic growth.

The decision to apply was taken in July 1961, with the formal application being made in the following month. From then on, the issue of the development of a political union, and British membership of both the existing Communities and the prospective union, were inextricably linked. These issues in turn were bound up with the tension between the French proposal for a political union on the one hand, and the existing structures of the Communities on the other. The picture was even further complicated by the potential impact of the political union upon the Atlantic Alliance. Within less than two years these linkages had brought about the downfall of both British membership and political union.

The committee on political union met in November 1961 under the chairmanship of the Frenchman Christian Fouchet. The French draft plan, focusing on the development of a common foreign and defence policy, immediately caused concern among the other five. In the first place the French plan clearly marked a step back from the level of integration already achieved by the Communities. According to article 6 of the French draft the Council was to take decisions unanimously. The European Parliament was to be weak. Even worse, the European Political Commission was to 'consist of senior officials of the Foreign affairs departments of each Member State'.[13] The proposed union was consistently intergovernmental in character. Moreover, article 16, envisaging a review three years after entry into force of the union, seemed to leave open the possibility of restructuring the existing communities in accordance with the intergovernmental model of the union. Subsequent negotiations brought forth a new version more acceptable to France's partners. De Gaulle, however, modified the revision, striking out elements he found unacceptable and adding new ones. He struck out the assertion that the union would strengthen the Atlantic Alliance, thereby confirming fears that he intended to draw Europe away from the United States. He also added economic policy to the list of the union's tasks, again seeming to confirm his intent to undermine the existing Community structures.[14] When the French refused to withdraw their revised proposal, the other five produced a counter-draft which contradicted the French proposal on all key issues.

A way forward seemed to open up as Adenauer and the Italian Prime Minister Fanfani extracted concessions from de Gaulle. He agreed to the inclusion of a statement affirming the union's commitment to the Atlantic Alliance and an assurance that the European Community was not to be weakened. Yet on 17 April 1962 the whole enterprise collapsed when the Netherlands and Belgium declared that they were unwilling to continue negotiations until Britain became a member of the Community.[15] De Gaulle's response came in the following month. In a press conference of 15 May 1962, he defended his conception of *l'Europe des patries* and attacked the idea of supranational integration. A supranational entity did not in fact exist, he claimed. It did not exist because there was no 'federator' to create it. More pointedly, he added that there might have been a federator, but not a European one. The target of his attack was unmistakable. The hypothetical federator could only be the United States.[16]

KENNEDY'S GRAND DESIGN

President Kennedy responded two days later, reaffirming American commitment to Europe and warning against any attempt to exclude the United States from Europe's affairs.[17] Kennedy's response reflected his own 'grand design' which was set out formally in his Independence Day speech of 4 July 1962.[18] In it he expressed support for a 'more perfect union' of Europe which would be an equal partner of the United States.[19] The idea of partnership embodied the long-standing desire to balance the Atlantic Alliance and European unity. It also reflected more immediate American concerns about economic trends and fears that the European Community might move in a protectionist direction. Within the American foreign policy establishment it represented a moderate position. There were advocates of a more Atlanticist strategy. That strategy was reflected in a resolution first introduced as early as 1949 and finally, in a much weakened version, signed by Eisenhower in September 1960. The resolution called for an investigation into an Atlantic union. Quite how far-reaching this strategy could be is evident from an article by former Secretary of State Herter in which he proposed a 'permanent High Council . . . to concert and plan, and in agreed cases to decide policy on matters of common concern to the Community as a whole'.[20]

The version which the Kennedy administration adopted was less expansive. It was also inconsistent. Kennedy did envisage the European Community as an equal economic partner within a liberal Atlantic framework. The Trade Expansion Act of October 1962 was designed to facilitate this objective. Not only did it give the President authority to reduce tariffs by 50 per cent, where the United States and the European Community accounted for 80 per cent of world exports of a product, it gave him authority to abolish the tariff entirely.[21] The latter provision would, however, only be of use if Britain became a member of the European Community. Economic equality was one thing. Military, that is nuclear, equality was different. Here, the Kennedy administration had no intention of allowing Europe to become an equal partner. The intent, rather, was to reduce the independence of European nuclear capability by subordinating it to the Atlantic Alliance. Indeed McGeorge Bundy, Kennedy's special assistant for national security, regretted that the United States had ever assisted the development of British nuclear capacity.[22] American hostility to independent European nuclear capacity was complicated by the adoption of a strategy of flexible deterrence which called into question the willingness of the United States to use nuclear weapons in Europe's defence. The solution, so the Kennedy administration believed, lay in a multilateral naval force.[23] A European nuclear capacity would in effect be subject to international and ultimately to American control.

This was of course anathema to de Gaulle, who was trying to salvage something from the collapse of his proposal for a European union. If the six could not be persuaded, the way forward, he concluded, lay in a bilateral agreement with the Federal Republic. Adenauer, who had grown tired of the political union wrangle, agreed when he met de Gaulle at Rambouillet in July 1962. Both also agreed that British entry into the Community was undesirable.[24] In the autumn they tried to co-opt Italy but Fanfani refused, having been won over to the Dutch stance.[25]

As de Gaulle and Adenauer prepared for a bilateral agreement the negotiations between the six and Britain crawled forward. Towards the end of the year they ground to a halt over agriculture. Macmillan's visit to de Gaulle on 15 December failed to bring about any improvement. Indeed, de Gaulle cast doubt upon Britain's readiness to commit herself to Europe. De Gaulle's underlying objection was that Britain was still too close to the United States, a suspicion which he found fully confirmed by the Anglo-American agreement at Nassau only days later. At the Nassau meeting Macmillan skilfully circumvented American pressure to fully integrate Britain's nuclear forces into the Atlantic Alliance. Moreover, Kennedy agreed to supply Britain with Polaris missiles. In return Britain's nuclear submarines were to be allocated to the proposed Atlantic multilateral force, but they could be withdrawn in the event that Britain felt that her national interests were threatened.[26] Polaris missiles were subsequently offered to France, though there was confusion about the terms of the offer. Moreover, at a key meeting on 29 December 1962 between Kennedy and the French Ambassador Alphand, the American President was 'non-committal' when Alphand explored the possibility of American assistance with the development of nuclear warheads.[27]

Early in the new year de Gaulle gave vent to all his suspicions and effectively vetoed British membership, in a press conference. After explaining that current British interests and policies were incompatible with the Community's he considered the prospect of a much enlarged Community. 'It is to be foreseen', he continued, 'that the cohesion of its members, who would be very numerous and diverse, would not endure for long, and that ultimately it would appear as a colossal Atlantic community under American dependence and direction ... '[28] France's partners had not been forewarned of de Gaulle's decision, nor, with the exception of Adenauer, did they agree with it. There was, however, little they could do. When the German State Secretary Lahr sought to persuade the French Minister Couve de Murville that the outstanding difficulties in the negotiations were resolvable, Couve de Murville declined to agree. It was, he claimed, 'clear to all the delegation for some time that a crisis would occur in January or February'.[29]

Both 'grand designs', that of Kennedy and that of de Gaulle, had been dealt a severe blow. The six, at the insistence of the Netherlands, would not proceed to political union without Britain and Kennedy's vision of partnership assumed that Britain would be a member of the European Community. Yet, despite the appearance of failure and stagnation, the Community had been making progress on a number of fronts. In May 1960 the Community had decided to accelerate its programme of tariff reduction. More importantly, agreement was finally reached, on 14 January 1962, on the framework of the Common Agricultural Policy. The agreement gave far more weight to the Council of Ministers than the Commission had wanted, opening up the way for agricultural Ministers to implement an expensive and protectionist policy, but it did facilitate the transition from stage one to stage two of the Rome Treaty.[30] In a landmark case decided in 1963 the European Court of Justice confirmed that Community law was directly effective in member states. As the Court explained, 'the Community constitutes a new legal order of international law for the benefit of which the states have limited their sovereign rights'.[31] Finally, economic growth continued to be impressive, reaching 5.3 per cent in 1961 and 4.8 per cent in 1962.[32]

KHRUSHCHEV'S ATTEMPT TO FORCE INTEGRATION IN THE EAST

The significance of these achievements was not lost on observers, including those in the eastern half of Europe. The Soviet Union initially responded to the flurry of developments in the west with the orthodox line that they merely demonstrated the reactionary and antagonistic nature of the western capitalist world. But in 1962 Khrushchev developed a new, more flexible, line.[33] This entailed not only a reinterpretation of the development of integration in the west but also an attempt to revive integration in the east. Khrushchev still emphasized that the European Community was tied to the 'aggressive NATO alliance' and insisted upon the 'profound internal contradictions' of capitalism, but, he continued,

> to refuse to exaggerate the strength of the adversary does not mean to ignore it.
>
> At the same time, we take cognizance of the objective tendencies toward internationalization of production which operate in the capitalist world and we design our economic measures accordingly. In this connection the question arises of the possibility of economic cooperation and peaceful economic competition not only between individual states with different social systems but also between their economic federations.[34]

Khrushchev appeared to answer his own question, declaring a willingness to improve trade agreements and even engage in co-operation in the development of raw materials and energy. But in all of these he referred to co-operation between 'countries'. There was in fact little prospect of co-operation between the European Community and Comecon so long as the former refused to deal with the latter on the grounds that Comecon had no authority over its members' trading policy. For their part, the eastern states refused, correspondingly, to recognize the *de jure* existence of the Community.

Nevertheless, Khrushchev's argument marked a significant departure in Soviet analysis. One of the conclusions he drew was that the socialist countries had to increase their integration in order better to compete. The obstacles to such integration had not changed, however, since the end of the previous decade. In fact the dispute between Romania and the more advanced members of Comecon had flared into the open again, with overt criticism of an east German economist in an article of March 1961. The Romanian criticism revealed the domestic ideological implications of the dispute, as well as the more obvious conflicts of interest between developed and developing nations. For, the Romanians argued, industrialization, especially through the development of heavy industry, promoted the formation of the working class and the dictatorship of the proletariat.[35] It was not only Romanian national interests that were at stake, but also the socialist character of the state.

The Soviet Union, aided by the German Democratic Republic and Czechoslovakia, continued to press for integration. The outcome, finally achieved in July 1962, was the Basic Principles of the International Division of Labour. Despite the emphasis upon the division of labour in its title, the document was a compromise. Some articles clearly emphasized integration, such as the assertion in article 3 that '[i]nterstate specialization implies concentrating production of similar products in one or several socialist countries'.[36] Others clearly reflected Romanian concerns, as did the commitment to 'steady elimination of historic differences in the economic development levels of individual countries'.[37]

Khrushchev was clearly dissatisfied with the compromise, for he promptly returned to the attack. The main focus of the article in which he reassessed the European Community was devoted to a call for further socialist integration. He castigated autarkic policies and called for 'the changeover from bilateral to multilateral planning and regulation of trade and payments'.[38] He insisted upon the need for economic plans embracing Comecon as a whole, for common projects, the co-ordination of national plans of capital investment, and the development of raw materials production. He even declared that the 'Soviet Union is prepared ... to cut down production of some kinds of manufactures if it proves more expedient to produce them in other countries'.[39] As Khrushchev refined his suggestions later in the year, the full implications became apparent. He was proposing nothing less than a supranational planning authority.[40]

Resistance from Comecon members, primarily but not exclusively Romania, seemed to bring the whole process to a halt at the conference of First Secretaries in the summer of 1963; a conference in which the Romanians did not participate.[41] Khrushchev, however, had not given up. In April 1964 he pushed for further integration of both Comecon and the Warsaw Pact. The Romanian response was prompt and blunt. In a declaration issued by the Romanian Central Committee the usual objections were rehearsed and the ideological significance of Khrushchev's proposals clearly set out:

> The idea of a single planning body for all CMEA countries has the most serious economic and political implications. The planned management of the national economy is one of the fundamental, essential and inalienable attributes of the socialist state – the state plan being the chief means through which the socialist state achieves its political and socioeconomic objectives ...[42]

Despite the rhetoric of socialist internationalism, the obstacles to the integration of socialist states were in some senses greater than those facing the capitalist west. Alongside the purely economic difficulties of co-ordinating plans was the fact that integration could not be left to a politically neutral market. Integration automatically meant an even greater sacrifice of sovereignty. But it was not purely the difficulties facing socialist states that brought Khrushchev's reforms to a halt in the spring of 1964. Economic nationalism had a long heritage in the region, a heritage the Romanians openly invoked.[43]

The attempt to put life into Comecon had largely failed. However, there were some institutional residues from Khrushchev's efforts. An Executive Committee, consisting of Deputy Prime Ministers, had been formed in 1962 and in July 1963 an International Bank for Economic Co-operation had been established. Interestingly, the Bank's charter specified the strict, and sovereign, equality of members and required unanimity for any decision.[44] The Soviet Union had also reverted to its earlier interpretation of the European Community. The prime reason for this sudden reversal was French rejection of British membership. Orthodoxy, contrary to Soviet expectations, had been confirmed. The capitalists were rent by their inherent contradictions.[45]

THE FRANCO-GERMAN AXIS AND THE LUXEMBOURG CRISIS

De Gaulle's veto of British membership was followed within days by the signature of a Franco-German Treaty. On the one hand the treaty marked the culmination of the Franco-German reconciliation which underpinned western European integration. Yet the treaty was also the remnant of a much grander design. The hour of its birth was not auspicious. According to the treaty both governments would consult each other before taking important foreign policy decisions, yet de Gaulle had just unilaterally wrecked the negotiations on British entry. Nor was the treaty universally welcome in Bonn. Ludwig Erhard spoke for the critics when he declared in an interview on 5 February 1963, 'Bilateralism is dead.'[46] The United States was no less blunt. Kennedy, 'in a noticeably bad mood' as the German Ambassador recorded, criticized the treaty 'repeatedly and clearly'.[47] Something was done to restore Atlantic relationships, and dilute the treaty, by the German Bundestag. In ratifying the treaty they added a preamble reaffirming commitment to the Atlantic Alliance and the European Community as well as asserting the desirability of British membership of the Community.[48] Other issues continued to cloud Atlantic relations. The negotiations on the multilateral force were making little headway. The French made clear to the Germans that they would not participate, affected to have no objection to German participation, but then suggested that the Germans consider whether or not this was merely another means to cloak American monopoly on nuclear weapons.[49] Another form of conflict, the so-called chicken war which raged from autumn 1962, was widely regarded as symbolic of the poor state of Atlantic relationships. The dispute arose over levies, imposed as part of the Common Agricultural Policy, upon American chicken exports to the European Community. The two sides did not settle their differences, via GATT mediation, until 22 November 1963, the day on which President Kennedy was assassinated.[50]

On the same day the new Chancellor of the Federal Republic, Ludwig Erhard, was in Paris on his first state visit, where Erhard and de Gaulle laid the basis for an agreement on agricultural issues and the conditions under which the Commission would negotiate within the Kennedy Round of GATT which finally opened in May 1964.[51] Despite past criticisms, of both de Gaulle and the European Community, Erhard as Chancellor strove to make a success of the Franco-German axis and to promote further integration. Erhard's attitude was not, of course, identical to Adenauer's. When Erhard met President Johnson in December he made it clear that there were differences on essential questions between France and Germany. Those differences, he said, had not always been made clear, since the relationship between Adenauer and de Gaulle had been 'emotional or sentimental'.[52]

Erhard's efforts to balance the Franco-German Treaty and the Atlantic Alliance while driving integration forward were tested in the summer and autumn of the following year. The key events took place in July. During his visit to Bonn, de Gaulle discussed with State Secretary Carstens the possibility of extending France's nuclear shield over Germany. The intent was to draw Germany away from the multilateral force and to cement the Franco-German axis. As Erhard explained to the American Ambassador, George McGhee, when Erhard had asked de Gaulle whether this meant that the French *force de frappe* would be European, it became clear that it would not. Erhard added that Germany would be dependent upon either the United States or France, and, significantly, he said to McGhee, 'I do not need to say with whom we feel safer.'[53] De Gaulle responded with a customary press conference, on 23 July, in which he was openly critical of the Federal Republic's foreign policy and complained that the Franco-German Treaty was not working.

During the remaining months of 1964 the French increased the pressure, with Pompidou warning that if the multilateral force led to a German–American military alliance France would consider this to be incompatible with the treaty.[54] But Erhard had 'given up' on 'the Europe of the two' and wanted to press forward with the six.[55] Erhard did press forward. In November 1964 the Federal Republic suggested that the six conclude an agreement, not a treaty, providing for intergovernmental co-operation. This, however, was to be a first stage. The second stage was much more ambitious, including the transformation of the European Parliament from a merely advisory body to one with real power.[56]

Of course Erhard still needed de Gaulle's co-operation for any progress among the six. Determined to prove his commitment to Europe, Erhard pushed through an agreement on cereal prices upon which the French were insisting, in the expectation that de Gaulle would be appreciative.[57] On the wider stage Britain muddied the waters at the beginning of December by proposing an Atlantic Nuclear Force which downgraded the multinational element and was seen by the Germans as far less satisfactory. Partly because of evident British hostility to the multilateral force, American interest in the idea was weakening. The United States declined to support an isolated German Foreign Minister, Schröder, at the Alliance's Council on 15–17 December, and then, at President Johnson's instruction, leaked American disinterest to the press.[58] De Gaulle added to German discomfort early in the new year by claiming that the German question was a 'European question', by which he meant it was to be solved by the Europeans alone. Yet Erhard still believed de Gaulle could be won round.[59] He had even gained the impression that de Gaulle had agreed to a Foreign Ministers' conference on improved integration in May, though Couve de Murville had ruled this out at the end of March.[60]

De Gaulle's underlying dissatisfaction with German policy was soon to be compounded by his dissatisfaction with the European Commission. The Commission had been requested by the 15 December Council to prepare proposals, for the financing of the Common Agricultural Policy after the end of June and the implementation of the agreement of January 1962, whereby the Community was to acquire its own resources. The latter, in turn, required consideration of the budgetary procedures to regulate these resources. Both at the time and in retrospect the Commission's proposals have been judged to have been over-ambitious.[61] The Commission did needlessly antagonize Paris by presenting its proposals to the Assembly first, but this was hardly the main issue. The proposals themselves would have brought a single market into operation in July 1967, with the Community bearing the cost of the Common Agricultural Policy. Expenditure was to be financed from the customs duties and levies which would be treated as the Community's own resources. The associated budgetary procedure would have given the Assembly the right to propose amendments which, if supported by the Commission, could only be overturned by a Council majority of five.[62]

A Franco-German meeting on 11–12 June 1965 left the French dissatisfied and the Germans in disarray.[63] Subsequently, on 22 June, Lahr for the Germans and Wormser for the French seemed to have reached agreement on a modified version of the Commission's package, but when the six met on 28 June this agreement unravelled.[64] Couve de Murville began to hint that a crisis was approaching and at 2 a.m. on 1 July broke off the negotiations. France proceeded to inflame the crisis by announcing, on 6 July, that she would not participate in the Community's institutions.

Although the disagreements over the financing of agriculture, and even more so the powers of the Assembly, were real enough, they were not unbridgeable. The negotiations were the victim of a much wider set of considerations concerning the future direction of integration, including the role of the Commission, and the Atlantic relationship. The preceding five years had seen protracted efforts by all parties to push integration, in both a European and an Atlantic sense, in the direction each desired. The crisis of 1965 was the expression of the incompatibility of the various grand designs for Europe's future. This became clear on 9 September in one of de Gaulle's press conferences. There, he referred to 'the persistent reluctance of the majority of our partners to bring agriculture within the scope of the Common Market, but also certain mistakes or ambiguities in the Treaties setting up the economic union of the Six. That is why the crisis was, sooner or later, inevitable.'[65] The treaties had been signed, he continued, before France's revival in 1958 and, consequently, did not pay sufficient regard to French interests. De Gaulle set all this in the broader context, denouncing the Commission, the hegemony of the superpowers and advocates of a 'federation designated European and which is in fact Atlantic', before ending with an invocation of Europe from the Atlantic to the Urals.[66]

There were, however, limits to de Gaulle's breach with his partners. When the other five refused to enter into any revision of the treaties de Gaulle pulled back and permitted the Community to resume functioning. The device which facilitated this was designated the Luxembourg Compromise, though in fact it was more of a statement of disagreement. While the other five declared that

> Where, in the case of decisions which may be taken by majority vote on a proposal of the Commission, very important interests of one or more partners are at stake, the Members of the Council will endeavour, within a reasonable time, to reach solutions which can be adopted by all the Members of the Council . . .[67]

France insisted that 'the discussion must be continued until unanimous agreement is reached'.[68] They then recorded the obvious fact that they disagreed. With the Luxembourg Compromise of January in place the financing of agriculture was quickly settled and a decision on the Community's own resources postponed.

At the Franco-German meeting in June 1965 the Germans sought to link agreement on agriculture with agreement on the Atlantic Alliance, specifically on participation in a nuclear planning committee which had been proposed by McNamara at the end of May.[69] The committee was another prospective solution to the problem of how to provide for some kind of European participation in nuclear strategy. France, however, declined participation on 9 July as debate about the committee and about the multilateral force increased. French refusal to participate was one more symbol of dissatisfaction with the arrangements within the Atlantic Alliance. Yet few anticipated the step which de Gaulle took the following year. On 21 February 1966 de Gaulle announced that France would reassert her sovereignty over all forces within its territory and indicated that it would withdraw from the integrated command structure of the Alliance. The decision was confirmed by letter on 7 March and France duly withdrew in July.

De Gaulle had long felt that France was not accorded a role of equality within the command structure of the Alliance and resented the affront to her sovereignty which he held the North Atlantic Treaty Organisation to pose.[70] But withdrawal from the organization did not mean, as de Gaulle made clear in his letter to Johnson, withdrawal from the North Atlantic Treaty.[71] The limits of the breach with the Atlantic Alliance became clear over the following two years. The Alliance had to adapt to the new climate of *détente*, which in part had facilitated de Gaulle's decision. Seeking to define its role in the new situation, the Alliance set up a committee under the Belgian Prime Minister Pierre Harmel. One of the key issues was whether or not the Alliance, in addition to its member states, should have a role in the management of *détente*. Couve de Murville asserted that it should not; the Alliance was a purely defensive arrangement. Yet the final report assigned the Alliance a dual task. Alongside military defence the Harmel report of December 1967 specified that the Alliance should work towards the solution of basic political questions. France signed the report.[72]

CRISIS AND COMPROMISE IN THE EAST

The difficulties of holding together the systems of integration in eastern Europe were both less severe and more severe. Romania had been able to limit Khrushchev's push for further integration and also successfully challenged his successors after Khrushchev fell from power in October 1964. Romania did not have to wait long to discover the new leaders' intentions. At the beginning of 1965 *Pravda* signalled that Kosygin and Brezhnev were seeking to give Comecon and the Warsaw Pact a higher profile. The two leaders continued to press the theme throughout that year. Finally, in May 1966, Ceauşescu replied, denouncing the existing blocs as 'an anachronism inconsistent with the independence and national sovereignty of peoples'.[73] This was bad enough, but Ceauşescu went further, threatening to open the Pandora's box of east European nationalism: 'Rumanian land – Moldavia, Transylvania – has been under foreign domination for many centuries'.[74] Both sides retreated within months. At the July 1966 Warsaw Pact meeting there was no progress on reform but there was a lengthy declaration in which the states repeatedly reaffirmed their commitment to Europe's existing borders and called upon other states to join in a 'conference on questions of European security and co-operation'.[75]

The solidity of the eastern bloc was confirmed the following year. During a visit to Poland in September 1967 de Gaulle publicly speculated upon a 'new vocation' for Poland. The words were vague but his intention was clear enough. De Gaulle was trying to tempt the Poles by holding out his vision of Europe from the Atlantic to the Urals. The Polish leader understood the implications and replied the following day, affirming Poland's commitment to the eastern bloc.[76] The risks of setting out on an independent road were made brutally clear in Czechoslovakia in 1968. In contrast to the 1956 Hungarian revolt there was no suggestion that Czechoslovakia intended to leave the Warsaw Pact. The Soviet Union, however, perceived a threat to its socialist identity. Czechoslovakia was invaded and the Brezhnev doctrine of 15 July deployed in justification. When 'hostile forces' seek to divert a country from the socialist path, that is no longer a purely internal matter. It is, Brezhnev asserted, of common concern.[77]

In both halves of Europe advocates of economic and military integration had met with considerable disappointment. Nationalist resentment at perceived superpower hegemony and fears of the loss of sovereign independence had induced displays of independence. Yet there were limits to these challenges. Even Czechoslovakia suffered more because of misjudgement of Soviet intentions than a desire to overturn the prevailing order. In 1968 the basic pattern, the institutions and in most respects the formal commitments and goals, were little different from when Europe's post-war architecture crystallized a decade earlier.

THE ENLARGEMENT OF THE COMMUNITY

By then Britain had renewed its application for membership under the Labour government of Harold Wilson. The decision had been especially difficult for a party marked by a long-standing antipathy to the Community. Among the critics of the decision, Douglas Jay pointed to the enthusiasm of the Conservatives who hoped, he claimed, to use entry to increase reliance upon indirect taxation, and to the enthusiasm of business circles whose real interest lay in using increased competition to undermine the trade unions.[78] Despite these traditional suspicions, the advantages of membership, and the lack of real alternatives, seemed overwhelming to others. Ironically Prime Minister Wilson was probably encouraged by the crisis in the Community and the weakening of its supranational elements. He even hoped that de Gaulle might become the prime supporter of British membership.[79]Alternatives to membership were canvassed, including the idea of a North Atlantic Free Trade Area. One study argued that this was in fact preferable on economic grounds, but had to conclude that it was 'a possibility rather than a probability'.[80] For de Gaulle the same was true of British membership of the Community. Eventually, on 27 November 1967, the British application was vetoed by de Gaulle, if anything in an even more damning manner than in 1963.

Once again his partners protested, not least because of his continued use of the press conference as a means of diplomacy.

De Gaulle's veto of November 1967 was not his final word. In the last months of his office there were signs that he might be prepared to reconsider. These culminated in a discussion with the British Ambassador to Paris, Soames, on 4 February 1969. In addition to expressing a more sympathetic attitude to British membership de Gaulle speculated upon European defence co-operation, and the possibility that the Atlantic Alliance might not last. In London the Foreign Minister Michael Stewart was suspicious of de Gaulle's motives. Wilson, in Bonn on a visit to the German Chancellor Kiesinger, revealed the contents of the conversation with Soames. This disclosure was soon followed by others and by public dispute between Britain and France about what had actually been said. The whole affair ended in animosity and bitterness.[81]

At this point de Gaulle had only a few more months in office left. After extensive domestic unrest and a misjudged referendum de Gaulle resigned. His successor, George Pompidou, was a former Gaullist Prime Minister and shared his predecessor's faith in the primacy of states. But he was also more strongly committed to the European Community, not out of any federalist inclination but out of 'necessity'.[82] The necessity arose from France's relationship with the Federal Republic of Germany. The underlying strength of the German economy was confirmed in 1969 by the eventual revaluation of the mark, which was preceded by the devaluation of the franc. Pompidou was even more concerned about the Ostpolitik of the new Chancellor Brandt whose SPD governed in coalition with the Free Democrats from September 1969. The Federal Republic's policy towards the east had already begun to change under the great coalition of the SPD and Christian Democrats. With Brandt's Chancellorship, however, the Federal Republic's policy became more assertive and dynamic. The new tone was evident in Brandt's reference to the 'two states in Germany'.[83]

Against this background Pompidou began to look to Britain as a potential counterweight to the more assertive Federal Republic. On the German side Brandt too looked to enlargement and integration of the Community to balance his new eastern policy and reassure nervous allies.[84] The breakthrough came at the Hague Summit of 1–2 December 1969. On the first evening Brandt reassured Pompidou that enlargement would not pose a threat to the Franco-German axis and showed understanding of French concerns about the financing of the Community's agricultural policy. The latter remained of great importance, and Pompidou was determined to see a final regulation of the financial issue before Britain entered the Community and gained the opportunity to influence the structure of agricultural finances.[85] The outcome was agreement on the linkage of 'completion', 'deepening' and 'enlargement' which Pompidou had sketched out earlier in a press conference on 10 July.[86] As agreed at the Hague, 'completion' meant the financing of agriculture from the Community's own resources. 'Deepening' entailed progress on two fronts, political co-operation and monetary union. With these agreed, enlargement, subject to successful negotiation, could take place.

The introduction of the Community's own resources and the associated budgetary procedures were quickly agreed upon, although not without some intense wrangling, especially over the powers of the Assembly within the new budgetary procedure. The outcome was the Treaty of Luxembourg, signed in April 1970, which amended the Treaty of Rome. According to the Luxembourg Treaty the Community was to acquire its own resources by 1975 and the Assembly's powers were expanded, albeit not to the extent desired by the Assembly.[87]

The financial settlement embodied in the Treaty of Luxembourg boded ill for Britain. Importing proportionally more from beyond the Community's frontiers, she would contribute more heavily to the Community than she would benefit through the Common Agricultural Policy. France, however, refused to allow Britain any influence over the terms of the financial settlement. When formal negotiations with the applicant countries, Denmark, Norway and Eire in addition to Britain, began in June 1970 a new government under the Conservative leader Edward Heath was in office in London. In the Scandinavian countries the strains imposed by the application of Denmark and Norway had brought about the demise of the proposed Nordek Treaty establishing a Nordic customs union. The main problem here was Finland's neutrality and its fear that this neutrality would, at least in the eyes of the Soviet Union, be compromised if it was linked through the Nordek Treaty to members of the European Community. The Finns sought to allay Soviet suspicion by offering to organize the conference on security and co-operation in Europe which the Warsaw Pact had called for. The Soviet Union was not reassured. Finally, although the Nordek Treaty was ready for signature, Finland declined to sign it amidst open disagreement between the President and the Prime Minister.[88] Once again Nordic co-operation had been undermined by the magnetic pull of broader processes of integration.

The negotiations with Britain made slow progress, seeming to come to a halt at the end of 1970. Once again doubts arose about French willingness to accept British membership, especially once the French press began to raise the question of the role of sterling. The suspicion was that unless this was reduced Britain would be unable to commit herself fully to the Community. Both the British and the French had been considering the desirability of direct talks between Heath and Pompidou since the summer or autumn of 1970. After careful preparation the two met on 20–21 May 1971. In contrast to the bitterness of the Soames affair of 1969, the meeting was a great success, with Pompidou concluding with an effusive declaration of support for British membership.[89] Thereafter progress was rapid, with the Accession Treaties being signed on 22 January 1972. Ratification duly followed in all cases save one. In a referendum of September 1972 Norwegian opponents of entry gained a narrow victory. The critics included not only agricultural and fishing interests but also sections of Norwegian urban society who disliked the image of a united Europe dominated by high-technology and business.[90]

While enlargement and completion had been achieved, uneven progress was made with the third of Pompidou's goals, deepening. The Davignon Report on political co-operation was ready in the summer of 1970 and was adopted at Luxembourg on 27 October. Care had been taken to avoid any appearance of a revival of the Fouchet strategy. Co-operation 'in the field of foreign policy' was to be strictly intergovernmental, but there was no apparent threat to existing institutions. The latter were barely mentioned, though the report did promise informal meetings with the Parliament and stated that 'The Commission will be consulted if the activities of the European Communities are affected by the work of the Ministers.'[91]

At the Ministers' first meeting in November 1970 one of the major topics on the agenda was the proposed conference on European security. The Warsaw Pact initiative had originally been regarded with suspicion as a device to split the western alliance since in its original form the intent was to have a strictly European conference, that is one excluding the United States and Canada. In the June 1970 Warsaw Pact memorandum, however, the two North American states were explicitly mentioned as members of the conference.[92] That the Ministers of the European Community sought to co-ordinate their stance was especially important for the Federal Republic. It would serve to alleviate fears that the treaties Bonn was negotiating with the eastern states symbolized a return to the Rapallo policy of the inter-war period.[93] That such fears were still present is evident from the reaction to Brandt's meeting with Brezhnev at Oreanda in the Crimea in September 1971. One French newspaper even described this as a 'second Yalta', a view not far removed from Pompidou's.[94]

THE DEBATE ON MONETARY UNION

The debate on monetary union was marked by more concrete differences, though this did not make them more tractable. The dispute, which has characterized the issue ever since, revolved around whether the co-ordination of economic policies or monetary integration, through fixed exchange rates, was to be given priority. These two diverging approaches were embodied in the views of the German Minister of Finance, Karl Schiller, and Raymond Barre. The report commissioned at the Hague, the Werner Report, sought to mediate between these two extremes but left neither side satisfied. Pompidou was upset by the supranational element of the Werner Report and responded with a press conference, on 21 January 1971, in which he proclaimed that Europe could only be united as a confederation of states. In his dismissal of 'technical organizations, of commissions' his rhetoric was little different from de Gaulle's.[95] Some compromise was achieved at the January Franco-German summit, where Brandt made concessions for the sake of his *Ostpolitik*, but the French and German positions diverged again as the international monetary system came under strain.

The Community's members had agreed in March 1971 to maintain their exchange rates within set bands, but this arrangement was disrupted by the persistent weakness of the dollar and the consequent decision by the United States to abandon the convertibility of the dollar into gold in August 1971. A second attempt, the so-called 'snake in a tunnel', which sought to link stability *vis-à-vis* the dollar with stability between European currencies, began operating in March 1972. It did not augur well for the system when Britain, Eire and Denmark were forced to abandon it in June, having only joined in May. Despite these difficulties, at the Paris summit of October 1972 the goal of monetary union was reaffirmed and an unrealistic goal of December 1980 set for the completion of economic and monetary union. The Paris summit also saw agreement to establish a Regional Development Fund. The issue of regional development, though raised by Italy during the negotiation of the Rome Treaty, had been largely neglected for the first two decades of the Community's existence. Enlargement put it back on the agenda. Eire, the poorest of the new members, stood to benefit, as did Britain. Indeed the main pressure for the Fund came from Heath, who sought to offset Britain's contribution to Community funds through the Regional Development Fund.[96] On other issues there was no agreement. The Netherlands pushed for institutional reform but was not supported by Brandt and was opposed by the British. The trend towards intergovernmentalism, evident from the Hague to the Paris summits, would not be reversed yet.[97] The summit also ignored the

German desire for some mechanism of consultation with the United States.[98]

European relations with the United States had lost their earlier intimacy as American policy became hesitant and inconsistent, and tensions arose over the volatile currency markets. Nor did the United States greet the faltering efforts of the Community's states to move towards political co-operation. Secretary of State Kissinger had already indicated a desire to address the problem in November 1972 when he declared that 1973 was to be the Year of Europe. Quite what that meant was not clear. Then in April 1973 he called for a new Atlantic Charter. His speech on this theme, however, was clumsy and provocative. 'The United States', he proclaimed, 'has global interests and responsibilities. Our European allies have regional interests.'[99] More concretely, Kissinger was demanding that the United States be consulted before the Europeans formulated a joint stance.

The European response was less than enthusiastic. While desultory talks on a joint Euro-American declaration proceeded, relationships worsened, especially under the pressure of the war which erupted in the Middle East in October. The associated oil crisis, where the Arab oil producers sought to use oil as a weapon to punish Israel's supporters, deeply divided the Atlantic partners and, indeed, the Europeans themselves. By then the Community was working on a declaration of its own which was approved at the Copenhagen summit in December. The Declaration on European Identity asserted that 'Europe must unite and speak increasingly with a single voice if it wants to make itself heard and play its proper role in the world.'[100] The significance of this was clear: the Community was asserting that it too had global interests. Whether the Community's states could speak with one voice was another matter. At the February 1974 energy conference called by President Nixon the divergent interests of the Community's states, most notably France and Germany was unmistakable. Helmut Schmidt and the French Foreign Minister, Jobert, were openly critical, with Jobert later describing the German as 'particularly unpleasant' but acknowledging that he had responded in kind.[101]

SOCIALIST VERSUS CAPITALIST INTEGRATION

Despite these tribulations western European integration continued to exercise influence on eastern Europe. As a member of the Hungarian Politburo put it:

> Unlike the countries of the European Common Market which have made considerable progress in economic integration, the C.M.E.A. countries are lagging behind in specialization of production co-operation even at the

> lowest level. How is one to explain that Common Market countries which are divided by capitalist contradictions have forged ahead in integration ... [102]

It was not only the embarrassment of lagging behind the imperialist rival that worried Comecon leaders. The rate of growth in productivity continued to fall. Comecon's share of world trade fell slightly in the second half of the 1960s, with its share in total world exports slipping from 10.6 per cent to 9.5 per cent. Even intra-bloc trade fell back from 63 per cent to 60.69 per cent. Other indicators of integration were no more encouraging. Poland, for example, exported some 22 out of 29 products which were the subject of Comecon specialization directives in 1963. In 1969 she did not manage to export a single one of some 79 such products.[103]

The failure to make the transition from extensive growths based upon additional capital and labour inputs to intensive growth based upon increased productivity, the unfavourable comparison with developments in the Economic Community and the need to restore unity in the wake of the disruption caused by the events of 1968, all combined to put integration back on the agenda. This time the debate was complicated by a new dispute about the best path to integration. The states more committed to domestic economic reform, especially Hungary, argued for the introduction of market-based integration. In the Hungarian case, as early as November 1968 there was explicit use of the Economic Community as a model with the suggestion that quotas should be abolished and trade liberalized.[104] In the following month the implications of this were made clear. Comecon would provide a framework in which agencies and enterprises within the states would deal directly with each other. Decision-making would be decentralized. The proximity to what was happening in the west was acknowledged by the Hungarian reformer Reszo Nyers, according to whom capitalist and socialist integration 'will be similar, in that economic efficiency, the measure of profitability, will come under the control of the international market in both cases'.[105] The Soviet Union, however, remained more committed to 'planned integration', that is, the co-ordination of national plans. The Soviets also had a more specific interest in the mobilization of joint investment for the extraction of raw materials and fuel. The Romanians, of course, continued to be suspicious of any threat to their sovereignty.

Nevertheless, some progress was made at the April 1969 Comecon Council when they agreed upon the establishment of new international organizations by 'interested parties according to necessity'.[106] Soon afterwards Interchim, an intergovernmental organization covering co-operation in chemicals, was founded, albeit with the notable absence of Romania.[107] Apart from this there was little progress, though in May 1970 there was an agreement to establish an investment bank. The agreement establishing the International Investment Bank was signed in July. The prime significance of the bank lay in the fact that for the first time there was provision for majority voting on some issues. Although Romania did not join initially she had accepted the principle of majority voting within a Comecon organization.[108]

This did not mean that Romania had abandoned the defence of sovereignty. This became clear as Comecon struggled to reach agreement on a new programme for integration. When agreement was reached the Complex Programme deserved its title. Intended to last for fifteen to twenty years, the programme set out a wide range of schedules for integration, but the reservations of the Romanians were clearly embodied in the text: 'Integration is taking place on the basis of complete voluntarism; it is not accompanied by the creation of supranational organs, and does not affect the activity of organizations so far as internal planning, finances, and economic accountability are concerned.'[109] On the other hand individual states would not be able to block integration. According to the concluding section 17, any state could declare its interest in a particular aspect of the programme but its refusal to participate would not prevent the others proceeding. The Comecon states were, in fact, proposing to embark on integration à la carte, where each could choose which elements to participate in according to its own judgement of its interests.

One of the most interesting aspects of the Complex Programme lay in the provision for 'international industrial associations', whose membership could include enterprises, with co-ordinating functions, and 'joint enterprises', with ownership of their own assets.[110] It had long been a notable weakness of Comecon integration that, compared with the European Community, the level of transnational co-operation was minimal. While the Complex Programme suggests a desire to remedy this, the obstacles were substantive. It was far from clear that genuine multinational enterprises were compatible with the assumption that all property belonged to the people of the particular state in question. Ironically, where legislation did exist which permitted joint enterprises, especially in Romania, this was more often used to cover joint enterprises with capitalist firms.[111]

Soviet interest in planned integration did not abate, and between 1973 and 1975 Comecon states drew up an 'Agreed plan for multilateral integration measures' which sought to co-ordinate 'special sections' within national plans devoted to integration.[112] This did bring some tangible benefits, primarily in the supply of energy, but it did not herald a new dawn of planned integration as its advocates had hoped. Of greater significance for the east European economies was the revision of prices implemented in 1975. The prime change here was the upward revision of Soviet fuel prices in the wake of the dramatic increases on the world market. Although the new Soviet prices were considerably higher, over 50 per cent higher for Hungary, they still remained below world market prices. The Soviet Union continued to trade under-priced raw materials for over-priced east European manufactures. According to the economist Paul Marer, the result was that the Soviet Union's European partners were an 'economic liability'.[113]

The revival of the debate on integration in the east was linked with a reconsideration of policy towards the European Community. The Soviet Union proceeded cautiously, but Brezhnev acknowledged, in 1972, that 'The Soviet Union is far from ignoring the actually existing situation in Western Europe, including the existence of such an economic grouping of capitalist countries as the European Common Market and its evolution.'[114] The fact that the Soviet Union did not 'ignore' the European Community did not, however, equal recognition of it. The problem was that the European Community persisted in taking a very dim view of Comecon on the grounds that it had no authority over its member states. Nevertheless, when approached by N. Fadeyev, the Commission did agree to a meeting which took place in February 1975, but the two sides could not even agree on a communiqué. At the time, the Commission, with considerable difficulty, sought to extend its authority over commercial policy, especially credit policy, in order to strengthen its hand in negotiations with the east European states. The underlying weakness of the latter soon became evident. In 1976 Romania entered into direct negotiation with the European Community about textile exports. Within months the Commission had granted Romania quotas. Ironically, the next major breach of the Comecon front was made by the Soviet Union. Faced with the possibility of exclusion from Community fishing grounds in 1977, it too entered into negotiations.[115]

THE CONFERENCE ON SECURITY AND CO-OPERATION IN EUROPE

While east–west relationships remained limited by the conflicting perceptions and goals of the European Community and Comecon, a new framework for co-operation had emerged in a broader context. At the beginning of the decade the Soviet Union continued to press for the long-desired European security conference. The western response was cautious, with the United States initially willing to leave the initiative to the Europeans. Among its European partners it was the Federal Republic of Germany which had the most to gain from such a conference, and from the associated proposals for a reduction of forces in Europe. Brandt had agreed to promote the conference during his negotiations on the August 1970 Moscow Treaty and reaffirmed this at his 1971 meeting with Brezhnev in Oreanda in the Crimea. At the latter meeting he pressed hard for talks on mutual and balanced force reductions, gaining Brezhnev's agreement. The negotiations could not, however, proceed without the consent of the United States, and it was Brezhnev and Nixon who effectively authorized them in May 1972.[116]

After protracted preliminary talks the conference opened in July 1973 and slowly worked its way to the Helsinki Final Act signed on 1 August 1975. During the preliminary talks it was agreed that each of the thirty-five participating states should be treated equally and hence each could exercise a veto. Despite this, complex compromises were eventually agreed. The Warsaw Pact obtained agreement that frontiers were 'inviolable', though it would have preferred the term 'immutable', ruling out even peaceful border changes. The west insisted upon the inclusion of extensive reference to human rights and confidence-building measures in the sections dealing with military security. The latter included, for example, notification of manoeuvres involving more than 25,000 troops.[117] The Final Act also included provision for a continuation of the process of consultation, but not for the creation of a permanent committee as desired by the Soviet Union. The Conference on Security and Co-operation in Europe was precisely that. There was no new international organization, no surrender of sovereignty. There was not even full agreement on the precise legal status of the Final Act.[118] But it did provide a new framework for co-operation and it did bridge the postwar division of Europe.

Participation in the conference had presented the European Community with what was to be a recurrent dilemma. Since the conference covered economic issues and hence had a bearing upon areas within the competence of the Community, the Commission asserted its right to be involved. On the other hand the Helsinki process was a conference of states and dealt primarily with issues which fell within the remit of European Political Co-operation in which the Commission had at most a limited role. The problem was resolved in September 1973 by assigning Commission representatives to the Danish delegation, Denmark exercising the Presidency of the Council of Ministers at the time.[119] The tension between the intergovernmental and the supranational elements of the Community was heightened at the end of the following year at the Paris summit.

THE TREND TOWARDS INTERGOVERNMENTALISM IN THE WEST

The Paris summit was very much the creation of Valery Giscard d'Estaing, who succeeded Pompidou after the latter's death in April 1974. Giscard was more committed to European integration than Pompidou but retained a suspicion of supranationalism. In the 1960s he equated the latter with an 'antinational' Europe, though he also recognized that there was a need for more than 'a Europe of alliances, a Europe of states' which he said could not withstand the blows of history.[120] His prime interlocutors at Paris were Helmut Schmidt and Harold Wilson, who had come to power committed to 'renegotiate' Britain's terms of entry to the Community and hold a referendum on continued membership. The Paris summit was a carefully prepared one, with Giscard concerned to ensure its success. In accordance with his wishes the discussions excluded the President of the Commission.

The prime point in the resulting communiqué stated simply that the 'Heads of Government have ... decided to meet, accompanied by the Ministers of Foreign Affairs, three times a year and, whenever necessary, in the Council of Ministers and in the context of political co-operation.'[121] With these bland words the summit announced the creation of what became known as the European Council. Its significance lay in the fact that it was an intergovernmental arrangement, though Commission representatives were allowed to attend. It was not a Community institution, for these could be created only by amending the Treaty of Rome. Its precise role was ambiguous. On the one hand the communiqué suggested that these meetings were to provide political direction and stimulus to further integration. Yet, as the Foreign Minister of the Netherlands warned, there was a risk that they could turn into a court of appeal 'which could paralyse the functioning of the General Council and of other councils of the Community'.[122] Balancing the intergovernmental character of the European Council, the Paris summit also agreed to move to direct elections to the European Assembly 'in or after 1978', though there were dissenting statements from Britain and Denmark, and to 'renounce the practice of making agreement on all questions conditional on the unanimous consent of the member States'.[123]

The first European Council after Paris was held in March 1975 in Dublin and dealt primarily with the British problem. The Labour Prime Minister Wilson sought to extract maximum publicity from the event, though the details had already been worked out, in order to placate domestic critics. He devoted special attention to the access of New Zealand dairy produce to the Community, leaving Helmut Schmidt to comment on this particular absurdity, 'Here we are talking about cheese and not a word has been said about unemployment and inflation.'[124] Having antagonized Britain's partners, Wilson then had to secure parliamentary approval of the agreement by courtesy of opposition votes and hold a referendum which confirmed membership by just over 67 per cent. The renegotiation, and even more so an attempt to circumvent Community unity at the forthcoming international energy conference, confirmed Britain's growing reputation as the Community's 'awkward partner'.[125]

The Paris summit had also decided that 'the time has come for the Nine to agree as soon as possible on an overall concept of European Union' and 'consequently' called for the Belgian Prime Minister, Leo Tindemans, to produce a report which would take into account a series of other reports from the Community's institutions.[126] Indeed, it would take little exaggeration to designate 1975 as the year of reports. For in addition to those already mentioned there was another report on monetary union (the Marjolin Report) and one commissioned by the Netherlands (the Spierenburg Report). The first of these to appear, the Marjolin Report, was a damning indictment of Community policy, or rather of the member states' lack of will. According to Marjolin, the problem in part was conceptual confusion. Economic and monetary union was being treated as if it were a mere extrapolation from the existing customs union, whereas it entailed in reality a transfer of authority to Community institutions which would border on political union. Yet member states showed no willingness to embark upon such a momentous transformation. Marjolin cited the pressing economic problems of the day and added, 'If not even a modicum of cohesion and unity can be established in opposition to these grave threats, there is not much point in continuing the discussion on EMU or European union.'[127]

The other reports dealt with a mixture of policy and institutional matters, seeking to balance the perceived need for greater integration against the patent difficulty member states were finding in making any progress. The Commission's Report of June 1975 considered, but rejected, solving the problem by regarding the Union 'as a network of special agreements involving all or only some of the Member States depending on the subject'.[128] Instead, it advocated the 'principe de subsidiarité' according to which 'the Union will be given responsibility only for those matters which the Member States are no longer capable of dealing with efficiently'.[129] The Tindemans Report of December 1975 sought to solve the problem in a different way, by allowing some member states to proceed at a faster pace than the others. But the report warned that 'This does not mean Europe à la carte: each country will be bound by the agreement of all as to the final objective to be achieved in common; it is only the timescales for achievement which vary.'[130] The prospect of graduated integration, as it came to be called, was already evident in the operation of the monetary snake. The fear, evident in both the Commission's report and that of Tindemans, was that divergent interests and centripetal forces would lead to a Europe à la carte which would undermine the integrity of the Community and make a nonsense of any notion of European union.[131] Little came of the Tindemans Report or of any of the others at this time. Giscard disliked the suggestion of additional powers for the Commission and Parliament. In an apparent reversion to earlier Gaullist notions, the French even speculated upon the creation of a political directorate. This met with predictable opposition and received no support from Schmidt.[132]

Agreement between Schmidt and Giscard was to form the basis for renewed monetary integration. The initiative was taken in 1977 by the new President of the Commission, Roy Jenkins. Jenkins took up monetary integration as the most obvious strategy of revitalizing integration and the role of the Commission. He was aware that none of the larger members was well-disposed to a Commission initiative, but decided that 'we . . . had to be prepared to go against them and to blaze a trail to a greater extent than we had done previously, however much this offended people'.[133] The initial response suggested considerable scepticism rather than offence. But then on 28 February 1978 Schmidt announced his conversion to a surprised Jenkins.[134] Schmidt had been persuaded of the virtues of further monetary integration by the continued decline in the dollar, which fell to 2.02 Deutschmarks in February, and by the failure of the Carter administration to do anything about it. The German Chancellor duly consulted Giscard, who shared his views about protecting European currencies from the destabilizing effects of the dollar and also hoped to use linkage with the Deutschmark to hold down inflation in France. Callaghan was noticeably less enthusiastic, but did agree, at the Copenhagen summit in April, to appoint one of three 'wise men' to prepare a report. The Bremen Report was in fact largely a product of Franco-German co-operation.[135]

The report was an ambiguous document which vaguely promised to place a European Currency Unit at the centre of the proposed system. This idea had been encouraged by Schmidt's speculation that German currency reserves might be used to back the scheme. The Bundesbank, however, which controlled the reserves, was adamantly opposed to this idea.[136] The ambiguity about the role of the ecu was linked to a dispute about whether a parity grid or a currency basket was to be used to trigger intervention. Underlying the technical details of the two lay a choice of considerable importance. The net effect of the basket system would be to increase the probability that Germany would have to bear the brunt of maintaining the system, whereas the parity grid would spread the burden, automatically putting pressure on the weaker countries as well.[137] Attempts to persuade Germany to play a leading role were widespread at this time, with Carter calling for Germany to act as the economic 'locomotive' which would pull the world economy out of recession. Carter's call was no more successful than the advocates of the basket system, with the Bundesbank standing firm.

Finally, at the Aachen Franco-German summit in September, Schmidt and Giscard agreed on a compromise Belgian proposal which in reality meant that the parity grid would dominate the system.[138] This still left protracted wrangling over the implications of the system for the Common Agricultural Policy and subsidies for Eire and Italy to facilitate their participation. Neither issue proved insuperable, though the negotiations threatened to collapse over relatively minor differences.[139] With these issues resolved, the European Monetary System came into being in March 1979. It was far from being a monetary union, though optimistic voices claimed that it was a step on the road to one.[140]

The negotiations had been complicated by the existence of other issues, among them the question of further enlargement. The new applicants, Greece, Portugal and Spain, had all recently begun the transition from authoritarian regimes and were seeking membership, in part, to bolster their fledgling democratic institutions. Greece and Portugal at least had vigorous supporters within the existing Community, in France and Britain respectively. But all of the applications were viewed with some trepidation. The reason for the concern was simple. Spain alone would swell the Community's agricultural work-force by 25 per cent.[141] The incorporation of these relatively poor countries would increase the burden on existing policies, especially on agriculture. It would raise also the more general question about the purposes of the Community, that is, to what extent it should have a strong redistributive function.

Some of the implications of this had been considered by the McDougall Report of April 1977. The report noted that Community expenditure was well under 1 per cent of GDP. By comparison, in existing federations federal public expenditure accounted for approximately a quarter of GDP and much of that went into regional redistribution which facilitated stability. The report focused on a less ambitious scenario, with the Community accounting for either 2–2.5 or 5–7 per cent, though this would still have been a dramatic increase from the current level. The underlying argument for considering such increases was, in part, that 'reducing the inequalities in per capita incomes between the various parts of the area . . . is a necessary part of economic union'.[142]

The Community's relatively small budget hampered it in other areas too. As the member states deprived themselves of tariff barriers to protect troubled industries, they resorted to an array of non-tariff barriers. In the declining industries of ship-building, steel and textiles this entailed extensive subsidies. Though well-aware that this undermined the principles of the common market as well as violating specific Treaty articles, the Commission was powerless to do much about it. In part the problem was a lack of authority, but a Community solution to the problems of structural adjustment was also impeded by a lack of funds.[143]

As the end of the decade approached, the inadequacies of the Community became the subject of two studies, one initiated by Jenkins, the other by Giscard. Jenkins was concerned by the cumbersome operation of the Commission itself and, in the summer of 1978, decided to appoint an independent group headed by Dirk Spierenburg. Giscard's proposal, announced in a letter of September, was perceived by the Commission as a direct attack upon itself, as a reversion to the old Gaullist idea of subordinating the Commission to a secretariat controlled by the member states, or even worse a directorate of the major European powers.[144] Those designated as the Three Wise Men, Robert Marjolin, Edmund Dell and Barend Biesheuvel, proved to be far too independent to suit Giscard, who quickly lost interest in the inquiry.

The Report of the Three Wise Men was submitted in October 1979, a month after the Spierenburg Report. Both sought to counter the weakening of the Commission's authority and made recommendations for streamlining its operations, including reducing the number of Commissioners. The Wise Men deplored the drift towards intergovernmentalism and called upon the Council to make more use of majority voting. Yet both reports reflected the intergovernmental mood, neither being ambitious. The Wise Men looked to the Council for improvement and sought to strengthen the position of the President of the Council.[145] Despite these proposals for institutional reform, the Wise Men located the Community's weakness in a failure of political will and of a clear sense of the Community's goal rather in the operation of its institutions.[146]

Despite the Wise Men's pessimism and dismissal of 'futuristic visions', they had noted the achievement that the Community embodied: 'The Community is a quite unprecedented creation. It may be less than a federation, or even less than a confederation, but it represents a great deal more than a traditional alliance or international organization.'[147] This was more or less the status which Giscard had assigned to Europe in the previous decade. It was a potentially unstable status because it left open the precise distribution of power and authority within the Community. The Community could continue the slide towards intergovernmentalism or it could 'advance' in either a confederal or federal direction. The direct elections to the European Parliament which took place in June 1979 pointed towards federalism in so far as they endowed the Community with direct legitimacy. Yet, if this was a step in the direction of federalism, it was a very small one. Parliament remained very much the junior partner in Community decision-making. It had acquired increased budgetary powers in 1970 and 1975, including the ability to reject the entire draft budget, but apart from this negative power it had little ability to influence the shape and size of the budget.[148] When the Parliament took advantage of the debate on institutional reform to advance claims to approve the Commission's programme, and to be consulted on all Commission initiatives, it was sharply rebuffed.[149]

The budget was also a focus of dispute between the member states. The problem lay in the amount of Britain's contribution. There was general willingness to do something to redress the problem, and Schmidt was especially sympathetic. The atmosphere, however, was not helped by the new British Prime Minister Margaret Thatcher. After a reasonable first summit in June 1979, she needlessly antagonized her partners at Dublin in November, belligerently demanding 'our money' back.[150] Such antics left little apparent prospect for even the modest expansion of the Community's budget suggested in the MacDougall Report.

ATLANTIC TENSIONS AND THE REVIVAL OF THE COLD WAR

Atlantic relationships fared little better at the end of the decade. The old dispute about the relative contribution of the United States and the Europeans to the collective defence of the west continued to provide a periodic point of dispute. This had been responsible partly for the formation of the Eurogroup within the Atlantic Alliance in 1968. The purpose was to co-ordinate the European contribution to defence on a loose, informal basis. Despite the lack of any institutional framework France predictably declined to join the group.[151] France did agree to join the Independent European Programme Group which emerged in 1976 and took over some of the functions of the earlier Eurogroup. The independent group arose in response to calls for the standardization of military equipment and sought to promote trade in military equipment between Europe and the United States. French membership reflected a more co-operative attitude towards the Atlantic Alliance under Giscard's Presidency. There were, however, limits to this. The addition of the word Independent was a concession to French sensitivities, as was the fact that the group did not meet at the Atlantic Alliance's headquarters in Brussels.[152] The reliance upon the United States combined with the fears of subserviency it brought, and the reluctance of the Europeans to accept supranational control in the field of defence, to ensure that these efforts would not extend beyond informal co-ordination. In that sense the rejection of the Defence Community back in 1954 continued to constrain European integration.[153]

Economic tensions added to the strains in Atlantic relationships, with the United States complaining about competition from subsidized European exports, including steel. For its part the Community sought some restriction upon the recourse to countervailing duties by the United States. Neither side was entirely satisfied by the compromise worked out during the Tokyo round of GATT.[154] It was not trade, however, but the broader considerations of security that caused the greatest concern. As the United States continued to make progress with the Soviet Union over arms control, setting limits to intercontinental ballistic missiles, the Europeans, especially the Federal Republic, worried about the perceived imbalance of forces at the European level, which was aggravated by Soviet intentions to deploy more modern intermediate range weapons. In October 1977 Schmidt expressed German concerns in a lecture to the International Institute for Strategic Studies. His intent was to push the United States towards incorporating intermediate weapons in the negotiations.[155] The outcome, after protracted negotiation, was the Atlantic Alliance's December 1979 'dual track' strategy, linking deployment of Pershing II and Cruise missiles in Europe to a commitment to negotiate the reduction of these weapons along with their Soviet counterparts.[156] Shortly after, the Soviet Union invaded Afghanistan, triggering a breakdown in the negotiations between the Soviet Union and the United States. Instead of the negotiated settlement Schmidt had wanted, he was confronted with a deterioration in relationships between the two blocs that developed into what commentators called the Second Cold War. Even before the dual-track decision, commentators were referring to the 'strained relationship' between the United States and Germany. In 1980 the relationship became even more strained.[157] The core of the problem lay in the fact that the United States could watch the deterioration in relations with the Soviet Union with relative equanimity. For the Federal Republic, the new atmosphere threatened the process of *détente* symbolized by the *Ostpolitik* of the 1970s and the Conference on Security and Co-operation in Europe. The distance from American perceptions was evident at the Franco-German summit of February 1980 where Europe's 'special responsibilities' were emphasized alongside affirmation of the Atlantic Alliance.[158]

While eastern Europe was not troubled by such evident strains, the economic prospects of the region were looking darker. Exports to the industrialized world remained relatively stagnant despite efforts to boost them, in part to offset the increasing hard currency debts which eastern Europe incurred in an ambitious attempt to switch to technologically based growth. The region was still dogged by the old problem of a profligate use of raw materials, with twice the energy consumption of western Europe per thousand dollars of GDP.[159] Moreover, as Europe slid into the Second Cold War the economic strains began to show in alarming form. The most heavily indebted east European state, Poland, announced that it could no longer meet the payments on its foreign debt.

Over the previous two decades both halves of Europe had witnessed efforts to accelerate integration, and both halves had witnessed resistance from member states. In the east the limits to diversity were much tighter and the costs of self-assertion much higher. But beyond the ideological conformity imposed in the interests of collective security, integration proved more difficult, both because of the inherent nature of the socialist enterprise and because of the burden of eastern Europe's historical legacy. In the west integration proved easier. Lacking a hegemonic power willing to impose its will by force, integration in the west was less extensive, leaving out some western European states, though the first enlargement of the European Community and the imminent prospect of further enlargement testified to the magnetic attraction of the integrated core countries. Integration proved easier so long as it was driven forward by market forces which could be treated as politically neutral. Efforts to extend integration beyond this base, into monetary union, structural adjustment or redistribution, quickly demonstrated that in the west too the sovereignty of the nation-state had not lost its arthritic grip.

NOTES

1. On these issues see van der Wee, *Prosperity and Upheaval*, especially pp. 48–54 and 450–62; Brian Tew, *The Evolution of the International Monetary System 1945–77* (London, 1977), pp. 112–16.
2. His biographer Jean Lacoutre sees it primarily as an assertion of national identity and history against the dictates of ideology. *De Gaulle. The Ruler 1945–1970* (New York, 1991), pp. 397–8. See also David Calleo, *The Atlantic Fantasy* (Baltimore, 1970), pp. 59–66; Ernst Weisenfeld, 'Europa vom Atlantik zum Ural', in Wilfried Loth and Robert Picht (eds), *De Gaulle, Deutschland und Europa* (Opladen, 1991), pp. 71–9; J. B. Duroselle, 'General de Gaulle's Europe and Jean Monnet's Europe', *The World Today*, **22** (1966), pp. 1–13.
3. See the very useful contribution by Ingo Kolboom, 'Charles de Gaulle und ein deutsch-französisches Missverständnis über Nation und Europa', in Loth and Picht (eds), *De Gaulle, Deutschland und Europa*, pp. 135–50, and Stanley Hoffmann, 'Obstinate or obsolete? The fate of the nation-state and the case of western Europe', *Daedalus*, **95** (1966), pp. 862–915.

4. On Rambouillet and the different impressions recorded by the two sides see Lacoutre, *De Gaulle. The Ruler*, pp. 338–9. More generally, see Hans von der Groeben, *The European Community. The Formative Years* (Brussels, 1985), pp. 89–91.
5. Edmund Jouve, *Le Général de Gaulle et la construction de l'Europe (1940–1966)* (Paris, 1967), Vol. 2, p. 242.
6. Von der Groeben, *The European Community*, p. 94.
7. European Parliament, *Selection of Texts*, p. 107. Pierre Gerbet suggests that the absence of any reference to economic matters may have reassured those fearful that the proposal would harm the Economic Community. 'In search of political union', in Ray Pryce (ed.), *The Dynamics of European Union* (London, 1987), p. 118.
8. Harold Macmillan, *Pointing the Way 1959–1961* (London, 1972), p. 325.
9. Winand, *Eisenhower, Kennedy and the United States of Europe*, p. 212.
10. The proposal came from the National Security Council. Eisenhower sanctioned it on 17 December 1960 (*ibid.*, p. 217).
11. See J. Young, *Britain and Europe*, pp. 74–6; J. Bruce-Gardyne and N. Lawson, *The Power Game* (London, 1976), pp. 38–62.
12. James Nicholson and Roger East, *From the Six to the Twelve* (Harlow, 1987), p. 8.
13. European Parliament, *Selection of Texts*, p. 113.
14. Lacoutre, *De Gaulle. The Ruler*, p. 349, quotes Ambassador Seydoux's claim that de Gaulle 'could not resist the temptation to add two or three little touches' but concedes that these affected issues vital to his partners. They were also vital to de Gaulle's conception of Europe from the Atlantic to the Urals.
15. Susan Bodenheimer argues that the differences between the six were bridgeable, that the Netherlands was the only member committed to British membership and could not have held out in isolation. The negotiations were wrecked, she concludes, more by bad diplomacy than a conflict of interests; 'The "political union" debate in Europe', *International Organization*, **21** (1967), pp. 24–54. Lois Pattison de Ménil, *Who Speaks for Europe?* (London, 1977), p. 72, blames 'the issue of the timing of the British entry', while Lacoutre, *De Gaulle. The Ruler*, p. 350, suggests that de Gaulle was losing interest in the union proposal. Bodenheimer's argument almost certainly underestimates the conflict of interest which was to surface again, weakening the Franco-German Treaty of 1963 and leading to the crises in the Communities (1965–66) and NATO.
16. Jouve, *Le Général de Gaulle et la construction de l'Europe*, pp. 266–7.
17. Winand, *Eisenhower, Kennedy and the United States of Europe*, p. 241.
18. It had already been put forward by State Department officials. See, for example, Georg Ball's 2 April speech in Weigall and Stirk (eds), *The Origins and Development of the European Community*, pp. 119–20.
19. Winand, *Eisenhower, Kennedy and the United States of Europe*, p. 240.
20. *Ibid.*, p. 199. On the 1960 resolution see pp. 196–7. For an analysis of the rhetoric surrounding the idea of an Atlantic community, see James Richardson, 'The concept of an Atlantic community', *Journal of Common Market Studies*, **3** (1964–5), pp. 1–22.
21. Winand, *Eisenhower, Kennedy and the United States of Europe*, pp. 184–5. Interestingly, Monnet disliked the 80 per cent clause because it pointed to complete free trade and threatened to make the Community's external tariff meaningless; *ibid.*, pp. 185–6.

22. According to Bundy, 'it is our guess that all merely national deterrents in the hands of powers of the second rank will become uneconomic and ineffective . . . ' quoted in William C. Cromwell, *The United States and the European Pillar* (New York, 1992), p. 21.
23. On flexible deterrence see James E. Stromseth, *The Origins of Flexible Response* (Basingstoke, 1988). There were in fact two versions: a land-based MRBM force favoured by General Norstad and the sea-based MLF force. The former was finally ruled out at the beginning of 1963. See Winand, *Eisenhower, Kennedy and the United States of Europe*, p. 216.
24. Schwarz, *Adenauer. Der Staatsmann*, pp. 737, 739, 763.
25. Gerbet, 'In search of political union', pp. 123–4; *Akten zur Auswärtigen Politik der Bundesrepublik Deutschlands 1963*, Vol. 1, doc. 136 (29 March 1963).
26. Winand, *Eisenhower, Kennedy and the United States of Europe*, pp. 315–20. For de Gaulle's attitude, see his *Memoirs of Hope* (London, 1971), p. 220.
27. Frank Costigliola, 'The failed design', *Diplomatic History*, **8** (1984), pp. 248–9. Richard Neustadt, *Alliance Politics* (New York, 1970), wrote that 'through a comedy of diplomatic errors he [de Gaulle] got contradictory signals . . . ', pp. 54–5.
28. Weigall and Stirk (eds), *The Origins and Development of the European Community*, p. 131.
29. Lahr, of course, denied this. *Akten zur Auswärtigen Politik der Bundesrepublik Deutschlands 1963*, Vol. 1, doc. 30 (17 January 1963).
30. Von der Groeben, *The European Community*, pp. 100–11. The agreement of 14 January was backdated to the end of 1961 in order notionally to adhere to the Treaty text.
31. Quoted in D. A. C. Freestone and J. S. Davidson, *The Institutional Framework of the European Communities* (London, 1988), p. 30.
32. Von der Groeben, *The European Community*, p. 141.
33. For the change, see David Forte, 'The response of Soviet foreign policy to the Common Market, 1957–1963', *Soviet Studies*, **19** (1967–8), pp. 373–86.
34. *Current Digest of the Soviet Press*, **35** (1962), p. 6.
35. Montias, *Economic Development in Communist Rumania*, p. 206.
36. Richard Vaughan, *Post-War European Integration* (London, 1975), p. 147.
37. *Ibid.*, p. 146. Montias identifies the provenance of other clauses, including those reflecting a specifically Soviet interest. *Economic Development in Communist Rumania*, pp. 210–11.
38. *Current Digest of the Soviet Press*, **36** (1962), p. 4.
39. *Ibid.*, pp. 3–4.
40. Robert S. Jaster, 'The defeat of Khrushchev's plan to integrate eastern Europe', *World Today*, **19** (1963), p. 517.
41. *Ibid.*, p. 521; Montias, *Economic Development in Communist Rumania*, p. 215.
42. Vaughan, *Postwar European Integration*, p. 149.
43. Montias, *Economic Development in Communist Rumania*, p. 231.
44. Schiavone, *The Institutions of Comecon*, pp. 151–2. The Bank was intended to facilitate multilateral trade and payments, but Hewett estimates that in the years 1964–8 only 2 per cent of Comecon trade was cleared multilaterally. *Foreign Trade Prices*, p. 15.
45. Forte, 'The response of Soviet foreign policy to the Common Market', p. 384.

46. Quoted by Ulrich Lappenküpper, ' "Ich bin wirklich ein guter Europäer". Ludwig Erhard's Europapolitik 1949–1966', *Francia*, **18.3** (1991), p. 99. For the text of the treaty, see Gasteyger (ed.), *Europe zwischen Spaltung und Einigung 1945–1990*, doc. 52.
47. *Akten zur Auswärtigen Politik der Bundesrepublik Deutschlands 1963*, Vol. 1, doc. 49 (23 January 1963). See also doc. 51 (24 January 1963), where American irritation about the proximity of the veto and the treaty is evident.
48. For de Gaulle's disappointment, see Horst Osterheld, *Aussenpolitik unter Bundeskanzler Ludwig Erhard 1963–1966* (Düsseldorf, 1992), p. 233.
49. *Akten zur Auswärtigen Politik der Bundesrepublik Deutschlands 1963*, Vol. 1, doc. 169 (16 May 1963).
50. Winand points out the link. *Eisenhower, Kennedy and the United States of Europe*, p. 302.
51. De Gaulle had set a deadline of the end of 1963 for agreement on these issues. Von der Groeben, *The European Community*, p. 149.
52. *Akten zur Auswärtigen Politik der Bundesrepublik Deutschlands 1963*, Vol. 3, doc. 486 (28 December 1963). The American record of Erhard's statement is even blunter. *FRUS*, 1961–1963, Vol. 15, doc. 249 (28 December 1963).
53. Osterheld, *Aussenpolitik unter Bundeskanzler Ludwig Erhard*, p. 101.
54. John Newhouse, *Collision in Brussels* (New York, 1967), p. 40.
55. Thus, Erhard to the Prime Minister and Foreign Minister of the Netherlands on 30 September. Osterheld, *Aussenpolitik unter Bundeskanzler Ludwig Erhard*, p. 111.
56. Walter Lipgens (ed.), *45 Jahre Ringen um die Europäische Verfassung. Dokumente 1939–1984* (Bonn, 1986), doc. 101.
57. Von der Groeben, *The European Community*, pp. 156–8.
58. *Ibid.*, p. 159; Osterheld, *Aussenpolitik unter Bundeskanzler Ludwig Erhard*, pp. 126–7; Stromseth, *The Origins of Flexible Response*, pp. 84–5. The leaked material appeared in the *New York Times* (21 December 1965).
59. For de Gaulle's press conference of 5 February 1965, see Lappenküpper, ' "Ich bin wirklich ein guter Europäer" ', p. 112. Erhard may have been misled by the January Rambouillet meeting with de Gaulle, despite having openly to state that Germany would not choose between France and the United States. Osterheld, *Aussenpolitik unter Bundeskanzler Ludwig Erhard*, pp. 138–46.
60. *Ibid.*, p. 184; Von der Groeben, *The European Community*, p. 161–2.
61. Newhouse, *Collision in Brussels*, p. 61, suggests that the Commission may have been encouraged by Dutch insistence on more democratic control in return for agreement on agricultural financing; Miriam Camps, *Europeans Unification in the Sixties* (London, 1967), p. 47, suggests they overestimated the importance of the agreement on cereal prices to France; while Robert Marjolin, *Memoirs*, p. 350, blames the Commission President, Hallstein. Von der Groeben, *The European Community*, p. 179, on the other hand, claims that the proposals were reasonable.
62. *Selections*, pp. 128–30. For a summary see Camps, *European Unification in the Sixties*, pp. 39–46; von der Groeben, *The European Community*, pp. 178–80.
63. Osterheld, *Aussenpolitik unter Bundeskanzler Ludwig Erhard*, pp. 204–7, blames the Germans, especially Lahr, for failing to reach agreement on financial regulations for the transitional period, 'the decisive point', and for raising additional demands.

64. On the agreement see Newhouse, *Collision in Brussels*, p. 106.
65. Quoted by Camps, *European Unification in the Sixties*, p. 81. The same theme of inevitability was invoked by Couve de Murville to justify the 1963 veto. See above, pp. 168–9.
66. Jouve, *Le Général de Gaulle et la construction de l'Europe*, pp. 353–8. Couve de Murville later called for a general revision of the treaties. Camps, *European Unification in the Sixties*, pp. 88–9.
67. *Selections*, p. 132.
68. *Ibid.*
69. Osterheld, *Aussenpolitik unter Bundeskanzler Ludwig Erhard*, p. 206; Nina Heathcote, 'The crisis of European supranationality', *Journal of Common Market Studies*, **5** (1966), p. 159.
70. France was given far less weight than the Anglo-Saxons in NATO. See *Akten zur Auswärtigen Politik der Bundesrepublik Deutschlands 1963*, Vol. 3, doc. 406 (31 October 1963); Calleo, *Atlantic Fantasy*, p. 29.
71. See the extract quoted in Grosser, *The Western Alliance*, pp. 211–12.
72. On the Harmel Report see H. Haftendorn, 'Entstehung und Bedeutung des Harmel-Berichtes der NATO vom 1967', *Vierteljahreshefte für Zeitgeschichte*, **40** (1992), pp. 169–222.
73. Remington, *The Warsaw Pact*, p. 84. I rely upon Remington for these events.
74. *Ibid.*, pp. 84–5.
75. Bucharest Declaration of 5 July 1966, in *Die Organisation des Warschauer Vertrages. Dokumente und Materialien 1955–1980* (Berlin, 1980), p. 90. See also Remington, *The Warsaw Pact*, p. 87.
76. Lacouture, *De Gaulle. The Ruler*, pp. 468–9. According to one of de Gaulle's aides, as de Gaulle was leaving Gomulka whispered to him, 'I hope it will be possible one day', *ibid.*, p. 469.
77. Gasteyger, *Europa zwischen Spaltung und Einigung*, doc. 62, p. 265. For Romanian fears at this time see Peter Bender, *East Europe in Search of Security* (London, 1972), pp. 118–19. Romania had earlier refused to sign a joint declaration on the non-proliferation treaty. Remington, *The Warsaw Pact*, p. 95; Neill Fodor, *The Warsaw Treaty Organisation* (Basingstoke, 1990), p. 88. On the conceptual link between 'internal' and external security see E. Rubin, 'The theory and concept of national security in the Warsaw Pact countries', *International Affairs*, **58** (1981–2), pp. 648–57.
78. Arter, *The Politics of European Integration in the Twentieth Century*, p. 150.
79. Young, *Britain and European Unity*, p. 89.
80. Uwe Kitzinger, *The Second Try. Labour and the EEC* (Oxford, 1968), pp. 161–4. This option was associated with the American Senator Jacob Javits, *ibid.*, pp. 156–27; Young, *Britain and European Unity*, p. 99.
81. See Lacouture, *De Gaulle. The Ruler*, pp. 475–7. This low point in Anglo-French relations was accompanied by French hostility to British attempts to promote European co-operation through the Western European Union which culminated in refusal to take part in meetings of the Union's Council of Ministers. Nicholson and East, *From the Six to the Twelve*, pp. 58–9.
82. Pierre-Bernard Cousté and François Visine situate Pompidou's view of Europe as 'necessity' between de Gaulle's view of it as a 'possibility' and Giscard d'Estaing's view of it as an 'essential priority'. *Pompidou et l'Europe* (Paris, 1974), pp. 10–11. On Pompidou see also Stéphanie Rials, *Les Idées politiques du Président Georges Pompidou*

(Paris, 1977), pp. 133–7; Eric Roussel, *Georges Pompidou 1911–1974* (Paris, 1994).

83. Arnulf Baring, *Machtwechsel* (Stuttgart, 1983), p. 247. The Federal Republic's policy had been to refuse to recognize the existence of the German Democratic Republic (Hallstein doctrine).

84. 'In reality *Ostpolitik* was one of our reasons for wanting progress in the West.' Willy Brandt. *People and Politics* (London, 1978), p. 254. See also Haig Simonian, *The Privileged Partnership* (Oxford, 1985), pp. 82–3. For the reactions of her allies, see Baring, *Machtwechsel*, pp. 260–3.

85. Brandt, *People and Politics*, p. 246.

86. Cousté and Visine, *Pompidou et l'Europe*, pp. 105–6.

87. For the Assembly's objections, see *Selections*, pp. 139–42.

88. Arter, *The Politics of European Integration in the Twentieth Century*, pp. 153–8.

89. See Alan Campbell, 'Anglo-French relations a decade ago: a new assessment', *International Affairs* **57** (1982), especially p. 436. On the issue of Sterling, Campbell notes that on 7 June 'to the astonishment of the Five the French Finance Minister expressed himself ... fully satisfied with the vague assurances on the subject offered by Geoffrey Ripon', *ibid.*, p. 438.

90. Arter, *The Politics of Euoropean Integration in the Twentieth Century*, pp. 175–8. For the referenda in Denmark and Ireland, see *ibid.*, pp. 163–73.

91. *Selections*, p. 149. See also Simon J. Nuttall, *European Political Co-operation* (Oxford, 1992), pp. 51–5.

92. *Die Organisation des Warschauer Vertrages*, p. 116. Nevertheless, Brandt still felt it important to record that at his September 1971 meeting with Brezhnev the Soviet leader did not raise any objection to American participation. Brandt, *People and Politics*, p. 352.

93. The relevant treaties were signed with the Soviet Union (August 1970), Poland (December 1970) and the German Democratic Republic (1972). There was also a Four Power Agreement on Berlin in 1971.

94. Simonian, *The Privileged Partnership*, p. 118. Images of the past continued to dog these developments. See, for example, the reassurance given to Pompidou by Helmut Kohl, the future Chancellor, that for the Christian Democrats 'the mere smell of Rapallo is mortal'. Quoted in Roussel, *Georges Pompidou 1911–1974*, p. 657.

95. Quoted in *ibid.*, p. 91. For the Barre and Schiller plans, see Peter Coffey, *The European Monetary System – Past, Present and Future* (Dordrecht, 1984), pp. 6–11.

96. *Selections*, pp. 244–5; Stephen George, *An Awkward Partner. Britain in the European Community* (Oxford, 1990), pp. 66–9.

97. Simonian, *The Privileged Partnership*, pp. 148–9. See also Nuttall, *European Political Co-operation*, who claims that political co-operation had been seen as a move towards broader integration but was locked into an intergovernmental framework at the Paris summit, pp. 73–4.

98. Simonian, *The Privileged Partnership*, p. 145.

99. Quoted in *ibid.*, p. 165. On the general deterioration in Atlantic relationships see J. Robert Schaetzel, *The Unhinged Alliance. America and the European Community* (New York, 1975).

100. *Selections*, p. 264. See also Nuttall, *European Political Co-operation*, pp. 89–90.

101. Quoted in Simonian, *The Privileged Partnership*, p. 235.

102. Quoted in Peter Marsh, 'The integration process in eastern Europe 1968 to 1975', *Journal of Common Market Studies*, **14** (1976), p. 319.
103. Z. M. Fallenbuchl, 'Comecon integration', *Problems of Communism*, **22** (March–April 1973), pp. 30–1.
104. H. W. Schaefer, *Comecon and the Politics of Integration* (New York, 1972), p. 18. On the relevance of the comparison see Werner Feld, 'The utility of the EEC experience for eastern Europe', *Journal of Common Market Studies*, **7** (1970), pp. 236–61.
105. Quoted in Schaefer, *Comecon and the Politics of Integration*, p. 24. On the contrast between planned and market integration see also Marsh, 'The integration process in eastern Europe 1968 to 1975', pp. 323–4.
106. Schaefer, *Comecon and the Politics of Integration*, p. 50.
107. Romania joined in December 1970, *ibid.*, p. 110.
108. *Ibid.*, pp. 98–100. Romania joined at the end of 1971, p. 110. For the text of the agreement, see *Dokumente RGW. Uber die Vertiefung und Vervollkommung der Zusammenarbeit und Entwicklung der sozialistischen ökonomischen Integration* (Berlin, 1971), pp. 222–32.
109. Quoted in Schaefer, *Comecon and the Politics of Integration*, p. 160.
110. On these forms of integration see Marie Lavigne, 'The problem of the multinational socialist enterprise', *ACES Bulletin*, **17** (1975), pp. 33–61.
111. *Ibid.*, pp. 44–6. On the comparison with the European community see Feld, 'The utility of the EEC experience for eastern Europe', pp. 245–8.
112. Peter Wiles and Alan Smith, 'The convergence of the CMEA on the EEC', in A. Schlaim and G. N. Yannopoulos (eds), *The EEC and Eastern Europe* (Cambridge, 1978), pp. 82–3; Marsh, 'The integration process in eastern Europe 1968 to 1975', pp. 329, 332–3. On the implementation of these measures see Schiavone, *The Institutions of Comecon*, p. 41; Alfred Zauberman, 'The east European economies', *Problems of Communism*, **27** (March–April 1978), p. 67.
113. Paul Marer, 'Has eastern Europe become a liability to the Soviet Union?', in Charles Gati (ed.), *The International Politics of Eastern Europe* (New York, 1976), p. 79.
114. Quoted in Peter Marsh, 'The Development of Relations between the EEC and the CMEA', in Schlaim and Yannopoulos (eds), *The EEC and Eastern Europe*, p. 35. For Soviet analysis of the Community, see John Pinder, 'Soviet views of western economic integration', in *ibid.*, pp. 107–26.
115. Marsh, 'The development of relations between the EEC and the CMEA', pp. 54–5, 61–2.
116. Brandt, *People and Politics*, pp. 333, 352–3; K. D. Bracher, W. Jäger and W. Link, *Geschichte der Bundesrepublik Deutschland. Republik im Wandel*, Vol. 5 pt 1 (Stuttgart, 1986), pp. 225–7; Hanrieder, *Germany, America, Europe*, pp. 203–4.
117. For the details see Kenneth Dyson, 'The Conference on Security and Co-operation in Europe: Europe before and after the Helsinki Final Act', in K. Dyson (ed.), *European Détente* (London, 1986), pp. 95–9. Dyson notes that the equality of all participants was a Romanian demand, p. 94.
118. John Erickson, 'The Soviet Union and European Détente', in *ibid.*, p. 188.
119. Nuttall, *European Political Co-operation*, pp. 110–11.
120. Cousté and Visine, *Pompidou et l'Europe*, p. 33. See also his advocacy of a European Senate and, albeit only in the long term, a 'federal constitution', pp. 33–9. Once in power Giscard exhibited more Gaullist tendencies and an obsessive concern

with his status *vis-à-vis* the Commission. See Roy Jenkins, *European Diary, 1977–81* (London, 1989).

121. *Selections*, p. 275. On the elaborate preparations see Emile Noel, 'Some reflections on the preparation, development and repercussions of the meetings between heads of Government (1974–75)', *Government and Opposition*, **11** (1976), pp. 20–6.
122. R. H. Lauwaars, 'The European Council', *Common Market Law Review*, **14** (1977), p. 29.
123. *Selections*, pp. 276–7.
124. Quoted in A. Morgan, *From the Summit to Council: Evolution in the EEC* (London, 1976), p. 25.
125. This is the title of Stephen George's study of Britain in the Community. See *An Awkward Partner* for details of the renegotiation, referendum and dispute over the energy conference, pp. 76–104.
126. *Selections*, pp. 277–8.
127. *Memoirs 1911–1986*, p. 364.
128. *Selections*, p. 309.
129. *Ibid.*
130. *Ibid.*, p. 377. For a discussion of the report, see J. D. B. Mitchell, 'The Tindemans Report – retrospect and prospect', *Common Market Law Review*, **13** (1976), pp. 455–84.
131. This would take Europe back to something like the position envisaged by Mitrany in the 1940s.
132. Simonian, *The Privileged Partnership*, pp. 261–5.
133. Record of a meeting with his *cabinet*, 2 August 1977, in Jenkins, *European Diary*, p. 135. Geoffrey Denton points out that one reason for a persistent interest in monetary union was the failure of flexible exchange rates to bring about any improvement. 'European monetary co-operation: the Bremen proposals', *The World Today*, **34** (1978), p. 438.
134 *Ibid.*, p. 224. For the scepticism, see Edmund Dell, 'Britain and the origins of the European monetary system', *Contemporary European History*, **3** (1995), pp. 1–60.
135. *Ibid.*, pp. 3–5. On British attitudes see George, *An Awkward Partner*, pp. 128–30.
136. Dell, 'Britain and the Origins of the European Monetary System', p. 10.
137. Dell provides an admirably clear description of the mechanisms, *ibid.*, pp. 24–7. See also Simonian, *The Privileged Partnership*, p. 283.
138 *Ibid.* On the Belgian compromise see Dell, 'Britain and the origins of the European monetary system', pp. 27–9.
139. See Jenkins' account of the December European Council, *European Diary*, pp. 349–53.
140. The British Secretary of Trade during much of the negotiations, Edmund Dell, claims it was not even that, 'Britain and the origins of the European monetary system', pp. 14–15. Coffey, *The European Monetary System*, was more optimistic from the vantage point of the mid-1980s.
141. D. Dinan, *Ever Closer Union?* (Basingstoke, 1994), p. 132.
142. *Selections*, p. 397.
143. See L. Tsoukalis and A. de Silva Ferreira, 'Management of industrial surplus capacity in the European Community', *International Organization*, **34** (1980), pp. 355–76.
144. Jenkins, *European Diary*, diary entries for 31 July, 14 September, pp. 299 and 311–12. A. N. Duff, 'The report of the three wise men', *Journal of Market Studies*, **19**

(1981), identifies an earlier Commission report of April 1978 as the cause of Giscard's initiative, pp. 238–40.

145. Duff, 'The report of the three wise men', pp. 241–50. On the trend towards intergovernmentalism see Marjolin's recollection, 'We felt almost completely at a loss to do anything about a trend of this kind. There was little more we could do than hope that the situation would not get any worse.' *Memoirs*, p. 369. For academic assessments, see Paul Taylor, 'Intergovernmentalism in the European Communities in the 1970s: patterns and perspectives', *International Organization*, **36** (1982), pp. 741–66; L.-J. Constantinesco, 'Die Institutionen der Gemeinschaft an der Schwelle der 80er Jahre', *Europarecht*, **16** (1981), pp. 209–39.
146. Marjolin, *Memoirs*, p. 365; Constantinesco, 'Die Institutionen der Gemeinschaft an der Schwelle der 80er Jahre', p. 213.
147. Quoted in Marjolin, *Memoirs*, p. 365. Murray Forsyth, *Unions of States* (Leicester, 1981), classified it as an economic confederation, pp. 183–7.
148. For a contemporary assessment, see David Coombes, *The Future of the European Parliament* (London, 1979).
149. Duff, 'The report of the three wise men', pp. 251–3.
150. For Thatcher's view of events, see Margaret Thatcher, *The Downing Street Years* (London, 1993), pp. 61–4 and 80–2. The atmosphere on 29 November is captured by Jenkins, who records the Danish Prime Minister 'calling out insults' while Schmidt pretended to be asleep. *European Diary*, p. 530.
151. So too initially did Portugal. Bernard Burrows and Geoffrey Edwards, *The Defence of Western Europen* (London, 1982), pp. 44–7.
152. *Ibid.*, pp. 51–2. On the French attitude to the Atlantic Alliance under Giscard see Michael M. Harrison, *The Reluctant Ally. France and Atlantic Security* (Baltimore, 1981), pp. 182–93.
153. On the enduring legacy of 1954 see Marjolin, *Memoirs*, pp. 370–1.
154. Stephen Woolcock, 'Atlantic trade relations', in Lawrence Freedman (ed.), *The Troubled Alliance* (London, 1983), pp. 89–91.
155. Dennis L. Bark and David R. Gress, *A History of West Germany*, Vol. 2 (London, 1993), pp. 310–11.
156. Hanrieder notes that 'the double-track decision marked the first time in NATO's history that the alliance undertook collective responsibility for procuring weapons'. *Germany, America, Europe*, p. 112.
157. See Marion Dönhoff, 'Bonn and Washington: the strained relationship', *Foreign Affairs*, **57** (1979), pp. 1052–64; J. Joffe, 'European–American relations: the enduring crisis', *Foreign Affairs*, **59** (1981), pp. 835–51.
158. Quoted in Simonian, *The Privileged Partnership*, p. 301.
159. Jan Winiecki, 'Are Soviet-type economies entering an era of long-term decline?', *Soviet Studies*, **38** (1986), p. 327. The 'developed market economies' did account for a greater share of Soviet exports (33 per cent in 1979 compared with 21.2 per cent in 1970), but not for east European exports (26.2 per cent in 1979 compared with 28 per cent in 1970). See L. Csaba, 'CMEA in a changing world', *Osteuropa-Wirtschaft*, **31** (1986), pp. 222–4.

7

The Triumph of the European Community?

INTRODUCTION

The 1980s opened with debate on the 'Eurosclerosis' which blocked further integration, tensions within the Atlantic Alliance and a revival of Cold War mentalities. Against this unpromising background the search for a way forward made little progress. One decisive development concerned French policy. The socialist government of President Mitterrand tried to pursue policies at variance with those of its economic partners. As the economic strains became apparent, the French government was faced with a choice between a retreat into isolation and abandoning its course in favour of continued integration. Mitterrand chose integration. The costs of a unilateral course were too great.

The pressures of the global economy also contributed to the Single European Act of 1986. Focused on market liberalization, this Act reflected the prevailing ideological climate. The very emphasis on the free market was problematic. Critics pointed to the prospects of increased regional disparities which would flow from the unhindered operation of the market. Others drew a slightly different conclusion: the single market would only work if there was further integration. Viewed from the outside, from the perspective of EETA and Comecon, the achievements of the single market were more impressive than its limitations. The pressure on both to reach an accommodation with the increasingly cohesive Community increased remorselessly.

Internally, the Community's agenda after 1986 was dominated by the issue of monetary union. The dominance of the Deutschmark was a powerful motive for integration in this field. Once again the only solution to the problem caused by German economic strength was to dilute it within a supranational framework. That strategy became even more urgent in 1989, when the end of the Cold War put German reunification on the agenda. German reunification, finalized in 1990, and further integration within the Community, embodied in the Maastricht Treaty of 1992, were closely entwined. The latter did not fulfil the vision of the ambitious President of the Commission, Jacques Delors, but its limitations drew less attention than the commitments it entailed.

The commitments were the focus of attention in the debate over the ratification of the treaty. Popular hostility, especially in Denmark, threw advocates of integration on to the defensive. They sought to placate fears of an emergent superstate through invoking the concept of subsidiarity. But subsidiarity was a two-edged sword. It could be used to justify both greater decentralization and greater centralization. The latter was clearly the only outcome of the proposed monetary union. Monetary union, however, could only be had under stringent economic criteria. The German Bundesbank stood guard against any weakening of the will. As the strains of meeting those criteria grew ever more apparent, the option of a multi-speed Europe re-emerged. Both the resort to subsidiarity and the idea of a multi-speed Europe were testimony to the strains of integration.

Further testimony was added by the enlargement of the Community. The EFTA states had no sooner agreed a European Economic Area with the Community, than they sought membership. Though not all finally joined, once again it was clear that enlargement meant some further loss of national power for all member states. If that was true for the admission of the small and prosperous EFTA states, the prospect of enlargement to the east, the realization of a Pan-European Union, was even more daunting. Yet, at the end of 1994, it was precisely that which was on the agenda.

THE SEARCH FOR A WAY FORWARD

It was the lack of progress within the framework of European Political Co-operation, and continuing strains within the Atlantic Alliance, which induced the German Foreign Minister Hans-Dietrich Genscher, at the beginning of 1981, to call for progress towards a European Union. That his prospects were not good was evident from French lack of interest in his initiative. Genscher, in fact, turned to the Italians for support, which he duly received from Foreign Minister Colombo. Although Colombo was supportive, his agenda was different. Whereas the Germans were interested primarily in Political Co-operation and salvaging the process of détente, the Italians were more interested in a declaration on economic integration. The ensuing compromise produced a decidedly ungainly document which the two ministers presented in November 1981.[1]

By then the member states had already taken modest steps towards strengthening Political Co-operation. The October 1981 London Report provided for a secretariat drawn from national foreign ministries and improved processes for consultation, but little more.[2] In the field of Political Co-operation the Genscher–Colombo proposals did not go a lot further, although they did include the formal incorporation of European Political Co-operation within their proposed European Union, and they did propose co-ordination of security policy. They also sought to improve the communication with Parliament, without endowing the latter with any additional power.[3]

The response from their partners was dilatory. Greece and Denmark were among the strongest opponents. France was largely indifferent, being more interested in her own proposals. The new French President, François Mitterrand, had launched the idea of a 'social European space' in June 1981, and in October the Minister for European Affairs, André Chandernagor, put forward a wide-ranging 'Memorandum' for the 're-vitalization' of Europe.[4] Neither won much support. It was not until June 1983 that the Genscher–Colombo proposal issued in a Solemn Declaration on European Union. The declaration disappointed those committed to further integration, while its vague verbosity reassured those who were opposed.[5]

France initially showed no more enthusiasm for another initiative, which came from the European Parliament. In June 1980 the veteran federalist Altiero Spinelli wrote to his fellow parliamentarians advocating an initiative and in the following month a small group met to plan their campaign. For Spinelli a prime aim was to wrest control of reform from the Council of Ministers, in which so many ambitious reforms had been watered down until little of substance was left. His intent was to form a coalition between the European Parliament and national parliaments which governments would be unable to resist.[6] Underlying Spinelli's efforts was the belief that the Community lacked both authority and democratic legitimacy. Those two central elements could be augmented, he argued, only by increasing the authority of the Commission and consequently the power of Parliament.[7]

The mobilization of a broad swathe of public opinion to establish the authority and legitimacy of a European Union was, of course, a long-standing strategy and ambition of federalists, going back at least to the ideas of Coudenhove-Kalergi.

Spinelli followed federalist tradition in another sense. The proposed European Union was to be a successor to the existing Community. The treaty would not merely amend the Rome Treaties, but would create a new legal body. Yet the Draft Treaty on European Union, which was approved by the European Parliament on 14 February 1984, stopped short of creating a federation. The Union would be a union of states, and revision of the treaty would require ratification by all member states.[8] The Draft Treaty also took over the existing institutions of the Community, including the European Council, seeking only to modify the balance between them. There was even provision for a national veto, albeit for only ten years. Differences within Parliament and sensitivity to the fears of governments combined to produce a document which was pragmatic in many respects.[9]

Despite these elements of caution the Draft Treaty was widely judged to be over-ambitious. Greece was adamantly opposed to institutional reform, and the Danish Parliament firmly rejected it. Even in Italy the treaty was approved as much for its symbolic value as for its concrete provisions.[10] Nor did the treaty have the impact upon the 1984 elections to the European Parliament which its authors had anticipated. One surprising source of support was Mitterrand. In a speech in May 1984 he supported the idea of an intergovernmental conference on a new treaty. Mitterand's support was qualified. His new treaty would entail revision of the existing Community, not the installation of a new union. It was, nevertheless, a dramatic declaration which even caught members of his own party off guard.[11]

Mitterrand's change of heart was in large part a product of the failure of the French socialists' ambitious expansionary programme. With the election of Mitterrand in 1981, the socialists embarked upon expensive social reforms and a nationalization programme that took the state's share of industrial investment up to 50 per cent.[12] Mitterrand's policy ran counter to the prevailing climate in France's major trading partners, where policies of retrenchment were dominant. In Britain an ideological commitment to the reduction of the role of the state in the economy was being implemented by the Thatcher government elected in 1979. The conservative trend was strengthened in 1982 when the coalition between the German Social Democrats and the Free Democrats broke up over the latter's demands for spending cuts. The contrast between French policy and her major partners could not have been clearer. Policy in the United States did not help. Although committed to reducing the role of government, the Republican Presidency of Ronald Reagan raised interest rates to fund its armaments programme, forcing European states to increase their rates. The strains on the French economy were manifested in an increasing balance of payments deficit and devaluations of the franc in October 1981 and June 1982. Within the French government, debate centred around a choice between a third devaluation, a turn to austerity and remaining within the European Monetary System or withdrawal from the Monetary System and a turn towards protectionism. In 1983 advocates of the former course, headed by Finance Minister Jacques Delors, finally won the argument.

Mitterrand's new-found enthusiasm for integration led to a more accommodating French attitude towards the vexed British budgetary question. There had been a provisional settlement in 1980, though Thatcher was induced to accept this only under pressure from her own ministers. This, however, did little to improve relationships between Britain and her partners. The tension between them surfaced in May 1982 when the British Minister of Agriculture invoked the national veto, only to find that the others refused to acknowledge it on the grounds that the issue, the level of agricultural prices, did not constitute a 'vital national interest'.[13] The gap between Britain and her partners was evident elsewhere, with Thatcher showing much more sympathy for Reagan's anti-Soviet rhetoric than her fellow Europeans. On some issues, though, the Community's member states co-operated against the United States, most notably over the dispute about a pipeline being built to deliver Soviet gas to western Europe. The United States had disliked this from the outset, but Reagan increased the pressure in response to the declaration of martial law in Poland in December 1981, which he believed was inspired by the Soviet Union. Six months later Reagan extended the United States' sanctions policies in a way that affected European companies. The Community responded by declaring that the American action was 'contrary to the principles of international law', and Thatcher joined in the general condemnation.[14]

Agreement on this issue did not symbolize greater willingness to co-operate over the budgetary issue. Mitterrand sought to push through a solution in the spring of 1984. At the Brussels summit of March, however, Thatcher remained obdurate, finally provoking Kohl into breaking off the discussions. In the wake of this débâcle the British governments considered withholding contributions to the Community budget while Mitterrand invoked the prospect of a two-speed Europe in his speech of 23 May. 'Some people', he noted, 'have talked about a Europe of different speeds or variable geometry. Such a step, which reflects a real situation, is one that we must take.'[15] Both sides then stepped back from this confrontational course.[16] Agreement followed at the Fontainebleau summit, in June, on the basis of a different formula which was, at most, marginally better for Britain.[17]

The success of the Fontainebleau summit was confirmed by agreement to establish two *ad hoc* committees, one to consider issues of European citizenship, the other to consider institutional matters. The year 1984 saw movement on other fronts, though its significance for the development of the Community was ambiguous. The Community's relationship with EFTA undoubtedly symbolized the comparative strength of the Community. Concerned that divergent economic policies between the Community and the EFTA states might undermine free trade in industrial products, EFTA had urged greater co-operation back in 1977. That initiative foundered amidst the turbulence at the end of the decade. The 1980s saw continuing progress on free trade, but also growing concern about a new, more protectionist mood in the global economy. Against this background a joint ministerial meeting was held in April 1984 and issued in a Joint Declaration which referred to 'dynamic European economic space'.[18] In order to maintain the momentum, regular meetings of officials began in September of 1984 and focused upon technical barriers to trade.

TOWARDS THE SINGLE MARKET

While the economic strength of the Community induced the EFTA states to seek an accommodation, the continued inability of the Community to develop a defence profile, or even to consolidate a common foreign policy induced some member states to look to other frameworks for co-operation. They found their alternative in the moribund Western European Union. There were other motives at work as well. Franco-German interest in a closer defence co-operation could, as both states knew, cause concern and a multilateral framework might help to dissipate suspicion. The result, in October 1984, was the Rome Declaration of the Western European Union. Great care was taken to reaffirm the importance of the Atlantic Alliance and to reassure the United States that the new initiative would not detract from broader defence co-operation. Despite this, the United States was suspicious, fearing the development of a European bloc.[19]

Europe's ambiguous relationship with the United States was one of the reasons behind the growing popularity of the idea of completing the project of a common market enshrined in the Treaty of Rome. In the middle of the 1980s the Community was still little more than a customs union, supplemented by an expensive and wasteful agricultural policy which catered for a tiny proportion of gross domestic product. The lack of thorough economic integration seemed all the more harmful in the light of the technological superiority of both American and, increasingly, Japanese industry.[20] Wisse Dekker of the electrical giant Philips was one of the most forthright of a host of business leaders who pleaded for the common market. According to Dekker,

> There is really no choice and the only option left for the Community is to achieve the goals laid down in the Treaty of Rome. Only in this way can

> industry compete globally, by exploiting economies of scale, for what will then be the biggest home market in the world today: *the European Community home market.*[21]

Earlier, in 1983, the Roundtable of European Industrialists had formed to promote integration, ironically under the chairmanship of Pehr Gyllenhammer of the Swedish firm Volvo.[22]

While businessmen helped to publicize these ideas, as they had done in the days of Emile Mayrisch, it was the Community's governments that were decisive in placing the issue on the official agenda. Their reasons for doing so were varied. German interest in the common market was longstanding and was shared by both government and opposition.[23] French interest was consolidated by the prospect of technological collaboration and the decisive change of policy in 1983. In Britain the Conservative government, invigorated by a recent electoral victory in 1983, was committed to deregulation and wanted to export this policy to the Community. Thatcher recalled that 'the Community's development as a free trade and free enterprise area ... was intended to fit in with our economic policy'. For good measure she also poured scorn on Conservatives who 'seem to accept that free markets are right for Britain but are prepared to accept *dirigisme* when it comes wrapped in the European flag'.[24] A less explicit but nevertheless powerful motive arose from the desire of governments to restrain growth in public expenditure: deregulation under the guise of integration could provide a convenient veil for domestically unpopular decisions.[25]

It was, then, not surprising that when the new President of the Commission, Jacques Delors, toured Europe's capitals to discuss avenues for a new initiative it was the completion of the common market that received general support.[26] Delors duly espoused the idea before the European Parliament and the Commission immediately began work on a draft. The process was sanctioned by the Council in March 1985 which called for a detailed programme. The ensuing White Paper, *Completing the Internal Market*, was a carefully constructed, if hurriedly written, document specifying over 300 measures and a timetable for their implementation by the end of 1992.

By the time the White Paper was published, the committee on institutional matters, established at the Fontainebleau conference, had produced its report. The Dooge Report starkly reflected the divisions among the states and effectively consisted of a majority report with numerous reservations being entered by Britain, Greece and Denmark. The minority countries objected to the abolition of the veto and to strengthening the Commission or Parliament. The British representative stuck by the slogan that 'institutions must be subservient to policies'.[27] At the Milan summit in June 1985 this was still the British position. It amounted to a desire to have the common market without institutional reform.

Britain tried to pre-empt the drive for treaty revision and institutional reform at the beginning of June, when the Foreign Ministers met at Stresa. Geoffrey Howe concentrated on Political Co-operation and also suggested a 'gentleman's agreement' whereby the states would endeavour to avoid recourse to the veto. In the event that they felt it necessary to invoke the veto, he suggested they should be obliged to justify their actions formally. This met with opposition from the Italians and the Benelux states, but the issue was still unresolved at the Milan summit.[28] At Milan the French and Germans muddied the waters by presenting a draft treaty on European Union which differed little from Howe's proposal. Both Mitterrand and Kohl seemed to be backing away from their earlier enthusiasm, though Kohl was being pushed hard by opposition accusations that his policy towards Europe was weak.[29] The choice appeared to lie between accepting the lowest common denominator and a more ambitious project which would simply repeat the divergence of the Dooge Committee. Determined to avoid either, the Italian Foreign Minster Andreotti proposed convoking an intergovernmental conference and Bettino Craxi moved a vote. France voted in favour reluctantly, while Britain, Greece and Denmark voted against. The others supported France. The use of majority voting at a European Council, was unprecedented. Thatcher was indignant, the Danish Prime Minister, Schlüter, said it amounted to 'rape', while Papandreou for Greece described it as a 'coup d'état'.[30] Despite the vigour of their protests they did duly attend the conference. For Thatcher the conference was a way of achieving the single market and there was fear of a two-speed Europe, a fear which was carefully stimulated by Mitterrand.[31]

This still left numerous issues open. Whether, given that it was an intergovernmental conference, the Commission would be able to attend was decided in July. The Commission would be party to the conference. There was, as yet, no decision about whether the conference would issue in a single act. When the conference opened in Luxembourg on 9 September 1985 Delors entered a plea for a single act. 'The Commission', he said, 'considers that the adoption of a single Treaty strengthening the concept of European Union and neither diminishing the future nor prejudging the developments ahead would be a valuable symbol of the resolve to attain European Union'.[32] It would also prevent a fragmentation of the Community's structure, though Delors did not rule out 'positive differentiation' allowing some member states to proceed faster than others.[33] Delors did eventually obtain the single treaty he desired, largely because of skilful linkage of the common market and institutional reform.

Both institutional reform and the content of the common market presented difficulties. The issue of majority voting was settled by complex compromises, which at least introduced majority voting for most of the measures implementing the single market. The extension of the powers of Parliament provoked opposition from Britain and Denmark. Here a compromise was found on the basis of a proposal by the German Foreign Minister, Genscher, who put forward a basket of measures, including consultation, co-operation and assent. The firmest of these, assent, was restricted to articles 237 and 238 concerning the accession of new members and association agreements respectively.[34] German initiative was also decisive in reaching agreement on the contentious issue of monetary union. Initially neither Britain nor Germany wanted any reference at all to a monetary capacity, and as late as 27 November Thatcher and Kohl maintained their opposition. The Germans, however, decided to compromise soon after and an isolated Britain was forced to salvage what it could in a text formulated by Germany and Britain. This was then accepted by the others, albeit only under considerable German pressure.[35]

The negotiation of the Single European Act was concluded with remarkable speed. It was far less ambitious than Parliament's Draft European Treaty or even the Dooge Report, but it did constitute a significant step forward. Quite how significant was not as yet clear. On returning to London Thatcher felt confident enough to reassure the House of Commons: 'I am constantly saying that I wish they would talk less about European and political union. The terms are not understood in this country. In so far as they are understood over there, they mean a good deal less than some people over here think they mean.'[36] As she later acknowledged, in this, she was wrong.

The Community had committed itself to creating an internal market which 'shall comprise an area without internal frontiers in which the free movement of goods, persons, services and capital is ensured'.[37] Advocates of market-based integration had assumed that the ensuing growth and the operation of comparative advantage would automatically guarantee benefits for all, and a gradual harmonization of living standards. Even in the Cecchini Report, which the Commission called for to demonstrate the advantages of the single market, the underlying assumption still reflected the old free-market principles. The Padoa-Schioppa Report of April 1994, which examined the consequences of the single market and the accession of Spain and Portugal, took a more robust view of the difficulties. According to Padoa-Schioppa,

> Regions tend towards an equalization of incomes per head as a result of the mobility of labour and capital only under severe and unrealistic conditions ... Any easy extrapolation of 'invisible hand' ideas to the real world of regional economics in the presence of market-opening measures would be unwarranted in the light of economic history and theory.[38]

While Padoa-Schioppa, a former Director General of the Commission, was forthright in his account of the problem, others issued damning indictments of Community policy. One critical appraisal described the Community's regional policy as 'liberal market tutelage' which misguidedly focused on infrastructural problems and threatened to reduce the ability of the poorer states and regions to address their problems.[39] Although this attack often presented Commission policy as less differentiated than it was, the underlying tensions were real enough. The budgetary constraints, which made the single market attractive to some, reduced the ability of governments and the Community to redress the problem of regional disparities, leaving only the threadbare assumption that growth would solve the problem. That tension became much more intense as monetary union, with the associated demands for even greater budgetary discipline, returned to the agenda.[40]

The reduction of integration to nothing more than an internal free market was not the ambition of the President of the Commission. Such a vision was, indeed, anathema to a man imbued with the spirit of personalism, a doctrine formulated precisely to counter the anomie of modern civilization. Nor was Delors' criticism of the free market solely a matter of ideology. Speaking in February 1987 he insisted that 'in economic terms, it is self-evident that a large market without internal frontiers could not be completed or operate properly unless the Community had instruments enabling it to avoid imbalances'.[41] Even among the governments more disposed to the free market there were limits to their fervour, although the line was drawn according to divergent national traditions. The most ideologically committed of the member states to the doctrine of the free market, Britain, still asserted a right to introduce regulation where the government deemed it to be in the public interest. Germany, in contrast, relied more upon statutory regulation implemented by independent agencies, and often flanked by extensive consultative mechanisms.[42] Under the slogan of the internal market there remained considerable scope for divergent conceptions rooted in domestic traditions and ideologies.

THE COMMUNITY, EFTA AND COMECON

It was not these internal difficulties and conflicts of vision which agitated the Community's neighbours but its successes and achievements, the simple economic weight of the Community and the uncertain implications of the Single European Act. There were fears in the United States that 1992 symbolized the emergence of 'fortress Europe', but improved exports which cut its trade deficit with the Community in half in 1988 diluted the threat. So too did the Community's agreement in May 1989 to allow American participation in the setting of standards for products.[43] The pressure was especially acute for the EFTA countries. They were even more dependent on trade than the Community states, and much of that trade was concentrated upon the Community. The latter took 55.9 per cent of EFTA exports in 1988 and supplied even more, 60.3 per cent, of its imports.[44] In the light of this the significance of the internal market was inescapable. As EFTA noted, 1992 posed 'a new challenge not only for the Community, but also for EFTA'.[45] The only possible response was to seek to deepen integration with the Community, extending co-operation into anything from services to education. In 1987 these efforts bore fruit, with Conventions facilitating the transport of goods and simplifying administrative procedures. EFTA was, however, in a much weaker position than the Community. Prior to the signing of these Conventions the Commissioner for External Affairs, Willy de Clerq, pointed out that the Community's policy would be based upon giving priority to internal Community integration preserving its autonomy, and assuring a balance between the concessions it made and those it was given.[46] These had in fact been the implicit guidelines of the Community ever since the debate on a free trade area in the 1950s. Then, as in the 1980s, the free trade states had no alternative other than to accept them. The pressure was much greater thirty years after the Community's formation. The remorseless logic of completing the internal market forced the EFTA states to bring their regulations into line with Community directives in whose formulation they had no part. As one observer noted, the outcome was that 'their *de jure* national sovereignty had lost much of its *de facto* value'.[47]

Eastern Europe was far less dependent upon the Community but nevertheless interested in reaching an agreement. Interest was increased by continuing and new obstacles to integration in the east. At the beginning of the decade the 'long-term target programmes', formulated in 1978 as the basis for a co-ordinated structural policy, were torn apart by the strains imposed by oil price rises and global recession.[48] Increased oil prices also meant that eastern Europe's indebtedness to the Soviet Union increased. The Soviet Union introduced a new problem by reducing the quantity of goods it proposed to trade. This presented special difficulties for a planning system predicated upon continual growth in trade. The custom had been to take the previous five years' trade figures as a base and bargain over the distribution of increased quantities available in the current planning period. The Soviet decision, consequently, undermined established habits.[49]

Alongside these new disruptions lay more deep-seated obstacles. Whereas the European Community could rely upon the Court to enforce integration measures, Comecon lacked an analogous organ. The significance of this was evident in the *cassis de Dijon* case of 1979 – when the Court of Justice struck down a German ban on a French liqueur which did not meet German standards. The underlying principle was that one member state must accept goods meeting the standards of another. This principle of mutual recognition was subsequently employed as a major instrument for completing the single market. Comecon suffered from the lack of any equivalent stimulus and even had difficulty enforcing the delivery of goods.[50]

It was not until the middle of the decade that Comecon responded with a series of meetings accompanied by Conferences of First Secretaries. The December 1984 summit had little impact, but was notable for an emphasis upon saving energy rather than the traditional strategy of solving the problem by producing more. In that respect it reflected the new climate.[51] At the Comecon Sessions of October 1987 and July 1988 there was considerable debate on decentralizing decision-making. This meant conceding more autonomy to individual enterprises, allowing them to enter into direct agreement with counterparts in other Comecon states.[52] Hungary, with its tradition of reform, was the most vocal advocate, though the Soviet Union pushed hard as well. Romania, predictably, and the German Democratic Republic were reluctant to embark upon this road. The outcome was disappointing, with less than one-half of 1 per cent of Soviet–Bulgarian and Soviet–Czechoslovak trade being carried out directly between enterprises.[53]

For some member states the economic strains had become almost unbearable. Poland had been faced with economic and social crisis at the beginning of the decade. Both Poland and Hungary continued to accumulate vast foreign debts, in the Hungarian case the debt in 1988 was just over double the 1980 figure.[54] The German Democratic Republic held its level of debt relatively steady but was finding increasing difficulty paying it, or paying for the fuel imports on which it was chronically dependent. In 1988 the Chairman of the State Planning Commission, Gerhard Schürer, told fellow members of the Politburo that the Democratic Republic was on the verge of bankruptcy.[55]

Despite mounting economic difficulties, the eastern bloc had made progress in other respects. By the end of 1988 Comecon had finally come to an accommodation with the European Community and Mikhail Gorbachev had steered the east towards a more co-operative relationship with the west. Gorbachev also facilitated a *rapprochement* between the two economic groups in May 1985. The Soviet Union, Gorbachev announced, was willing to discuss specific issues with the member states to 'the extent that the countries of the Community function as a political entity'.[56] In the following September Comecon's Secretary General, Vyacheslav Sychov, offered a draft declaration in which the two would recognize each other 'in the context of their respective competencies'.[57] For the Community this meant that Comecon was dropping its old demand for a trade agreement between the two organizations which the Community had always opposed, on the grounds that Comecon did not have any authority over its members' trade. It was consistent with the Community's stance that it insisted upon parallel negotiations with the member states of Comecon for a 'normalization of relations'.[58] This was conceded by Romania in March 1986 and by the others in May.[59] The subsequent negotiations lasted for two years, partly because the Community insisted on sufficient progress on the bilateral agreements and partly because of disagreements over the status of West Berlin. Nevertheless, the willingness of the east Europeans to compromise eventually led to the Joint Declaration of 24 June 1988. In a variation on the formula suggested by Sychov, the Community and Comecon agreed to 'develop cooperation in areas which fall within their respective spheres of competence and where there is a common interest'.[60] Six days later Hungary and the Community initialled a trade and co-operation agreement. As in its negotiations with EFTA, the Community had more to offer and less to lose than its negotiating partners. In both cases it successfully exploited that advantage to preserve or gain recognition of its status. It made no concessions which detracted from its symbolic or institutional integrity. The Community was triumphant.

Inevitably the Community exercised little influence within the framework of the Conference on Security and Co-operation in Europe. That process had fallen victim to the revived Cold War antagonisms. At the middle of the decade meetings were still being held, but with little apparent prospect of success. The appointment of Gorbachev brought a mixture of old and new themes. He invoked the idea of a common European home, but with the implication that while the Soviet Union was part of this home the United States was not. The anti-American tinge, and even more so the idea that the Soviet Union no longer had any aggressive ambitions, appealed to many, including German social democrats who argued for the removal of nuclear weapons from Germany. For others the reduction of nuclear weapons, especially in the radical form mooted at the September 1986 Reykjavik summit between Reagan and Gorbachev, conjured up the old fears of being abandoned by the United States and left at the mercy of superior Warsaw Pact conventional forces. But September also brought a major breakthrough at the Stockholm Conference on Confidence and Security Building Measures. There the Soviet Union agreed to allow on-site inspection of conventional forces. This heralded a phase of rapid development in the negotiations. The Warsaw Pact had already proposed negotiation on the reduction of conventional forces in its Budapest declaration in June, which the Atlantic Alliance agreed to in December. A year later the Intermediate-Range Nuclear Forces agreement committed the two superpowers to the withdrawal of all INF weapons from Europe. There was now no doubt that the situation had radically changed.[61]

Gorbachev's rhetoric changed too. In a series of interviews and in his book *Perestroika*, published in 1987, he invoked the image of the common European home and disavowed any intent to drive a wedge between western Europe and the United States. The relationship between the two, he conceded, was 'a political reality'.[62] In this he was right. The improved relationship between the superpowers did prompt the Europeans to consider greater co-operation among themselves. In 1987 Kohl and Mitterrand agreed to establish a joint Franco-German brigade and a Defence and Security Council. At French insistence the brigade was not placed under the Atlantic Alliance's integrated command. Thatcher saw this as a threat to the Alliance, while the Italian Prime Minister Giovanni Goria saw it as a threat to genuine European co-operation. In reality it was not substantive enough to be the latter, and neither Mitterrand nor Kohl had any desire to dispense with the Atlantic Alliance.[63] The same ambiguity, the desire to strengthen European co-operation mixed with hesitancy for fear of alienating the United States, was evident in the Western European Union's October 1987 Platform on European Security Interests.[64] The only major change came the following year, with the entry of Spain and Portugal into the Western European Union, though this did nothing to reduce the uncertainty about its long-term purpose, its relationship to the Atlantic Alliance, and the role of European Political Co-operation.[65]

CONSOLIDATING THE SINGLE MARKET AND THE DEBATE ON MONETARY UNION

The attempt to invigorate the Western European Union had been welcomed by Delors, though his attention was focused on a series of initiatives aimed at consolidating the single market. The first sought to combine a solution to regional disparities and a solution to the Community's growing financial crisis. The former was being demanded by the southern member states as compensation for implementing the single market, while the latter was the inevitable product of constraints on Community revenue combined with a lack of sufficient constraint on expenditure, especially agricultural expenditure.[66] The Commission's proposals, set out in 'Making a Success of the Single Act', were presented in February 1987. The initial response from the Council at Brussels in June was unsympathetic. Thatcher was predictably hostile to increased revenue, protective of budgetary rebates and insistent upon greater controls on expenditure. Kohl was cautious, for Germany, as always, would have to pay for any increases. Chirac too was unwilling to pay for 'cohesion'. The Copenhagen Council in December met against the background of a failure to fulfil the constitutional commitment to set a budget in October for the following year and signally failed to make any progress. Yet, in February 1988, at a special summit called by Kohl, agreement was reached. Thatcher conceded increased expenditure, including the new principle of setting a limit for the Community's own resources in terms of a percentage of gross national product. The package as a whole was not significantly different from the Commission's proposals.[67]

The next Commission initiative was more dramatic and even more difficult to carry through. Monetary union had long been on the agenda and the Community was officially committed to bringing it about. The Single European Act had brought little more than a symbolic change to the monetary system, which was far removed from the concept of monetary union. The change in attitude behind the new initiative was facilitated by the logic of the single market. In June 1988 the Community agreed on the liberalization of capital markets as a part of progress towards the single market. That meant that France and Italy could no longer defend their currencies by exchange controls as they had been accustomed to doing.[68] France already had additional reasons for favouring monetary union. Devaluation of the franc at the beginning of 1987 emphasized the inadequacies of the existing Monetary System, as well as being a blow to French pride. Modifications of the system in September brought some improvement but still left France dissatisfied, as did the Franco-German Economic Council on which agreement was reached in November. In its original form ministers were to meet along with the heads of the Bundesbank and the Banque de France. On finally learning of this, the Bundesbank quickly mobilized opposition to this attempt to place the German bank, which was independent, on a footing with the Banque de France, which was under government control. Kohl was forced to reassure the Bundesbank that the Economic Council would not impinge upon the autonomy of the Bank.[69] The French had indeed sought to use the economic Council to exercise some influence over the Bundesbank and hence the Deutschmark. It was becoming clear that the only way this goal could be attained was via monetary union.

The key link was made by the German government in March, when Finance Minister Stoltenberg indicated that agreement on the liberalization of capital markets would open up the possibility of progress towards monetary union. It was precisely this linkage which underlay the June 1988 Hanover Council. By then Delors was already trying to mobilize a consensus.[70] There were, of course, severe limits to any consensus. Thatcher's hostility to monetary union was well known and Britain still remained outside the Monetary System. At the Hanover Council there was considerable support for a study of a European Central Bank. This was opposed by Paul Schlüter of Denmark, with Thatcher's support. Together they managed to exclude any reference to a central bank, but they could not block the appointment of a group, chaired by Delors, to report on monetary union.[71]

The Hanover Council also agreed on the reappointment of Delors, though Thatcher did so with reluctance. Her growing antipathy to the Commission's President was to be fuelled by another initiative. In a speech to the European Trade Union Confederation on 12 May 1988, Delors argued for a revival of the Community's social dimension, and for 'social dialogue and greater social cohesion' through an enhanced role for trade unions.[72] He presented this as a corollary of the single market. It was also consistent with his vision of a just and stable social order. To Margaret Thatcher it was anathema. At Hanover she was dismissive: 'Talk of dialogue with the social partners is old fashioned.'[73] But as Delors continued to extol the virtues of the social dimension, Thatcher became increasingly irritated, especially when Delors addressed the British Trades Union Congress in September. In the same month Thatcher effectively gave her reply in a speech at the College of Bruges. 'We have not', she proclaimed, 'successfully rolled back the frontiers of the state in Britain only to see them reimposed at a European level, with a European superstate exercising a new dominance from Brussels.'[74]

The Delors *Report on Economic and Monetary Union in the European Community* was ready in April 1989. It followed the earlier Werner Report in proposing a three-stage process, beginning with an emphasis upon economic convergence and the incorporation of all currencies into the exchange rate mechanism. Stage two would see the creation of a European System of Central Banks, which would take over management of monetary policy in stage three, when exchange rates were to be locked together.[75] Inevitably, German preferences strongly marked the report. As head of the Bundesbank, Karl Otto Pöhl easily gained the inclusion of two vital principles. First, the 'System would be committed to the objective of price stability.'[76] Second, the Bank's Council 'should be independent of instructions from national governments and Community authorities'.[77] The broader implications were set out by Pöhl. Monetary union entailed such a transfer of sovereignty that '*it would be bearable only in the context of extremely close and irrevocable political integration* [italics in original]'.[78]

It was, of course, this kind of implication that so horrified Thatcher. But at the Madrid Council of June 1989 she felt unable to block agreement on an intergovernmental conference on monetary union. She had even been badgered into conceding British entry into the exchange rate mechanism by her own ministers, albeit only under certain conditions. As far as the intergovernmental conference was concerned, she could do little more than issue a declaration that Britain would not agree to any automatic transition from stage one to stage two.[79]

THE PROSPECT OF GERMAN REUNIFICATION

This was the last European Council before the transformation in eastern Europe inaugurated an 'acceleration of history' and undermined the post-war European architecture.[80] The Community had been watching the progress of reform in eastern Europe, seeking to use its economic leverage to encourage the reformers and penalize the hardliners.[81] The Community had also been given the task of co-ordinating western aid to eastern Europe by the G7 summit of June 1989. But none of this prepared the Community for the shock of November. Faced with a flight of its citizens from the Democratic Republic, massive protests, and the clear withdrawal of support from the Soviet Union, the communist authorities opened the Berlin wall. Kohl was caught off guard by the speed of events and had to abandon his visit to Poland and rush to Berlin. By the end of the month he had seized the initiative. In his ten-point plan of 28 November Kohl announced that the Federal Republic was ready to 'develop confederative structures between the two States in Germany, with the object of then creating a federation, that is, a national federal system in Germany'.[82]

Kohl had consulted none of his Community partners. Only shortly before his announcement both the British and French Foreign Ministers had declared that reunification was not on the immediate agenda.[83] Mitterrand was especially irate at the lack of consultation. But it was not merely lack of consultation that worried him. Both France and Britain regarded the prospect of reunification with less than enthusiasm. As the editor of the newspaper *Die Zeit* complained, their attitude resembled that of Christians to the prospect of heaven: 'Every pious Christian wishes to get to heaven, but none of them wants it to happen too soon.'[84] More prosaically, Regis Debray, one of Mitterrand's advisers, speculated upon the need to re-create a Franco-Russian alliance to counter a reunified Germany. That this was more than speculation is suggested by Mitterrand's visit to the Soviet Union in December, when he tried to persuade Gorbachev to block reunification.[85]

Kohl, however, was not to be deflected. Aware of the concerns of his neighbours, he sought to reassure them by putting increasing emphasis upon the link between German reunification and increased Community integration. The implication was that a reunified Germany would pose no threat if it was even more closely tied into the Community. A formula embodying this logic was accepted at the Strasbourg European Council in December, albeit not without some haggling. The Community gave its formal blessing to 'unity through self-determination' which had to be 'placed in the perspective of European integration'.[86] The Council also agreed to open the intergovernmental conference on monetary union the following December in Rome. During the discussions on monetary union, Kohl made clear his desire to see more power given to the Community's Parliament. The idea of further institutional reform would soon be given added impetus by a co-ordinated German–Commission initiative.

Delors led the way in his address to Parliament on 17 January. After setting out the challenges facing the Community, he proclaimed that 'we need an institutional structure that can withstand the strains'.[87] He specified that this meant more power for both Commission and Parliament, and sought to ward off fears of centralization by invoking 'the principle of subsidiarity . . . as a counterweight to the natural tendency of the centre to accumulate power'.[88] Delors' speech was warmly welcomed by both Kohl and Genscher on the same day. An alliance between the Federal Republic and the Commission was not, however, sufficient. As on previous occasions it took a Franco-German alliance to force the pace of developments. This became possible after the March elections in the Democratic Republic which saw a victory for Kohl's political allies and forced Mitterrand into accepting the inevitability of reunification. The revival of Franco-German co-operation resulted in a joint letter of 17 April in which Kohl and Mitterrand called for an intergovernmental conference on political union to run parallel with the conference on monetary union. It was this issue which dominated the Dublin European Council in April that had been called to discuss German reunification. An intergovernmental conference was endorsed a little later at a second Dublin Council in June.

These developments were largely welcomed by the United States' administration under George Bush, though the prospects of closer European integration brought the familiar call to strengthen Atlantic co-operation at the same time. The call for a New Atlanticism came from Secretary of State James Baker on 12 December 1989. France responded with equally familiar suspicion.[89] The United States suggested the desirability of new institutional arrangements or a treaty. Both of these went too far for the Europeans. Eventually the idea of a joint declaration, put forward by Genscher, was taken up. The declaration of November 1990 added nothing new. The United States could not even agree on a reference to a 'stable international financial system', construing this as impinging upon its freedom to control the dollar.[90] With the Europeans refusing to accept anything which implied American tutelage, and the United States equally unwilling to contemplate any restriction upon its own sovereignty, the two sides were dependent upon largely *ad hoc* adjustments to regulate their interdependence.

THE INTERGOVERNMENTAL CONFERENCES

The following month the two intergovernmental conferences opened. There had been substantial preparation for the conference on monetary union but much less on political union. Throughout the year the positions on monetary union had been clarified and some revealed as untenable. This applied above all to Britain. At first Britain tried to argue that the liberalization of capital movements did not require monetary union at all. Following the economist Friedrich Hayek, the British government upheld the virtues of competition between the different national currencies. This attempt to find a market solution to a problem, exchange rate instability, which was aggravated by progress towards a single market, met with little enthusiasm. It was seen as little more than a 'diversionary tactic'.[91] A variation on the market solution was tried by Chancellor of the Exchequer John Major when he proposed introducing a 'hard ecu' in the summer of 1990.[92] This fared a little better and was taken by some as evidence that Britain was at least showing some interest, but its fate was sealed in November when Pöhl dismissed it as the 'worst possible recipe for monetary policy'.[93] Britain had already joined the exchange rate mechanism, in October, at a rate which the Bundesbank considered too high. Any expectation that this indicated a fundamental change in British attitudes was soon proved to be false. At the Rome European Council of 27–28 October, Kohl pushed hard for a commitment to enter on stage two of monetary union on 1 January 1994. Thatcher was isolated and again had to resort to a unilateral declaration distancing Britain from the common position of the other member states.

Thatcher's often dramatic assertion of a stance opposed to that of Britain's partners had become a point of major dispute within her own cabinet. It had already led to the resignation of Chancellor Nigel Lawson and now led to the resignation of Foreign Secretary Geoffrey Howe. Worse still, Howe's resignation speech was a powerful indictment of her policy towards Europe, deploring her 'retreat into a ghetto of sentimentality about our past'.[94] Two weeks later Margaret Thatcher's hold on power was gone. For the first time a Prime Minister of a member state of the Community had been overthrown by her own party as a result of disputes over policy towards the Community.

FINALIZING GERMAN REUNIFICATION

Part of Kohl's enthusiasm to press ahead at Rome was derived from the impending all-German elections of December 1990, following on from reunification in October. The previous year this outcome had appeared neither certain nor so imminent. Both members of the communist regime and their critics responded to Kohl's ten-point plan of November 1989 with an appeal 'For our country – the preservation of the independence of the GDR'.[95] The regime's critics, at their first formal meeting with the government, similarly referred to their country's 'autonomy and continued development'.[96] Their hopes lay in the formulation of a 'third way' between capitalism and the authoritarian socialism of the Democratic Republic. A distinctive socio-economic identity was indeed the only justification for a state independent from the Federal Republic. The point had been made earlier by a defender of the old order in the Democratic Republic. 'What entitlement to existence', he asked, 'would a capitalist GDR have alongside a capitalist Federal Republic? None, of course.'[97] Economic collapse and continued massive migration to the Federal Republic ruled out whatever slight chances a 'third way' had. Against the advice of the Council of Experts, the cabinet decided, on 7 February 1990 to implement monetary union between the two states. Kohl also overruled the experts, in this case the Bundesbank, in setting the exchange rate for monetary union which duly took place on 1 July.[98] German monetary union was to exert a significant influence on the broader debate on monetary union. Pöhl noted that the 'crass extreme example' of the former could not be compared to European monetary union, but he also pointed to the high unemployment and public expenditure induced by German monetary union. The implication was clear. Excessive haste on the European level would lead to disaster.[99]

The Commission had been more realistic than Kohl in estimating the difficulties of unifying such divergent economies, but the Commission also proved to be supportive of unification and the incorporation of the new territories into the European Community. The key lay in persuading the Federal Republic's partners to treat the enlargement of Germany as a special case which did not require any treaty amendment. This was achieved at the Dublin European Councils in April and June. Community law became applicable to the new *Länder* on the date of unification, 3 October 1990. This too marked a great triumph for the Community, both as a specific institution which coped with the speed of developments and as an instrument for the integration of the Federal Republic into the west. Integration of the Federal Republic, after all, had been an important strategic purpose of the varied efforts to promote western European integration in the 1940s and 1950s. The Federal Republic's takeover, for that was what it was, of its alter ego in the east seemed to be justification of that course of action.

Kohl's domestic political strategy had also proved successful, with the government coalition winning the December elections. Shortly afterwards the European Council at Rome opened and launched the intergovernmental conferences. In the conference on monetary union the Commission had to defend its proposals against attacks from both France and Germany, as well as, of course, from Britain. The French government's confederal inclinations were evident in the suggestion that the Council of Finance Ministers be given a greater role. As with the earlier attempt to endow the Franco-German Council with authority, this posed a threat to the Bundesbank's vision of an independent monetary authority. The result was that Delors was supported by both the Germans and the smaller states and could fend off the French initiative.[100]

DELORS' VISION UNDER ATTACK

On another issue, however, France and the Commission were allies. Both wanted to see a European central bank installed at stage two. But when the German draft was presented in March the central bank was firmly relegated to stage three. The consternation this caused was evident when Delors prompted his spokesman to accuse the Germans of abandoning commitments made at Rome in October. The accusation was inaccurate in so far as they had agreed merely to establish a 'new monetary institution'.[101] Kohl brushed aside Delors' insinuations, but the Germans were, as usual, far from united. While Genscher could agree with the French Foreign Minister Roland Dumas that the central bank should be established at stage two, Pöhl insisted that it should not.[102] A solution was found in June 1991 which essentially confirmed the harder German position. There would be no central bank until stage three, but, by way of compensation, stage three could be introduced as early as 1996.[103] The Bundesbank then stepped up its insistence on rigorous convergence criteria for a transition to stage three. Its underlying strategy, and the points of dispute, remained the same. The Bundesbank was determined to wrest control of monetary policy from the politicians and to prevent any loss of control over the Deutschmark until the member states' economies were in a position to bear the strain of full monetary union.

While the negotiations on economic and monetary union slowly made progress, those on political union stagnated. Progress on both was necessary, for Kohl was insistent that without political union there would be no economic and monetary union. The Commission's draft for political union included an interesting attempt to reshape the structure of Community legislation. The Commission proposed a 'hierarchy of norms' which distinguished 'laws' from 'regulations' and other acts: 'Laws shall determine the fundamental principles, general guidelines and basic elements of the measures to be taken for their implementation . . . [while] . . . Implementation may be entrusted in whole or in part to the Member States, acting in accordance with their own constitutional requirements.'[104] The intent was to extract Parliament from the morass of detail. The proposal would also promote subsidiarity. This would have contributed to one of the goals of the conference, increasing the efficiency of the Community, but it met with little sympathy from member states.[105]

These laws were to be subject to a new procedure of co-decision involving the Council and Parliament, but here the Commission soon found itself on the defensive. France put forward the idea of a Congress drawn from national parliaments, with the clear intent of strengthening the confederal element. The Germans, reflecting their domestic parliamentary procedures, proposed a committee of conciliation which would bring together representatives of the Council and Parliament, but not the Commission. Delors perceived both as a threat to the Commission and, in April, he berated the Parliament for its support for such schemes. Why, he demanded, 'have you accepted a system which . . . risks plunging Community institutional processes into endless palavering between Council and Parliament at the expense of efficiency'?[106]

Delors found discussion of the common foreign and security policy equally frustrating. His ambition was for the Community effectively to absorb the Western European Union. A proposal from Genscher and

Dumas in February 1991 did not envisage such a rapid development, but it too held out the prospect of eventually incorporating the Western European Union. These speculations quickly prompted a reaction from the United States, with Ambassador Taft warning that 'US public opinion will not understand any proposal which aims at replacing NATO by a different mechanism'.[107] Britain, strongly supported by Denmark, the Netherlands and Portugal, opposed anything which would weaken the Atlantic Alliance. Western European Union, they argued, should serve as a bridge between the Community and the Alliance. Consequently, the Community should not acquire its own defence policy. The issue was especially sensitive, since the Alliance was in the middle of its own crisis of identity as it struggled to find a new role in the post-Cold War world. That made Europe's Atlanticists even more vigorous, while Delors was left complaining that if Europe persisted in acting 'as though it has a protector or an insurance contract, then this will signal its absolute historical decline'.[108]

The biggest threat to Delors' vision came from Luxembourg, whose April draft sketched out a European Union consisting of three pillars.[109] One would be formed by the existing Community with the addition of economic and monetary union. The second would be the common foreign and security policy, and the third would cover internal and judicial affairs. Delors struck back, seeking at least to build in language preserving the existing *acquis communautaire* and a commitment to a federal future. In this he had some success at the Dresden meeting of Foreign Ministers in June, though this did little more than provoke an apoplectic response from Britain to the use of the word 'federal'.

The major attempt to redirect negotiations to Delors' original conception came from the new Dutch Presidency of the Community. With Prime Minister Ruud Lubbers and Foreign Minister Hans van den Broeck distracted by the crisis in Yugoslavia, the new Dutch paper was strongly influenced by the federalist junior minister Piet Dankert. The Netherlands' draft rejected the three pillars of the Luxembourg draft, reverted to the idea of a unified Community, and also strengthened the powers of Parliament. It did deviate from the Commission's preferences in two respects. First, in accordance with traditional Dutch Atlanticism, the importance of the Atlantic Alliance was reaffirmed. Second, there was no reference to the new 'law' which formed the heart of the Commission's hierarchy of norms. The reaction of the Netherlands' partners on 30 September was almost uniformly hostile. Only Belgium offered consistent support. Dutch Atlanticism antagonized France, while Britain, Denmark and Portugal resented the attempt to revive a more federal structure. Even those sympathetic to the ideas in the paper saw it as a lost cause and an irritating waste of time. Faced with such wide opposition, the Netherlands retreated and began work on a modified version of the Luxembourg draft. Belgium tried to gain at least a commitment to bring the two non-Community pillars within the framework of 'Community mechanisms and institutions' at the beginning of December, but in vain. A European Union consisting of three pillars was now the only plausible outcome.[110]

That still left a considerable amount to disagree on. The conditions of economic and monetary union remained contentious. Here again the Netherlands had raised the stakes in a draft presented in September. This provided for a minimum of six countries proceeding to stage three in 1996. It was, as an Italian official pointed out, 'the first time that an EC paper had stated from the very beginning that there would be two groups'.[111] Italy was one of the countries which, by implication, would not be ready for full monetary union in 1996. In a sense, all the Netherlands was doing was drawing out the consequence of persistent economic divergence within the Community. The consequence was a two-speed Europe. Again there was only a single supporter of the Netherlands' draft, this time Germany, and Finance Minister Wim Kok quickly retreated. The Netherlands was eventually successful in finding a formula for dealing with British reluctance to enter into a commitment to full monetary union. Britain would, in fact, be exempt from any commitment to proceed to stage three.[112]

Spain, supported by the poorer members of the Community, was still pressing, unsuccessfully, for extensive provisions on economic and social cohesion. These had been set out in a memorandum of 5 March 1991 in which Spain emphasized that 'the national budget discipline rules which will be incorporated in the New Treaty ... will undoubtedly limit the member States' spending ability which, for the less prosperous Member States, will make it difficult to provide the necessary infrastructure for the development of the private sector'.[113] Again, it was the prospect of a two-speed Europe which drove the Spanish to insist on cohesion. It was the cost of cohesion that inspired the equally firm resistance of the wealthier member states, leaving Prime Minister Filipe Gonzalez threatening to refuse to sign the treaty if there was inadequate provision for cohesion.[114]

Social policy again cast Britain in the role of the awkward partner. Here the Commission's strategy was to promote 'social dialogue' between industry and labour by holding out the threat of legislation, and then offering industry and labour the opportunity to conclude 'framework agreements' to pre-empt legislation.[115] When the Luxembourg draft reduced the employers' room for manoeuvre, by conceding them only a right to consultation before legislation was passed, the employers confederation, UNICE, discovered a new enthusiasm for the Commission's proposals. The latter entailed acceptance of Community-wide bargaining with the trades unions, but at least it staved off the threat of extensive legislation.[116] All of this met with the unreserved hostility of Britain's Conservative governments.

THE EUROPEAN ECONOMIC AREA

While the Community's states were locked in dispute over the future direction of the proposed European Union, negotiations with the EFTA states had finally produced an agreement on a European Economic Area. Negotiations had begun in 1990, largely in response to the application for membership by Austria the previous July and the prospect of yet further applications by members of EFTA. Delors' intent was to pre-empt enlargement by offering a free trade area covering the whole of western Europe. His fear was that enlargement would be used as an excuse for avoiding deepening the Community's integration. It was, indeed, this prospect which induced support for enlargement in Britain.

The negotiations on the European Economic Area proved to be complex, and ground to a halt in September 1991 over disputes concerning fishing rights, the transit of heavy goods vehicles, and contributions to the Community's structural funds. In the end, however, the Community's negotiating partners had too much to lose by failing to come to an agreement and the Commission made a few concessions to settle the agreement before the impending Maastricht summit which was to conclude the intergovernmental conferences. After a final sixteen-hour session, the negotiations were brought to a conclusion on 22 October. Ironically, when the negotiations began only Austria had declared for membership of the Community. The others saw the Economic Area as a way of gaining entry to the single market without having to accept the other aspects of Community membership. The problem was that the single market involved accepting a mass of Community legislation, over which they had no control, and the certainty of yet further legislation, over which they would have very limited influence. The Commission did agree to a joint court to deal with disputes, but even this was struck down in December by the Community's court, on the grounds that it infringed its integrity, forcing a renegotiation of the treaty. By then, however, the European Economic Area was seen as an antechamber to membership and the Swedish Prime Minister Carl Bildt greeted the agreement with the proclamation, 'Now we can go full speed ahead into the EC.'[117]

THE MAASTRICHT TREATY

The intergovernmental conferences were concluded two months later at Maastricht in December 1991. The success of Maastricht owed much to the Prime Minister of the Netherlands, Ruud Lubbers, who extracted compromises in bilateral discussions. Kohl gave way on the cohesion fund, opening up the way for Spanish acceptance of the treaty. On economic and monetary union, the others held firm while Britain concentrated on its 'opt out'. Major did make concessions on the extension of majority voting and on increased powers for the European Parliament. However, he refused to concede any ground on the social chapter.[118] The outcome was that Major was able to exclude the chapter from the Treaty on European Union, but he could not prevent the others going ahead with a Protocol on Social Policy which allowed them 'to have recourse to the institutions, procedures and mechanisms of the Treaty' to implement an attached Agreement on Social Policy.[119]

The Treaty on European Union reflected the divergent views and compromises even in those parts to which all member states subscribed. Although Article C referred to a Union which 'shall be served by a single institutional framework', the Union in fact consisted of three distinct pillars as outlined in the Luxembourg draft. The two new fields of action, the Common Foreign and Security Policy and Judicial and Home Affairs, bore a distinctly intergovernmental stamp. They were, for example, explicitly exempt from supervision by the Court of Justice.[120] Yet in both there was also provision that the 'Commission shall be fully associated', and Commission initiative was at least permitted.[121] Moreover, the Council could decide, albeit only unanimously and case by case, to act by a qualified majority. On the other hand, even within the European Community, the intergovernmental element was strengthened by giving the Council quasi-judicial and executive powers over progress towards monetary union.[122] These did not affect the autonomy of the proposed central bank, but did signify that France had been able to wring some concessions from Germany. Predictably, the European Parliament did not gain as much as it had hoped. It was denied any real power in Common Foreign and Security Policy, and Judicial and Home Affairs. In these, as in relation to the Bank, Parliament had little more than a right of consultation. Yet it did benefit from a new co-decision procedure which allowed Parliament to reject legislation in certain areas and from the extension of the assent procedure.[123]

For all its limitations and ambiguities, the Maastricht Treaty seemed to have committed the member states to a degree of integration even greater than the Single European Act. The key lay in monetary union and the loss of control over national currencies which had often been seen as a symbol of state sovereignty. It was true that the flanking pillars were far less ambitious, but even they marked an advance into new fields, and the Common Foreign and Security Policy reconciled the desire for European co-operation and the countervailing reluctance to abandon Atlanticism.[124] Delors moved quickly to consolidate the momentum, as he had six years earlier after the Single European Act. The result was the appropriately titled *From the Single European Act to Maastricht and Beyond: The Means to Match Our Ambitions*, which was presented in February 1992. The 'means' included a large increase in expenditure on the structural funds, and increase in Community revenues. The Common Agricultural Policy was also to grow, but would decline as a percentage of Community expenditure.[125]

Reform of the agricultural policy had been on the agenda since February 1991 under the guidance of the Commissioner for Agriculture, Ray MacSharry. MacSharry did not enjoy the support of Delors, and agriculture was always an issue guaranteed to raise the political temperature both within the Commission and in member states. Nevertheless, after the customary marathon negotiating session on 21 May 1992, agreement was finally reached. The most important element of the reforms was that, while farmers would continue to be subsidized, they would be paid directly rather than receiving the subsidy through artificially inflated prices.[126] This entailed openly accepting that much of the Community's rural population was being maintained for social or environmental reasons rather than for economic ones. The reforms also meant that the incentive to produce more, to benefit from the higher prices, was diminished and Community agricultural prices could move towards world market prices. That in turn facilitated agreement with the United States. But it did not guarantee it, for the United States and the Community were locked in dispute over oil seed. When MacSharry was on the point of agreement, he was overruled by Delors. An irate MacSharry then resigned and the United States announced trade sanctions. Under pressure from Britain and Germany, Delors agreed to restart the negotiations and MacSharry was reappointed. With concessions from both sides, the Blair House agreement was concluded on 20 November. The dispute was significant not just because of its impact on relations between the Community and the United States, but also because it demonstrated the passions which agricultural matters incited, passions disproportionate to the economic importance of the agricultural sector. Delors was not merely indulging in rhetoric when he railed against the United States and proclaimed that 'I'm not going to be an accomplice to the depopulation of the land.'[127]

THE RATIFICATION DEBATE AND SUBSIDIARITY

The dispute with the United States was a relatively minor crisis compared with events within the Community. The storm broke with the Danish referendum on Maastricht on 2 June 1992. By the narrow majority of 50.7 per cent the Danes rejected the treaty. Some consolation came from the Irish referendum at the end of the month, when 69 per cent voted in favour. A referendum in France, which was not really necessary, produced a much more marginal result in September, with 51 per cent voting 'yes'. The Danish result presented the most immediate problem, including the question whether the treaty could enter into force without ratification by Denmark. The Community resolved the problem by refusing to be deterred, holding out the prospect of proceeding without Denmark, while allowing the Danish government to negotiate protocols exempting them from the rigours of stage three of economic and monetary union and from participation in discussions on defence issues. With these in place, Denmark held a second referendum, in May 1993, and secured support for ratification.

The ratification crisis also had more long-term implications. Danish, French and Irish voters had probably been more influenced by domestic considerations than by their estimation of the Treaty on European Union.[128] Nevertheless, the results were taken by critics as evidence that Maastricht was a treaty too far. Some even questioned whether they indicated that European integration, which had been pushed forward by political elites and technocrats, was incompatible with democracy.[129] Delors sought to dilute the challenge by increased emphasis upon the principle of subsidiarity. This had aready been enshrined in the Treaty on European Union. According to Article 3b,

> In areas which do not fall within its exclusive competence, the Community shall take action, in accordance with the principle of subsidiarity, only if and in so far as the objectives of the proposed action cannot be sufficiently achieved by Member States and can therefore, by reasons of the scale or the effects of the proposed action, be better achieved by the Community.[130]

Subsidiarity was soon on the agenda at the Lisbon Council in June 1992, shortly after the first Danish referendum, and was the focus of a special summit in Birmingham in October. In Lisbon both Delors and Major sang the praises of subsidiarity, though the summit did little to clarify what it meant. In part at least, Major and other government leaders were, as the Italian Environment Minister Carlo Ripa di Mena pointed out on the eve of the Birmingham summit, using subsidiarity as a means to berate the Commission and divert attention from their own unpopularity.[131] At Birmingham they all agreed on the platitude that 'decisions must be taken as closely as possible to the citizen'.[132] It was not until the Edinburgh Council of December that they produced something more substantive. According to the Edinburgh Council, Community action was warranted where

> the issue under consideration has transnational aspects which cannot be satisfactorily regulated by action by Member States; and/or actions by Member States alone or lack of Community action would conflict with the requirements of the Treaty ... or would otherwise significantly damage Member States' interests; and/or the Council must be satisfied that action at community level would produce clear benefits by reasons of its scale or effects compared with action at the level of the Member States.[133]

Quite what these guidelines would mean was far from clear. The varying principles clearly differed in the scope they left to the Community. At Edinburgh the Commission seemed to be following the new spirit of the times and presented a list of proposed and existing legislation where it said Community action was not appropriate. The Commission's new modesty did not convince everyone, with a sceptical British newspaper commenting that some of these measures were 'so arcane that officials could not be found to explain what they were'.[134]

The real difficulty was that the concept of subsidiarity had been torn from the concept in which it had been formulated. A product of Catholic social theory, it described the obligations of higher levels of authority to support lower ones, down to the family and parish, where the latter could not fulfil their tasks unaided. The original moral dimension was largely ignored in the debates in 1992, to the irritation of those who recalled that the concept originally had such connotations.[135] It was not, however, the absence of a specifically moral dimension that mattered, but the absence of any social and political theory specifying what the appropriate levels of authority were.

The concept of subsidiarity was being invoked, in fact, to act as a substitute for a European constitution. It was being invoked to allocate competencies to different levels of decision-making. Different states, however, had widely differing conceptions of what the appropriate levels were. For the most centralized member state of the Community, Britain, the most desirable level of decision-making was the nation-state, and subsidiarity was to be used to wrest control from the Community. For most other member states a more flexible response was evident. Subsidiarity might indeed mean restoring power to the nation-state, but it might also mean devolving it to regional units within the nation-state. It was this ambiguity which alarmed some British conservatives. For Nigel Lawson, 'What the Brussels Commission wants to do is to destroy the nation state – both ways. Not just through taking far more powers to the centre, to

Brussels. But also by devolving powers, and they decide which powers it will be, to the lowest levels.'[136]

In Germany, it was not Brussels which decided on the distribution of power, but a deal between the *Länder* and the federal governments. As part of the ratification process the *Länder* had insisted upon a strengthening of their influence upon Germany's policy towards the Community, including a right of veto for the *Bundesrat* over any transfer of sovereignty to the Community and extensive obligations upon the federal government to consult the *Bundesrat.*[137] The new emphasis upon regionalism had already found its way into the Maastricht Treaty with the creation of the Committee of Regions. This body was given only 'advisory status', and some member states showed a marked reluctance even to appoint representatives to the Committee.[138] Nevertheless, the Committee did eventually meet in March 1994. It proved to be a cumbersome body, with members representing anything from impotent local authorities in Britain to the powerful land of Nordrhein-Westfalen in Germany. Regional representatives did not rely purely on the new, and weak, Committee, but assiduously lobbied the Commission, which in turn cultivated its relations with them.[139]

MONETARY UNION AND A MULTI-SPEED EUROPE

While the concept of subsidiarity and the Committee of Regions pointed to a possible decentralization of power, economic and monetary union, again in accordance with the concept of subsidiarity, pointed towards centralization. The year 1992 proved, however, to be no kinder to economic and monetary union. The bankers continued to worry about the details. The Governor of the Danish central bank, Erik Hoffmeyer, complained that the Maastricht Treaty was dangerously asymmetrical, consigning responsibility for monetary policy to a central bank while fiscal powers would remain dispersed among the member states.[140] It was, however, in part the failure of the central bankers to co-ordinate their actions which led to a crisis in September. Even more important were the underlying economic and monetary strains. Faltering growth in the early 1990s did not augur well. High German interest rates, the product of the costs of reunification and the decline of the dollar, created tension within the exchange rate mechanism. Amidst growing acrimony between the British Chancellor and the Bundesbank, speculators mounted an attack on sterling. On 16 September, 'black Wednesday', the crisis came. Sterling was forced to abandon the exchange rate mechanism. Public recriminations followed, dragging Anglo-German relations to their lowest point since the foundation of the Community. Economic and monetary union appeared to be in tatters.

This was not the end of the exchange rate crisis. The following summer a similar scenario unfolded, with the franc being the prime target of speculation. Again the Bundesbank refused to cut interest rates, and again the recriminations followed. In June, when the French Finance Minister, Edmond Alphandéry, criticized Bundesbank policy and suggested that a forthcoming meeting would see 'joint discussion of the conditions for a concerted reduction in French and German rates', the Germans cancelled the meeting.[141] In the ensuing crisis the franc was kept within the exchange rate mechanism only by the expedient of widening the bands to cater for its weakness. The French press lashed out in all directions. The Bundesbank council was accused of 'acting like provincial managers'.[142] The monetary crisis was depicted as a battle between two cultures, between 'Anglo-Saxon' speculators, for whom currencies were mere commodities, and a continental tradition according to which the currency was something more.[143] The national currency was evidently still a symbol of sovereign statehood. It was not only French commentators who cited cultural differences as key issues. According to one German commentator the Maastricht strategy of monetary union, based on an extension of the practices of the Bundesbank, was flawed. The Bundesbank's authority rested not only on its statute but also on the length of its experience and a 'quite specific "horror of inflations" ' in Germany.[144]

These strains naturally refocused attention on economic convergence as a criterion for monetary union. In April 1994 the central bankers invoked 'a new realism' and insisted that there would have to be internal reform before there was any prospect of monetary union.[145] An alternative strategy was to place the emphasis upon the restoration of economic growth. It was this to which Delors had turned his mind. At the June 1993 Copenhagen European Council he was able to persuade member states to sanction preparation of a White Paper on unemployment, competitiveness and growth. Some of the ideas which Delors considered, including a shorter working week and a reduction in overtime, met with suspicion from several member states and outright hostility from the British Chancellor Kenneth Clarke, who dismissed them as folly.[146] But when Delors presented his package, Major found much that he could agree with. Both Major and Kohl were highly cautious about the ambitious borrowing plans for energy and transportation projects. Faced with the assertion that there were no 'miracle cures' for unemployment, Major could only agree. There was indeed much in the White Paper that fitted in with a British Conservative emphasis upon small businesses and competitiveness. There was also frequently a difference of emphasis. When the White Paper praised small businesses and argued that 'The organization of work in a standardized way, frequently in huge production units, has distanced the individual from the results of his work', Delors the personalist was still evident.[147]

Despite the underlying differences of social and economic philosophy, the persistence of high unemployment and its attendant social costs induced the Essen European Council, in December 1994, to back much of Delors' White Paper. So long as the costs could be kept within bearable limits, or decisions on costs postponed, it was in many ways easier to agree on projects for the improvement of infrastructure, improved training and the reduction of non-wage labour costs, than it was to agree on the institutional and fiscal consequences of monetary union. Economic and monetary union was, however, still the goal of the Community, with the emphasis upon strict adherence to the convergence criteria.

Whether all member states would be in a position to fulfil the convergence criteria remained very much in doubt. That continued to induce speculation on a multi-speed or two-tier Europe. The French European Affairs Minister, Alain Lamassoure, went as far as to suggest that those who did proceed to monetary union should constitute 'new founding members of Europe'.[148] Since this status would be defined, it seemed, by a declaration rather than a new treaty, his remarks did not provoke much reaction. That could not be said of two German proposals, later in the year, which set out diverse futures for Europe. The first arose from the Bertelsmann Foundation, in June, and did not therefore represent official government policy, though former ministers and current government advisers were involved. The proposal was for a bicameral Community in which Council and Parliament enjoyed equal status. It represented the old federalist vision, including provision for a new treaty to replace all the existing ones and to specify the respective competence of the Community and its members.[149] The second proposal appeared in September and came from the Christian Democratic Union and Christian Social Union. This openly espoused a two-speed Europe centred around a hard core including Germany, France and the Benelux countries. Italy, one of the founding members of the Community, was notably absent. Although the proposal came from Germany's main governing parties, Foreign Minister Klaus Klinkel promptly asserted German commitment to the progress of the whole Union and described terms like variable geometry as unhelpful. He also stated that 'I have always said that we will need to address the question as to whether or not the slowest ship should continue to determine the pace of the convoy.'[150] In some respects the Community was already operating at variable speeds. On monetary union, social policy and on border controls, a multi-speed Community was a reality. But the more the Community integrated, the higher the stakes became and the higher the costs of being left behind.

ENLARGEMENT

While deepening integration posed problems, so too did widening the Community. At the Lisbon Council in 1992 member states agreed to enter into negotiations with the EFTA states, after the ratification of Maastricht and the associated budgetary package which Delors had presented in February. Two years later the negotiations were complete. Not all of the original candidates had survived. The Swiss ruled themselves out by declining to ratify even the agreement on the European Economic Area, and the Norwegians eventually voted against ratification of the accession treaty. That left Austria, Sweden and Finland as new members. Enlargement from twelve to fifteen brought with it the question of the balance of power within the Community, and especially the number of votes needed to block measures where qualified majority voting took place. Here Spain joined Britain, in what Spanish ministers themselves described as an 'unholy alliance', to try to maintain the old blocking majority. In the end they had to accept a face-saving compromise. Where the old majority existed, 'the Council will do all within its power to reach, within a reasonable time and without prejudicing obligatory time limits . . . a satisfactory solution that can be adopted by at least 68 votes.'[151] Britain and Spain thought the compromise gave them too little, the European Parliament that it gave them too much. But so long as the other member states stood firm neither could do anything other than refuse to ratify the treaties and wreck the imminent enlargement. Neither was willing to go so far.

The Essen European Council in December 1994 was the last Council of the twelve. At Essen the twelve braced themselves for yet further enlargement. Confirming decisions taken earlier in the year, the Council resolved to accept new member states from eastern and central Europe as soon as these were in a position to fulfil the associated obligations. There was one further major condition. Negotiations could not begin until 'the institutional assumptions for a frictionless functioning of the Union' were established at the intergovernmental conference which they were due to hold in 1996, in accordance with the provisions of the Maastricht Treaty. Once again deepening and widening were being linked, but whether this would issue in a Union closer to the outline of the Bertelsmann Foundation or that of the German Christian Democrats was still to be decided.

Essen was also the last summit for Delors and Mitterrand, both of whom had played a major role in the revival of the Community's fortunes over the previous decade. In December 1994 the Community dominated western Europe. It stood out as the most successful forum of integration in Europe in the twentieth century. Neither its western rival, the European Free Trade Association, nor its eastern European rival, Comecon, had proved its equal. Critics could point to rows over fish and heavy goods traffic, to the absurdities of the Comecon Agricultural Policy and impassioned, and often equally absurd, defence of national sovereignty. Yet as the history of European integration shows, the Community was still a remarkable achievement. Its complexity and imperfections were the inevitable product of constructing a half-way house between the Europe of nation-states and the federation which would constitute the United States of Europe. Few were foolish enough to wish to return to the former, but there was no majority for the latter. The Community's complexity also derived from its asymmetrical development. Still primarily an economic power, and still restricted to western Europe, it had to exist in a wider environment. Even with its three pillars, it formed only part of Europe's architecture.

NOTES

1. Nuttall, *European Political Co-operation*, pp. 183–6. For an extent to which German–American relationships had soured, see the public dispute of June 1980 in Bark and Gress, *A History of West German*, Vol. 2, pp. 318–19.
2. For the details, see Nuttall, *European Political Co-operation*, pp. 178–80.
3. *Selections*, pp. 492–7. For an analysis, see Joseph H. H. Weiler, 'The Genscher-Colombo Draft European Act: the politics of indecision', *Journal of European Integration*, **6** (1983), pp. 129–53, especially his concluding comment: 'It is a sign of the very malaise that even their anemic proposals, once processed by the normal intergovernmental procedure, will emerge so watered down that their fate ... will matter little to the real problems faced by the Europe of the Ten', p. 153. It was an accurate prediction.
4. *Selections*, pp. 501–20. For the background, see Alistair Cole, *François Mitterrand. A Study in Political Leadership* (London, 1994), pp. 119–20; E. Z. Haywood, 'The French socialists and European institutional reform', *Journal of European Integration*, **12** (1989), pp. 122–5.
5. See Margaret Thatcher's comment: 'I took the view that I could not quarrel with everything, and the document had no legal force. So I went along with it', though she added, 'the linguistic skeleton on which so much institutional flesh would grow was already evident'. *The Downing Street Years*, p. 314.
6. On the initiative and its underlying rationale see R. Cardoza and R. Corbett, 'The crocodile initiative', in J. Lodge (ed), *European Union: The European Community in Search of a Future* (New York, 1986), pp. 15– 46; M. Burgess, 'Altiero Spinelli, federalism and the EUT', *ibid*, pp. 14–85.
7. *Ibid.*, p. 183.
8. Article 84, Draft Treaty establishing the European Union.
9. Burgess encapsulates the treaty well in the phrase 'federalism without federation', 'Altiero Spinelli, federalism and the EUT', p. 183.
10. For national responses, see R. Bieber, J.-P. Jacqué and J. H. H. Weiler (eds), *An Ever Closer Union* (Luxembourg, 1985), pp. 177–304.
11. Cole, *François Mitterrand. A Study in Political Leadership*, pp. 125–6; Haywood, 'The French socialists and European institutional reform', pp.132–6.

12. On this and subsequent developments see Cole, *François Mitterrand*, pp. 33–6; Michael M. Harrison, 'Mitterrand's France in the Atlantic system', *Political Science Quarterly*, **99** (1984), pp. 237–41; H. Unterwedde, 'Wirtschafts- und Sozialpolitik unter Mitterrand 1981–1991', *Aus Politik und Zeitgeschichte*, **47–48** (1991), pp. 16–25.
13. Young, *Britain and European Unity*, p. 142.
14. Quoted in Cromwell, *The United States and the European Pillar*, p. 120. For Thatcher's account, see *The Downing Street Years*, pp. 253–6.
15. *Bulletin of the European Communities*, **5** (1984), p. 138.
16. Thatcher blamed 'Euro-enthusiasts' in her own party for undermining this option, *The Downing Street Years*, p. 539. See also George, *An Awkward Partner*, pp. 157–8.
17. *Ibid.*, pp. 154–7; Paul Taylor, 'The new dynamics of EC integration in the 1980s', in J. Lodge (ed.), *The European Community and the Challenge of the Future* (London, 1989), pp. 4–7.
18. *Bulletin of the European Communities*, **4** (1984), p. 10. See also Finn Laursen, 'The Community's policy towards EFTA', *Journal of Common Market Studies*, **28** (1990), p. 312. On the new protectionism and Community-EFTA relations see T. Pedersen, 'EC-EFTA relations', in G. Edwards and E. Regelsberger (eds), *Europe's Global Links* (New York, 1990), p. 99.
19. Cromwell, *The United States and the European Pillar*, pp. 173–4.
20. W. Sandholtz and J. Zysman emphasize the Japanese challenge, '1992: recasting the European bargain', *World Politics*, **42** (1989), pp. 105–6.
21. Quoted in *ibid.*, p. 117. Sandholtz and Zysman place great emphasis upon the role of business interests. Andre Moravcsik argues that at least some business groups had been pressing for this for a long time, hence, '[g]iven their persistence, what needs to be explained is why governments finally listened'. 'Negotiating the Single European Act', in Robert O. Keohane and Stanley Hoffman (eds), *The New European Community* (Boulder, 1991), p. 65.
22. Sandholtz and Zysman, '1992: recasting the European bargain', p. 117.
23. See Helmut Schmidt, *A Grand Strategy for the West* (New Haven, 1985).
24. *The Downing Street Years*, p. 546.
25. See the comment from an Italian businessman, 'The most we can hope for is that 1992 straightens us out.' Quoted in Sandholtz and Zysman, '1992: recasting the European bargain', p. 112. For French interest in this argument, see Georges Ross, *Jacques Delors and European Integration* (Cambridge, 1995), p. 258.
26. Ross, *Jacques Delors and European Integration*, p. 30.
27. Malcolm Rifkind in September 1983, quoted in George, *An Awkward Partner*, p. 177. This had also been the French refrain before Mitterrand's conversion to institutional reform. See Cole, *François Mitterrand*, pp. 124–5.
28. On the Stresa meeting see George, *An Awkward Partner*, pp. 179–80; Jean de Ruyt, *L'Acte unique européene* (Brussels, 1989), pp. 57–9.
29. On this domestic pressure see Haywood, 'French socialists and European institutional reform', pp. 141, 143.
30. *Ibid*, pp. 143–4; de Ruyt, *L'Acte unique européene*, pp.61–2.
31. Thatcher, *Downing Street Years*, p. 551; Taylor, 'The new dynamics of EC integration in the 1980's, p. 10.
32. *Bulletin of the European Communities*, **9** (1985), point 1.1.1, p. 8.
33. *Ibid.*, p. 9.

34. De Ruyt, *L'Acte unique européenne,* pp. 72, 121–38.
35. De Ruyt states that the German position changed because the Netherlands persuaded them that it was a political necessity. R. Corbett, 'The 1985 Intergovernmental Conference and the Single European Act', in Pryce (ed.), *The Dynamics of European Union,* points to French and Italian liberalization of exchange controls as facilitating the German compromise, p. 247.
36. *The Downing Street Years,* p. 557. Compare Delors' reassurance to the European Parliament 'that the Intergovernmental Conference is a progressive compromise. It is up to us to turn it into a dynamic compromise.' *Bulletin of the European Communities,* **12** (1985), p. 9.
37. Article 13, Single European Act.
38. T. Padoa-Schioppa, *Efficiency, Stability and Equity* (Oxford, 1987), p. 93. For criticism of Cecchini, see Tony Cutler *et al., The Struggle for Europe. A Critical Evaluation of the European Community* (New York, 1989), p. 76; U. Bullmann and D. Eissel, ' "Europa der Regionen" Entwicklung und Perspektiven', *Aus Politik und Zeitgeschichte,* **20–1** (1993), p. 4. See also L. Tsoukalis, *The New European Economy* (Oxford, 1991), pp. 82–3.
39. Cutler *et al., The Struggle for Europe,* pp. 78–105.
40. See Bullman and Eissel, ' "Europa der regionen" Entwicklung und Perspektiven', pp. 5–6.
41. Quoted in Ross, *Jacques Delors and European Integration,* p. 41. For a more ideological expression, see his comments in an interview in 1993: 'I reject a Europe that would be just a market, a free trade zone without a soul, without a conscience, without a political will, without a social dimension.' *The Guardian* (19 October 1993). On the diversity of goals hidden beneath the slogan of the single market see Michael Kreile, 'Politische Dimensionen des europäischen Binnenmarkts', *Aus Politik und Zeitgeschichte,* **24–5** (1989), pp. 25–35.
42. On this see Stephen Woolcock, Michael Hodges and Kristin Schreiber, *Britain, Germany and 1992. The Limits of Deregulation* (London, 1991), especially their observation that at the macroeconomic level the German approach is likely to prevail 'for the simple reason that none of the member-states are prepared to see a transfer of discretionary power to the EC', p. 9.
43. Youri Devuyst, 'European Community Integration and the United States: toward a new Transatlantic relationship?', *Journal of European Integration,* **14** (1990), pp. 10–12.
44. Philippe G. Nell, 'EFTA in the 1990s: the search for a new identity', *Journal of Common Market Studies,* **28** (1990), p. 329.
45. Quoted in Laursen, 'The Community's policy towards EFTA', p. 314.
46. *Ibid.,* p. 315.
47. Nell, 'EFTA in the 1990s', p. 352.
48. Jozef M. van Brabant, 'The demise of the CMEA – the agony of inaction', *Osteuropa-Wirtschaft,* **36** (1991), p. 238.
49. L. Csaba, 'CMEA and the challenge of the 1980s', *Soviet Studies,* **40** (1988), pp. 267–8. Csaba argues that the real problem with oil was not the price but the insatiable demand of economies with inadequate constraints on raw material consumption, *ibid.,* pp. 268–9.
50. *Ibid.,* pp. 272–3.
51. *Ibid.,* p. 275.
52. On these meetings see Brabant, 'The demise of the CMEA', pp. 24–6.

53. *Ibid.*, p. 245.
54. See *Financial Times* (24 January 1990) and Statistisches Bundesamt, *Country Reports. Central and Eastern Europe 1991* (Luxembourg, 1991), p. 140.
55. H.-H. Hertle, 'Der Weg in den Bankrott der DDR– Wirtschaft', *Deutschland Archiv*, **2** (1992), pp. 127–44. Günter Mittag claimed he was aware that the Democratic Republic was at the point of economic catastrophe in 1987. *Der Spiegel*, **37** (1991), p. 92. Schürer recalled Mittag as a dogmatist.
56. Quoted in Barbara Lippert, 'EC-CMEA relations: normalisation and beyond', in Edwards and Regelsberger (eds), *Europe's Global Links*, p. 123. The novelty lay in Soviet recognition of the Community's political role.
57. John Pinder, *The European Community and Eastern Europe* (London, 1991), p. 24.
58. *Bulletin of the European Communities*, **2** (1986), point 2.2.21.
59. The Community announced this as 'a fundamental change in relations'. *Bulletin of the European Communities*, **5** (1986), point 2.2.37.
60. *Official Journal of the European Communities*, Series L, 157. See also the description of the decision of the east Europeans to send diplomatic missions to the Community as 'an unprecedented act of formal recognition from the Eastern European countries'. *Bulletin of the European Communities*, **6** (1988), point 1.5.3.
61. On Gorbachev's common European home see Neil Malcolm, 'The "common European home" and Soviet foreign policy', *International Affairs*, **65** (1989), pp. 659–76; on the CSCE see Vojtech Mastny (ed.), *The Helsinki Process and the Reintegration of Europe 1986–1991* (New York, 1992); on German reactions see Bark and Gress, *A History of West German*, Vol. 2, pp. 465–74, 481–88.
62. Quoted in Malcolm, 'The "common European home" and Soviet foreign policy', p. 666. For more expansive comments, see M. Gorbachev, *Perestroika* (London, 1987), pp. 190–209.
63. Werner J. Feld, 'Franco-German military cooperation and European unification', *Journal of European Integration*, **12** (1989), pp. 151–64.
64. For an assessment, see P. Tsakaloyannis (ed.), *Western European Security in a Changing World* (Maastricht, 1988). See especially Howe's speech of 16 March 1987 in which he alternately cast doubt on and affirmed his faith in American commitment to Europe, ibid., pp. 141–48.
65. Michael Clarke, 'Evaluating the new Western European Union: the implications for Spain', in Kenneth Maxwell (ed.), *Spanish Foreign and Defense Policy* (Boulder, 1991), pp. 165–86. Spain had joined the Atlantic Alliance in 1982 but, given the hostility of the Socialist Party, subsequently held a referendum which confirmed membership. See Bruce George and Mark Stenhouse, 'Western perspectives of Spain', *ibid.*, pp. 63–113, especially the comments on Prime Minister Gonzalez's attempt to link continued membership with entry into the European Community, pp. 96–7.
66. For the details, see Michael Shackelton, *Financing the European Community* (London, 1990), pp. 10–12.
67. Dinan, *Ever Closer Union?*, p. 153 and George, *An Awkward Partner*, p. 190, describe Thatcher's behaviour as surprising. In her memoirs she states simply that she had got as much out of her partners as she could, *Downing Street Years*, p. 737. According to Lord Cockfield, *The European Union. Creating the Single Market* (London, 1994), Thatcher's belated concessions 'rankled deeply', p. 139.
68. Kenneth Dyson, *Elusive Union: The Process of Economic and Monetary Union in Europe* (London, 1994), pp. 120–1.

69. *Ibid.*, pp. 123–4.
70. See his comments on 23 June reported in the *Financial Times* (24 June 1988). On Stoltenberg and the linkage see Dyson, *Elusive Union*, pp. 127–8.
71. Thatcher, *Downing Street Years*, p. 740. Her problem was that the 'linguistic skeleton' of monetary union already existed, *ibid.*, pp. 741–2.
72. *Bulletin of the European Communities*, **5** (1988), point 1.1.4.
73. *The Guardian* (28 June 1988).
74. Thatcher, *Downing Street Years*, pp. 744-5.
75. *Report on Economic and Monetary Union in the European Community* (Luxembourg, 1989), pp. 34–40. On similarities and differences between the Werner and Delors reports see Dyson, *Elusive Union*, pp. 130–2.
76. *Report on Economic and Monetary Union*, p. 25.
77. *Ibid.*, p. 26.
78. *Ibid.*, p. 136.
79. Thatcher, *Downing Street Years*, pp. 709–13, 750–2. She did extract a few minor concessions. See Dyson, *Elusive Union*, pp. 135–6.
80. Delors used this and similar phrases on several occasions. See, for example, *The Guardian* (25 January 1990).
81. See 'EEC uses carrot and stick strategy on Eastern bloc', *The Guardian* (25 April 1989).
82. Quoted in Renata Fritsch-Bournazel, *Europe and German Reunification* (New York, 1992), p. 19.
83. Gerd Langguth, 'Die deutsche Frage und die Europäische Gemeinschaft', *Aus Politik und Zeitgeschichte*, **29** (1990), p. 19; Cole, *François Mitterrand*, p. 135.
84. Quoted in Renata Fritsch-Bournazel, *Europe and German Reunification*, p. 173.
85. Stephen F. Szabo, *The Diplomacy of German Unification* (New York, 1992), p. 50. See also Cole's assessment that Mitterrand 'remained attached to a bipolar vision of the world, shaped by an inability to escape from the logic of the cold war, and an incomprehension of the revolutionary changes in eastern Europe', *François Mitterrand*, p. 152.
86. Quoted in Fritsch-Bournazel, *Europe and German Reunification*, p. 59. For the haggling, see the *Financial Times* (9 December 1989).
87. *Bulletin of the European Communities*, Supplement 1 (1990), p. 12.
88. *Ibid.*, p. 13. According to one of his advisers, his ambition was that the Commission should resemble the government of the Federal Republic but with weaker powers, *The Guardian* (18 January 1990).
89. Devuyst, 'European Community integration and the United States', p. 16. For Bush's enthusiastic support of further integration, see his press conference at the December NATO summit, *The Guardian* (5 December 1989).
90. Duvuyst, 'European Community integration and the United States', p. 26.
91. Dyson, *Elusive Union*, p. 137. See also the criticism of the Italian Treasury Minister, Guido Carli, 'There is no example in historical experience of a stable regime of fixed exchange rates which co-existed with free capital movements and "competing" monetary authorities.' He ruled out the pre-1914 gold standard because controls were utilized. *Financial Times* (17 January 1990).
92. Dyson, *Elusive Union*, points to the similarity with the competing currency plan, pp. 141–2.

93. For a qualified welcome of Major's initiative, see the comments of Wilfried Guth of the Deutsche Bank, *Financial Times* (8 October 1990); for Pöhl's rejection, see *Financial Times* (10 November 1990).
94. *Financial Times* (14 November 1990).
95. *The Guardian* (30 November 1990).
96. Quoted in Uwe Thayson, *Der Runde Tisch* (Opladen, 1990), p. 50.
97. Quoted in Fritsch-Bournazel, *Europe and German Reunification*, pp. 84–5.
98. On these disputes see Michael Kreile, 'The political economy of the new Germany', in Paul B. Stares (ed.), *The New Germany and the New Europe* (Washington, 1992), pp. 68–71; Barbara Lippert and Rosalind Stevens-Ströhmann, *German Unification and EC Integration* (London, 1992), pp. 40–4.
99. *Financial Times* (21 September 1990).
100. Dyson, *Elusive Union*, p. 147.
101. *Ibid.*, p. 154; Charles Grant, *Delors. Inside the House That Jacques Built* (London, 1994), p. 182. Ross describes Delors' 'theatrical indignation' as a ploy to deter the Germans from an alliance with the British rather than a serious attempt to obtain a central bank at stage two, *Jacques Delors*, p. 87.
102. *Financial Times* (20 March 1991 and 23 March 1991).
103. Ross, *Jacques Delors*, pp. 154–5; Dyson, *Elusive Union*, p. 156. The proposal had been made by the Luxembourg Presidency in April, *Financial Times* (24 April 1991).
104. *Bulletin of the European Communities*, Supplement 2 (1991), p. 117.
105. There was even opposition within the Commission. See Ross, *Jacques Delors*, pp. 100–1.
106. *Ibid.*, p. 148. See also p. 104 and Enrico Martial, 'France', in Finn Laursen and Sophie Vanhoonacker (eds), *The Intergovernmental Conference on Political Union* (Maastricht, 1992), p. 121.
107. Quoted in Ross, *Jacques Delors*, p. 94. On the Genscher-Dumas proposal see Panos Tsakaloyannis, '"The acceleration of history" and the reopening of the political debate in the European Community', *Journal of European Integration*, **14** (1991), pp. 97–8; Laursen and Vanhoonacker (eds), *the Intergovernmental Conference on Political Union*, pp. 333–5.
108. *Financial Times* (5 August 1991). See also Ross, *Jacques Delors*, pp. 146–8.
109. The ideal of three pillars was suggested by the French Foreign Office. See Martial, 'France', p. 124.
110. Sophie Vanhoonacker, 'Belgium and European political union', in Laursen and Vanhoonacker (eds), *The Intergovernmental Conference on Political Union*, pp. 45–6. For Commission disenchantment, see *Bulletin of the European Communities*, **11** (1991), point 1.1.1.
111. *Financial Times* (13 September 1991).
112. Dyson, *Elusive Union*, p. 156.
113. In Laursen and Vanhoonacker (eds), *The Intergovernmental Conference on Political Union*, p. 339.
114. Alberto Gil Ibanez, 'Spain and European political union', in *ibid.*, p. 109.
115. *Bulletin of the European Communities*, Supplement 2 (1991), Articles 118 and 118b, pp. 126–7.
116. Ross, *Jacques Delors*, pp. 150–2.
117. *Financial Times* (23 October 1991).

118. Stubbornness on this point was related to domestic policies. The Conservative government had abandoned most of the commitments and policy techniques it had espoused on entering office. Social policy was the one major exception.
119. *Treaty on European Union* (Luxembourg, 1992), pp. 196–201.
120. On the importance of this see Robert Harmsen, 'A European union of variable geometry: problems and perspectives', *Northern Ireland Legal Quarterly*, **45** (1994), p. 111. But note that Article M, in the words of M. R. Eaton, allows the Court to 'police the borderline between the Community pillar' and the new areas. 'Common foreign and security policy', in David O'Keeffe and Patrick M Twomey (eds), *Legal Issues of the Maastricht Treaty* (London, 1994), p. 233.
121. Articles J.8, J.9, K.3.2, K.4.2. See Harmsen, 'A European union of variable geometry', p. 112.
122. *Ibid.*, p. 113; D. R. R. Dunnett, 'Legal and institutional issues affecting economic and monetary union', in O'Keeffe and Twomey (eds), *Legal Issues of the Maastricht Treaty*, pp. 141–2.
123. The areas included the internal market and environmental action programmes. See Dinan, *Ever Closer Union?*, pp. 280–1, for a list of areas and summary of the complex co-decision procedure. The major extension of the assent procedure covered certain types of international agreements.
124. It was welcomed by Manfred Wörner, Secretary General of the Atlantic Alliance, and by the United States. *The Guardian* (12 December 1991).
125. Ross, *Jacques Delors*, pp. 198–9; Grant, *Delors*, p. 211.
126. *Financial Times* (22 May 1992).
127. Grant, *Delors*, p. 172. See also his comments in March, 'The rural world has developed around farmers, who are, at the same time, producers of goods, creators of civilisation and gardeners of nature', *ibid.*, p. 173.
128. Mark Franklin, Michael Marsh, Lauren McLaren, 'Uncorking the bottle: popular opposition to European unification in the wake of Maastricht', *Journal of Common Market Studies*, **32** (1994), pp. 455–72; Cole, *François Mitterrand*, pp. 159–62; Arter, *The Politics of European Integration in the Twentieth Century*, pp. 212–16.
129. The point is raised by Wolfgang Kowalsky, 'Europa vor der Herausforderung zivilisierter Innenbeziehungen', *Aus Politik und Zeitgeschichte*, **3–4** (1995), pp. 20–1.
130. Article 3b, *Treaty on European Union* (Luxembourg, 1992).
131. *Financial Times* (16 October 1992).
132. *Financial Times* (17 October 1992).
133. In Andrew Duff (ed.), *Subsidiarity within the European Community* (London, 1993), p. 120.
134. *Financial Times* (14 December 1992). See also *Bulletin of the European Communities*, **12** (1992), point 1.23.
135. See the complaint of A. Oostalander quoted in Kees van Kersbergen and Bert jan Verbeek, 'The politics of subsidiarity in the European union', *Journal of Common Market Studies* **32** (1994), p. 224.
136. Lars C. Blichner and Linda Sanglot, 'The concept of subsidiarity and the debate on European cooperation: pitfalls and possibilities', *Governance*, **7** (1994), p. 294. On the hypocrisy of the British government in invoking subsidiarity to deny power to the Community, while refusing to concede it to local or regional government, see Andrew Scott, John Peterson, David Millar, 'Subsidiarity: a "Europe of the regions" v. the British constitution', *Journal of Common Market Studies*, **32** (1994), pp. 47–67.

137. See Hans Hoffman, 'Grundgesetz und Europäische Union', *Aus Politik und Zeitgeschichte*, **52–3** (1993), pp. 33–9.
138. For the Maastricht provisions, see Articles 198a–c. For the reluctance, see *The Guardian* (7 October 1993).
139. See the reports in *Das Parlament* (8 April 1994).
140. *Financial Times* (11 May 1992).
141. *Financial Times* (25 June 1993).
142. *Financial Times* (2 August 1993).
143. This underestimated the symbolic significance of national currencies to some Anglo-Saxons. See Thatcher's proclamation on 30 October 1990 that it would be wrong to 'abolish the pound sterling, the greatest expression of sovereignty'. Quoted in Geoffrey Howe, *Conflict of Loyalty* (London, 1994), p. 644.
144. Peter Bohley, 'Europäische Einheit, föderatives Prinzip und Währungsunion', *Aus Politik und Zeitgeschichte*, **1** (1993), p. 44.
145. *Financial Times* (9 April 1994).
146. *Financial Times* (24 November 1993). See also Grant, *Delors*, p. 265.
147. *Bulletin of the European Communities*, Supplement 6 (1993). For the suggestion that action concerning unemployment might resolve the Community's crisis of legitimacy, see Kowalsky, 'Europa vor der Herausforderung zivilisierter Innenbeziehungen', p. 23.
148. *Financial Times* (16 April 1994).
149. *The Guardian* (21 June 1994).
150. Embassy of the Federal Republic of Germany, Press Release 103/94 (7 September 1994). For reports of the proposals and reactions to them, see *Financial Times* (3 September 1994, 9 September 1994, 14 September 1994, 16 September 1994, 29 September 1994).
151. *Bulletin of the European Communities*, **3** (1994), point 1.3.28.

8

The New European Architecture

INTRODUCTION

In 1989 the basis of Europe's post-war architecture began to crumble. The next year, in July, the Atlantic Alliance proposed to the Warsaw Pact 'a joint declaration in which we solemnly state that we are no longer adversaries and reaffirm our intention to refrain from the threat or use of force against the territorial integrity or political independence of any state'.[1] While the end of the Cold War, symbolized by the Alliance's declaration, was widely welcomed, pessimists suggested that the development was not an unalloyed blessing. Compared with the first half of the twentieth century, the postwar years had been remarkably stable. The Germans, whether living in an authoritarian communist state or a democratic capitalist state, had posed no threat, nor shown any inclination to do so. The territorial borders which the Alliance promised to respect had been stable. No state had been annexed and no new ones created. For all its faults, the system in which two external superpowers divided and dominated Europe had given Europeans a stability they had been patently unable to achieve on their own.

When German reunification was placed on the agenda in 1989 the deep-seated suspicions of her neighbours were evident. The main potential obstacle was the Soviet Union. But the Soviet Union lacked the will, and the ability, to prevent reunification and membership of a reunified Germany in the European Community. More surprisingly, the Soviet Union also conceded the membership of reunified Germany in the Atlantic Alliance. The old Soviet strategy, trading unity for neutrality, lay in tatters. The old western strategy, linking German revival with European and Atlantic integration, was reconfirmed.

German reunification was accompanied by the development of an economic and security vacuum in the east. The new regimes in eastern Europe insisted on dismantling the institutions of the socialist commonwealth. Dismantling the old order proved easier than inaugurating a new one. Attempts to solve the problem by strengthening regional integration in the east, either with or without the Soviet Union, met with limited success. The potential consequences of disintegration were dramatically illustrated by the crisis in Yugoslavia, which also cruelly exposed the weakness of the European Community.

Developments in Yugoslavia seemed to herald a return of Europe to its old instability.[2] The revival of the demons of nationalism was one of the problems which confronted the newly strengthened Conference on Security and Co-operation in Europe. Hopes that the Conference might provide a pan-European security structure were, however, doomed from the start. For the states of east Europe, integration into the west was a more attractive proposition.

Here entry into the Council of Europe, the weakest of the western fora, proved comparatively easy. Integration into the economic and military core of western Europe was much more problematic. The European Community proved to be cautious even in matters of trade and aid. The Community's hesitancy, the qualifications and escape clauses in the much-vaunted Europe Agreements, focused attention on the Community's failure to live up to the challenge. Yet in a broader historical perspective the Community's response contrasted favourably with the indecision and indifference shown by the west in the inter-war years.

Now, in the 1990s, the agenda was different. The eastern states wanted not just trade concessions but to join the victors of the Cold War. By the end of 1994 enlargement of the European Community and, much more equivocally, of the Atlantic Alliance, was on the agenda. But expansion of either brought back old problems of where exactly Europe's borders lay. There was no prospect that Europe, or the Atlantic, could be expanded until they were synonymous with the Conference on Security and Co-operation, with Europe from Vancouver to Vladivostok. Anything less extensive automatically meant either perpetuating the old divisions, or drawing new divisions to replace the old ones. Over four years after the Atlantic Alliance proclaimed the end of the Cold War, fear of drawing new divisions still hindered the attempt to abolish the old.

THE CHALLENGE OF GERMAN REUNIFICATION

The division of Germany had been the corner-stone and symbol of the division of Europe, the containment of Germany the prime benefit claimed by defenders of Cold War Europe. A united Germany posed a threat whether it was a member of one of the alliances, for then it would alter the balance of power, or it was a member of neither, for then it would be a 'loose cannon' which might be tempted to play off one side against the other. Nor did a united Germany pose only a security threat.

A united Germany, it was assumed, would be economically even stronger and would exercise at least an informal hegemony over the states of central and eastern Europe.

For the latter the new Europe meant changes in international institutions, socio-economic transformation and a reorientation of trade to the west. That in turn brought with it the old questions about the relationship between the relatively undeveloped east and the advanced west. Indeed the discrepancies were in some respects even greater than in the inter-war period, for western Europe's peripheral countries had narrowed the gap between themselves and their more advanced neighbours, while the gap between the more advanced eastern countries and the west had remained substantial. Spain, for example, could boast a per capita income of $12,670 in 1991 whereas the Czech Republic had only $7,570. Whereas the modernized Spain relied upon agriculture for only 5 per cent of its GDP, the Czech Republic depended upon agriculture for 8 per cent.[3] As in previous periods of reconstruction, the transformation soon proved more difficult than anticipated, leaving a Polish commentator to warn that the 'emergence of Latin American forms of dependence along with authoritarian and corrupt regimes is sadly very probable'.[4]

German reunification combined both the geo-political security problems and those of economic transformation. Reunification had been offered periodically in the past by the Soviet Union, at the price of the neutralization of Germany. Initially, the Soviet response to the prospect of reunification was similar, even in terminology, to that of the Federal Republic's allies. Shortly after the opening of the Berlin wall Gorbachev affirmed that reunification 'is not a matter of current politics'.[5] According to Kohl's adviser Horst Teltschik, only days later, on 21 November, a Soviet official indicated that confederation was one of the options being discussed in Moscow. This encouraged Kohl to launch his ten-point plan on 28 November. If the Soviet Union was considering confederation, it was clearly in no hurry to see it brought about. The official response to Kohl's ten-point plan was that it 'could only lead to confusion'.[6] In December Gorbachev continued to stress the obstacles to reunification and the importance of the Democratic Republic as a Soviet ally. A little later his Foreign Minister, Eduard Shevardnadze, conceded that it could join the European Community if it wished, but he too emphasized the Democratic Republic's importance to the Warsaw Pact and insisted that the Democratic Republic could not leave the Pact while the Federal Republic remained in the Atlantic Alliance.[7]

Alliance membership was equally vital to the United States since its relationship to the Federal Republic was the linchpin of American strategy towards the Atlantic Alliance.[8] It was not only fear of a united

Germany as a loose cannon that motivated the United States, or even continued fears about Soviet military strength. As Assistant Secretary of State Seitz put it, the Alliance, with Germany in it, enabled the United States to 'play an active role in shaping the emerging political and security architecture of Europe'.[9] Germany's importance had been made strikingly evident in May 1989 when President Bush described the Federal Republic as America's 'partner in leadership'.[10] It was also evident in December 1989 when Secretary of State Baker called for a new Atlanticism. Baker placed German unification in the context of linkage between American and European security, a prominent role for the Alliance in managing arms reduction and creating a new approach to security which would reassure the east, and use of the Conference on Security and Co-operation to promote broader east–west co-operation. By then the United States was committed to reunification. The object, however, was to control the process and ensure that American interests were preserved.

It was the United States that devised the diplomatic framework within which reunification was achieved. The formula 2 + 4 was suggested by two American officials, Robert Zoellick and Dennis Ross. The two Germanies would negotiate the internal aspects while they, together with the four wartime allies, the United States, the Soviet Union, France and Britain, would deal with the broader issues. Both the Atlantic Alliance and the Conference on Security and Co-operation were excluded on the grounds that they were too large.[11] This strategy appealed to Kohl, who was anxious to avoid a large gathering which could take on the form of a belated peace conference, and bring with it unwanted claims for compensation from Germany's wartime enemies.

Relations with Poland were especially important here. By the Warsaw treaty of 1970 both states had recognized that the Oder–Neisse line constituted Poland's western border. There was, however, a question mark over the legal status of this given the residual rights of the wartime victors, a question mark which was enlarged when the Federal Constitutional Court ruled that territories east of the line, which had belonged to Germany before 1939, still legally formed part of Germany.[12] Little practical notice was taken of this. But when Poland pressed for a treaty to finalize the border issue in 1989 Kohl was evasive. Although several excuses were offered, his real reason was to placate right-wing elements sympathetic to associations of Germans who had been expelled from the east at the end of the Second World War. Kohl's position was even more exposed because his own Foreign Minister clearly was prepared to proceed to full and final recognition of the border.[13]

Germany's border was one theme in Foreign Minister Genscher's speech of 31 January 1990. With an eye to the forthcoming election in the

Democratic Republic in March, he declared that the 'first joint act by the two freely elected German parliaments and governments must be a declaration guaranteeing the frontiers of all our neighbours'.[14] The bulk of his speech was, however, devoted to reassuring the Soviet Union, without weakening the principles of the German position. Thus, he stated that a united Germany would be a member of the Atlantic Alliance. Neutrality was not an option. But he promised the Soviet Union that there would be no eastward expansion of the Alliance. The whole process would take place within the framework of strengthening the European Community and the Conference on Security and Co-operation.

The day before Genscher's speech Gorbachev abandoned his earlier emphasis upon the 'reality' of two German states. Of unification he said, 'In principle, no one puts it in doubt.'[15] That there were, as yet, limits to Gorbachev's concessions was evident from the proposal which the leader of the Democratic Republic brought back from Moscow on 1 February. According to this, confederation would lead to full unity, and to neutrality.[16] Yet when Kohl and Genscher visited Moscow, Gorbachev agreed reunification was on the agenda and that the timing was a matter for the Germans, albeit with the qualification that its external implications had to be sanctioned by the four wartime allies. In fact Kohl and Genscher were rapidly gaining control over the reunification process.[17]

February saw agreement on the 2 + 4 framework at the Ottawa 'Open Skies' conference.[18] The framework was not seen as the most desirable by all of Germany's neighbours. Both Britain and France preferred restricting the issue to negotiations among the four great powers. Foreign Minister Gianni de Michelis demanded Italian participation in the talks, but was not supported by his own Prime Minister.[19] Most worried of all were the Poles. The otherwise adroit Kohl inflamed their suspicions by insisting that only a united Germany could issue guarantees of borders and by linking the guarantee with Polish renunciation of any claims for reparations.[20] Both Britain and France supported the Polish position, as indeed did many in Germany, including President von Weizsäcker. Faced with mounting domestic and foreign criticism, Kohl abandoned the link between border guarantees and reparations, acknowledging that 'mistakes were made on all sides, including by me'.[21] Kohl made an even more substantive concession on 14 March when he agreed that Poland could participate in the 2 + 4 talks on the border issue.[22]

The latent fears which the fact and speed of the reunification process roused were most crudely exposed by a British Minister, Nicholas Ridley, in July. His immediate target was the Community's monetary policy, which he described as a 'German racket'. He recalled Britain's traditional concern with the balance of power, which was more necessary than ever 'with Germany so uppity' and the 'French behaving like poodles'.[23] The remarks led to his resignation, but both the crudity of the sentiment and the concern with the balance of power were shared by the Prime Minister and considerations of the balance of power were widely spread among the British foreign policy establishment.[24] Yet the traditional language of the balance of power was of little use to Germany's partners in the Community. Anti-German alliances to redress the balance were hardly plausible. The only solution was the one offered by Kohl: further European integration.

Balance of power considerations were of greater relevance in gaining Soviet acceptance of reunification. It was also important to Germany's western allies that the strength of the west *vis-à-vis* the Soviet Union be maintained. For the Atlantic Alliance that meant agreement on a Conventional Forces in Europe treaty, setting limits to troop levels and armaments. Agreement on conventional forces was made a condition of the Conference on Security and Co-operation in Europe which was planned for November.[25] The Soviet Union wanted the conference to consolidate the security and co-operation process by giving it an institutional framework. This was a well-established Soviet goal, but one which had traditionally been resisted by the Atlantic Alliance, especially by its Anglo-Saxon members. Now, however, they were beginning to accept it as part of a package for the new European architecture.[26]

GERMAN MEMBERSHIP OF THE ATLANTIC ALLIANCE AND THE NEW EUROPEAN ARCHITECTURE

Soviet interest in the conference was linked to its opposition to German membership of the Atlantic Alliance. In April Foreign Minister Shevardnadze suggested that a reunified Germany could be a member of both the Atlantic Alliance and the Warsaw Pact for a transitional period while both alliances transformed themselves into political rather than security organizations. Security issues would then become the concern of a new Conference on security and Co-operation in Europe, into which Germany would be incorporated 'as an equal partner'.[27] The following month Shevardnadze suggested uncoupling internal reunification and settlement of its external consequences. The former could proceed while the latter would be postponed until agreement was reached on a new pan-European security order. During the transitional period the four great powers would retain their rights over Germany. While the conciliatory Genscher showed some interest in the offer, Kohl's rejection of it on 9 May was blunt.[28] The underlying reasons for the vigour of Kohl's response had been made clear earlier: 'The first important principle is that

Germany must not be singled out ... Singling out Germany means neutralising it. Then you will turn the geographic centre of Europe into a ghetto – a policy which would be catastrophic.'[29] In this Kohl was following Adenauer's stance during the negotiations on the European Defence Community almost forty years earlier. Germany would accept restrictions upon her sovereignty in the interests of European security, but Germany would not accept an institutional arrangement which discriminated against her.

Yet Kohl, again following Adenauer, was not entirely rigid in this, as became clear at his meeting with Gorbachev in the middle of July. The German–Soviet meeting was greatly aided by two initiatives, one from the United States and one from the Atlantic Alliance. The American initiative occurred during Gorbachev's visit to Washington in May. Bush offered the Soviet Union 'Nine Assurances' on German reunification, including German economic assistance to the Soviet Union, a new, less threatening Alliance strategy and a new, institutionalized Conference on Security and Co-operation. The aim was to persuade Gorbachev to accept German membership of the Atlantic Alliance. On this point he was evasive, but Bush and Gorbachev were able to agree on settling the arms reduction talks and the shape of the new Conference.[30]

The second initiative was the Atlantic Alliance's London Declaration. In addition to the offer of a joint declaration ending the antagonistic posture of the Atlantic Alliance and the Warsaw Pact, the London document included a key clause on nuclear weapons. With a withdrawal of Soviet forces and the treaty on conventional forces, the Alliance 'will be able to adopt a new NATO strategy making nuclear forces truly weapons of last resort'.[31] This came close to the commitment, long desired by the Soviet Union, not to use nuclear weapons as a first resort. True, it was qualified, at British insistence, by the statement that 'there are no circumstances in which nuclear retaliation ... might be discounted'.[32] Britain and France were concerned about the reliability of American commitment to Europe and about their status as great powers and, on both counts, were reluctant to accept restrictions on their nuclear arsenals. Nevertheless, Shevardnadze and Gorbachev were delighted and responded to the Alliance's offer within the hour. Their haste reflected a desire to pre-empt any opposition from their own hardliners, especially in the light of the forthcoming Party Congress. Opposition at the Congress proved less vigorous than they had expected. Shortly afterwards Kohl flew to the Soviet Union.[33]

Agreement on the outstanding issues was reached quickly. Gorbachev accepted Germany's membership of the Atlantic Alliance in return for a promise that neither nuclear weapons nor non-German Alliance forces would be deployed in the territories of the former Democratic Republic. Kohl also accepted limits on the new Bundeswehr and offered economic assistance to facilitate the withdrawal of Soviet troops. Germany's allies, especially the United States, were surprised by the speed with which agreement was reached. Once again Kohl had seized the initiative and won. On 16 July 1990 he returned to Germany in triumph. The following day the last significant problem was resolved within the 2 + 4 framework. Germany agreed to a treaty guaranteeing the Oder–Neisse line, and agreed to conclude a second treaty of 'friendship and good neighbourliness'.[34] There was a final last crisis as Britain, insensitive as ever to the issue at stake, declared that the treaty was unacceptable because it restricted the right of the Alliance to hold manoeuvres on German territory. An additional 'minute' was drafted as a compromise and the Treaty on the Final Settlement with Respect to Germany was signed on 12 September 1990.

By the Final Treaty the wartime allies ended 'their rights and responsibilities relating to Berlin and to Germany as a whole ... The united Germany shall have accordingly full sovereignty over its internal and external affairs.'[35] The treaty acknowledged Germany's right to belong to alliances and incorporated the provisions on the limits on the German army worked out by Gorbachev and Kohl. Article 1 also confirmed that 'The united Germany and the Republic of Poland shall confirm the existing border between them in a treaty that is binding under international law.'[36] Germany was duly united as a sovereign state on 3 October.

The following month the two other main elements of the jigsaw fell into place. The Treaty on Conventional Armed Forces in Europe was signed on 19 November and on 21 November thirty-four states signed the Charter of Paris for a New Europe. The Paris Charter created the new institutionalized Conference on Security and Co-operation in Europe which the Soviets, and others, had called for. But the new structures disappointed Havel's hopes for a 'pan-European structure which could decide about its own security system'.[37] The weakness of the Conference arose partly from its sheer size and partly from the fact that the western powers had no intention of seeing the Atlantic Alliance dissolved into a collective security system. This was true even for the Alliance's most reluctant member, France. For France the task was still to balance the need for American support against any future Soviet threat on the one hand, and the desire for independence and the development of a European security system on the other hand. The latter was enough to make France a supporter of the Conference; the former was enough to make France a defender of the Alliance.[38]

The outcome was a weak institutional structure. The Paris Charter provided for a Council, consisting of Ministers of Foreign Affairs, which would meet at least once a year. A Committee of Senior Officials was established to prepare for Council meetings and implement decisions with the aid of a Secretariat. The only other two institutional innovations indicated the diversity of the tasks in which the Conference had become embroiled. One was a Conflict Prevention Centre whose tasks were largely restricted to monitoring and consultation. The other was an Office for Free Elections with similar tasks in its field.[39] The Paris Charter did not provide even for the transformation of the Conference into an international organization, let alone endow it with supranational elements. Yet this was the only forum which covered the entirety of Europe. At the same time as this part of Europe's architecture was being reformed other elements of the European home were beginning to crumble.

THE DEMISE OF COMECON AND THE WARSAW PACT

The first to go was Comecon. A commission had been appointed to examine reform in 1988 and its report was due for consideration at two meetings in 1989. The first, however, was cancelled and the second postponed until January 1990. By then the agenda of some member states had changed radically. The week before the January meeting Václav Klaus announced that he would propose the dissolution of Comecon and threatened that Czechoslovakia would withdraw if the others did not agree.[40] At the meeting itself the Soviet Union argued for reform, including transition to trading in hard currencies from the beginning of 1991. That was dismissed as 'disastrous' by the Czechoslovak Deputy Prime Minister. The problem was that it would mean an immediate and substantial rise in the cost of energy which the east European states imported from the Soviet Union. Such considerations encouraged the Poles to argue for a new regional organization and a longer transition period, while the Hungarians emphasized the possibilities of co-operation between Hungary, Poland and Czechoslovakia.[41] The outcome was yet another reform commission.[42]

Ironically, after forty years of attempted integration, Comecon debate focused on an arrangement similar to the western Organisation for European Economic Co-operation established in 1948, but without the massive inflow of aid which the United States had provided for western Europe. In the west, experts suggested a Central European Economic Union, possibly incorporating the Soviet Union, and a more restricted Central European Payments Union.[43] Hungarian speculation on tripartite co-operation with Poland and Czechoslovakia suggested there might be some future for the latter. But when the idea of a payments union was taken up by the Community's Commissioner for External Affairs, Frans Andrieson, in April 1990, it met with suspicion. The east Europeans suspected it as either an attempt to revive Comecon or as a poor man's club.[44] There were other underlying problems. If Poland, Hungary and Czechoslovakia proceeded on their own the union would account for between 7 and 12 per cent of their exports; too small a percentage to cushion them from the pain of economic reconstruction, let alone provide the basis for renewed integration. If the union was enlarged to include the Soviet Union it would account for a much larger percentage of trade, but the Soviet Union had hardly begun to dismantle its command economy and it was difficult to see how the union could work until it did.[45]

The pain of reconstruction was severe, more severe than expected. As eastern Europe struggled to introduce market economies production began a rapid decline. In 1990 net material product fell by 3.1 per cent in Czechoslovakia, 13 per cent in Poland and 13.6 per cent in Bulgaria.[48] Unemployment was beginning to emerge and inflation was gathering pace, reaching catastrophic levels in Poland and Yugoslavia. Regional trade fell by between 18 and 21 per cent.[47] It was this that maintained efforts to find an alternative to the old Comecon, but there was little enthusiasm among the more advanced eastern European countries. At the beginning of 1991 the member states formally agreed to dissolve Comecon and replace it with a looser, co-ordinating body. The Czechoslovak Minister Vladimir Dlouhy promptly used the occasion to dismiss the proposed successor organization as irrelevant and to assert that bilateral trade links were quite sufficient.[48] As he proclaimed, it was the end of Comecon. The only incentive which the Soviet Union had to offer its partners was cheap energy, but with the transition to world market prices in January 1991 and the associated abandonment of the transferable rouble, this incentive vanished. The final rites were performed in June.[49]

Whereas Czechoslovakia was the most vigorous advocate of the dissolution of Comecon, Hungary was the most vocal critic of the Warsaw Pact. Reform of the Pact had been on the agenda since 1987 as the Soviet Union emphasized a defensive military strategy and improved security co-operation in Europe, both of which would facilitate a reduction in defence spending. Hungary and Poland took the opportunity to reduce their defence budgets and force levels. These reforms did not, in the minds of the Soviet military, presage the dissolution of the Pact. If anything, they were taken as requiring greater integration within the Alliance. As late as May 1990 General Pyotr Lushev could contemplate the withdrawal of 'this or that country', but not the dissolution of the Pact itself.[50]

By then the Soviet Union had been confronted with demands for the withdrawal of its troops from Hungary, Poland and Czechoslovakia, though Poland's position, given the uncertainty over the Oder–Neisse line, was equivocal.[51] The Hungarians reached agreement with the Soviet Union on 10 March. Soviet forces were to be withdrawn from Hungary by the end of June 1991. Again Hungary led the way at the Political Consultative Committee in June, openly calling for the dissolution of the Pact. Gorbachev pleaded that this was premature. Poland wanted to retain it and Czechoslovakia to transform it into a political organization.[52] Soon after this meeting Czechoslovakia moved over to the Hungarian camp after realizing that its preferred solution, the dissolution of both the Pact and the Alliance in favour of a pan-European structure, was not on the agenda. Poland, somewhat less nervous about Germany, joined them and the three began to co-ordinate their call for a dissolution of the Pact. At the Paris conference in November the Hungarian Prime Minister Jozef Antall was already indicating that dissolution was merely a matter of time.[53] The Soviet Union, however, continued to postpone another summit for which the central European states were pressing. Their sense of urgency was increased at the turn of the year by two events. First, Foreign Minister Shevardnadze resigned in December and warned that the Soviet Union was in danger of sliding into a new authoritarianism. Shevardnadze's warning seemed to be confirmed by the Soviet resort to force to repress moves towards independence in Lithuania and Latvia.

ATTEMPTS TO FILL THE VACUUM IN THE EAST

Faced with this deterioration in the political climate, the Foreign Ministers of the three central European countries met at Budapest on 21 January 1991 to express their concern at developments in the Baltic republics. In the following month the leaders of these states met at Visegrád on 15 February. Visegrád was of symbolic importance as the meeting-place of the monarchs of Poland, Hungary and Bohemia in 1335, a fact which their modern counterparts duly recorded. More importantly, they cited their common predicament as one of the reasons for consultation on security matters and co-operation on economic and ecological problems. Significantly, they concluded with the declaration 'that their co-operation in no way disrupts or limits their existing relations with other states, nor is it in any way directed against the interests of any other state'.[54] The loosening of the eastern bloc had encouraged widespread speculation upon the future architecture of central Europe, including a suggestion as early as January 1990 from Zbigniew Brzezinski for a Polish–Czech confederation. This, along with another suggestion from Henry Kissinger for a neutral bloc consisting of the three states, recalled schemes of the inter-war period and the Second World War.[55] Their most common element was the formation of a bloc to guard against either, or both, Soviet or German expansion. None of the three in February 1991 wished to embark upon that perilous road, or even to be suspected of wishing to do so.

This did not mean that their consultation was entirely symbolic. They were co-ordinating their efforts to dissolve the Warsaw Pact. Three days before the Visegrád meeting Gorbachev conceded. According to a Soviet official, the Soviet Union would seek bilateral treaties with former members of the Warsaw Pact but did not intend to seek a collective replacement for it.[56] On 25 February the Political Consultative Committee met to disband the Warsaw Pact. At the end of March the military agreements, command structure and institutions were abolished. The collapse of the institutional architecture of the eastern bloc had taken a bare eighteen months. As with German reunification, with which the developments in Comecon and the Warsaw Pact were related, the sheer pace of change left states on both sides of the old Cold War divide disorientated. The predicament of the members of the Visegrád Triangle was well put by Havel on 21 March in a speech to the Atlantic Alliance: 'our countries are dangerously sliding into a certain political, economic, and security vacuum'.[57]

The Soviet Union attempted to fill at least part of that vacuum by negotiating bilateral treaties with the former members of the Pact. The Soviet Union used this opportunity to try to prevent any unwelcome developments by including in the treaties the provision that the parties should not 'take part in any type of alliance directed against either of them'.[58] The purpose was to prevent any eastward expansion of the Atlantic Alliance. That possibility had been raised by Hungary back in February 1990, only to be dismissed by the Alliance.[59] The Soviet strategy did lead to a treaty with Romania in April 1991. There was also some sympathy for a similar treaty in Bulgaria, but the strength of opposition from the anti-communist parties proved sufficient to block it. Among the Visegrád states there was no interest at all. The Soviet initiative served only to give them added reason to maintain their co-operation.

The Visegrád Triangle was not the only forum for regional co-operation. As far back as 1978 regions of Italy, Austria, Hungary and Yugoslavia had begun to co-operate on issues of common concern. This low-level, pragmatic co-operation, designated the Alpine Adriatic group, developed against the background of increasing interest in the revival of a *mitteleuropäisch* cultural identity.[60] It was only with the transformation of eastern Europe, however, that this forum acquired a higher profile. In November 1989, at the initiative of the Hungarians and Italian Foreign Minister de Michaelis, the national governments of the states became parties to the co-operation process. The following May Czechoslovakia joined the group, now renamed the Pentagonal. They soon parcelled out policy areas, with each state co-ordinating a working party in a different area, the environment for Austria, and minorities and migration for Hungary. One aspect of its broader significance was captured by de Michaelis' description of the Pentagonal as a 'region of small and medium sized nations between Germany and Russia'.[61] De Michaelis had been worried by the pace of German unification and Italian exclusion from the 2 + 4 talks and looked to the Pentagonal as an alternative framework for Italian foreign policy. The Italian Minister showed little enthusiasm for Polish membership, and this was postponed until the Dubrovnik summit of July 1991. For Poland, as for the other former members of the eastern bloc, the Hexagonal, as it was now called, served a mixture of purposes. Alongside the pragmatic ones associated with particular policy areas stood above all else the fact that it served as yet another opening to the west and as a way of enlisting Italian support for this cause. Regional, central European co-operation, despite the surrounding aura of a restoration of Mitteleuropa, was no substitute for the real centres of integration, the European Community and the Atlantic Alliance. It was this fact which explains the otherwise strange praise for the Hexagonal from the Hungarian Foreign Minister, Géza Jeszensky. After citing various projects upon which agreement had been reached, he added that they 'prove that it is possible to establish close co-operation among the countries and regions of the area without the need to raise it to the level of political integration or any type of bloc'.[62]

THE CRISIS IN YUGOSLAVIA

The prospects of the Hexagonal were further weakened by the outbreak of civil war in one of its members, Yugoslavia. With the relaxation of the constraints imposed by the eastern bloc the demons of nationalism were loose once again. They had been barely concealed in the last years of the old regime. In 1986 the Serbian Academy of Sciences and Arts issued a memorandum complaining that not all nations within the Republic were equal: 'The Serbian nation, for example, has no right to its own state. Large parts of the Serbian nation, which live in other Republics, have, in contrast to national minorities, no right to their own language, alphabet and cultural organizations'.[63] Three years later the future Croatian leader, Franjo Tudjman, published a book in which he railed against 'world Jewry' as the source of his nation's ills.[64] The nationalists were given their opportunity by the strains imposed by economic transformation, which saw industrial production fall by 11 per cent in 1990, and by the inherent divergence of interest between Yugoslavia's constituent republics. The relatively prosperous Slovenia, with a per capita export level more than double that of any other Republic, sought substantial cuts in the federal budget, especially that for the Serbian-dominated army.[65]

As calls for independence in both Slovenia and Croatia grew ever louder, both the European Community and the United States sought to discourage the break up of the Yugoslav federation, affirming that they would not recognize any secession. Undeterred, Slovenia and Croatia declared independence on 25 June 1991. The federal army responded and sought to hold Slovenia within the federation by force. Confronted with the outbreak of violence, the European Cummunity sought to mediate. The efforts to develop a common foreign and security policy within the intergovernmental conference gave the trio of Foreign Ministers representing the Community confidence. Indeed Jacques Poos, Luxembourg's Foreign Minister, proudly, if unwisely, proclaimed that 'this is the hour of Europe, not the hour of the Americans'.[66] At first Poos' confidence seemed justified, as an armistice was negotiated early in July. But by the end of the month conflict between Croats and the Serbian minority in Croatia, backed by units of the federal army, was escalating. This time the Community faced a much more intractable problem.

The prospects for the Community's intervention were not aided by the evident differences between its member states. The newly unified Germany pressed hard for recognition of Croatia and Slovenia while its more cautious partners agreed to appoint a committee, under the French jurist Robert Badinter, to assess the claims for recognition. Both Kohl and Volker Rühe drew parallels between self-determination for the Germans and self-determination for Croatians and Slovenians.[67] More importantly, Germany threatened to act unilaterally, forcing the Community, in a desperate attempt to preserve the façade of unity, to recognize Croatian and Slovenian independence. While Slovenia arguably met the Community's own criteria, it was doubtful whether Croatia did. Worse still, both the Commission and Badinter supported recognition of another Yugoslav Republic, Macedonia, which the Community did not recognize because of opposition from Greece. The disarray within the Community was blatant. The position grew even worse as Bosnia-Hercegovina sought to follow its northern neighbours. Again the Community recognized the aspirant state, which promptly succumbed to an intense civil war. The divisions within the Community were now supplemented by open recrimination, with the French Foreign Minister Dumas openly blaming German haste for the escalation of the conflict.[68]

THE CONFERENCE ON SECURITY AND CO-OPERATION AND THE PROBLEM OF MINORITIES

The disintegration of Yugoslavia was part of a wider trend which called into question the euphoria of the previous two years and the prospects of wider and deeper European integration. It reflected both the persistence of historic antagonisms and the complexity of the ethnic map, and, more importantly, the failure of the developmental nationalism which characterized the region in both its pre-war and its communist phases.[69] Neither the Community nor any of the other institutions of Europe's new architecture had been prepared for this development. The Community was still predominantly an economic body whose first steps towards a Common Foreign and Security Policy unfortunately coincided with the débâcle over Yugoslavia. The Atlantic Alliance was groping for a new role with the end of the Cold War but still bore the marks of its history as a military alliance orientated towards conventional or nuclear warfare. The Council of Europe had served well as a forum for the promotion of human rights but had made little progress with the even more difficult issue of minority rights. The Conference on Security and Co-operation in Europe had been designed as an instrument of detente and consolidated, by the Paris Charter, in a spirit of *rapprochement*.[70]

Ironically, at the 1990 Copenhagen Conference, Yugoslavia was one of five sponsors of a proposed code of rights for minorities including the 'right to an appropriate form of self-government on the territory in which they live'.[71] Romania, which had a substantial Hungarian minority, replied that there were no such things as minority rights, only human rights.[72] Alongside disagreements of principle were clashes about the fate of particular minorities, with Yugoslavia expressing concern about Macedonians in Bulgaria. The latter denied that there was a Macedonian people and countered by inquiring about the fate of Bulgarians living in the Yugoslav Republic of Macedonia.[73] Despite these disputes the Copenhagen Conference did agree on a text incorporating minority rights.

Even more striking were two agreements in the following year. In June 1991, at the first meeting of the Council established by the Charter of Paris, the parties agreed they could meet to discuss emergencies without the consent of the state in which the emergency was deemed to exist. The mechanism was promptly invoked to discuss the Yugoslav crisis but, beyond condemning the conflict, the Conference could do little more than delegate monitoring and mediation to the European Community.[74] Yet the decisions taken in June were of symbolic significance, in that they indicated that the Conference considered the internal affairs of member states to be of legitimate concern to all members. This breach of the principle of the unanimity of sovereign states was soon to be followed by others. At the Moscow Conference, in December, the states declared 'that the commitments undertaken in the field of the human dimension of the CSCE are matters of direct and legitimate concern to all participating States and do not belong exclusively to the internal affairs of the State concerned'.[75] The same Conference also provided for sending missions of experts to countries without their consent, though it had no mechanism at all for enforcing such a decision.

Germany's suggestions that sanctions should be applied against non-compliant states had been rejected at Moscow. At the Prague Conference of 1992 there was a more substantial breach of the principle of unanimity, but only a slight concession to German demands for sanctions. The Council, or Committee of Senior Officials, could take action 'in the absence of the State concerned' but '[s]uch actions would consist of political declarations or other political steps to apply outside the territory of the State concerned'.[76] While willing to approve the principle of intervention, by declaring internal issues to be matters of international concern, the Conference was unwilling to endow itself with the means for enforcing its will. Nor was the breach of the principle of unanimity as far-reaching as it appeared. Although the 'State concerned' could not block action, that still left the need for agreement among the rest. That this was possible was demonstrated by the suspension of Serbia-Montenegro from the Conference in July 1992. That it was not likely to be a frequent occurrence was demonstrated by the failure to obtain a 'consensus-minus-one' on other occasions.[77]

At Prague the Foreign Minister of the Netherlands, Hans van den Broek, suggested the creation of a High Commissioner for Minorities. The idea was taken up at the Helsinki Conference in March–July. Agreement on a High Commissioner was reached, but only with some trepidation and several qualifications. France drew attention to its constitutional commitment to 'the equality of all its citizens without distinction as to origin, race or religion', while Turkey declared that it would recognize as minorities only those it chose to.[78] Britain reserved the right to exclude the High Commissioner, but promised to do so 'only when absolutely necessary'.[79] Nevertheless, the High Commissioner was given substantial independence to instigate inquiries and issue warnings about national minorities issues where 'the High Commissioner concludes that there is a *prima facie* risk of potential conflict'.[80] By the end of the year the Conference had agreed on the former Foreign Minister of the Netherlands, Max van der Stoel, as High Commissioner. Six months later he was dealing with issues arising from Russian minorities in the newly independent Baltic states, the Hungarian minorities in Romania and Slovakia, and the Albanian minority in Macedonia. Lacking any authority to impose solutions, let alone power to enforce them, the Commissioner was reliant upon the good will of the parties concerned.[81]

As the Conference sought to adjust to the post-Cold War Europe, its development exhibited a clear trend. According to its Secretary General, the Conference 'is giving increasing emphasis to early warning and conflict prevention'.[82] He referred to the High Commissioner on National Minorities as evidence that 'preventive diplomacy can be instrumental in defusing tensions', but also noted that missions sent to Serb-controlled Kosovo, Sanjak and Vojvodina had been expelled in August 1993.[83] The Conference was becoming a multifaceted organization consisting largely of fora for discussion and the exchange of information. With the addition of an Economic Forum and the Forum for Security Co-operation at Helsinki in 1992, the Conference sought to build on and expand its remit. While the extent of its activities and the frequency of meetings helped to develop a network of communication, this kind of 'cobweb integration' worked best within regions like the Nordic area with a shared cultural identity and a low incidence of crises.[84] In contract, the Conference's agenda was strewn with crises stretching from the Balkans to the Baltic and even to the republics which had broken away from Moscow. Early expectations that it would develop into a pan-European collective security organization had been unrealistic. The member states had no obligation to go to the defence of victims of aggression, even if they could agree on who the aggressor was. That in turn was difficult to determine in conflicts which pitted different ethnic groups of the same state against each other.[85] Conscious of its own limitations, the Conference looked to other elements of Europe's architecture to intervene where it could not.

INTEGRATION WITH THE WEST

A more prominent role was played by the older western-based institutions. The Atlantic Alliance in the security field and the European Community in the economic field were bound to be the major actors. The Council of Europe also played a significant role. In the light of its focus on human rights, the Council was well-placed to act as a gatekeeper for wider integration with the west. Admission to the Council of Europe was seen as a precondition, and admission required demonstration of applicants' democratic credentials. That proved easier for some than others. Hungary gained membership as early as November 1990, but Romania had to wait almost another three years. Initial optimism about Romania's transition to democracy evaporated in June 1990 as opponents of the ruling National Salvation Front came under attack from pro-government mobs.

As well as redeeming its now tarnished reputation, Romania had to reassure the Council that its new constitution and its treatment of minorities conformed to the requirements of the Council. In constitutional matters Romania was aided, and scrutinized, by the Commission for Democracy through Law, established just before the June riots. It was, however, the question of minority rights which proved to be the most contentious.[86] Attacks on Gypsies and discrimination against the Hungarian minority were high on the agenda. This was reflected in the June 1992 Charter for Regional or Minority Rights which linked the protection and promotion of minority languages with 'the principles of democracy and cultural diversity'.[87] Later in the same year the Council's Vienna summit agreed to draw up a protocol supplementing the Convention on Human Rights which would deal with minorities. Just before the Vienna summit of October, Romania became a member of the Council. The residual doubts were evident in the very ceremony to mark Romania's entry. Romania, Secretary General Catherine Lalumière pointed out, was entering an organization 'which had a duty to remain vigilant'.[88] The degree of vigilance needed in some of the new members was evident from the fact that Slovakia had managed to gain entry in June only after promising to repeal legislation which discriminated against its Hungarian minority.[89] International scrutiny of minority rights was bound to be contentious, for it affected conceptions of national identity as well as formal issues of sovereignty. That the Conference on Security and Co-operation and the Council of Europe were able to exert some influence was testimony to the desire for integration with the west.

Membership of the Council of Europe was a symbol of successful transition from the authoritarianism of the communist regimes, a symbol of the 'return to Europe'. It was also a necessary precondition of entry into the European Community. It was a necessary precondition, but far from a sufficient one. The east European states did have supporters in the Community, including Thatcher, who proposed that 'the Community should declare unequivocally that it is ready to accept all the countries of eastern Europe', though she added the qualification, 'when democracy has taken root and their economies are capable of sustaining membership'.[90] Her advocacy, in August 1990, aroused the suspicion that she merely wanted to fend off further integration within the Community by widening membership.[91] In August 1990 the Community was indeed in no hurry to admit even the principle of an eastward expansion. Initially, it focused on trade and aid. In both cases the Community's action failed to live up to the accompanying rhetoric.

TRADE AND AID

The Community's policy towards the east lagged behind the pace of events. On the eve of the revolution in eastern Europe the Community had only the outlines of a common policy and had only begun the process of normalizing its relations with the member states of Comecon. The latter suffered more discrimination than the Community's other trading partners. When Hungary, Poland and Romania had joined GATT in the 1960s and 1970s the Community insisted upon protocols sanctioning its quotas against state trading countries.[92] In the light of Romania's relatively independent foreign policy it had benefited, since 1974, from the Generalized System of Preferences which the Community conceded to developing countries. It was, however, the only member state of Comecon to do so. Ironically, Hungary, which had embarked on economic reforms earlier than the others, benefited from none of the Community's battery of preferences, leaving it facing tariff barriers higher than those imposed upon either developed or developing economies as well as an array of non-tariff barriers.[93] Hungary's position was improved by the Trade and Co-operation Agreement in September 1988, but all this did was to remove some of the quota restrictions upon Hungarian goods. Others, especially in steel, textiles and agricultural goods, remained. This became the model for subsequent trade and co-operation agreements. Czechoslovakia at first obtained only a trade agreement in September 1989, though this was upgraded in May 1990, following free elections earlier in the year. Community criticism of the treatment of minorities by both Bulgaria and Romania led to the suspension of negotiations, delaying the agreements until May 1990 and October 1990. With the agreement with Romania in place, the Community came to the end of its first phase of adjustment to the new Europe.

The Community had also embarked upon an aid strategy to facilitate the economic reforms in eastern Europe. At the July summit of the G7 states the Commission was given the broader task of co-ordinating western economic aid. The programme initially was restricted to Poland and Hungary, hence the acronym Phare.[94] It was, however, extended to the other eastern European countries in May 1990. Aid had been an important part of Europe's post-war reconstruction, and the analogy between 1947 and 1989 was soon the subject of widespread speculation. According to the *Financial Times*, 'What is emerging ... is a package – no less comprehensive for lacking the name of Marshall – of trade concessions, financial aid, micro-economic advice and technical know-how.'[95] Nor was it merely observers who drew the analogy. Czechoslovakia's new foreign Minister, Jiri Dienstbier, travelled to Harvard, the site of General Marshall's 1947 offer, to launch his plan for reconstruction. Dienstbier proposed that the west provide sixteen billion dollars, which would be credited to the Soviet Union for the purchase of goods from Czechoslovakia, Hungary and Poland. The idea of bolstering trade between the eastern states with western aid had clear parallels with the original Marshall Plan. But the idea was not even universally supported by the Czechoslovak government. Finance Minister Klaus, suspicious of any attempt to prop up Comecon, dismissed a similar plan as 'a delay on our way to a normally functioning economy'.[96] Nor was the United States willing to play its former role. As Secretary of Commerce Robert Mossbacher put it, 'We just cannot afford it.'[97] Despite the fact that Dienstbier's proposal attracted more immediate attention than Marshall's original speech, the second Marshall Plan failed to materialize.

To more critical observers, the analogy between 1947 and 1989, upon which calls for a new Marahall plan were based, was flawed. The differences were evident in the implications for Czechoslovakia. The prescription of European co-operation in 1947 meant integration with the west as both its Czechoslovak advocates and Stalin knew. A similar prescription in 1989 or 1990 might have meant giving priority to integration within the east. In that sense Klaus was right. There were also underlying economic differences. In 1947 western Europe had the institutions and mechanisms of a market economy, even if they were still distorted by wartime regulations. Western Europe's problems were the dislocation caused by the war and the chronic imbalance in trade with the United States. In 1989 and 1990 eastern Europe was only beginning to build the structures of a market economy and was burdened by an economic history which had bequeathed internationally uncompetitive industries. Worse still, whereas there were signs of at least an incipient recovery in western Europe in 1947, eastern Europe had entered a precipitous decline in 1990 and 1991. There were even doubts about whether eastern Europe could absorb aid on the scale of the Marshall Plan.[98] Ironically, the ideological climate was also less tolerant. In the 1940s the United States, for all its eulogies to the American way and the virtues of competition, was prepared to tolerate practices of which it disapproved in the interests of social stability and increased production and trade. The western powers, including the Community, were now more insistent upon socio-economic transformation. Aid would be granted in return for 'clear commitments regarding the rule of law, respect for human rights, the establishment of multiparty systems, the holding of free and fair elections in the course of 1990, and economic liberalization with a view to introducing market economics'.[99] For their part, the east Europeans also saw their salvation in market economics. There was pressure from both sides to let building the institutions of the free market take precedence over both production and employment. There were of course limits, both practical and ideological, to the pace of reconstruction. Václav Klaus, the ardent critic of Comecon, advocated 'small practical steps' because 'it is not true (as is often a priori assumed) that as soon as public sector institutions are dismantled or weakened, the private sector will rush in'.[100]

The pace of economic reform was one of the issues which divided the western powers during their negotiations about a new bank to support economic transformation in the east. The initiative for the bank came from Mitterrand. His adviser, Jacques Attali, drew up a strategy for a new bank which would take over all of the Community's existing aid programmes. Even after the European Bank for Reconstruction and Development had been established, in much more modest form, the ambitious Attali proclaimed that the Bank 'will be the embryo of a larger Europe and a larger European entity'.[101] The bank was in reality too restricted a tool for such a grandiose vision. The first blow to Attali's strategy came at Strasbourg in December 1989 when the Community agreed to launch the new bank. It would not take over existing programmes but run alongside them. Nor would it be a purely European institution. As with previous initiatives the French government had intended to use the bank to promote a European identity, separate from the United States. France's partners, however, insisted upon American membership.[102]

The United States was not enthusiastic about the proposal at all, but nevertheless agreed to take part in the negotiations where differences between France and the United States were prominent. France argued that the bank should be involved in lending to support macroeconomic reform and wanted to give the bank a broad and flexible remit. The United States, suspicious of French *dirigisme*, argued that this would impinge upon the World Bank and the IMF and that the lending of the new bank should be restricted to the private sector. Underlying the latter demand was American fear that the bank would prop up the old economic structures of the east, delaying reform. For the same reason the United States wanted to curtail the Soviet Union's rights within the bank. The Americans won the first point when it was agreed that the bank should not stray into the field of macroeconomic reform. The French were more successful in insisting that private capital would be insufficient to fund the required investments in infrastructure and hence some lending to the public sector was necessary. The ensuing compromise set a limit of 40 per cent of lending for the public sector, the remainder being tied to private-sector projects. On the remaining points of disagreement the American view prevailed. The United States became the largest shareholder, with 10 per cent of the total, and the Soviet Union was restricted to borrowing no more than what it contributed in hard currency. With these issues resolved, the Charter of the European Bank for Reconstruction and Development was signed in May 1990.[103]

The retreat from Attali's goals continued when the bank was established, not least because of Attali's own errors of judgement. The bank was slow to make loans, though this in part resulted from its restrictive mandate. Obliged to charge market rates for its loans to the private sector, the bureaucratically unwieldy bank was not the most attractive source of credit. Yet when Attali sought to gain approval for less stringent lending criteria the United States refused to consider the suggestion. With only 620 million ecu committed in April 1992, out of its original capital of 10 billion, Attali was left complaining that the 'Bank has more money than it has projects'.[104] A little over a year later, amidst recurring scandal about the bank's expenditure on its own offices and officials, Attali resigned.[105] Under the new management of Jacques de Larosière, a former director of the IMF, the bank's reputation improved. With increased lending and 70 per cent of commitments in 1994 devoted to the private sector, criticism abated. But there was a price for the praise which was then given to de Larosière. In his own words, 'we are a bank and we have to behave as a bank. We have a profit and loss account. We are judged by the markets.'[106] During each of the three major phases of reconstruction, after both world wars and again after the end of the Cold War, ideas of an investment-led boom, organized by either international banks or by private consortia backed by governments had flourished. On each occasion disputes over the size of each member's contributions and wrangling over the terms of reference had proved to be the major obstacles. Even when an institution did emerge it was so restricted both in the scale of its operations and its terms of reference that it was a pale shadow of the original ambitions.

THE EUROPE AGREEMENTS

According to Czechoslovak Prime Minister Marion Calfa, it was not credit that his country needed but access to Community markets.[107] Greater access was forthcoming in the so-called Europe Agreements which were negotiated in 1991. The initiative for these had come from the Commission in August 1990, the same month as Thatcher called for an eastward expansion of the Community. But in recommending these new agreements the Commission noted that membership was not one of their objectives. After the Council had sanctioned the idea of these agreements, negotiations begun in late December 1990. The Commission's programme for 1991 maintained the reserve about expansion. Using the language of variable geometry, the Commission described the creation of the European Economic Area as the second pillar of Europe while the proposed Europe Agreements would constitute the third pillar.[108] The negotiations proved as difficult as usual, and the toughness of the Community's tactics left some of its negotiating partners disillusioned. The Czechoslovak Foreign Minister, Dienstbier, recalled that

> when the talks reached the final stage we suddenly realized how many conditions and restrictions were put before us. We suddenly realized that the tough rules of the market and competition were being applied everywhere where solidarity should rule in the first place. And when we eventually reached compromises on our exports of textiles, steel and meat, the extent of which absolutely cannot threaten the EC markets, we had to face another condition – either you will allow the transit through your territory of a quite unbearable number of tractor trailers or one of the twelve participants will not sign the association agreement.[109]

Europe Agreements were signed with Hungary, Poland and Czechoslovakia in December 1991, though the latter had to be renegotiated after Czechoslovakia dissolved. The new Agreements with the Czech Republic and Slovakia were not signed until October 1993, after those with Bulgaria and Romania. Despite the diverse economic predicament of the east European countries, the Agreements were substantially the same. The only significant difference was that those negotiated in 1993 contained provisions on human and minority rights in the preamble.[110]

The Europe Agreements and the Interim Europe Agreements, which came into force in 1992 and 1993, provided for the creation of a free trade area between the Community and the signatory state over a transitional period of a maximum of ten years. For products not covered by special provisions this meant the abolition of Community tariffs and quantitative restrictions on the day the Interim Agreements came into force.[111] In an attempt to cushion the east European states against competition from the advanced Community member states, their tariffs and quantitative restrictions were to be abolished in stages during the transitional period. The extent of trade covered by special provisions showed the reluctance of some of the Community's member states to increase access to their markets. Special provisions covered between 44.5 per cent of Bulgarian industrial exports to the Community and 74.6 per cent of Romanian industrial exports. The products covered by these provisions included basic industrial products, textiles and clothing, and coal and steel. Agricultural products were also subject to special provisions. These were, of course, areas where the Community was traditionally most protectionist and areas where the east European countries were likely to be competitive. They also covered products which constituted an important share in east European exports to the Community. Steel, textiles and agricultural products, for example, constituted 35 per cent of the joint exports of Hungary, Poland and Czechoslovakia. By comparison those exports constituted a mere 2 per cent of the Community's total import bill for those products.[112]

Hesitancy by the Community was also evident in provisions allowing the parties to introduce protection where there was 'serious disturbance to the markets' for agricultural products, where dumping occurred, where increased imports caused 'serious injury to domestic producers' or 'serious disturbances in any sector of the economy or difficulties which could bring about serious deterioration in the economic situation of a region'.[113] In the early years of the Europe Agreements recourse to these measures was not in fact extensive. Anti-dumping cases declined, with only two being recorded in 1993. Products affected were concentrated in steel and chemicals and constituted less than 1 per cent of the Community's imports from its Europe Agreement partners.[114] There was some concern that the fear of anti-dumping measures would deter foreign investors, though the most striking characteristic of direct foreign investment was the way in which it was heavily skewed. Hungary and the Czech Republic were by far the main beneficiaries. The discrepancies were especially striking when expressed on a per capita basis. From this perspective, per capita direct foreign investment in Hungary amounted to an average of 130 dollars for 1992–93, whereas for Poland the figure was 11 dollars, with Romania and Bulgaria attracting only half the Polish figure.[115] It was, therefore, no surprise when Polish Prime Minister Waldemar Pawlak complained about the paucity of investment from the Community, which, he noted, was exceeded by that of the United States.[116]

A more worrying trend was evident in the balance of trade. The Community's new partners showed a fairly persistent and growing trade deficit with the Community, with the temporary exception of 1990 when the extension of the Generalized System of Preferences provided a boost to their exports. Only the Czech Republic proved relatively immune to the general deterioration. For the others the discrepancy in their trade with the Community contributed to balance of payments deficits, which reached 3.2 billion dollars in Hungary in 1993. Critics pointed out that, having exhausted the advantages of trade liberalization offered by the Community while scarcely having begun the process of modernization, the prospect was for a continuation of the imbalance.[117]

The Europe Agreements had consolidated earlier Community concessions but, as Jiri Dienstbier noted, at a price. While the Czech Republic, historically the most advanced of the Europe Agreement states, responded quite strongly, the strains upon the others were all too evident.

The Europe Agreements did contribute towards increased regional integration between the Visegrád states. Co-operation between the Visegrád states had been driven forward largely by security considerations. At the October 1991 Cracow summit, an offer by Poland to extend the range of co-operation by creating a free trade area was rejected. The disagreement, however, really only concerned the timing of a free trade area rather than the principle itself.[118] The underlying pressure for economic co-operation was steadily increasing. Trade between the three states had dropped dramatically, with Hungary's trade with the other two falling by 60 per cent in 1991. Part of the problem lay in the new tariffs which they had introduced. Having relied upon state control to regulate trade under the communist regimes the transition to market economies, accompanied by the general enthusiasm for liberal economics, left them with low tariffs and an absence of the more sophisticated non-tariff barriers prevalent in the west. Poland reacted by increasing its average tariff level in August 1991 from 4 to 5 per cent to 16 per cent. Only Czechoslovakia persisted with a moderate tariff, though even it introduced new controls on agricultural products.[119] The position was made worse by the Europe Agreements. Implementation of these would mean that the Visegrád states would have been charging higher tariffs on goods imported from each other than on those from the Community. There was also a prospect that this arrangement would have acted as a deterrent to foreign investment.[120] Under these external pressures the Visegrád states moved slowly towards a free trade agreement which was eventually signed in December 1992. The impact of the Europe Agreements was evident in Hungary's announcement of the free trade agreement according to which 'customs duties and quotas will be lifted in three stages from March 1, 1993 to 2001, under the pattern of the association agreements concluded with the European Community'.[121] The Hungarian Minister of International Economic Relations, Béla Kádár proudly proclaimed that the agreement 'indicates that the East European peoples can shape their own fate and settle their own problems'.[122] The claim was at best partially justifiable. Indeed the Visegrád states had no desire to be left to settle their problems on their own. That was evident in the statement by Klaus the following January that the Visegrád group 'was an artificial process created by the West'.[123] That claim was even more dubious. The Visegrád group had arisen as a response to their relations with the Soviet Union. But underlying Klaus's assertion was recognition that the fate of the three countries did not lie entirely in their own hands and that, from the perspective of all three, their future lay in the west.

PUTTING ENLARGEMENT ON THE AGENDA

This aim had been clear from the outset. It was not only a matter of the economic advantages of membership but also the return to Europe, to which eastern Europe's leaders frequently referred. For eastern Europeans the fear was that the iron curtain would be replaced by what Foreign Minister Jeszensky in December 1990 called a 'Wall of Prosperity or Wall of Welfare'.[124] Even optimistic assumptions about growth rates in the more advanced eastern economies of the Visegrád four, led to the prediction that it would take those states thirty years to reach 75 per cent of the Community's average income.[125] According to the European Bank for Reconstruction and Development, what was needed was growth rates similar to those on the Pacific Rim, but its chief economist noted 'no one is predicting that type of growth in eastern Europe'.[126]

Their common predicament was one reason for the co-operation between the Visegrád states. As Foreign Minister Jeszensky put it, they were all 'sitting together in the waiting room of the European Community'.[127] It was also a factor which divided the Visgrád states from Bulgaria and Romania. Hence, when the latter sought to join the Visegrád group early in 1991 the answer was negative.[128] The Visegrád states presented themselves as more economically advanced and as culturally and politically more 'European'. The implication was that they deserved to be the first to enter the Community. The Community, however, was showing little sign of being willing to let them out of the waiting room.

The Community was distracted by the problems over Maastricht and the apparent hostility to deepening integration within its existing population. Yet the eastern European states did have advocates, most prominently Germany. Kohl promised Czechoslovakia that Germany would play this role during the signing of the German–Czechoslovak Treaty in February 1992. During the Bundestag debate on the Maastricht Treaty he argued that the states of the Visegrád group must be given the prospect of membership in the 'foreseeable future'. On that occasion he added that it was unacceptable for Germany to constitute the eastern border of the European Community and sought to reassure the Poles that their country lay in 'Mitteleuropa', not eastern Europe.[129] There was some evidence of movement in the Europe Agreements signed in December 1991. In the Agreement with Hungary the preamble included the equivocal statement 'HAVING IN MIND that the final objective of Hungary is to become a member of the Community and that this association, in the view of the parties, will help to achieve this objective'.[130] The equivocation, that the Community agreed the association would help to achieve a goal it would not acknowledge as its own, was revealing.

Pushed by the Commission and by Germany, the Community finally, and reluctantly, accepted the principle of membership. At the June 1993 Copenhagen Council the Community

> agreed that the associated countries in central and eastern Europe that so desire shall become members of the European Union. Accession will take place as soon as an associated country is able to assume the obligation of membership by satisfying the economic and political conditions required.
>
> Membership requires that the candidate country has achieved stability of institutions guaranteeing democracy, the rule of law, human rights and respect for and protection of minorities, the existence of a functioning market economy as well as the capacity to cope with competitive pressures and market forces within the Union. Membership presupposes the candidate's ability to take on the obligations of membership including adherence to the aims of political, economic and monetary union.[131]

It was an imposing list of preconditions. Indeed it was a list which, if applied strictly, several present members of the Community would have had difficulty meeting. Reaction to the Copenhagen Council in east Europe was mixed. Not only had the Community declined to specify precise conditions and a timetable, it had lumped together all the 'associated countries' without any differentiation. The Visegrád strategy had been based on the assumption that the Community would recognize the privileged status of its members *vis-à-vis* Romania and Bulgaria. The Community's refusal to draw the desired conclusion encouraged Klaus's suspicion that regional co-operation merely lengthened the time the Czech Republic would have to spend in the waiting room, though this time he was backed by Havel, who had been one of the keenest advocates of a joint approach through the Visegrád group.[132]

At the end of 1993 the British and Italian foreign Ministers, Douglas Hurd and Beniamino Andreatta, pressed for closer co-operation with the associated states in the fields of common foreign and security policy, and justice and home affairs. The immediate cause of their initiative was the results of the election in Russia which produced a swing to the right and alarm in eastern Europe.[133] While Germany was concerned that developments in Russia, especially the rise of the nationalist politician Vladimir Zhirinovsky, distracted attention from the need to integrate east Europe, they probably did more to spur on a review of policy towards the east and agreement on the Anglo-Italian plan of the previous December.[134] Although the June Council in Corfu was largely taken up by wrangling over Delors' successor, it did call upon the Commission and the Presidency to report 'on the strategy to be followed with a view to accession'.[135] In *The Europe Agreements and Beyond* the Commission took up the idea of a 'structured relationship' which had been suggested at the Copenhagen Council the preceding year.[136] The Commission elaborated on this at greater length in a subsequent report. The 'structured' relationship was to be a framework for dialogue covering all three pillars of the European Union. At the same time the Commission reiterated the Community's support for intra-regional co-operation among the associated states, noting that this 'will be economically beneficial and will help to accelerate accession'.[137] In fact the Visegrád states had already agreed to accelerate their planned Central European Free Trade Area at their Prague meeting in February.[138]

Encouraged by the new climate, first Hungary, on 1 April, and then Poland, on 8 April, applied for full membership. The Czech Republic preferred to wait until after its Parliament had ratified the new Europe Agreement, and argued that the timing of an application for membership was less important than preparing the country for the obligations of accession.[139] Later in the year, in October, the Polish Foreign Minister also exhibited flexibility. While expressing a preference for simultaneous negotiations with all of the applicants, he said that 'it is not to be ruled out that some are judged ready to join before others', and added, 'I would not worry, if for example, the Czech Republic joined before Poland because once one central European state is a member it will help the accession of the others.'[140] The general trend was confirmed by the European Council at Essen in December 1994. The Council still refused to offer a timetable for accession, but the presence of ministers from the associated states in Essen was symbolic. Moreover, the Council endorsed the Commission's strategy of 'structured relations' as the main instrument in preparation for accession.

The Essen Council marked another success for Helmut Kohl. After the reunification of his own nation, the unification of Europe with which he had associated it had moved a step nearer. But as he pointed out to the associated states, they would have to bear the main burden of preparing their economies for accession.[141] That burden was still enormous. At the Community's first enlargement Denmark and Britain had joined a customs union complemented by a Common Agricultural Policy. Both had been members of the wealthy western European heartland throughout the century. At the last enlargement Spain and Portugal had joined a more integrated Community but had been given long transition periods and had benefited from considerable transfers within the Community. Both also had much longer experience of free trade in industrial goods. The associated east European states were faced with the prospect of a Community characterized by economic and monetary union and were starting from an even less favourable position than previous new members.[142] Furthermore, even if they benefited from an extensive transition period, they were unlikely to benefit from transfers similar to those conceded to Portugal and Spain. The first enlargement had taken twelve years from application to accession. The prospect was that it would take at least as long for the new applicants.

TOWARDS AN EASTERN EXPANSION OF THE ATLANTIC ALLIANCE

Doubts also hung over their prospective membership of the Atlantic Alliance. That some at least would seek membership had been clear even before the institutions of the old order in the east had been demolished. Only Romania had signed the bilateral treaties by which the Soviet Union had sought to fill the security vacuum in the east. Fearful of Germany, Poland had hesitated about decisively opting for the west, but with guarantees on the Oder–Neisse border she was free to join Hungary and Czechoslovakia in burying the Warsaw Pact. Membership of the Atlantic Alliance was an obvious solution to the power vacuum, but it faced two obstacles: the hostility of the Soviet Union and the unwillingness of existing Alliance members to extend the commitments which they offered to each other. The key commitment, article 5 of the treaty, for which the west Europeans had fought so hard in 1948 and 1949, had been formulated at the time of the height of American power and the clear perception of a common threat from the Soviet Union. The latter, however, had disappeared as the 1990 London Declaration acknowledged. The Alliance in fact was faced with inquiries about membership when it was uncertain of its own purpose in the new, post-Cold War world.

The Alliance moved slowly to adjust. A review was launched in 1990 to re-examine the Alliance's strategic concepts, in which France decided to participate in March 1991. There had been some indication the previous year that France might reconsider its equivocal commitment to the Alliance, but the initiative had foundered during the Key Largo meeting between Bush and Mitterrand in April.[143] Mitterrand found much to be suspicious of in 1991. The decision to create a Rapid Reaction Force found little favour in Paris.[144] Nor was Mitterrand entirely happy with the outcome of the November Rome summit which sanctioned a new strategic concept. It was not so much the strategic concept that irritated Mitterrand as the formulation of a new political role for the Alliance. Of this he commented, 'I did not know it had a political role. I am surprised it has a new one.'[145] Despite traditional French hostility to the idea of a political role for the Alliance, the Rome Declaration invited the former members of the Warsaw Pact to a joint meeting to discuss forms of co-operation, including 'annual meetings with the North Atlantic Council at

Ministerial level in what might be called a North Atlantic Cooperation Council'.[146]

The assembled states duly accepted the offer, including the formation of a North Atlantic Co-operation Council, on 20 December 1991. The complications of the new Europe were evident in the fact that the Soviet Ambassador asked for all references to the Soviet Union to be removed from the agreement.[147] This was not an expression of his dissatisfaction with the document, but reflected the effective replacement of the Soviet Union by the Commonwealth of Independent States at Minsk in October. The complexity of the new Europe was also evident in a statement of the Atlantic Council the day before the creation of the Co-operation Council. Under the heading of 'A Security Architecture for Europe', the Alliance declared that 'The peace and security of Europe will increasingly depend on a framework of interlocking institutions which complement each other, since the challenges we face cannot be comprehensively addressed by one institution alone.'[148] Europe's security had always been beyond the capacity of a single institution. Nor was the idea that security could be managed best by 'a framework of interlocking institutions' new. That had been the intent during discussions of a European Defence Community in the 1950s. The novelty, and contrast with the earlier debates, lay in the fact that the 'framework of interlocking institutions which complement each other' was meant to be pan-European. The problem lay in the fact that there was a dearth of institutions in eastern Europe and hence that eastern Europe's states looked to membership of the Alliance to fill the vacuum, and consequently threatened to overburden the Alliance. Not even Russia was exempt from this temptation, as Boris Yeltsin's letter to the inaugural meeting of the Atlantic Co-operation Council, suggesting Russian membership of the Alliance, demonstrated.[149]

The slight difference in approach adopted by the Western European Union revealed some of the problems of interlocking institutions. The Union had rejected a German proposal for a Co-operation Council during November, though it did agree to establish a dialogue at ministerial level with Russia and the eastern European states. The Union, given a new profile by the Maastricht Treaty, did not want to move too far ahead of the Atlantic Alliance for fear of implying that the Alliance was dispensable. Yet nor did it merely want to duplicate the activities of the Atlantic Alliance in the east.[150] The position of the Union was made more difficult by the inevitable tensions in Atlantic relationships which accompanied every debate on its future role. For its Secretary General this was a time of great opportunity. Writing in April 1992, he proclaimed that the 'Alliance's new strategy, agreed in Rome, created an opportunity for Europeans to regain the ground which had been lost when the European

Defence Community failed in 1954. The Maastricht Summit succeeded in seizing this opportunity.'[151] This was, to say the least, a considerable exaggeration. The failure in 1954 was a failure to create a European army which would facilitate German rearmament. Maastricht did not seek to create a European army and the German security problem in 1990, just as in the mid-1950s, was solved by membership of the Atlantic Alliance rather than a European security organization. The Western European Union was still a subordinate element of Europe's architecture. Its dilemma lay in finding a way of expanding its role without undermining the more important Atlantic Alliance.

The Alliance's difficulty in adjusting to the new agenda was rooted in its very origins. Conceived as a defensive alliance, it lacked the legitimacy to intervene where the security of its own members was not threatened. A way out of this dilemma seemed to offer a solution to another problem, namely the weakness of the Conference on Security and Co-operation. At its Oslo Council in June the Alliance's members agreed 'to support, on a case-by-case basis, in accordance with our own procedures, peacekeeping activities under the responsibility of the CSCE, including by making available Alliance resources and expertise'.[152] That in turn helped to define the role of the Conference on Security and Co-operation as the most comprehensive element of the new architecture and hence as well placed to provide a source of legitimacy for intervention by other organizations.[153] When the Alliance became involved in Bosnia, under the mandate of the United Nations, the difficulties of this kind of relationship soon became apparent. In May 1993 Manfred Wörner acknowledged that the Yugoslav crisis was forcing a change in approaches to peacekeeping. He also warned that the Alliance did not see 'its role mainly as that of a "sub-contractor" for international peacekeeping duties ... especially where the conditions for success are absent, where it believes that the mandate and rules of engagement are inadequate, and where it cannot exercise unity of command'.[154] Disagreements over precisely these issues had marred the Alliance's involvement in Bosnia, hence it came as no surprise when the Athens Council of June adopted guidelines for peacekeeping which reflected Wörner's concerns. The Alliance still held to the principle of supplying forces for the United Nations or the Conference on Security and Co-operation, but clearly intended to exercise more caution.

Another kind of symbiosis was used to try to bolster the Western European Union without weakening the Alliance. As always, French susceptibilities were important here. France had alarmed the United States by persuading Germany to agree to expand the Franco-German brigade into a 35,000 man corps, but was also being much more conciliatory towards the Atlantic Alliance. The *rapprochement* was led by the Defence Minister Pierre Joxe, though Mitterrand was more cautious.[155] The tension between the new *rapprochement* and the traditional desire to enhance a European defence identity autonomous from the Alliance was evident in French reactions to the decision of the January 1994 Atlantic Council. In Brussels the Council agreed 'to make collective assets of the Alliance available, on the basis of consultations in the North Atlantic Council, for WEU operations undertaken by the European Allies in pursuit of their Common Foreign and Security Policy'.[156] While strengthening the Western European Union pleased Mitterrand, the fact that the Combined Joint Task Force, as it came to be known, required the sanction of the Atlantic Council did not, for it clearly inhibited the autonomy of the former. France's response to the Task Force was marked by traditional goals in other respects. French representatives emphasized the need for a 'political design to give direction to the defence effort and for the need for the Europeans to develop their own planning and intelligence capacities. But they warned against adopting 'the principles of NATO's integrated military structure', preferring to 'opt for cooperation rather than integration'.[157]

Traditional French goals were evident in another initiative which was launched by Edouard Balladur in April 1993. The intent was to emphasize the European regulation of stability and the prominence of France in that process.[158] The proposed Pact on Stability in Europe was taken up by the European Community in June with the intent of holding an inaugural conference in the next year. The pact itself was to consist of a series of bilateral and multilateral agreements covering minorities, the inviolability of borders and the promotion of neighbourly relations. All these were to be 'ratified' by the inaugural conference and then 'forwarded to the CSCE, which will act as its guardian'.[159]

While west European initiatives were hampered by relations with the western superpower, east European initiatives were constrained by Russia. The east European states did not share French hesitancy about the Alliance's integrated command structure. As with the issue of membership of the European Community, membership of the Alliance both united the eastern Europeans and divided them. While Havel supported the idea of the expansion of the Alliance into a pan-European security organization, some of the arguments he invoked for Czech membership clearly distinguished between different categories of east European state. According to Havel, 'The Czech Republic, Hungary, Poland and Slovakia – and Austria and Slovenia as well – clearly belong to the western sphere of European civilisation.'[160] That left several states which, by implication, did not.

The clamour for membership was led by Poland, and in 1993 the main obstacle to membership, Russian opposition, seemed to evaporate. During a visit to Warsaw Yeltsin agreed that Polish membership did 'not run counter to the interests of any state, including Russia'.[161] The Poles had become increasingly anxious during 1993 about developments in Russia, and especially about the assertion that Russia had special rights and responsibilities in the 'near abroad'. Although the latter signified the territories of the former Soviet Union, it seemed to be symbolic of a more assertive Russian policy.[162] Relieved at Yeltsin's agreement, Poland promptly called upon the Alliance for a commitment on membership. Manfred Wörner seemed receptive, stating that 'NATO is not a closed shop' and expressing his view that it was now time to offer 'a more concrete perspective' to those who wished to join.[163] Yeltsin, however, had acted despite the warnings of his advisers and was soon under pressure from his generals to retract his concession. At the end of September Yeltsin announced his opposition to any eastward expansion of the Alliance and offered instead a joint Alliance–Russian guarantee of east Europe as an alternative.[164]

Confronted with this reversal, Wörner sounded more cautious, emphasizing the need to take into account considerations of Russian security concerns. As well as trying to reconcile east European and Russian pressures, Wörner was trying to suppress doubts about the long-term viability of the Atlantic Alliance. He criticized both isolationist sentiment in the United States and advocates of a purely European security strategy, and pointed out that the Alliance's members had been 'brutally reminded that their security is indivisible' twice in this century.[165] It was the American Secretary of Defense Aspin who ordered a compromise to deal with security fears in the east at a special meeting at Travemuende on 20 October. Membership was not on the immediate agenda. Instead he suggested practical working agreements with individual countries under the slogan of 'partnerships for peace'.[166] Even before the Travemuende meeting the Polish press had speculated upon the possibility of a third betrayal of Poland by the west. By the new year Walesa was openly accusing the west of desertion.[167]

Poland, however, had little choice but to accept the proffered Partnership for Peace agreement. The partnerships had been ratified at the January 1994 Atlantic Council. The Council did 'reaffirm that the Alliance remains open to the membership of other European countries', but focused on the partnership idea.[168] Following previous practice, the partnerships were offered to all non-Alliance members of the Co-operation Council, as well as to other participants in the Conference on Security and Co-operation. As on previous occasions this lack of discrimination disappointed some. The Visegrád states saw it as a failure to recognize their privileged status, while Russia too objected to being placed on a par with inferior powers. They did all sign the agreements, though in the case of Russia not until June 1994.[169] By then the Conference on the Pact for Security and Stability had been held in Paris, in May. The Conference added to the dense network of treaties which characterized the new Europe, but did nothing to resolve the complexity of its architecture.[170] Indeed, earlier in the same month Europe's architecture received a new component as the Western European Union offered a 'consultation forum' analogous to the Alliance's Co-operation Council.[171]

OLD AND NEW DIVISIONS

Neither the Alliance nor the Western Union felt able to offer the east European states the one thing that really mattered, that is membership. In the autumn both Volker Rühe for Germany and his American counterpart William Perry seemed committed to forcing the issue and inviting the Visegrád countries to become members of the Alliance. Following Yeltsin's visit to Washington in September, however, the United States retreated. When the Alliance members met, Rühe found himself isolated as Perry described membership of the Visegrád states as 'entirely premature'.[172] Instead, the United States placed its hopes in a strengthening of the Conference on Security and Co-operation at its forthcoming meeting in December in Budapest. The persistent attraction of the Conference was, of course, its simple extent. As a joint German–Dutch proposal of May put it, the Conference had 'an overriding responsibility for the prevention of new divisions in Europe'.[173] For so long as attention was focused on the Conference, new divisions were indeed avoided, but old ones remained in place. Short of transforming itself into a full-blown security organization on a par with, and hence as a replacement for, the Atlantic Alliance, the Conference could not sweep away the division of Europe which was embodied in the existence of an Atlantic Alliance. For the east European states that meant the perpetuation of the division of Europe which they ascribed to Yalta. The alternative, to extend the Alliance eastwards, meant to create a new division, a division at the border of the former Soviet Union.

The December round of meetings brought little relief from the discordance caused by these intractable problems. Just before the Budapest summit of the Conference on Security and Co-operation in December, the Atlantic Alliance met amidst continuing speculation upon its imminent demise and disagreement over policy on Bosnia. That issue divided Kohl and Mitterrand. Kohl favoured lifting the embargo on the supply of armaments to the Bosnian government, and only failed to press the case in return for Mitterrand's agreement to inviting the east Europeans to the Community's Essen Council.[174] The Conference on Security and Co-operation was no more successful, leaving the Hungarian President, Arpad Concz, to record the regret of member states that they had not been able even to agree upon 'the right formulations to express our stand on the situation in Bosnia-Hercegovina'.[175] Failure to agree upon policy contrasted sharply with the consensus that the Conference needed to be strengthened. That consensus extended to transforming the conference into the Organization for Security and Co-operation in Europe, though the summit emphasized that this did not affect the commitments of member states.[176]

Compared with the previous two major transformations of Europe, the end of the Cold War had witnessed remarkably little violence. That states were able to adjust, albeit imperfectly, was due in no small measure to the reassurances and prospects provided by the international institutions which were unevenly scattered across the European landscape. Europe was characterized by a network of fora for multilateral co-operation. The authority of these fora, the sacrifice of sovereignty, or lack of it, varied almost as extensively as their membership. The major difficulty remained the relationship between them all. The Atlantic Alliance's judgement that 'the challenges we face cannot be comprehensively addressed by one institution alone' remained valid, but its vision of 'a framework of interlocking institutions which complement each other' glossed over the confusion of overlapping jurisdictions and commitments which were Europe's historical legacy.[177]

NOTES

1. *London Declaration on a Transformed Atlantic Alliance*, 5–6 July 1990.
2. For sketches of a fragmented Europe, see John J. Mearsheimer, 'Back to the future: instability in Europe after the Cold War', *International Security*, **1** (1990), pp. 5–56; Adrian Hyde-Price, *European Security beyond the Cold War: Four Scenarios for the Year 2010* (London, 1991), pp. 226–36; Barry Buzan *et al.*, *The European Security Order Recast: Scenarios for the Post-Cold War Era* (London, 1990), pp. 229–52. For an emphasis upon nationalism, see Marcin Krol, 'A Europe of nations or a universalist Europe?', *International Affairs*, **66** (1990), pp. 285–90.
3. Richard E. Baldwin, *Towards an Integrated Europe* (London, 1994), p. 166. These comparisons are affected by the post-1989 industrial decline in eastern Europe. Nevertheless, an earlier comparative study noted: 'All Central-Eastern European planned economies' positions deteriorated relative to Austria, Italy, Spain and Greece in the 1937–1980 period, save Bulgaria.' Eva Ehrlich, 'Contests between countries: 1937–1986', Conference Paper, Fourth World Congress of Soviet and East European Studies (1990), p. 17.

4. Wojtek Lamentowitcz, 'Nationale Interessen und europäische Integration', *Europäische Rundschau* **2** (1993), p. 39.
5. *The Guardian* (16 November 1989).
6. Szabo, *The Diplomacy of German Unification*, p. 45. For Teltschik's comments, see *ibid.*, p. 38.
7. *Ibid.*, pp. 45–6; *Financial Times* (20 December 1989).
8. This is strongly emphasized by Frank Costigliola, 'An "arm around the shoulder": the United States, NATO and German reunification, 1989–90', *Contemporary European History*, **3** (1995), pp. 87–90.
9. Quoted in *ibid.*, p. 102.
10. *Ibid.*, p. 95.
11. Szabo, *The Diplomacy of German Unification*, p. 58.
12. Werner Weidenfeld and Karl-Rudolf Korte (eds), *Handwörterbuch zur deutschen Einheit* (Bonn, 1991), pp. 521–2.
13. Haral Müller, 'German foreign policy after unification', in Stares (ed.), *The New Germany and the New Europe*, pp. 146–7. For the emotions this raised, see the debate in the Bundestag, *Das Parlament* (1 December 1989).
14. Speech at a conference of the Tutzing Protestant Academy on 31 January 1990.
15. *Financial Times* (31 January 1990).
16. Szabo, *The Diplomacy of German Unification*, p. 56.
17. *Ibid.*, pp. 62–4; *Financial Times* (12 February 1990). Genscher's option of alliance membership but no alliance deployment in the territories of the Demooratic Republic was discussed, apparently inconclusively.
18. The 'Open Skies' conference formed part of the negotiations on armaments reduction and allowed for aerial inspection.
19. Fritsch-Bournazel, *Europe and German Unification*, pp. 157–8; Szabo, *The Diplomacy of German Unification*, p. 61.
20. *Financial Times* (5 March 1990).
21. *Financial Times* (7 March 1990).
22. *The Guardian* (15 March 1990); Szabo, *The Diplomacy of German Unification*, pp. 74–5.
23. Quoted in Fritsch-Bournazel, *Europe and German Unification*, p. 156.
24. The crudity of sentiment was evident in the so-called Chequers affair in March. The best guide to this is Gordon A. Craig, 'Die Chequers-Affäre von 1990', *Vierteljahreshefte für Zeitgeschichte*, **39** (1991), pp. 611–24.
25. By Douglas Hurd, *The Guardian* (3 April 1990). On the Alliance's view see Manfred Wörner's comments in Mastny (ed.), *The Helsinki Process and the Reintegration of Europe 1986–1991*, pp. 255–7.
26. *Ibid.*, doc. 64 and 66.
27. *The Guardian* (12 April 1990).
28. *The Guardian* (10 May 1990). See also Szabo, *The Diplomacy of German Unification*, p. 83.
29. *Financial Times* (2 April 1990).
30. Szabo, *The Diplomacy of German Unification*, pp. 85–7.
31. Quoted in *ibid.*, p. 92.
32. *Ibid.*
33. *Ibid.*, pp. 95–7.

34. *Financial Times* (18 July 1990). On American surprise at the results of the Kohl–Gorbachev meeting see Costigliola, 'An "arm around the shoulder" ', pp. 107–8.
35. Article 7, Treaty on the Final Settlement with Respect to Germany, Press and Information Office of the Embassy of the Federal Republic of Germany.
36. Arcticle 1, *ibid.*
37. Address to a joint session of the United States Congress, 21 February 1990, Orbis Press Agency.
38. Stefan Fröhlich, 'Umbruch in Europa', *Aus Politik und Zeitgeschichte,* **29** (1990), p. 42.
39. See *Bulletin of the European Communities,* **11** (1990).
40. *Financial Times* (5 January 1990).
41. *Financial Times* (10 January 1990); *The Guardian* (January 1990).
42. On this see Jozef M. van Brabant, 'Renewal of cooperation and economic transition in Eastern Europe', *Studies in Comparative Communism,* **24** (1991), p. 159.
43. The main advocate of these ideas was Jozef M. Van Brabant. See his 'On reforming the trade and payments regimes in the CMEA', *Jahrbuch der Wirtschaft Osteuropas,* **14** (1990), pp. 7–30.
44. Giles Merrit, *Eastern Europe and the USSR. The Challenge of Freedom* (London, 1991), p. 109.
45. H. Matejka, 'East–West European integration', Conference Paper, Fourth World Congress for Soviet and East European Studies, July 1990, pp. 21–3.
46. Pinder, *The European Community and Eastern Europe,* p. 52.
47. Merrit, *Eastern Europe and the USSR,* p. 96.
48. *Financial Times* (7 January 1991).
49. Libor Roucek, *After the Bloc: The New International Relations in Eastern Europe* (London, 1992), p. 8.
50. Andrew A. Michta, *East Central Europe after the Warsaw Pact* (New York, 1992), pp. 46–55.
51. *Financial Times* (19 January 1990). Roucek, *After the Bloc,* refers to Polish requests in February that Soviet troops remain, p. 5.
52. Michta, *East Central Europe after the Warsaw Pact,* p. 140. According to Michta, Polish and Czechoslovak attitudes were influenced by pressure from the Atlantic Alliance to proceed cautiously for fear of aggravating Soviet insecurity, *ibid.,* pp. 138–40.
53. *Financial Times* (21 November 1990).
54. Ministry of Foreign Affairs, Hungary, Press Release 4/1991 (15 February 1991). On the Visegrád Summit see Rudolf L. Tökes, 'From Visegrád to Kraków: cooperation, competition, and coexistence in central Europe', *Problems of Communism,* **6** (November–December 1981), pp. 100–14.
55. Jan Obrman, 'Czechoslovakia overcomes its initial reluctance', *RFE/RL Research Report,* **23** (June 1992), p. 20.
56. *Financial Times* (13 February 1991); Tökes, 'From Visegrád to Kraków', p. 105.
57. Quoted in *ibid.,* p. 108.
58. Quoted in Roucek, *After the Bloc,* p. 6.
59. Michta, *East Central Europe after the Warsaw Pact,* p. 146.
60. See Moritz Csáky, 'Österreich und die Mitteleuropaidee', *Europäische Rundschau,* **2** (1986), pp. 99–107.

61. *The German Tribune* (12 August 1990). On these developments see also Rudolf Stamm, 'Die Pentagonale als Beitrag zur Annäherung in Europa', *Europäische Rundschau,* **2** (1991), pp. 35–41; Ernst Sucharipa, 'Die Pentagonale', *Europäische Rundschau,* **3** (1990), pp. 25–34.
62. Address to the Hungarian Parliament on 15 October 1991, Ministry of Foreign Affairs, Current Policy No. 38/1991.
63. Quoted in Wolf Oschlies, 'Ursachen des Krieges in Ex-Jugoslawien', *Aus Politik und Zeitgeschichte,* **37** (1993), p. 8.
64. *Ibid.*
65. *Financial Times* (5 July 1991).
66. Quoted in Dinan, *Ever Closer Union?,* p. 490.
67. G. Edwards, 'European responses to the Yugoslav crisis: an interim assessment', in R. Rummel (ed.), *Towards Political Union* (Boulder, 1992), p. 176.
68. On the Community's policy see Marie-Janine Calic, 'Jugoslawienpolitik am Wendepunkt', *Aus Politik und Zeitgeschichte,* **37** (1993), pp. 11–20. On the reasons for Greek opposition to recognition of Macedonia see Jens Reuter, 'Makedonien-der jüngste Staat auf der Europäischen Landkarte', *ibid.*, p. 28.
69. In this I follow Dieter Senghaas, 'Vom Nutzen und Eland der Nationalismen im Leben von Völkern', *Aus Politik und Zeitgeschichte,* **31–2** (1992), pp. 23–32.
70. On the importance of this see Andrei Zagorski, 'New institutions and structures of the CSCE: adjusting to the new Europe', *Paradigms,* **2** (1992), pp. 12–25.
71. Mastny (ed.), *The Helsinki Process and the Reintegration of Europe 1986–1991,* doc. 73.
72. *Ibid.*, doc. 76.
73. *Ibid.*, doc. 78. See also doc. 77 for Greek concern. This was a continuation of disputes at the end of the Second World War. See above, chapter 2.
74. *Financial Times* (21 June 1991, 3 July 1991); *The Guardian* (11 September 1991).
75. *Document of the Moscow Meeting of the Conference on the Human Dimension of the CSCE* (Moscow, 1991), p. 29. On the Berlin Conference see Zagorski, 'New institutions and structures of the CSCE', pp. 12–13.
76. CSCE, *Second Meeting of the Council* (Prague, 1992), p. 15. On Prague see C. Antis, 'CSCE Mark II', *NATO Review,* **2** (1992), pp. 18–23. For a critical assessment focusing on Yugoslavia, see Nicholas Wheeler, 'The human rights and security agenda', in G. Wyn Rees (ed.), *International Politics. The New Agenda* (London, 1993), pp. 133–57.
77. Rob Zaagman and Hanie Zaal, 'The CSCE High Commissioner on National Minorities: prehistory and negotiations', typescript, pp. 8–9, forthcoming in U. Bloed (ed.), *The Challenges of Change* (The Hague, 1994).
78. *Ibid.*, p. 12. Turkey continued to reiterate this. See Budapest Summit 1994, Journal No. 2.
79. Zaagman and Zaal, 'The CSCE High Commissioner on National Minorities', p. 14.
80. CSCE, *Helsinki Documents 1992* (Helsinki, 1992), p. 20. Konrad J. Huber stresses that this was the first time an official of the Conference could act without express permission, 'Preventing ethnic conflict in the new Europe', in Ian M. Cuthbertson and Jane Leibowitz (eds), *Minorities: The New Europe's Old Issue* (Boulder, 1993), p. 295.
81. For Max van der Stoel's perception of his role, see 'Die KSZE und die Minderheitenfrage', *Europa-Archiv,* **22** (1994), pp. 629–34, especially the statement

that 'The High Commissioner is not an instrument for the protection of minorities or a kind of ombudsman who acts in their name', p. 632.

82. Speech by the Secretary General of the CSCE, Dr Wilhelm Höynck, at the NATO Seminar in Brussels on 7 March 1994.
83. *Ibid.*
84. On 'cobweb integration' in the Nordic region see Nils Andrén, 'Nordic integration', *Cooperation and Conflict*, **3–4** (1967), pp. 1–25; Bengt Sundelius and Claes Wiklund, 'The Nordic community: the ugly duckling of regional cooperation', *Journal of Common Market Studies*, **18** (1979), pp. 59–75.
85. Heinz-Jürgen Axt, 'Auf dem Weg zur kollektiven Sicherheit? Die KSZE nach Erweiterung und Institutionalisierung', *Europäische Rundschau*, **1** (1993), pp. 83–99, answers the question in his title with a firm no. Secretary General Höynck evidently felt a little uncomfortable with this, for, having stated that the Conference did not provide security guarantees, he invoked the idea of 'indivisible security' which 'should ... mean that no State will be left alone if its security is threatened.' Speech at the Royal Institute of International Affairs (London, 18 May 1994).
86. Aurel Zidaru-Barbulescu, 'Romania seeks admission to the Council of Europe', *REF/RL Research Report*, **2** (1993), pp. 11–16, especially p. 15.
87. Council of Europe, *European Charter for Regional or Minority Languages* (Strasbourg, 5 October 1992). For restrictions on which languages qualified, see *European Charter for Regional or Minority Languages. Explanatory Report* (Strasbourg, 7 July 1992), paragraph 30.
88. *Financial Times* (8 October 1993). On the Council's involvement with minority rights see Klaus Schumann. 'The role of the Council of Europe', in Hugh Miall (ed.), *Minority Rights in Europe* (London, 1994), pp. 87–98.
89. *Financial Times* (6 October 1993). Hungary sought first to delay Slovak entry then to mobilize the Czechs to press Slovakia on minority rights, neither successfully. Alfred A. Reisch, 'The central European initiative: to be or not to be?', *RFE/RL Research Report*, **34** (1993), pp. 33–4.
90. *Financial Times* (6 August 1990).
91. This was encouraged by her assertion that the European states 'have not thrown off central command and control in their own countries only to find them reincarnated within the European Community', *ibid.*
92. Pinder, *The European Community and Eastern Europe*, p. 27; Dan Horovitz, 'EC–Central/East European relations: new principles for a new era', *Common Market Law Review*, **27** (1990), pp. 265–6.
93. Alfred Tovias, 'EC–Eastern Europe: a case study of Hungary', *Journal of Common Market Studies*, **29** (1991), pp. 293–4. Tovias emphasizes that both political motives and fear of Hungarian competition were at work.
94. Poland Hungary: Aid for Economic Reconstruction (Phare).
95. *Financial Times* (8 December 1989).
96. *The Guardian* (24 May 1990).
97. *Ibid.*
98. Economic Commission for Europe, *Economic Survey of Europe in 1989–1990* (New York, 1990), pp. 5–26.
99. Quoted in Steven Weber, 'Origins of the European Bank for Reconstruction and Development', *International Organization*, **48** (1994), p. 11.

100. Václav Klaus and Tomas Jezek, 'The evolutionary approach', *Financial Times* (13 December 1989). For a survey of early progress and the associated problems, see Hugh Miall, *Shaping the New Europe* (London, 1993), pp. 39–47.
101. *The Guardian* (15 November 1990).
102. Weber, 'Origins of the European Bank for Reconstruction and Development', p. 15.
103. For a detailed survey of the negotiations, see *ibid.*, pp. 17–23.
104. *Financial Times* (13 April 1992, 15 April 1992).
105. *Financial Times* (26 June 1993).
106. *Financial Times* (29 December 1994).
107. *Financial Times* (13 January 1990).
108. *Bulletin of the European Communities*, Supplement 1 (1991), p. 21.
109. Lecture at St Anthony's College, Oxford University, 11 December 1991.
110. See *European Economy*, Supplement A, No. 7 (July 1994), p. 16.
111. There is a concise summary of provisions in *European Economy, ibid.*
112. Christina Mastropasqua and Veria Rolli, 'Industrial countries' protectionism with respect to eastern Europe', *World Economy*, **17** (1994), p. 167. For a more detailed breakdown, see *European Economy*, Supplement A, No. 7 (July 1994), pp. 4–5.
113. Europe Agreement between the European Communities and the Republic of Hungary, Articles 21, 29 and 30, *Official Journal of the European Communities*, No. L347/7–8 (31 December 1993).
114. *European Economy*, Supplement A, No. 7 (July 1994), p. 11.
115. *European Economy*, Supplement A, No. 3 (March 1994), p. 5.
116. His complaint was expressed during a visit to the Commission on 3 February 1994, *Europa–Archiv*, **22** (1994), p. D649.
117. See Andras Inotai, 'Die Beziehungen zwischen der EU und den assozierten Staaten Mittel – und Osteuropas', *Europäische Rundschau*, **3** (1994), pp. 27–9; Franz-Lothar Altmann and Cornelius Ochmann, 'Mittel – und Osteuropa auf dem Weg in die EU', *Europäische Rundschau*, **1** (1995), pp. 51–2.
118. *East European Reporter*, **1** (1992), p. 44; David Shumaker, 'The origins and development of central European cooperation: 1989–1992', *East European Quarterly*, **27** (1993), p. 362. Some accounts accept more optimistic Polish reports and date agreement from the Cracow summit.
119. Altmann and Ochmann, 'Mittel – und Osteuropa auf dem Weg in die EU', pp. 52–3; Karoly Olicsanyi, 'The Visegrád Triangle's free-trade zone', *RFE/RL Research Report*, **2.3** (1993), p. 20.
120. *Ibid.* On the impact on foreign investment as well as the special problems facing a free trade area between them see Baldwin, *Towards an Integrated Europe*, pp. 128–39.
121. Ministry of Foreign Affairs, Newsletter 616/1992 (22 December 1992).
122. *Ibid.*
123. Quoted in Jan B. de Wedenthal, 'EC keeps central Europe at arm's length', *RFE/RL Research Report*, **5** (January 1993), p. 29.
124. Ministry of Foreign Affairs, Republic of Hungary, Current Policy, No.4/1991.
125. Baldwin, *Towards an Integrated Europe*, p. 168.
126. *Financial Times* (22 September 1993).
127. Ministry of Foreign Affairs, Republic of Hungary, Current Policy, No. 6/1992.
128. Alfred A. Reisch, 'Hungary sees common goals and bilateral issues', *RFE/RL Research Report*, **23** (1992), p. 30; Roucek, *After the Bloc*, p. 24.

129. *Financial Times* (28 February 1992); *Das Parlament* (1 January 1993).
130. *Official Journal of the European Communities*, No. L347/3 (31 December 1993).
131. *Bulletin of the European Communities*, **6** (1993), point 1.13.
132. Chritoph Royen, 'Die "Visegrád"-Staatengruppe: Zu früh für einen Nachruf', *Europa-Archiv*, **22** (1994), p. 639. M. Hatschikjan discerns a more positive response from Hungary, 'Foreign policy reorientations in central Europe', *Aussenpolitik*, **1** (1994), p. 55.
133. *The Guardian* (21 December 1993).
134. *Financial Times* (29 January 1994, 31 January 1994, 7 March 1994).
135. *Bulletin of the European Communities*, **6** (1994), point 1.13.
136. *The Europe Agreements and Beyond*, COM (94) 320 final.
137. COM (94) 361 final (27 July 1994), p. 4.
138. With a view to its completion in 1997. Christian Meier, 'Cooperation initiatives in eastern central Europe', *Aussenpolitik*, **45** (1994), pp. 260–1.
139. Interview with the Czech Foreign Minister, Jozef Zieleniec, 23 May 1994, in *Europa-Archiv*, **22** (1994), p. D652.
140. *The Guardian* (1 November 1994).
141. *Financial Times* (12 December 1994).
142. See Baldwin, *Towards an Integrated Europe*, pp. 140–51.
143. On the French decision to join the review see *Financial Times* (16 March 1991). On the Key Largo meeting see Julius W. Friend, 'U.S. policy toward Franco-German cooperation', in Patrick McCarthy (ed.), *France–Germany, 1983–1993* (New York, 1993), p. 167.
144. Anand Menon, 'From independence to cooperation: France, NATO and European security', *International Affairs*, **71** (1995), p. 24.
145. Quoted in *ibid.*, p. 23.
146. *Rome Declaration on Peace and Cooperation* (November 1991), paragraph 11. For a survey of the summit, see Manfred Woerner, 'NATO transformed: the significance of the Rome summit', *NATO Review*, **6** (1991), pp. 3–8.
147. NATO Prsss Communiqué M–NACC–1(91)111(Rev) (20 December 1991).
148. NATO Press Communiqué M–NAC–2(91)110 (19 December 1991).
149. *Financial Times* (21 December 1991).
150. Andrzej Podraza, *The Western European Union and Central Europe: A New Relationship* (London, 1992), p. 29. Podraza recommended a division of tasks between the two. While the Atlantic Alliance should retain its policy of not discriminating between the former members of the Warsaw Pact, the Union should pursue a policy of differentiation, pp. 32–5. See especially his quotation of a Polish official, 'NATO's (and the WEU's) policy of non-differentiation ... is broadly seen in the countries of Central Europe as proof of lasting Yalta-like, Western-supported division of Europe', p. 35.
151. Willem van Eekelen, 'WEU's post-Maastricht agenda', *NATO Review*, **2** (1992), p. 17.
152. Ministerial meeting of the North Atlantic Council in Oslo, Final Communiqué, 4 June 1992, paragraph 11.
153. Speech by the Secretary General of the CSCE, Dr Wilhelm Höynck, 7 March 1994.
154. NATO Press Service, Speech by the Secretary General of NATO, Mr Manfred Wörner, 10 May 1993.

155. On the corps see Philip Gordon, 'The Franco-German security partnership', in McCarthy (ed.), *France–Germany, 1983–1993*, pp. 152–54. For Joxe's views, see *Financial Times* (30 September 1992); Menon, 'From independence to cooperation', pp. 25–6.
156. NATO Press Communiqué, M-1(94)3 (11 January 1994).
157. Jean-Marie Guéhenno, 'France and the WEU', *NATO Review*, **5** (1994). p. 12. The Gulf War had revealed French deficiencies in the intelligence field. See Menon, 'From independence to cooperation', p. 21.
158. The idea was first presented by the French Ambassador to Germany in March. Franz H. U. Borkenhagen, 'Geteilte Sicherheit in Europa?', *Aus Politik und Zeitgeschichte*, **26–7** (1994), p. 19.
159. *Bulletin of the European Communities*, **12** (1993), point 1.16.
160. *The Guardian* (19 October 1993).
161. *Financial Times* (27 August 1993). See also Alfred Reisch, 'Central Europe's disappointments and hopes', *RFE/RL Research Report*, **3** (1994), p. 21.
162. On Polish fears see Joana Radzyner, 'Auf halbem Weg. Polens europäische Integration', *Europäische Rundschau*, **1** (1994), pp. 34–6.
163. NATO Press Service, Speech by the Secretary General of NATO Mr Manfred Wörner, 10 September 1993.
164. Reisch, 'Central Europe's disappointments and hopes', p. 24.
165. NATO Press Service, Speech by the Secretary General of NATO, Mr Manfred Wörner, 6 October 1993.
166. *The Guardian* (21 October 1993); Michael Mihalka, 'Squaring the circle: NATO's offer to the East', *RFE/RL Research Report*, **3** (1994), pp. 3–4.
167. Reisch, 'Central Europe's disappointments and hopes', p. 25. On the Polish press see Radzyner, 'Auf halbem Weg', p. 35. The first two betrayals were identified as Munich and Yalta.
168. NATO Press Communiqué, M–1(94)3 (11 January 1994).
169. On the basis of a package which, according to the Russian Foreign Minister reflected 'Russia's size, importance and capabilities'. Andrei Kozyrev, 'Russia and NATO', *NATO Review*, **4** (1994), pp. 3–6.
170. On the Conference see *Europa-Archiv*, **13–14** (1994), pp. D398–D409.
171. See *Europa-Archiv*, **17** (1994), pp. D489–D495.
172. *Financial Times* (2 October 1994).
173. Embassy of the Federal Republic of Germany, Press Release 48/94 (24 May 1994).
174. *The Guardian* (1 December 1994).
175. *CSCE Newsletter*, **11** (21 December 1994).
176. *Ibid.*
177. NATO Press Communiqué M–NACC–1(91)111(Rev) (20 December 1991).

Concluding Reflections

According to the economic historian Carl Strikwerda, 'scholars may by forgiven for imagining that a century or so from now, the years from 1914 to 1989 may be seen as a painful period in which Europe groped to rediscover the cooperative route it had begun to take before World War 1'.[1] His speculation was based upon economic trends in heavy industry, especially the development of multinational enterprises and labour migration. If persuasive, it could be said to vindicate the nineteenth-century advocates of the triumph of commerce over the pursuit of glory by Europe's warrior class. Integration here is brought about by economic logic and self-interest, save when it is distorted by governments who embark upon protectionist strategies or foreign adventures to the disadvantage of fellow citizens.

Economic logic and self-interest were not unequivocal guides. Even where they pointed to integration, that integration was sometimes perceived as limited and defensive, intended to protect a given area from wider competition. This was always one possible purpose of a customs union. For the nineteenth-century Magyar landowners in the customs union of the Dual Monarchy, as for many of the European Community's farmers, a customs union meant protected markets and inflated prices. Similarly, advocacy of a customs union in inter-war Europe was commonly intended to provide protection from the ravages of competition from the United States. Disputes about the advantages and disadvantages of greater or lesser protection were about more than material gains and losses. They affected the kind of society and socio-economic structure within the customs area. At the beginning of the twentieth century, even in an economy as advanced as that of the German Reich, a liberal tariff regime was denounced on the grounds that it would lead to the destruction of the Agrarian-State. For these critics of a liberal tariff, unrestrained industrialization was undesirable on both economic and social grounds. It would, they claimed, induce the industrially advanced states forcefully to prevent others from following them on the path of industrialization.

Competition would ruin German markets and lead to unemployment and revolution, while on a broader front it would lead to international war.[2] Although the idea of an Agrarian-State lingered on, it was no longer a viable option for Europe's states. Even the 'blood and soil' ideology of National Socialist Germany foundered on the reality of an industrialized modern state. In the long run Jean Monnet was right in insisting that protectionism meant a retreat into 'the rut of limited, protected production' and economic 'Malthusianism'.[3]

Strikwerda's choice of 1989 only partly reflected this economic thesis. It was more of a response to the end of the Cold War and to the apparent triumph of democracy. For some nineteenth-century advocates of integration the two went hand in hand, with parliamentary democracy as the precondition of integrating all of Europe's states, as well as being the appropriate political form for a commercial society. Ironically, in 1989 the triumph of democracy was associated with a European Community which was coming under increasing criticism for its 'democratic deficit'. Defined as 'the gap between the powers transferred to the Community level and the control of the elected parliament over them', the deficit weakened democracy in two ways.[4] Most obviously, the weakly developed European Parliament had limited control, even after the Maastricht Treaty. The transfer of powers also weakened the domestic parliaments of the Community, not merely because they lost sovereign control over policy areas but because they lost control over their own ministers. The latter operated in a complex policy-making world inhabited by civil servants and ministers who met in closed sessions. There were some feeble attempts to win back ground for the parliamentarians of the member states, through, for example, the first of the Assizes which brought together representatives of the European Parliament and the national parliaments in November 1980.[5] Nevertheless, Community legislation took place largely in a democratic no man's land between democratic control at national and at Community level.

This did not matter so long as European integration inspired little popular interest and even less popular passion. The lack of popular enthusiasm was one of the most striking features of the history of integration. All of the efforts to gain popular support for European integration failed dismally. The failure of Coudenhove-Kalergi's attempt to build a mass membership European union, which would force governments into uniting, foreshadowed the fate of subsequent efforts. Even at the end of the Second World War Spinelli's hope of capitalizing on discredited nationalism and the evident impotence of the isolated nation-state was disappointed. Forty years later, when Parliamentarians, including Spinelli, sought to turn the election of 1984 into a debate on the Draft

Treaty establishing the European Union, they were no more successful. Integration within the Community was a product of agreements between Europe's political elites. The popular legitimacy of the Community was dependent upon the domestic legitimacy of those elites. As they fell into discredit, an attitude towards the Community best characterized as benign indifference gave way to a more sceptical and suspicious one.[6]

The Community had not been devised as a democratic institution. Indeed, such feeble democratic provision as existed was added as an afterthought. The lack of democracy has been ascribed to the technocratic ethos of the Community's founders, with much of the blame laid at the feet of Jean Monnet.[7] There had been a strong technocratic stream in advocacy of European integration, less out of authoritarian inclinations, though those did exist, than out of a distrust of political leaders beholden to volatile and self-interested electorates. But this was only part of the reason. A technocratic element, that is first the High Authority of the Coal and Steel Community and then the Commission, was necessary to resolve the problem caused by the disparity in size and power between Europe's states. Once a full-scale federal state was rejected, that left only a confederation of states or some hybrid as a possibility. A confederation could not be had on the basis of full equality, for that would have privileged smaller powers, especially if majority voting was allowed, or larger powers if weighted majority voting was allowed. Provision for both could be made if either threat was mitigated by some neutral actor independent of the member states, and hence beyond democratic control.

Not only was democracy practically ignored in the construction of the European Communities, a distinctly anti-democratic element had been built in because of those considerations, considerations which had little to do with general trends towards or away from democracy and a great deal to do with the historical peculiarities of the European system of states. In Comecon, where democratic considerations were irrelevant, the failure to conjure up some such solution left the organization dependent upon consensus, like the western Organization for European Economic Co-operation before it, and condemned Comecon to an ineffectual struggle to escape from this defect of its birth. Comecon's problem was even greater than the Community's, for the disparity in the distribution of power between its member states was proportionately greater. The same applied to the two military alliances. Here considerations of democracy were traditionally weaker, when present at all. The Atlantic Alliance and the Warsaw Pact moved in the sphere which John Locke reserved for the 'federative' function of government, by which he meant a kind of activity, largely synonymous with foreign affairs, which by its nature was not subject to law.[8]

While 1988 could be interpreted as a resumption of pre-1914 economic trends and aspirations for democracy, it also invoked fears of the return of the demons of nationalism. Earlier, the nineteenth-century Italian nationalist Mazzini had claimed that national self-determination would be the solution of Europe's ills. Wars arose, he claimed, precisely because of a denial of national self-determination. Once all nations were free, a European brotherhood of nations would result. That perspective became increasingly difficult to maintain. The expansionist nationalism of the pan-Germans revealed one of the less benign faces of nationalism. In central Europe Germans and non-Germans alike calculated their respective 'national assets', by which they meant the individuals incorporated, willingly or not, into the respective nations. Statisticians marshalled their figures like generals for the coming battle of population growth. Victory would go to the nation which outbred its competitors. Before 1914 these underlying conflicts erupted into open warfare in the divisive and bloody squabbles of the new Balkan states. It was memories of the latter that were invoked when Yugoslavia disintegrated amidst bitter ethnic cleansing.[9]

Although post-Cold War Europe seemed to be reviving the trends and hopes of the nineteenth century, both attitudes and realities had been shaped by the intervening years. This was true even of nationalism, which had fallen into discredit among advocates of integration. For Spinelli, writing from a fascist prison, nationalism had been 'a powerful stimulus to progress. It had helped overcome narrow-minded parochialism and created a much wider feeling of solidarity against foreign oppression.'[10] But this progressive function had been replaced by a drive for domination. The judgement of the German opponent of the Nazi regime, Helmuth von Moltke, was even harsher: nationalism had simply been a colossal error. Although there were far fewer such critics of nationalism, let alone advocates of a European national identity, than defenders of the sovereign state pretended, nationalism had been tainted by the excesses of the first half of the twentieth century. Here the Second World War was more decisive than the First. In the wake of the First World War remnants of Mazzini's faith in the benign efforts of self-determination persisted, along with vengeful and revisionist nationalisms. In the wake of the Second World War, nationalism was much more muted. Few European states had escaped the experience of defeat. The most common experience was of liberation by external armies, not victory. Even the Germans were 'liberated', if only from themselves.[11] In the German case nationalism had been discredited by the crimes of the Third Reich and could not be invoked without calling into question the entire post-war order. In the Federal Republic this dual embarrassment induced a turn to 'constitutional patriotism': not the nation but the democratic values embodied in the Basic Law were upheld as the proper object of patriotic devotion.[12] While the circumstances of the German nation were unusual, aggressive nationalism in western Europe in general was reserved for Europe's colonies.[13] In eastern Europe the end of the war witnessed a vindictive flourish of nationalism, directed mainly, but not exclusively, against German minorities, but was then subdued by the new communist regimes.

Nationalism had so lost its rigour that speculation upon its obsolescence became commonplace. The memories of the super-heated nationalism of the Second World War were strong enough to make nationalistic outbursts unrespectable. The unease that arose in response to assertions of national identity lay behind Václav Klaus's plea that 'the idea of Europe should not be built on an all too simplistic rejection of nationalism. We should recognize the legitimacy of national sentiment and need not be ashamed of it.'[14] But Klaus's nationalism was moderate. The last outburst of violent Czech nationalism had taken place at the end of the Second World War when Germans, irrespective of their political leanings, had been driven from liberated Czechoslovakia. By the 1990s Czech intellectuals could reflect upon German–Czech relations, acknowledge the contribution which the Germans had made to Czech culture, and lament the loss which their departure signified. There were less benign echoes of the past when Slovaks recalled their independence during the Second World War, an independence which had been bought at the cost of Nazi occupation of the Czech lands. But the separation of the Czech and Slovak halves of Czechoslovakia was smooth enough to warrant the label the 'velvet divorce'.[15] Discrimination against minorities was common in eastern European states, notably so in Slovakia, Romania and Bulgaria, but only in the former Yugoslavia and the Commonwealth of Independent States did ethnic antagonism lead to bloodshed. In Poland, the Czech Republic, Slovakia and Hungary there was more willingness to deal with the problems of minorities by means of treaties, and no apparent prospect of a resort to force.[16]

The most dramatic change was, of course, the emergence of institutionalized integration and the associated sacrifice of aspects of state sovereignty. While the Cold War ensured that this integration was fractured into western and eastern forms, the experience of both the Second World War and the earlier inter-war period were decisive in persuading elements of Europe's political elites, especially west Europe's political elites, to contemplate integration as a solution. It was, after all, only in the light of the 'disintegration' of Europe's economy during the inter-war period that the term 'integration' as opposed to union or federation became prevalent.[17] Terminological novelty in itself was not particularly important, but the experience it referred to was.

The conversion to integration was neither universal, automatic nor unequivocal. France first tried older policies and sought to gain Anglo-American support for the control of Germany. Only when this was not forthcoming did France take the initiative which led to the European Coal and Steel Community. These and numerous other similar instances have led the British historian A. S. Milward to argue that 'Integration was not the supercession of the nation-state by another form of governance as the nation-state became incapable, but was the creation of the nation-states themselves for their own purposes, an act of national will.'[18] From this perspective the

> evolution of the Community's political machinery had little to do with European federalism or with abstract demands for a European constitution as a desirable thing in itself, because the programme of the European federalists was irrelevant to immediate political needs. Many of them in any case, perhaps the majority, were opposed to the domestic policies of the nation-states.[19]

Domestic agendas, whether the modernization of the French economy under the Monnet plan or the pursuit of deregulation by the Thatcher government in Britain, did play a major role in shaping policies towards the form of integration. The limited success of the federalists in imposing their vision of politics is equally undeniable. But ideas of 'another form of governance' were not as insignificant as Milward suggests. In advocating integration Monnet did seek to obtain French national goals by other means, but he was genuine in his assertion of the 'independence of the Authority *vis-à-vis* Governments and the sectional interests concerned' which was the 'precondition for the emergence of a common point of view which could be taken neither by Governments nor by private interests'.[20] Similarly, west German officials and ministers supported integration, first to gain acceptance for the restoration of the country to a position of equality, and later to ensure the unification of the two German states. But west German statesmen and officials did support the development of a more federalist form of governance. In doing so they drew on Germany's federalist tradition. The peculiarities of German history and the country's relative economic strength in postwar Europe were added reasons for looking beyond the nation-state.[21]

The evolution of the Community was not driven forward, as the self-avowed functionalists had hoped, by a process of 'spill-over', where initial, partial integration exposed problems and contradictions, partly of its own creation, and subsequently led to further integration in an attempt to resolve these.[22] External shocks were much more important.[23] It was the disintegration of the post-war monetary order backed by the United States that put monetary union on the agenda. It was continued international monetary instability that kept it there, despite the disappointments of efforts even to co-ordinate exchange rates, let alone bring about genuine monetary union. It was enlargement, including the enlargement brought about by the reunification of Germany, that on each occasion brought forth renewed integration. External shocks alone were not sufficient. There was always the option of seeking a purely national solution. Only when the socialist government of Mitterrand was confronted with the failure of its initial strategy did it turn to renewed integration, and even then a retreat to a more protectionist stance was favoured by some.[24] The more integrated the Community became, and the longer it endured, the higher the risks and the potential penalties of a turn to protectionism. The extent and longevity of integration had never been a guarantee against protectionist or secessionist sentiment. But it was a deterrent.

The Community's erratic progress on the road of integration was greatly aided by the decision to embark upon market-based integration in the Economic Community. Contrary to the expectations of the functionalists, sectoral integration proved difficult. An extension of it beyond the Coal and Steel Community brought with it the prospect of complex bargaining, sector by sector, which gave maximum scope to the 'sectional interests concerned'. The difficulties this entailed were evident in the other half of Europe. The integration of planned economies within Comecon entailed something similar to sectoral integration in the west. The co-ordination of plans, the specialization of production, meant taking specific and overt decisions about who was to gain and who was to lose. Yet this was not the only difficulty which was more acute in the east than in the west. In the planned economies the sovereignty of the state was much more closely bound up with the economy. Those states drew their legitimacy from their ownership of the means of production. To surrender control over the fate of industries meant a direct sacrifice of sovereignty.

The same consequence set limits to integration within the two military alliances and helped bring down the planned European Defence Community. Control over its armed forces was closer to the heart of the state and its claim to sovereignty. De Gaulle and the Romanians made this explicit, but it was true for the others as well. The obstacles to a sacrifice of sovereignty within the alliances were compounded by the fact that any sacrifice was bound to be asymmetrical. There was no prospect of the hegemonic superpowers accepting the restraints upon their own freedom of action which they advocated for their smaller allies. Within the European Community, where the salience of activities was lower, there was a rough symmetry within the key Franco-German axis. It was only a rough symmetry. The underlying inferiority of France acted as a periodic stimulus to initiatives aimed at managing that inferiority by gaining control over German resources, even if that meant accepting equivalent restrictions upon itself. While the Franco-German axis enjoyed a privileged status within the Community, it had not, to de Gaulle's disappointment, been tightly enough welded together to act autonomously. For France, therefore, the Franco-German axis constituted one possibility of maximizing leverage within broader frameworks, that is, within the Community and within the Alliance. The existence of those frameworks fundamentally affects the conduct of policy for all of their members. As one commentator put it, 'Today, a country's influence is determined by the extent to which it can mobilise (or prevent) coalitions between states in the network of multinational organizations and bilateral relations able to resolve international problems which cannot by resolved by individual states.'[25] The Franco-German axis functioned primarily as the basis of a prima-facie coalition within the European Community. Comecon lacked an equivalent axis. Even excluding the Soviet Union, there were no two states with sufficient common interest and rough equality of resources to drive the organization forward.

When Comecon and the Warsaw Pact dissolved, the echoes of the pact were loud, if not entirely clear. Mostly it was images of the inter-war and immediate post-1945 years that were invoked. On the security front, the hostility of Moscow to an eastern expansion of the Atlantic Alliance, the hesitancy of the Alliance, and then signs of a more assertive Russia, combined to conjure up the image of *Zwischeneuropa,* of an 'intermediate zone of lesser security' between a Russian sphere of influence and the security of the Alliance.[26] Some argued that the plausibility of this scenario depended upon the extent of the threat from Russia. That Russia had abandoned all imperial ambitions seemed doubtful. With a defence budget estimated at 11.4 per cent of GDP, Russia had the means to attempt to assert its will. The proclamation of Russian interests in the 'near abroad' as well as the invocation of a clash of cultures in its conflict with Chechenia seemed evidence of the ambition.[27] While these developments did pose an implicit threat to the Baltic states with their substantial Russian populations, their implications for the former member states of the Warsaw Pact were less clear. But then the plausibility of *Zwischeneuropa* depended less upon the existence of a direct threat and more upon the absence of positive guarantees. Arguably, the same had been true in western Europe in the 1940s. Positive evidence of aggressive Soviet intent was less important than the fear of being abandoned, in western Europe's clamour for an Atlantic treaty.

The greatest evident threat to eastern Europe came from economic problems which were hardly soluble by military means.[28] Here too images of the past were conjured up. Schemes of regional co-operation from the inter-war years were invoked along with the even more powerful image of the Marshall Plan. The fate of the former pointedly revealed their limited appeal in the new Europe. They had failed for want of support from the west. This time, however, the west, that is the European Community, was able to act as a more or less cohesive unit. In the inter-war years the protectionist climate, and even more so divisions within the west, had all but precluded a positive response. Having resolved its internal differences, at least in relative terms, western Europe was able to offer eastern Europe what it had asked for in vain during the depression: access to markets. The hesitancy associated with sensitive industries and agricultural markets, the fear that the safeguard clauses would be used to reintroduce protection, caused irritation and recrimination. Even more striking was the paucity of aid compared with the generosity of the United States in the Marshall Plan. Yet the Marshall Plan was not the appropriate point of comparison, and not only because the nature of the process of reconstruction was different. The more relevant comparison lay in the inter-war years when feuding west Europeans had abandoned the east to its fate.

The greatest contrast of all lay in the role of Germany. In the 1930s Germany had been the predator who took advantage first of the economic weakness of *Zwischeneuropa*, and then of its insecurity, to launch a bid for world power. In the 1990s Germany has been the strongest advocate of an eastern extension of both the European Community and the Atlantic Alliance. As Defence Minister Rühe put it in October 1993, it was in no one's interest to see the emergence of an unstable *Zwischeneuropa*, nor was it in Germany's interest to be the 'eastern border state of a prosperity zone'.[29] German interest in the east was matched by its willingness to contribute more to the western aid programme than its partners, providing approximately half of the total. Germany's share in trade constituted over half of the Community's total trade with eastern Europe.[30]

The end of the Cold War, reunification, and the evaporation of the threat from the east combined to increase Germany's potential freedom of manoeuvre as well as its sheer economic weight. That in itself was enough to cause concern in France. Differences over the former Yugoslavia seemed to confirm the risks.[31] In Poland, France sought to balance German involvement by participation in triangular co-operation between

France, Germany and Poland. But France could match neither German levels of trade, investment or aid.[32] Critics argued that France suffered from continued pretensions to play a role on the world stage which exceeded its capacity.[33]

France's policy towards Europe had been based upon a grand design, in which the Federal Republic would follow France's lead in bringing Europe together within a framework which would enhance Europe's, and hence France's, role within the world. This grand design had been fundamentally flawed from the start. Its precondition was a divided Germany, with a militarily weak Federal Republic fearful of the Soviet bloc. That weakness was supposed to tempt the Federal Republic to accept French protection as part of the grand design. But it was that same weakness which made the Federal Republic look to the United States. The French nuclear deterrent was never any substitute for the American nuclear arsenal. Even in conventional forces, France simply lacked the necessary resources. It was for that reason that French Generals ultimately had preferred to rearm Germany within the framework of the Atlantic Alliance rather than the European Defence Community. They needed the Anglo-Saxons to contain Germany. With the end of the Cold War the preconditions of the French grand design evaporated, leaving France with a more flexible but also a less certain orientation.[34]

While a united Germany was called on to play a role commensurate with its economic strength and new-found freedom of manoeuvre, each initiative or ill-chosen phrase brought suspicion and recrimination. In Germany itself, officials and parliamentary leaders complained of a lack of vision concerning Germany's wider role. In the words of Wolfgang Schäuble, 'The majority of our population, and sadly also our elites, would rather be left in peace.'[35] The post-war European architecture had provided the Federal Republic with a relatively stable framework and foreign policy orientation. There had been periods of alarm, notably the Berlin crisis, and initiatives, notably Willy Brandt's *Ostpolitik*. The latter, however, despite the fears that it induced, consolidated rather than challenged the basic architecture. Within the security of this overarching framework, the Federal Republic concentrated upon expanding cultural contacts and economic exchanges, that is, upon lessening the significance of the boundaries of Cold War Europe rather than calling them into question. The response of the reunified Germany to the new demands of the 1990s was to expand the two bodies which had provided it with security and prosperity. But it was far from clear that either the Community or the Atlantic Alliance was equal to the task.

For the Community, the problem lay in the desire to deepen integration and in doubts about the economic and institutional impact of enlargement. For the Alliance, the problem lay in accepting new obligations. In principle both were willing, and some member states were even eager. But to extend either meant to change the dividing line in Europe, or, as Russia feared, to exclude her from Europe. The cultural isolation of Russia from Europe had taken place in the nineteenth century, when critics linked its imperial vocation with its suppression of democratic reform and national independence. That isolation was periodically legitimated by references to even earlier historical developments which were in vogue again in post-Cold War Europe. In a provocative article, the American political scientist Samuel Huntington suggested that 'The most significant dividing line in Europe . . . may well be the eastern boundary of Western Christianity in the year 1500.'[36] Without invoking ancient religious divisions, and without seeking to identify new lines of conflict, a German political scientist, Otto Czempiel, argued for a division between an expanded Community and the Commonwealth of Independent States. He warned against expanding the Alliance since this would be too provocative. But the Community, as both an economic and a security organization, should extend to incorporate eastern Europe, including, 'one distant day', the Baltic states. If, he continued, the Commonwealth of Independent States developed structures analogous to those of the Community, then 'two great federations will arise in Europe'.[37] This was essentially the vision of the prophet of pan-Europe, Coudenhove-Kalergi. Divisions within the west, above all Franco-German enmity, which he recognized as decisive, along with the reality of the Soviet Union as a centralized empire, insured that his vision remained purely a vision during his own lifetime.

Seventy years after the publication of Coudenhove-Kalergi's *Pan-Europa,* doubts remained about whether Russia could manage to combine democratization and an imperial vocation. For all the speculation upon new tensions in the Franco-German relationship, there was no doubt that the enmity which had rightly concerned Coudenhove-Kalergi was a thing of the past. Franco-German reconciliation was an achievement, brought about by integration first within the Coal and Steel Community, then bolstered by the Economic Community. In a long-term perspective this achievement stood on a par with the end of the Cold War. Europe divided by the Cold War had overshadowed the specifically European origins of conflict and pressed European integration into the service of that divide. But, as the German Foreign Minister Klaus Klinkel argued, the fall of the iron curtain had not mitigated the need for integration. The latter, he insisted, was not a product of conflict between east and west, but of a 'centuries-long civil war in Europe'.[38]

Further integration raised the question of how the Community could be inserted into a broader European architecture. There was little prospect for the foreseeable future that the European federation envisaged by Coudenhove-Kalergi would replace the fragments of Europe's architecture by a single, integrated structure. The single structure, the United States of Europe, had been the federalists' answer all along. The end of the Cold War lessened some obstacles but increased others. The strains of maintaining structural integrity had already become evident in the Maastricht 'opt-outs', encouraging speculation about a multi-speed Europe. The prospect of enlargement towards the east inflamed that speculation. Early attempts to deal with the strains, notably the Tindemans Report of 1975, emphasized the maintenance of common goals and allowed only divergent timescales for their achievement. Another alternative was Europe à la carte, but this was officially taboo and in some senses misleading. It had always been clear that Europe à la carte would not entail a random selection from the menu of integration. The preferences of some states would tend to coincide. The real choice was between maintaining common goals and the development of a two-speed Europe. The latter really meant the emergence of a core Europe with a dependent periphery. Politically, core Europe would be anchored around the Franco-German axis. Economically, it would coincide in large part with the concentration of population and wealth which had characterized Europe for centuries, stretching from the Low Countries along the Rhine to northern Italy.[39]

That was where the European Community had begun, with the original six members of the Coal and Steel Community. In 1951 as in 1994, the emergence of core Europe induced the others to look for strategies of regulating their relationship with the core, and of ensuring that it was contained within some wider framework. Core Europe, in fact, had produced the first debate on Europe's architecture, a debate which had continued through to the end of the 1950s. None of those strategies had been successful. Britain had tried to solve the problem of its isolation by subordinating all of the fora of integration, both broad and narrow, to the most comprehensive forum, the Council of Europe. There was confusion on the British side about how tight that subordination should be. While some clearly favoured an attempt to control the core, others professed that they intended no threat to the integrity of core Europe and merely wanted some mechanism for bridging the gap. The British attempt failed because the latter was vague and aroused suspicion that the real intent was the former. No more success was had with the attempt to dilute core Europe within a wider free trade area, for that too would have denied core

Europe the integrity that it desired. The perceived threat posed by core Europe was only a partial one. Militarily, it had no pretensions, at least not after the failure of the Defence Community and so long as de Gaulle's ambitions remained unfulfilled. Nevertheless, the peripheral states of western Europe were forced sooner or later to escape their isolation by seeking membership of the core Communities.

In the debate on Europe's new architecture forty years later, elements of the earlier strategies resurfaced. There were, of course, significant differences. The most comprehensive forum was the Conference on Security and Co-operation in Europe, which embraced not only all of Europe but North America and parts of Asia. Moreover, the suggestion was not that the Community might be subordinate to the Conference, but that the Atlantic Alliance should be. The similarity lay in the response. The Alliance, as earlier the Community, refused to sacrifice its integrity.

During these debates, first western Europe, or rather western Europe and the Atlantic community, and then a 'Europe' stretching from Vancouver to Vladivostok, were left trying to build 'a framework of interlocking institutions which complement each other'. They were locked into this strategy for two reasons. Firstly, no single institution was able to absorb the others. Officials of the United States had speculated upon the possibility of an all-embracing Atlantic Alliance at the end of the 1940s, but this was never realistic, and most were relieved when France rescued them from their embarrassment by launching the Schuman Plan. Václav Havel's hope that the Conference on Security and Co-operation might become a pan-European security structure, displacing both of the Cold War military alliances, was also unrealistic. The second reason was that 'the challenges we face cannot be comprehensively addressed by one institution alone'. That too had been evident in the postwar development of Europe's architecture. According to the men behind the Marshall Plan, the prime threat to western Europe was economic, not military. Internal instability rather than external aggression was the challenge to security. Western Europeans, or at least enough of them, were not persuaded, and insisted upon the entangling alliance. Similarly, the greatest security challenge to post-Cold War eastern Europe was economics, not military. Again, the prospect of economic salvation was not enough. At the end of 1994 the Community, despite its pretensions to raise its security profile, showed little inclination to do without the Alliance. What was on offer was, at most, a duopoly of the Community and the Alliance. Neither, however, was intended to include Russia, and little solace was provided by membership of the Organization for Security and Co-operation in Europe.

These problems were sometimes couched in terms of the prospective enlargement of Europe. When asked to comment on this issue, Václav Klaus confessed that he was puzzled.

> It seems to me, however, that Europe cannot be enlarged. Europe is as it is, and as it always was, and the authors of the title had in mind, probably, the enlargement not of Europe but of some European institutions only. The difference is important. Some of us tend to underestimate it and . . . [that] . . . is an error.[40]

He did not, of course, mean to deny that Europe had changed in some respects. His objection was to the equation of Europe with its international institutions, and especially the triumphant western institutions which the Czech Republic aspired to join. From the Czech perspective their country's membership of Europe was a fact of geography, of history and of culture. From a broader perspective, the same point was valid. Europe's history and culture, and even the issue of the extent of its integration, was not merely the history of its international institutions or even their prehistory. But at the same time the wider ramifications of European integration, or disintegration, had always been reflected through disputes about international institutions. The existence of those institutions in 1994, and the reconciliation between the western European powers which they enshrined, was the most striking and evident difference between Europe then and a century earlier.

NOTES

1. Carl Strikwerda, 'The troubled origins of European economic integration: international iron and steel and labor migration in the era of World War 1', *American Historical Review*, **98** (1993), p. 1108.
2. Kenneth D. Barkin, *The Controversy over German Industrialization 1890–1902* (Chicago, 1970).
3. Quoted in Weigall and Stirk (eds), *The Origins and Development of the European Community*, p. 58.
4. Shirley Williams, 'Sovereignty and Accountability in the European Community', in Keohane and Hoffmann (eds), *The New European Community*, p. 162.
5. Martin Westlake, 'The European parliament, the national parliaments and the 1966 intergovernmental conference', *Political Quarterly*, **66** (1995), pp. 59–73.
6. Even in Germany. See K. Michael Prince, 'Germany, Europe and the dilemma of democratic legitimation', *Aussenpolitik*, **1** (1995), pp. 3–13.
7. Featherstone, 'Jean Monnet and the "democratic deficit" in the European Union', pp. 149–70.
8. 'And though this *federative Power* in the well or ill management of it be of great moment to the commonwealth, yet it is much less capable to be directed by antecedent, standing, positive Laws, than the *Executive* . . . ', Peter Laslett (ed.), *John Locke. Two Treatises of Government* (Cambridge, 1963), p. 411. The same does

not apply, of course, to the conception of a federative power concerned with the internal affairs of a commonwealth.

9. On the comparison see Max Jacobson. 'Frieden und Stabilität-eine Fata Morgana?', *Europa-Archiv*, **11** (1994), p, 307.
10. Altiero Spinelli and Ernesto Rossi, *The Ventotene Manifesto* (London, n.d.), p. 19.
11. The issue of the meaning of the end of the war for the Germans and whether it can be meaningfully described as liberation is a fraught one. See the comments by James Morgan in *Financial Times* (23 April 1995) and Hermann Glaser, '1945: Befreiung von der NS-Gewaltherrschaft', *Aus Politik und Zeitgeschichte*, **1–2** (1995), pp. 3–10.
12. See Jürgen Gebhardt, 'Verfassungspatriotismus als Identitätskonzept der Nation', *Aus Politik und Zeitgeschichte*, **14** (1993), pp. 29–37; Roland Hahn, 'Die Idee der Nation und der Lösung der deutschen Frage', *Aus Politik und Zeitgeschichte*, **29** (1990), pp. 3–12.
13. On this see Hoffmann, 'Obstinate or obsolete? The fate of the nation-state and the case of western Europe', pp. 870–2.
14. Václav Klaus, 'Die Tschechische Republik und die Integration Europas', *Europäische Rundschau*, **3** (1994), p. 5.
15. See Stephen Iwan Griffiths, *Nationalism and Ethnic Conflict. Threats to European Security* (Oxford, 1993), pp. 25–32.
16. Hence Griffiths's 'cautious optimism', *ibid.*, p. 123.
17. Herbst, 'Die zeitgenössische Integrationstheorie und die Anfänge der europäischen Einigung 1947–1950', p. 171. For a brief assessment of the legacy of the years before 1945, see Peter Stirk, 'The preconditions of European integration: observations on the years 1918–1945', in W. A. F. Camphuis and C. G. J. Wildeboer Schut (eds), *Europese Eenwording in Historisch Perspectief* (Zaltbommel, 1991), pp. 174–85.
18. Milward, *The European Rescue of the Nation-State*, p. 18. For a survey of the historiographical debate, see P.-H. Laurent, 'Historical perspectives on early European integration', *Journal of European Integration*, **12** (1986), pp. 89–100.
19. Milward, *The European Rescue of the Nation-State*, p. 445.
20. Quoted in Weigall and Stirk (eds), *The Origins and Development of the European Community*, p. 59.
21. British ministers and officials more or less consistently ignored the British federal tradition.
22. Functionalist theories are typically complex and rarely rigorous. For two attempts to clarify the issues, see Paul Taylor 'Functionalism: the approach of David Mitrany', in A. J. R. Groom and Paul Taylor (eds), *Frameworks for International Co-operation* (London, 1990), pp. 125–38 and R. J. Harrison, 'Neo-functionalism', in *ibid.*, pp. 139–50.
23. See A. S. Milward and Vibeke Sorensen, 'Interdependence or integration? A national choice', in Milward *et al.*, *The Frontier of National Sovereignty*, pp. 22, 29.
24. For a survey of approaches, see Robert O. Keohane and Stanley Hoffmann, 'Institutional change in Europe in the 1980s', in Keohane and Hoffmann (eds), *The New European Community*, pp. 1–39.
25. Peter Schmidt, 'French security ambitions', *Aussenpolitik*, **4** (1993), p. 343.
26. Lothar Rühl, 'Jenseits der "Partnerschaft für den Frieden". Ein neue Demarkationslinie durch Europa?', *Europa-Archiv*, **4** (1994), p. 105.

27. See H. Magenheimer, 'Sicherheitspolitik und Machtgestaltung in Europa', *Aus Politik und Zeitgeschichte*, **6** (1995), pp. 10–11.
28. *Ibid.*, p. 9.
29. Speech in Prague, 8 October 1993, *Europa-Archiv*, **3** (1994), p. D102.
30. Embassy of the Federal Republic of Germany, Press Release 22/93 (11 March 1994). The figures are for 1992.
31. Rudolf Scharping, 'New challenges for Franco-German cooperation', *Aussenpolitik*, **1** (1994), pp. 3–9.
32. Valérie Guérin-Sendelbach and Jacek Rulkowski, '"Euro-Trio" France–Germany–Poland', *Aussenpolitik*, **3** (1994), pp. 246–53, especially the warning that 'Germany and France should not view their policy of support *vis-à-vis* Poland/Eastern Europe as a zero-sum game', p. 253.
33. André Brigot, 'Frankreich und Europa', *Aus Politik und Zeitgeschichte*, **42** (1994), pp. 34–8.
34. On the idea that the end of the Cold War undermined the French vision of Europe see Ole Waever, 'Three competing Europes: German, French, Russian', *International Affairs*, **66** (1990), pp. 477–93.
35. Quoted in *Die Zeit* (12 May 1995). See also Christian Hacke, 'Deutschland und die Weltordnung. Zwischen innenpolitischer Überordnung und aussenpolitischen Krisen', *Aus Politik und Zeitgeschichte*, **46** (1992), pp. 3–16.
36. Samuel P. Huntingdon, 'The clash of civilizations?', *Foreign Affairs*, **3** (1993), p. 30. Huntingdon notes that this was suggested by William Wallace, *The Transformation of Western Europe* (London, 1991), though Wallace's statements were more moderate. See p. 17.
37. Otto Czempiel, 'Bausteine einer europäischen Friedensordnung', *Europa-Archiv*, **4** (1991), p. 99.
38. *Das Parlament* (1 January 1993).
39. On this core Europe see Wallace, *The Transformation of Western Europe*, pp. 21–8. Changes in Italian politics raised the prospects of Italy's exclusion. See Josef Jenning, 'Europa braucht verschiedene Geschwindigkeiten', *Europa-Archiv*, **18** (1994), p. 533.
40. 'The future shape of Europe and its position in the world (Václav Klaus's Notes), Davos, 21.1.94', Ministry of Foreign Affairs, The Czech Republic, Press Release No. 02/94 (11 February 1994).

Selected Bibliography

This bibliography is largely restricted to English-language material and is intended as a guide for those who are approaching the topic for the first time. Preference has been given to books rather than articles. Readers requiring more detailed material should consult the notes.

Among the general surveys, Derek Heater, *The Idea of European Unity* (Leicester, 1992) goes back to the medieval origins. Surveys with as broad a chronological span as the present work are David Arter, *The Politics of European Integration in the Twentieth Century* (Dartmouth, 1993) and R. Vaughan, *Twentieth Century Europe* (London, 1979). For comparable documentary collections, see D. Weigall and P. Stirk (eds), *The Origins and Development of the European Community* (Leicester, 1992) and R. Vaughan (ed.), *Postwar Integration in Europe* (London, 1976). Economic trends and the problem of minorities are surveyed in Sidney Pollard, *The Integration of the European Economy since 1815* (London, 1981) and Raymond Pearson, *National Minorities in Eastern Europe 1848–1945* (London, 1983). The idea of Mitteleuropa is dealt with in H. C. Meyer, *Mitteleuropa in German Thought and Action* (The Hague, 1955) and Peter Stirk (ed.), *Mitteleuropa. History and Prospects* (Edinburgh, 1994). For details of the German bid to implement the idea, see the classic work of Fritz Fischer, *Germany's Aims in the First World War* (London, 1967). The inter-war period is still comparatively neglected, but Carl H. Pegg, *Evolution of the European Idea 1914–1932* (Chapel Hill, 1983) provides a detailed examination of the groups favouring integration in the 1920s. There are useful contributions in the following collections: Andrea Bosco (ed.), *The Federal Idea*, Vol. 1 (London, 1991): Preston King and Andrea Bosco (eds), *A Constitution for Europe* (London, 1991); and Peter M. R. Stirk (ed.), *European Unity in Context: The Interwar Period* (London, 1989).

For a general survey of the Nazi New Order, see Arnold Toynbee and Veronica Toynbee (eds), *Hitler's Europe* (London, 1954). M. L. Smith and Peter M. R. Stirk (eds), *Making the New Europe* (London, 1990) provides a more recent survey of diverse aspects of unity and disunity in the period. There are several invaluable documentary collections for this period, especially W. Lipgens (ed.), *Documents on the History of European Integration*, Vols 1 and 2 (Berlin, 1985 and 1986). For Allied policy, see *Dokumente zur Deutschlandpolitik*, I. Reihe. The documents are in the original English. Economic developments are covered by A. S. Milward. See especially his *The Fascist Economy in Norway* (Oxford, 1970) and *The French Economy: War, Economy and Society 1939–1945* (London, 1977). The idea of the Resistance and exiled governments can be followed through the *Documents on the History of European Integration.* Piotr S. Wandycz, 'Recent traditions of the quest for unity', in J. Lukaszewski (ed.), *The Peoples' Democracies after Prague* (Bruges, 1970), pp. 37–93, provides a good survey of developments in eastern Europe during the war and into the postwar period.

The literature on the second half of the 1940s is voluminous, though significant gaps remain. Wilfried Loth, *The Division of the World 1941–1955* (London, 1988) provides a good general survey. W. Lipgens, *A History of European Integration,* Vol. 1: 1945–1947 (Oxford, 1982) is an extremely detailed study of those years. The Marshall Plan continues to attract attention. Michael Hogan, *The Marshall Plan* (Cambridge, 1987) is a substantial contribution. A. S. Milward, *The Reconstruction of Western Europe 1945–51* (London, 1984) is an economic history which emphasizes European resistance to integration and casts doubt on the importance of the Marshall Plan. Coverage of developments in eastern Europe is much thinner. For some interesting recent works, see O. A. Wested *et al.* (eds), *The Soviet Union in Eastern Europe, 1945–89* (Houndmills, 1994), pp. 9–25. For the origins of Comecon, see J. M. Brabant, 'Another look at the origins of east European economic cooperation', *Osteuropa Wirtschaft,* **24** (1979), pp. 243–66. The standard account of the Council of Europe remains A. H. Robertson, *The Council of Europe* (London, 1956). The origins and development of NATO are better served. See, for example, Timothy P. Ireland, *Creating the Entangling Alliance* (Westport, Conn., 1981), and F. H. Heller and J. R. Gillingham (eds), *NATO: The Founding of the Atlantic Alliance and the Integration of Europe* (New York, 1992).

A good starting-point for developments in the 1950s is provided by the memoirs of two key participants: J. Monnet, *Memoirs* (London, 1976) and Robert Marjolin, *Memoirs 1911–1986* (London, 1989). Key documents are gathered in European Parliament, *Selection of Texts Concerning Institutional Matters of the Community from 1950–1982* (Luxembourg, n.d.). Series of diplomatic papers include *Documents on British Policy Overseas,* Series 2, though this series has not yet progressed very far, and *Documents diplomatique française* and *Foreign Relations of the United States.* For the European Coal and Steel Community, see K. Schwabe (ed.), *Die Anfänge des Schuman-Plans 1950/51* (Baden-Baden, 1988), which includes contributions in English, and R. Poidevin and D. Spierenburg, *History of the High Authority of the European Coal and Steel Community* (London, 1994). The best general guide to the ill-fated European Defence Community remains Edward Fursdon, *The European Defence Community* (London, 1980). On the Rome Treaties see A. S. Milward, *The European Rescue of the Nation-State* (London, 1992); A. S. Milward *et al., The Frontier of National Sovereignty. History and Theory 1945–1992* (London, 1993); Hanns-Jürgen Küsters, *Fondements de la communauté économique européene* (Luxembourg, 1990); E. Serra (ed.), *The Relaunching of Europe and the Treaties of Rome* (Baden-Baden, 1989). On the free trade area debate Miriam Camps, *Britain and the European Community* (London, 1964) still provides the authoritative account. For the Atlantic dimension, Alfred Grosser, *The Western*

Alliance (London, 1980) gives an excellent overview while Pascaline Winand, *Eisenhower, Kennedy and the United States of Europe* (New York, 1993) provides detail. For a general survey of integration in the east, see Michael Kaser, *Comecon* (Oxford, 1965). G. Schiavone, *The Institutions of Comecon* (London, 1981) is a good guide to institutional developments, while J. Montias, *Economic Development in Communist Rumania* (Cambridge, Mass., 1967), despite its narrow remit, goes to the heart of the disputes.

There are a number of surveys of the European Communities. D. Dinan, *Ever Closer Union?* (Basingstoke, 1994) prefaces his institutional survey with a substantial historical account. Hans von der Groeben, *The European Community. The Formative Years* (Brussels, 1985) is a good account of the years up to and including the Luxembourg crisis. See also the older, but still valuable, John Newhouse, *Collision in Brussels* (New York, 1967) and Miriam Camps, *European Unification in the Sixties* (London, 1967). The enlargement of the Communities is covered by James Nicholson and Roger East, *From the Six to the Twelve* (Harlow, 1987). While Winand's book covers the early years of Euro-Atlantic tensions, William C. Cromwell, *The United States and the European Pillar* (New York, 1992) focuses on the later years. Much of the most useful literature on Comecon is to be found in the journals, but see H. W. Schaefer, *Comecon and the Politics of Integration* (New York, 1972) and A. Schlaim and G. N. Yannopoulos (eds), *The EEC and Eastern Europe* (Cambridge 1978). The revival of integration under the Franco-German aegis is covered by Haig Simonian, *The Privileged Partnership* (Oxford, 1985). For the British perspective, see Stephen George, *An Awkward Partner. Britain in the European Community* (Oxford, 1990). The literature on policy areas within the Community is very large. For two good guides to areas emphasized in this work, see Simon J. Nuttall, *European Political Co-operation* (Oxford, 1992) and Peter Coffey, *The European Monetary System – Past, Present and Future* (Dordrecht, 1984). The contributions to K. Dyson (ed.), *European Détente* (London, 1986) provide diverse perspectives on that theme.

Paul Taylor, 'The new dynamics of EC integration in the 1980s', in J. Lodge (ed.), *The European Community and the Challenge of the Future* (London, 1989) provides a succinct survey of the main developments. Detailed perspectives on the Draft Treaty are in R. Bieber, J. -P. Jacqué and J. H. H. Weiler (eds), *An Ever Closer Union?* (Luxembourg, 1985). Retrospective assessments of the 1980s are in Robert O. Keohane and Stanley Hoffman (eds), *The New European Community* (Boulder, 1991). An influential, if disputed, interpretation of the drive towards the Single European Act is W. Sandholtz and J. Zysman. '1992: recasting the European bargain', *World Politics*, **42** (1989), pp. 95–126. For the negotiations, see Jean de Ruyt, *L'Acte unique européenne* (Brussels, 1989). For the ideas behind the single market, see T. Padoa-Schioppa, *Efficiency, Stability and Equity* (Oxford, 1987). Tony Cutler *et al.*, *The Struggle for Europe. A Critical Evaluation of the European Community* (New York, 1989) bears out the sub-title. For an attempt to draw a balance, see L. Tsoukalis, *The New European Economy* (Oxford, 1991). On the influence of Delors see Charles Grant, *Delors. Inside the House That Jacques Built* (London, 1994) and Georges Ross, *Jacques Delors and European Integration* (Cambridge, 1995), which focuses on the period between the Single European Act and the Treaty on European Union. In addition to this, for the Treaty on European Union see two invaluable works: Kenneth Dyson, *Elusive Union: The Process of Economic and Monetary Union in Europe* (London, 1994) and Finn Laursen and Sophie Vanhooker (eds), *The Intergovernmental Conference on Political Union* (Maastricht, 1992). For an analysis of the Treaty, see David O'Keeffe and Patrick M. Twomey (eds), *Legal Issues of the Maastricht Treaty* (London, 1994). There is a growing literature on the impact of German reunification. Two books completed soon after the event remain helpful: Renata Fritsch-Bournazel, *Europe and German Reunification* (New York, 1992) and Paul B. Stares (ed.), *The New Germany and the New Europe* (Washington, 1992). For the Community's relations with its European competitors, see the special issue of the *Journal of Common Market Studies*, **28.4** (1990) for EFTA, and John Pinder, *The European Community and Eastern Europe* (London, 1991). For the Comecon's problems, the best guides are two articles: L. Csaba, 'CMEA and the challenge of the 1980s', *Soviet Studies*, **40** (1988), pp. 218–38 and Jozef M. van Brabant, 'The demise of the CMEA – the agony of inaction', *Osteuropa-Wirtschaft*, **36** (1991), pp. 234–54. A useful collection of documents on the Conference on Security and Co-operation in Europe is supplied by Vojtech Mastny (ed.), *The Helsinki Process and the Reintegration of Europe 1986–1991* (New York, 1992).

Developments after 1989 relating to the New European Architecture have to be followed through specialist literature, official publications and the press. There are, however, some good guides. Adrian Hyde-Price, *European Security beyond the Cold War: Four Scenarios for the Year 2010* (London, 1991) is an early sketch which is still worth reading, as is Ole Waever, 'Three competing Europes: German, French, Russian', *International Affairs*, **66** (1990), pp. 477–93. See also Libor Roucek, *After the Bloc: The New International Relations in Eastern Europe* (London, 1992) and Andrew A. Michta, *East Central Europe after the Warsaw Pact* (New York, 1992). David Shumaker, 'The origins and development of central European cooperation: 1989–1992', *East European Quarterly*, **27** (1993), pp. 351–73, is succinct. Giles Merrit, *Eastern Europe and the USSR. The Challenge of Freedom* (London, 1991) deals with the Community's response to the east. Richard E. Baldwin, *Towards an Integrated Europe* (London, 1994) is an excellent analysis of the problems confronting eastern enlargement of the Community. The new agenda is surveyed in Hugh Miall, *Shaping the New Europe* (London, 1993) and Hugh Miall (ed.), *Minority Rights in Europe* (London, 1994).

Index